**Fodor's**

# WALT DISNEY WORLD®
# FOR
# ADULTS

## *The Original Guide for Grown-Ups*

RITA AERO

Fodor's Travel Publications, Inc.
New York • Toronto • London • Sydney • Auckland

Copyright © 1996 by Rita Aero

Fodor's is a registered trademark of Fodor's Travel Publications, Inc.

All rights reserved under International and Pan-American Copyright Conventions.
Published in the United States by Fodor's Travel Publications, Inc., a subsidiary of Random House, Inc., New York,
and simultaneously in Canada by Random House of Canada Limited, Toronto. Distributed by Random House, Inc., New York.

*No maps, illustrations, or other portions of this book may be reproduced in any form without written permission from the publishers.*

ISBN 0–679–03081–6

SPECIAL SALES: Fodor's Travel Publications are available at special discounts for bulk purchases for sales promotions or premiums. Special editions, including personalized covers, excerpts of existing guides, and corporate imprints, can be created in large quantities for special needs. For more information, contact you local bookseller or write to Special Markets, Fodor's Travel Publications, 201 East 50th Street, New York, NY 10022. Inquiries from Canada should be directed to your local Canadian bookseller or sent to Random House of Canada, Ltd., Marketing Department, 1265 Aerowood Drive, Mississauga, Ontario L4W 1B9. Inquiries from the United Kingdom should be sent to Fodor's Travel Publications, 20 Vauxhall Bridge Rd., London SW1V 2SA.

MANUFACTURED IN THE UNITED STATES OF AMERICA

10 9 8 7 6 5 4 3 2 1

| | | | | | |
|---|---|---|---|---|---|
| Adventureland | Audio-Animatronics | Captain EO | Circle-Vision 360 | Disneyland | EPCOT |
| EPCOT® Center | Fantasyland | Magic Kingdom | Magic Kingdom® Park | Mickey Mouse | Mickey's Starland |
| PeopleMover | Space Mountain | Typhoon Lagoon | Walt Disney | Walt Disney World | Walt Disney World® Resort |
| Blizzard Beach | Disney's Boardwalk | Disney Institute | | | |

Jim Henson's Muppet*Vision 3D is copyright © 1991 Henson Associates, © Disney.

*Map Design:* Harry Driggs

*Art Director:* Rita Aero

*Senior Editor:* Stephanie Rick

*Orlando Editor:* Jane Cartelli

*Research Editor:* Colleen Sumser

*Consulting Editor:* Rick Namey

*Copy Editor:* Carolyn Miller

*Fodor's Editor:* Karen Cure

*Index & Proofing:* Elin Chadwick

*Editing Associates:* Jan Haag, Sharon Hennessey, Janet Hutchison

*Research Associates:* Larry Cartelli, Robin Clauson, Bob Richmond

*Jacket Design:* Fabrizio LaRocca

*Jacket Photos:* Flamingo, Bill Nosh/FPG International; Water, Color Box/FPG International; Lemon, Color Box/FPG International; Golf, John Callanan/Image Bank; Fireworks, Philip M. Derenzis/Image Bank

*Symbol Font Design:* Bill Tchakirides, U-Design Type Foundry, Hartford, CT

*Electronic Prepress:* Dan Everard, RR Donnelley & Sons Co.

*Travel Coordinator:* Rebecca Gardener, Travel Advisors, Mill Valley, CA

*Electronic Rights:* Immedia Publishing, Sausalito, CA & San Francisco, CA

*Legal Counsel:* Sheldon Fogelman, Richard Rosenberg

*Special Contributions:* Wendy Justus, John Sumser, Bob Mervine, Vicki Valentine, Terrie Namey, Connie Gay, Bonnie Ammer, Jeff Weiss, Dawn Chesko, Leslie Doolittle, Amy Sadowsky, Jacki Diener, Don Capozzo, Camille McDuffie, Maribeth Riggs, Holly Stiel, Paul Kuhn, David Pool, Mace Dailey, Allan Rinkus, Stephen Haight, Cynthia VanEvery, Ashley Brown, Kelly Ozanne, Phillip Knowlton.

# CONTENTS

# WALT DISNEY WORLD FOR ADULTS

Things have really changed at Walt Disney World since the last edition of this book was published just two short years ago! At that time, the idea of Walt Disney World as an adult vacation destination was met with some surprise and more than a few raised eyebrows. Since then, however, The Disney Company has thrown itself into an unprecedented expansion and has spent more than two billion dollars positioning Walt Disney World as exactly that — a vacation destination for adults.

So what's new at Walt Disney World? A number of outstanding attractions have been added to the theme parks, such as The Twilight Zone Tower of Terror and ExtraTERRORestrial Alien Encounter, and 1996 ushers in a new era of recreation and entertainment for adult visitors. Disney's BoardWalk is opening — an attraction area fashioned after Atlantic City's boardwalk of the 1930s — with several nightclubs, a dance hall, and ESPN's sensational Sports World complex. Pleasure Island, another adult enclave, is expanding as well, with the addition of Planet Hollywood, House of Blues, and other celebrity-owned entertainment clubs. Appearing throughout Walt Disney World are sophisticated new restaurants that emphasize fresh seasonal foods and entertaining preparations, and in the near future, you will see world-class chefs such as Wolfgang Puck establishing restaurants at Walt Disney World.

The budget-priced All-Star Resorts opened recently, as did the rustically splendid Wilderness Lodge. Several premier resorts are opening as well, including the long awaited BoardWalk Inn. At Hotel Plaza, a number of hotels have changed hands and been fully remodeled, and Buena Vista Palace Resort and Spa is launching a luxurious full-service spa that is clearly geared to adult visitors. The Disney Institute is also making its debut. This combined resort and learning center offers "discovery vacations" to adults and families with older children, with programs that range from the performing arts to cardiovascular fitness.

Blizzard Beach, Disney's newest and most inventively designed water park, splashed on the scene in 1995; and Disney's International Sports Complex, under construction nearby, will feature a professional baseball stadium and facilities for more than twenty-five individual and team sports competitions. Walt Disney World is fast becoming a premier sports vacation destination with such events as its nationally televised marathon and the opening of its Indy 200 race track. With more than 25,000 hotel rooms and five championship PGA golf courses, Walt Disney World is by far the largest golf resort in the world, and is host to hundreds of professional tournaments each year, including the PGA Tour's biggest, the Walt Disney World/Oldsmobile Golf Classic.

Acknowledged as the world's number one honeymoon destination, Walt Disney World joined the growing trend in destination weddings when it premiered its new Wedding Pavilion, where unforgettable wedding events are meticulously carried out from beginning to end. And because Walt Disney World is the most popular vacation destination for military personnel, The Disney Inn was recently transformed into Shades of Green, the first Armed Forces Recreation Center located in the continental United States.

Most of these new developments at Walt Disney World are designed primarily for adult visitors. Adults traveling without young children represent half of all visitors, and given its soaring attendance figures, that makes Walt Disney World the number one adult vacation destination on the planet. In this new edition of *Walt Disney World for Adults,* all of these new and coming attractions have been thoroughly researched and included. The book has grown dramatically in scope, but the features that readers have found so useful were carefully preserved: The theme park restaurants have full-page review with up-to-date sample menus; and the full-page hotel reviews offer comprehensive, detailed information about resort amenities, recreation facilities, access to transportation, and tips on the best room locations.

The ratings for hotels and restaurants have been updated, however, based on the latest research of the WDW for Adults Team and on the many responses to the Reader Survey in the prior edition. Because our readers requested ratings for the resort restaurants, these now appear in a new expanded section. Our readers also demanded information about hotels outside of Walt Disney World, so we scouted the area for accommodations that would appeal to adults and added a new section, "Off-Site Hotels." In fact, readers' comments and opinions have modified a number of ratings in this new edition. We've also included many useful and sometimes surprising tips that our readers wanted us to passed along.

All maps have been updated and enhanced, and we still believe they are the smartest, easiest-to-use maps that you will find in any Walt Disney World guidebook. Several new maps have also been added, including maps that are not available at Walt Disney World. Each map indicates the locations of the best telephones and rest rooms, as well as cocktail lounges, cafes, and banking services.

*Walt Disney World for Adults* is designed to help you preplan and organize your trip so that you'll have the best vacation possible in the world's most complex playground. I will never forget the first time I arrived at Walt Disney World, completely unprepared for the immense world of possibilities I encountered. It was exciting, to be sure, but quite overwhelming. It was this early experience that inspired the book's 4-Day Vacation itineraries and the mix-and-match Mini Tours of the attractions. They have been extensively field-tested by both younger and older adults, as well as families with older children. You'll find many touring strategies to choose from, and they are the key to an enjoyable, carefree vacation.

This new edition of *Walt Disney World for Adults* continues to provide the essential travel information it is known for, including a complete guide to all sports and outdoor activities; concise descriptions of the dinner show menus and entertainment; and all those hard-to-get insider tips on everything from navigating the Orlando International Airport and selecting ground transportation to Walt Disney World, to strategies for making reservations, parking, traveling in groups, finding discounts, selecting child care services, traveling with disabilities, and much more.

We are very proud of this new edition. The members of the team that put it together, happen to be card-carrying perfectionists. We challenged ourselves to create the most accurate, up-to-date guide to Walt Disney World available anywhere. We know who our competition is, we know how hard we worked, and we're willing to bet we accomplished our goal, and then some.

We also realize that the continuing appeal of this guide is due in large part to our readers. To convey our gratitude, we created a coupon page in the back of the book with discounts designed exclusively for *Walt Disney World for Adults* readers. Look these coupons over; you will see that they are special and quite valuable. The businesses that are offering them have done so because they, too, realize that our readers are a loyal, thoughtful, unique audience. We hope you can use them on your next vacation and would love to hear from you when you return. ◆

# How to Use This Book

This book is designed to provide you with the strategies you need to take full advantage of your Walt Disney World vacation and get the most out of the time and money you will spend there. It will allow you to plan ahead of time where you will spend each day, and help you make to advance reservations at nearby restaurants, book special-interest tours, and attend sports and entertainment events that may be going on during your visit.

First-time visitors to Walt Disney World can be easily overwhelmed by its massive size and the seemingly endless entertainment choices that are available. Often visitors are unprepared to take full advantage of their recreation options and take control of their vacation time. They end up following the crowds, standing in long lines, being turned away from already booked restaurants and dinner shows, and they remain unaware of the many activities, events, and unique opportunities that are offered. Repeat visitors, too, can often get caught up in the herd mentality if they do not have a preplanning strategy.

## ATTRACTIONS

Begin by glancing through the first section, "Attractions." Familiarize yourself with the theme parks and recreation sites so you can decide in advance what you would like to see and do. Notice, too, the half-day tours included with each attraction. By combining these tours, you can create your own custom vacation. For example, you may want to combine a morning tour and lunch at Disney-MGM Studios with an evening tour and dinner in the World Showcase at Epcot Center.

## 4-DAY VACATIONS

Continue to the next section, "4-Day Vacations," which has three detailed special-interest tours for adults. Each 4-Day Vacation can be expanded or modified, and each suggests a range of accommodations that are ideal for that itinerary. If you find a 4-Day Vacation that matches your special interests, simply follow its schedule's preplanning and reservations countdown to departure. When you arrive, your reservations will all be made, so you can relax and have a good time. If you do not find a vacation itinerary that works for you, if you are staying fewer than four nights, or if you are attending a convention that demands part of your day, use the half-day tours in "Attractions" to design your own itinerary. Create a schedule that shows where you will be each day, so you can follow up with restaurant and entertainment reservations. Except for toll-free numbers, all phone numbers listed in the book require a 407 area code if you call from outside the area.

## TICKETS & TIMING

Once your vacation schedule has taken shape, turn to "Tickets & Timing" to make sure you're traveling at a time when the weather is pleasant and the parks are not overcrowded, or at a time when there are special activities and events that appeal to you. If you are traveling during peak attendance times, you will probably not be able to see as many attractions, although at these times there are many more celebrity appearances, parades, and fireworks shows to take advantage of and enjoy. Tickets & Timing also indicates the value seasons, those times of year when resort rates are at their lowest.

## HOTELS

Once you know when you're traveling, move on to "Hotels," which features complete reviews of the Walt Disney World resorts and selected off-site hotels. There are advantages to staying at a WDW resort, and in many ways it can make your vacation a simpler and more complete experience. WDW resort guests have unlimited access to the extensive internal transportation system, and they have extended reservation privileges at golf courses and special entertainment events. The off-site hotels that are listed offer larger accommodations and exceptional value. Look for a hotel that provides easy access to the activities and attractions you plan to visit most. Consult the map on page 10 for hotel locations, and book well in advance of your trip.

## RESTAURANTS AND DINING EVENTS

The next two sections, "Restaurants" and "Dining Events," will help you decide where and when to dine. Remember, WDW is spread out over many miles, so select restaurants near locations where you will be touring, or dine at your hotel if you want to relax and enjoy the resort amenities and recreation facilities.

## SPORTS

If you prefer an active vacation, or if you enjoy outings in nature or sports events, you can find out about your options in the "Sports" section. There is a wide array of recreational choices at Walt Disney World, including boating, bicycling, tennis, waterskiing, and nature walks. If you would like to play one of Walt Disney World's five PGA golf courses, be sure to make advance reservations.

## TOURING TIPS

Finally, look through "Touring Tips," which is filled with vacation strategies from experienced Walt Disney World visitors. You'll find tips on discount travel, group vacations, local transportation, parking, babysitting, and much more. There is also a description of services available for travelers with disabilities.

## READER'S TIPS AND SURVEY

The tours and itineraries have been field-tested at various times of the year, and the ratings that appear throughout this book reflect a consensus of reviewers and readers. We are interested in *your* experiences and opinions, as well. If you would like to add your voice to the ratings and touring tips, fill out the Reader Survey in the book after you return from your vacation and tell us about your trip.

## VACATION DISCOUNT COUPONS

Before you make your final plans, look through the vacation discounts at the back of the book. In the Orlando attractions area, coupons are a dime a dozen, but the discounts that appear here are unique and *very valuable.* They were carefully selected for adult travelers to Walt Disney World, and most participants have never offered discounts before. You won't see many of these elsewhere. Enjoy them and have a great trip! ◆

# ATTRACTIONS

The Walt Disney World theme parks and attractions are located throughout the forty-three-square-mile resort, separated by acres of forests, wilderness areas, lakes, and waterways. Close to 150 miles of road traverse Walt Disney World, with nearly thirty resort hotels located on the property. Although the land, like all of Florida, is flat, the landscaping is such that visitors never really see their recreation destination until they actually arrive there. Two striking exceptions are the immense eighteen-story silver geosphere at Epcot Center and The Twilight Zone Tower of Terror attraction at Disney-MGM Studios, which are both visible from many areas of Walt Disney World.

The major attractions include the Magic Kingdom (modeled on the original Disneyland in California), Disney-MGM Studios, and Epcot Center (which is divided into two theme parks: the World Showcase and Future World). The other attractions described in this chapter are Typhoon Lagoon, Blizzard Beach, Pleasure Island, Discovery Island, Disney's BoardWalk, Disney Village Marketplace, and Fort Wilderness & River Country. All rides and entertainment events are rated for adult tastes, and services at each attraction are also listed, including information for visitors with disabilities. Most attractions also include one or more half-day tours for adults.

✳

## HOW TO USE THE HALF-DAY TOURS

The half-day tours, at the end of each chapter, are designed especially for first-time visitors to Walt Disney World, although return visitors will also find the touring strategies useful. At the Magic Kingdom, World Showcase at Epcot, Future World at Epcot, and Disney-MGM Studios, the half-day tours are oriented to either the morning or evening, since lines tend to be long in the afternoons. At Discovery Island, Fort Wilderness & River Country, Blizzard Beach, and Typhoon Lagoon, there are both morning and afternoon tours, since these attractions can be great midday getaways. Pleasure Island and Disney's BoardWalk feature evening tours that explore the nightclubs and entertainment events. Most tours include lunch or dinner as part of the overall experience, and each specifies the best time of year to use it. In general, most of these tours will work best during low- to moderate-attendance times (see "Crowds & Weather," page 128). The theme parks charge admission, so you will want to plan your ticket purchase based on the length of your stay and how much you would like to see and do (see "Admissions," page 127).

The half-day tours allow you to design and plan a custom vacation at Walt Disney World based on your interests and past experiences. Since most of the tours are designed in three- to six-hour modules, you can mix and match in a single day the theme parks and attractions that appeal to you. You can also combine the half-day tours with many of the entertainment events and activities that are available outside the theme parks (see "Dining Events," page 205, and "Sports," page 213). If you're visiting WDW for a convention, seminar, or special event, you will find that the half-day tours allow you to experience the best that a particular theme park offers in the limited time available to you. If you are planning to stay four days or longer, you may want to follow one of the special-interest 4-Day Vacations that begin on page 107. These detailed vacation itineraries incorporate the best of the attractions and many of the entertainment events and recreation options that are available throughout Walt Disney World. ◆

# ATTRACTIONS

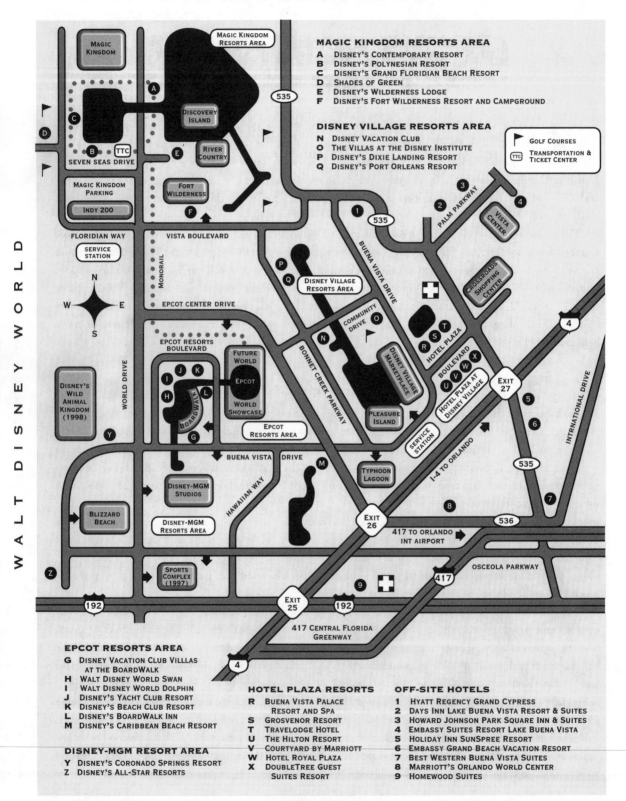

WALT DISNEY WORLD

**MAGIC KINGDOM RESORTS AREA**
- A DISNEY'S CONTEMPORARY RESORT
- B DISNEY'S POLYNESIAN RESORT
- C DISNEY'S GRAND FLORIDIAN BEACH RESORT
- D SHADES OF GREEN
- E DISNEY'S WILDERNESS LODGE
- F DISNEY'S FORT WILDERNESS RESORT AND CAMPGROUND

**DISNEY VILLAGE RESORTS AREA**
- N DISNEY VACATION CLUB
- O THE VILLAS AT THE DISNEY INSTITUTE
- P DISNEY'S DIXIE LANDING RESORT
- Q DISNEY'S PORT ORLEANS RESORT

GOLF COURSES
TTC TRANSPORTATION & TICKET CENTER

**EPCOT RESORTS AREA**
- G DISNEY VACATION CLUB VILLLAS AT THE BOARDWALK
- H WALT DISNEY WORLD SWAN
- I WALT DISNEY WORLD DOLPHIN
- J DISNEY'S YACHT CLUB RESORT
- K DISNEY'S BEACH CLUB RESORT
- L DISNEY'S BOARDWALK INN
- M DISNEY'S CARIBBEAN BEACH RESORT

**DISNEY-MGM RESORT AREA**
- Y DISNEY'S CORONADO SPRINGS RESORT
- Z DISNEY'S ALL-STAR RESORTS

**HOTEL PLAZA RESORTS**
- R BUENA VISTA PALACE RESORT AND SPA
- S GROSVENOR RESORT
- T TRAVELODGE HOTEL
- U THE HILTON RESORT
- V COURTYARD BY MARRIOTT
- W HOTEL ROYAL PLAZA
- X DOUBLETREE GUEST SUITES RESORT

**OFF-SITE HOTELS**
1. HYATT REGENCY GRAND CYPRESS
2. DAYS INN LAKE BUENA VISTA RESORT & SUITES
3. HOWARD JOHNSON PARK SQUARE INN & SUITES
4. EMBASSY SUITES RESORT LAKE BUENA VISTA
5. HOLIDAY INN SUNSPREE RESORT
6. EMBASSY GRAND BEACH VACATION RESORT
7. BEST WESTERN BUENA VISTA SUITES
8. MARRIOTT'S ORLANDO WORLD CENTER
9. HOMEWOOD SUITES

10

# WALT DISNEY WORLD OVERVIEW

Walt Disney World lies south of Orlando on Interstate 4, about a thirty-minute drive from the Orlando International Airport. This sprawling forty-three-square-mile playground contains eleven distinct theme parks and recreation areas, nearly thirty resorts, a dozen lakes with miles of interconnected waterways, and five PGA golf courses — all surrounded by wilderness areas, wetlands, forests, and conservation areas. It's a self-contained, self-sustaining world with its own telephone system, power plant, waste management and recycling center, transportation system, and a computer control center linked with three Disney-owned space satellites that coordinates every aspect of this vacation paradise. There are five main resort areas in Walt Disney World, each with themed resort accommodations spanning a range of prices and amenities.

**MAGIC KINGDOM RESORTS AREA:** This area, at the northernmost point of Walt Disney World, incorporates the Magic Kingdom, Fort Wilderness & River Country, Discovery Island, Magnolia Golf Course, and Palm Golf Course. Bay Lake, WDW's largest lake, is located here, along with Seven Seas Lagoon and the Fort Wilderness Waterways. A fourteen-mile monorail system connects several of the resorts in this area with the Magic Kingdom and Epcot Center. The resorts located here include Disney's Polynesian Resort, Disney's Contemporary Resort, Disney's Grand Floridian Beach Resort, Disney's Fort Wilderness Resort and Campground, Disney's Wilderness Lodge, and Shades of Green.

**EPCOT RESORTS AREA:** Located in the center of Walt Disney World, the Epcot Resorts Area incorporates Epcot Center and Disney's BoardWalk, and is adjacent to Disney-MGM Studios. Water launches, trams, or buses provide transportation between the resorts in this area and Epcot Center and Disney-MGM Studios. There are three small recreational lakes here: Stormalong Bay, Crescent Lake, and Barefoot Bay. The resorts located here include Disney's Beach Club Resort, Disney's Yacht Club Resort, Disney's Caribbean Beach Resort, Walt Disney World Dolphin, and Walt Disney World Swan. Opening mid-1996 are Disney's BoardWalk Inn and Disney's BoardWalk Villas.

**DISNEY VILLAGE RESORTS AREA:** The Disney Village Resorts Area incorporates Pleasure Island, Typhoon Lagoon, Disney Village Marketplace, Osprey Ridge Golf Course, Eagle Pines Golf Course, and Lake Buena Vista Golf Course. Water launches provide transportation between the resorts in this area and Pleasure Island and Disney Village Marketplace. Buena Vista Lagoon is located here and feeds into the meandering Disney Village Waterways. The resorts located here include Disney Vacation Club, Disney's Dixie Landings Resort, Disney's Port Orleans Resort, and The Villas at the Disney Institute.

**DISNEY-MGM RESORTS AREA:** This area, at the southernmost point of Walt Disney World, incorporates Disney-MGM Studios, Blizzard Beach, Disney's new International Sports Complex, and its fourth major theme park, Disney's Wild Animal Kingdom, opening in 1998. The Disney-MGM Resorts are serviced by buses, and include Disney's All-Star Sports and Music Resorts, (and soon-to-be-added Movies resort). In 1997, Disney's Coronado Springs Resort will open here.

**HOTEL PLAZA AT DISNEY VILLAGE:** Hotel Plaza is located adjacent to the Disney Village Resorts Area. The resorts in this area are on WDW property, but are privately owned. Hotel shuttle buses provide transportation to the attractions. The resorts located here include Buena Vista Palace Resort and Spa, The Hilton Resort, Grosvenor Resort, Hotel Royal Plaza (which may become a Holiday Inn Crown Plaza), Courtyard by Marriott, DoubleTree Guest Suites Resort, and Travelodge Hotel. ◆

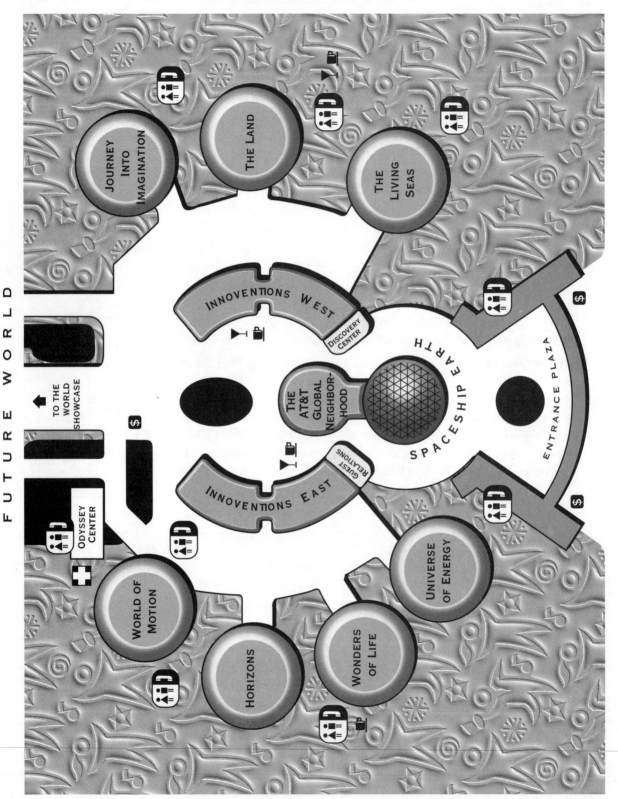

FUTURE WORLD

JOURNEY INTO IMAGINATION

THE LAND

THE LIVING SEAS

INNOVENTIONS WEST

DISCOVERY CENTER

THE AT&T GLOBAL NEIGHBORHOOD

SPACESHIP EARTH

ENTRANCE PLAZA

GUEST RELATIONS

INNOVENTIONS EAST

TO THE WORLD SHOWCASE

ODYSSEY CENTER

WORLD OF MOTION

HORIZONS

WONDERS OF LIFE

UNIVERSE OF ENERGY

# FUTURE WORLD AT EPCOT

Walt Disney's Experimental Prototype Community of Tomorrow, better known as Epcot Center, is distinguished by Spaceship Earth, the enormous silver geosphere at its entrance. The front half of Epcot Center is occupied by Future World, where eight themed pavilions present informative attractions on topics such as transportation, energy, communications, agriculture, and health. Most are of considerable interest to adults. A number of pavilions are actually ongoing experiments designed to test innovations in energy management, food production, and waste and water recycling. Many of the technologies developed here have been incorporated into day-to-day operations at Future World and throughout Walt Disney World. Future World's most recent attraction is Innoventions, which offers visitors scores of entertaining hands-on exhibits that demonstrate emerging technologies that are affecting the everyday lives of ordinary people.

**WHEN TO GO:** If you prefer a morning visit, arrive at Epcot's Main Gate about one half hour before the scheduled opening time so you can enjoy some of the popular attractions before the park gets crowded. Spaceship Earth and Innoventions East and West generally open one half hour before the rest of the park officially opens. The Future World pavilions and attractions are most accessible after 4 PM, as crowds begin to leave; however, Future World generally closes before the World Showcase, usually at 7 PM. Check operating hours at Guest Services in your resort, or call 407 824-4321.

**HOW TO GET THERE:** Future World is located at the main entrance to Epcot Center. The large Epcot parking lot is free to guests at WDW resorts (other visitors are charged about $7). The parking lot is serviced by trams. WDW buses travel between Epcot Center and all WDW resorts, theme parks, and the Transportation and Ticket Center (TTC). The monorail system services Epcot Center from the TTC, the Magic Kingdom, and the following resorts: Contemporary, Polynesian, and Grand Floridian. Future World can also be entered by way of the World Showcase through the International Gateway from the following resorts: Dolphin, Swan, Yacht Club, Beach Club, and BoardWalk.

✳

## ATTRACTIONS

✗✗✗ – Good entertainment.  ✗✗ – Enjoyable for most visitors.  ✗ – Of limited appeal.

**EPCOT'S ENTRANCE PLAZA:** As visitors enter the sprawling Entrance Plaza and pass by its sleek tripod sculpture fountain, they face the huge, multifaceted, 180-foot-high silver geosphere housing Spaceship Earth. The geosphere, clearly visible from any part of Epcot, serves as a point of orientation. The Entrance Plaza is the site of many of Epcot's services, including the Tour Window, bank, wheelchair rentals, lockers, camera center, and American Express financial services.

✦ *Spaceship Earth* — World-renowned science fiction writer Ray Bradbury and the Disney designers collaborated to design this ride, which actually travels inside the Epcot geosphere. Spaceship Earth has been updated with a new musical score, narration, and finale. Visitors journey through the history of communication, from the earliest cave paintings to the printing press, and from the age of radio to the future of satellite communications. The lifelike Audio-Animatronic figures, carefully researched dioramas, and the new planetarium visualization of the universe make Spaceship Earth one of Future World's not-to-be-missed experiences. Duration: 17 minutes. ✗✗✗

**THE AT&T GLOBAL NEIGHBORHOOD:** This exhibit hall, located behind Spaceship Earth, lets visitors experiment with the communications technologies of the future. Several small living room–like areas allow visitors to explore interactive television. Simulatorlike devices at Ride the AT&T Network allow visitors to travel through the fiber optics of the AT&T Worldwide Information Network. ✘✘

**INNOVENTIONS EAST:** Located in one of a pair of large semicircular buildings facing the Fountain of Nations at the center of Future World, Innoventions East houses exhibits that change frequently and focus on tomorrow's consumer goods. Here, manufacturers showcase new products and give visitors a chance to try some of them out. Recent exhibits include time-saving appliances and gadgets, virtual reality and other interactive multimedia systems, an on-line *Encyclopedia Britannica,* lessons in using a computer to edit home videos, and a tour of an electronically managed "smart" house, complete with a handprint-triggered lock on its front door. A futuristic store, Centorium, sells clothing, books, videos, and Disney merchandise. Guest Relations is located in the first entryway to the building, and the WorldKey Information Service is in an alcove nearby. The Electric Umbrella Restaurant is also located here. ✘

**INNOVENTIONS WEST:** Across the Fountain of Nations from Innoventions East, a mirror-image structure houses Innoventions West. Here, the personal entertainment and communications systems of the future are the focus. Recent exhibits include wireless digital musical instruments and sound systems, computers and voice recognition systems, and a variety of educational and entertainment software and high-tech toys. Sega of America, Inc., has showcased its latest game systems here; InfoByte has offered a virtual walkthrough of Rome's Basilica of St. Peter's as it was in the fifteenth century, to demonstrate the concept of virtual-travel-anywhere-anytime museum exhibits; and AT&T lets visitors fax postcards to anyone in the world, and communicate with each other in the pavilion using wrist phones. Pasta Piazza Ristorante and Fountain View Espresso & Bakery are also located here. ✘

✦ *Walt Disney Imagineering Labs* — An attraction during the day, this area is a design laboratory at night for the Disney Imagineers, who develop and design new attractions for Walt Disney World. A recent demonstration presented the efforts involved in designing a virtual-reality experience. Visitors selected at random were fitted with virtual-reality helmets, which let them "fly" through Agrabah on Aladdin's magic carpet. The audience followed the flight on overhead monitors. This technology will be used in an upcoming attraction at Disney-MGM Studios. Duration: Approximately 20 minutes. ✘✘

✦ *Epcot Discovery Center* — Here, visitors can gather background and technical information about many of the exhibits at Epcot Center and throughout Walt Disney World. Interested visitors can request data at the Ask Epcot desk, where an attendant has access to a databank on specific topics, such as how many people Walt Disney World employs or how DACS, the central computer control system at WDW, works. This is the place to ask any and all Disney-related questions. The center may be moving to a new location in the near future. ✘

✦ *Resources for Teachers* — Visiting teachers will find a wide array of educational materials and resources here designed to enhance their knowledge on a variety of subjects. Printed educational materials and programs, previews of educational software, and access to professional education journals are provided. A computer network allows educators to exchange ideas with other teaching professionals throughout the world. Resources for Teachers may be moving to a new location in the near future. ✘

**UNIVERSE OF ENERGY PAVILION:** Housed in a pyramidal building surfaced with mirrors, the Universe of Energy is a traveling theater that is part ride, part film, and total technical marvel. There is always a crowd at this popular pavilion; however, the attraction accommodates about six hundred people at a time, so lines disappear quickly. During peak hours, longer waits are the norm.

✦ *Universe of Energy* — Just inside the pavilion, visitors watch a short film about the types of energy currently in use and under development. They are then seated in what seems to be a large theater, where a second film begins. At this point, all similarity to a standard theater ends. The room breaks apart into six large traveling vehicles that take visitors on a journey through a primeval world populated with prehistoric beasts wallowing in swampy waters, flapping ominously overhead, or locked in mortal combat. Erupting volcanoes spew lava, and thick fog wafts across the vehicles' paths. The Audio-Animatronic figures, some of the largest ever built, are stunning in their detail, and ambient special effects include warm tropical air carrying whiffs of sulfur from nearby volcanic eruptions. This attraction is scheduled for an update in the near future. Duration: 45 minutes. ✗✗

**WONDERS OF LIFE PAVILION:** Just beyond the Universe of Energy pavilion, where a steel DNA sculpture looms near a gigantic golden dome, is the Wonders of Life pavilion. This pavilion houses the Fitness Fairground exhibition center, the AnaComical Players theater, and three popular attractions: Body Wars, Cranium Command, and the film *The Making of Me.*

✦ *Body Wars* — In this thrill ride, visitors are miniaturized and injected into a human body to retrieve a technician investigating the effects of a splinter. Naturally, problems develop and visitors find themselves hurtling along in the circulatory system, hoping to be rescued themselves. The theater is actually a flight simulator that moves, tilts, and rocks dramatically during the show. The seat belts provided are a definite must for this ride, which is not for those prone to motion sickness. Some health restrictions are enforced. Long lines are the norm at almost any hour. Duration: 5 minutes. ✗✗✗

✦ *Cranium Command* — One of the funnier attractions in Future World, this show opens with a preshow cartoon introducing the Cranium Command, a specialized corps of Brain Pilots trained to run the systems that make up the human body. Those who fail get stuck running the bodies of chickens, as the loudmouth training sergeant continually reminds his cadets. Visitors then enter a multimedia theater, where they follow Buzzy, the youngest Cranium Command cadet, on his first venture into a truly frightful environment: the body and mind of a twelve-year-old boy on a typical school day. The clever humor strikes on an adult level. Cranium Command is hidden in the back of the pavilion, so lines are generally short. The animated preshow helps to make the rest of the show clear. Duration: 18 minutes. ✗✗✗

✦ *The Making of Me* — This light and humorous film tells visitors all about the facts of life. Created for a younger audience, *The Making of Me* once aroused considerable controversy because of its open approach to the topic of sex and reproduction, which culminates with superb, though graphic footage of the stages of pregnancy from initial conception through birth. Lines are common at this attraction because of the theater's small size. Duration: 14 minutes. ✗✗

✦ *AnaComical Players* — The actors and comedians in this small open theater in the Fitness Fairground put on an improvisational comedy performance, tagging a member of the audience to appear as a contestant in a game show about health. Duration: 15 minutes. ✗

◆ *Fitness Fairground* — This large and lively exhibition center presents a collection of both serious and lighthearted exhibits that focus on lifestyles and personal health. Visitors can try out the latest workout and fitness-monitoring equipment, receive personalized suggestions for improving their health and well-being, and learn about the latest medical and health breakthroughs. Despite the fact that some of the exhibits seem a bit preachy, this attraction always attracts a crowd. A gift shop features health-oriented books and other items for visitors in a shopping mode. ✗

**HORIZONS PAVILION:** The large building next to the Wonders of Life pavilion that looks like a giant flying saucer is the Horizons pavilion. Enclosing the domed OmniSphere theater, with one of the largest movie screens in the world, the pavilion is dedicated to an engaging ride and show that explore how we will live and work in the twenty-first century. In the near future, a new attraction is planned for this pavilion, based on space travel and employing thrilling special effects to create the illusion of a journey through outer space to the distant galaxies.

◆ *Horizons* — Visitors board four-passenger vehicles to explore past and current speculations about the future. Starting with visions from the past, such as Jules Verne's imaginary flight to the moon, visitors travel through time until they reach the present in the OmniSphere theater. Here, they are treated to dramatic images of new technologies in action. Turning to the future, twenty-first-century lifestyles are presented as visitors travel through convincingly futuristic environments. The pavilion is scheduled for a complete redesign and is often closed; however, it may open again temporarily in 1996 and early 1997. Duration: 15 minutes. ✗✗

**WORLD OF MOTION PAVILION:** This massive wheel-shaped pavilion, covered in stainless steel, houses It's Fun to be Free, a ride through the past, present, and future of transportation, as well as the Trans-Center, where transportation-related exhibits and the latest models of GM vehicles are on display. The pavilion is scheduled to close in early 1996 and reopen in 1997 with a completely new attraction based on an auto test track and possibly a new pavilion name. (See "Coming Attractions," page 22.)

◆ *It's Fun to be Free* — This charming ride explores the many modes of transportation evolved by humans. The highly detailed sets and chaotic scenarios use props that include genuine artifacts from the eras they depict. Audio-Animatronic figures reflecting the vagaries of human nature lend realism to this ride. As they travel into the future of transportation, visitors are treated to a magnificent view of a dazzling, soaring cityscape linked by aerial trains and exotic vehicles. This ride will close in 1996 and be replaced with a new attraction featuring a high-speed test track. Duration: 15 minutes. ✗✗

◆ *TransCenter* — Visitors can enter this line-free exhibition center at any time through doors on the far side of the pavilion. TransCenter presents a number of transportation exhibits, including a whimsical animated film about alternatives to the internal combustion engine, displays on fuel conservation and aerodynamics, and a very clever assembly-line robot. TransCenter also gives visitors an up-close look at concept cars and even lets them climb into the driver's seat of the very latest models of full-featured GM vehicles. The TransCenter may close in 1996, possibly reopening in 1997 with similar features but a new name. ✗✗

**JOURNEY INTO IMAGINATION PAVILION:** This pavilion is housed in a pair of leaning glass pyramids fronted by unpredictably spurting and leaping fountains. It features the Journey Into Imagination attraction, a ride that explores the creative process; the Magic Eye Theater's special 3-D movie presentation; and The Image Works exhibition center, a hands-on electronic playground.

✦ *Journey Into Imagination* — An eccentric adventurer named Dreamfinder and his purple sidekick Figment lead visitors on a flight of fancy, exploring the realms where imagination and ideas flourish: music, art, theater, literature, science, and technology. Huge, fanciful sets are interspersed with laser effects and bursts of music. There is an underlying structure to the sequences in the ride, but it is not particularly clear to most first-time visitors, who find it fairly disjointed and sometimes boring. This attraction is probably best enjoyed as a purely sensory experience. If you are not particularly fond of cuteness, skip it. Duration: 14 minutes. ✘

✦ *Magic Eye Theater — Honey, I Shrunk the Audience* — The attraction begins with a preshow film about the significance of imaginative process. Visitors are then given 3-D glasses and enter a theater where they become the audience that the movie characters address directly. The "Imagination Institute" is presenting the Inventor of the Year Award to Wayne Salinsky (the main character from the popular movies *Honey, I Shrunk the Kids* and *Honey, I Blew Up the Kid*). During the show, a variety of mishaps occur and the audience is unexpectedly reduced to the size of insects, experiencing a rush of harrowing and thrilling mayhem. The 3-D effects are enhanced by exceptional sound, motion, visual, and sensory effects. This attraction is definitely worth seeing, even with a wait; however, arriving early in the day or late in the afternoon may alleviate waiting in long lines. Duration: 25 minutes. ✘✘✘

✦ *The Image Works* — This recently updated high-tech electronic environment is a playground of light, sound, color, and video. Recent hands-on exhibits include neon light tunnels, electronic paint boxes, and lasers with artistic skills. A nearby shop sells a variety of film and a small selection of cameras, lenses, and videotapes. The Image Works appeals primarily to children, who can spend vast amounts of time in the area. However, adults who like simple razzle-dazzle and have time to spare may find this active gallery worth a look, especially if they can elbow their way to the controls of an exhibit. ✘

**THE LAND PAVILION:** Food and farming — past, present, and future — are explored in this pavilion, the largest at Future World. The massive tri-level building, with its glass roof and greenhouses, is a combination science experiment and theme attraction. The Land pavilion houses the Harvest Theater film attraction, the Food Rocks stage show, the Living with The Land boat ride, and the Greenhouse Tour. Also in the pavilion are The Green Thumb Emporium (a gift shop selling gardeners' goodies), the Sunshine Season Food Fair food court, and The Garden Grill Restaurant, one of two full-service restaurants in Future World.

✦ *Living with The Land* — Located on the lower level of the pavilion, this recently revamped boat ride is a pleasant, relaxing, and informative journey through the history of agriculture. A Cast Member travels with visitors through several ecological biomes, including a tropical rain forest; a hot, harsh desert; and a replica of the American prairie, depicting a small family farm at the turn of the century. As they cruise through The Land's impressive experimental greenhouses, visitors learn about applied future technologies in agriculture. Much of the produce and fish grown in the greenhouses is served in The Garden Grill Restaurant. Duration: 13 minutes. ✘✘✘

✦ *Harvest Theater — Circle of Life* is a new 70mm film presented at the Harvest Theater. Simba, Timon, and Pumbaa, characters from the Disney film *The Lion King*, examine the interrelationship between humans and the land. The movie portrays Timon and Pumbaa as land developers creating "Hakuna Matata Lakeside Village," with Simba stepping in to tell his father's tale of the human creatures who often forget that everything is connected in the great Circle of Life. Combined with the animated fable is a series of spectacular images, some beautiful and some nightmarish, depicting environmental scenes from around the world. Some of this footage is taken from *Symbiosis,* the movie that was formerly presented here. Overall, the film provides good entertainment, while presenting this serious topic. Duration: 20 minutes. ✘

✦ *Food Rocks* — Host Füd Wrapper and a cast of singing and dancing Audio-Animatronic fruits, vegetables, and other foods — including stars such as Pita Gabriel, The Peach Boys, and Chubby Cheddar — present a musical revue based on the basic food groups and nutrition. Variations of familiar lyrics and tunes and the transformation of popular stars into vegetables is really quite humorous. Food Rocks turns a lesson in nutrition into an unexpectedly enjoyable experience. Duration: 13 minutes. ✘✘

✦ *Greenhouse Tour* — This walking tour takes up where the Living with The Land boat cruise leaves off. Covering many of the same topics, the tour explores them in greater depth, with an emphasis on the experiments underway in the greenhouses. Visitors glimpse cutting-edge research laboratories, including the Biotechnology Lab, take an informative walk through several experimental greenhouses, and have a chance to ask questions and pick up horticultural tips from the tour guides, all of whom hold degrees in agricultural fields. The daily tours are limited to ten people and depart from the Greenhouse Tour Desk on the lower level of the pavilion every half hour between 9:30 AM and 4:30 PM. Reservations are required and should be made early in the day, since the tour is popular and fills quickly. Only same-day reservations are taken, which must be made in person at the Greenhouse Tour Desk. The price of the tour is about $5 for adults ($3 for children). Duration: 45 minutes to 1 hour. ✘

**THE LIVING SEAS PAVILION:** The rippling façade of this massive pavilion suggests a natural shoreline, complete with crashing waves. Here, visitors experience life under the oceans. The Living Seas houses one of the world's largest saltwater aquariums, as well as a marine mammal research center, living reef, and numerous exhibits on marine topics. The Living Seas Gift Shop features marine-themed gifts, and the Coral Reef Restaurant offers diners a dramatic view of the aquarium as they eat.

✦ *Caribbean Coral Reef Ride* — This attraction is a pavilion-wide experience that is only partially a ride. After a short dramatic film on the interrelationship between humans and the ocean, visitors descend in the Hydrolator (a simulated elevator ride) to the ocean floor, where they board Seacabs for a trip to Sea Base Alpha, an underwater research facility. Here, visitors can take some time to view the more than two hundred species of sea life in the aquarium, watch the sleepy manatees and other residents of the Marine Mammal Research Center, and explore the exhibits on aquaculture and ocean ecosystems. A marine biologist is on hand to answer questions. Duration: 20 minutes; visitors may explore Sea Base Alpha as long as they wish. ✘✘✘

✦ *Dolphin Exploration & Education Program (DEEP)* — Held in the backstage area of The Living Seas pavilion, this educational tour lets visitors learn all about dolphins and even participate in ongoing dolphin research. In the Marine Mammal Center, visitors get an up-close look at the dolphins (but are not allowed to touch them), and even converse with them — the dolphins reply using a special keyboard. By the end of the session, visitors have enough knowledge to be able to contribute their own observations of the dolphins' behavior to the data being collected by the center's marine biologists. DEEP, limited to ten people, departs Monday through Friday at 9 AM from the Tour Garden in Epcot's Entrance Plaza. Reservations are required, must be made at least two days ahead, and can be made up to forty-five days in advance (407 939-8687); the cost is about $45. Duration: 3 hours. ✗✗

## SPECIAL EVENTS AND LIVE ENTERTAINMENT

*Live entertainment is scheduled throughout the day until about 6 PM at various Future World sites. As you enter the park, pick up an entertainment schedule at Guest Relations in Innoventions East. Schedules are also available at most Future World shops.*

**ILLUMINATIONS:** This sensational fireworks, laser, music, and water show occurs over the World Showcase Lagoon nightly, between 8 and 10 PM, depending on the time of year. There is no really good viewing area in Future World, since the show is oriented to the World Showcase. For a good view, visitors need to arrive at the World Showcase at least one half hour before show time. Some of the best viewing locations close to Future World are along the World Showcase Lagoon from Mexico to China and, on the opposite side of the Lagoon, from the United Kingdom to the bridge promenade in front of France. Duration: 20 minutes. ✗✗✗

**HOT ITEM:** *Solar-Powered Lawn Mower* — This small machine is easy to miss as it goes about mowing a small grassy area in Future World, so keep your eyes open. Even though it might be pushing it a bit to call this live entertainment, this preprogrammed, self-sufficient robot is a working example of tomorrow's technology functioning in today's world. ✗✗

## FULL-SERVICE RESTAURANTS

*All WDW visitors can make restaurant reservations up to sixty days in advance. Same-day reservations should be made as early as possible at the WorldKey Information Service at Innoventions East; at the WorldKey Information Service kiosk near the Germany pavilion in the World Showcase; or at the restaurant itself. Smoking is not permitted. See "Restaurants," page 163, for reviews and reservation information.*

**THE LAND PAVILION:** *The Garden Grill Restaurant* — This pleasant, intimate restaurant is furnished with comfortable booths and revolves slowly during the meal, taking diners past several ecosystems, including rain forest, desert, and prairie environments. Family-style Character Meals are served here, hosted by Farmer Mickey, featuring traditional American cuisine including chicken, steak, and fish. Beer, wine, and spirits are served. Open for breakfast, lunch, and dinner; reservations necessary.

**THE LIVING SEAS PAVILION:** *Coral Reef Restaurant* — The giant aquarium in The Living Seas pavilion forms one wall of this atmospheric, dimly lit restaurant. Tables are arranged in tiers so that everyone has a clear view. On arrival, guests receive picture cards to help them identify the marine life they are watching. The menu features fresh seafood. Beer, wine, and spirits are served. Open for lunch and dinner; reservations necessary.

FUTURE WORLD

## COCKTAIL LOUNGES AND CAFES

*A number of refreshment stands in Future World serve snacks and fast food. Those listed below are especially pleasant and make ideal rendezvous spots. Two are located in the World Showcase, but they are directly adjacent to Future World. For before-dinner cocktails, try the lively Rose & Crown Pub in the nearby United Kingdom pavilion in the World Showcase.*

**INNOVENTIONS EAST:** *Electric Umbrella Restaurant* — This counter service restaurant is open for lunch and dinner. The menu features chicken sandwiches, burgers, and salads. Visitors can find seating inside or outside. Coffee, beer, and hot chocolate are available. 🍽️🍸

**INNOVENTIONS WEST:** *Pasta Piazza Ristorante* — This counter service restaurant offers all-day dining, from an early-morning omelette or pastry to an evening meal of pasta, pizza, and salad. There are dining tables indoors and outside on the terrace. Coffee, beer, and wine are available. 🍽️🍸

*Fountain View Espresso & Bakery* — Open earlier and later than most restaurants in Future World, this is an ideal spot for that early-morning cappuccino and pastry or for a glass of wine or beer in the evening. The outdoor terrace provides a wonderful view of the periodic water-show performances at the Fountain of Nations. 🍽️🍸

**THE LAND PAVILION:** *Sunshine Season Food Fair* — Several fast-food booths line one side of this food court and offer pasta, barbecued chicken, soup, salad, and some the best ice cream in Future World. Also available are coffee, beer, wine, and frozen alcoholic beverages. The Sunshine Season Food Fair is at its busiest between 11 AM and 2 PM, and between 5 and 7 PM, when it is mobbed with crowds. 🍽️🍸

**UNITED KINGDOM PAVILION IN THE WORLD SHOWCASE:** *Rose & Crown Pub* — Several fine British ales are on tap in this busy and beloved hangout of World Showcase veterans. Along with beverages, pub snacks such as Stilton cheese and Scotch eggs are offered. Visitors who order snacks or drinks at the bar can carry them to the outdoor terrace adjacent to the Rose & Crown Dining Room. A traditional high tea is served at 3:30 PM; same-day reservations are required, and can be made at the restaurant itself or at the WorldKey Information Service, located at Innoventions East. 🍽️🍸

**MEXICO PAVILION IN THE WORLD SHOWCASE:** *Cantina de San Angel* — This outdoor cafe overlooking the World Showcase Lagoon serves Mexican fast food such as burritos and tostadas, as well as frozen Margaritas, beer, coffee, hot chocolate, and churros. If you arrive well before IllumiNations begins, the Cantina is a great viewing spot for the show. 🍽️🍸

## SERVICES

**WORLDKEY INFORMATION SERVICE:** This interactive information and reservation system is headquartered at Innoventions East, where visitors arrive early in the day to make restaurant reservations. There is also a WorldKey Information Service kiosk located near Germany in the World Showcase. The system's simple-to-use touch-screen computer terminals offer detailed information about all of Epcot Center, including schedules for the day's events and shows. By touching the words *Call Attendant*, visitors can speak directly to a Guest Relations representative to make restaurant reservations.

**REST ROOMS:** Public rest rooms are located outside Epcot Center's Main Gate; on either side of the Entrance Plaza, near Spaceship Earth; on the far side of Innoventions East; and outside the Journey Into Imagination pavilion. There are fairly deserted rest rooms in The Land pavilion, next to The Garden Grill Restaurant; and in The Living Seas pavilion, in the entrance hall to the Coral Reef Restaurant.

**TELEPHONES:** Public telephones are located on either side of the Entrance Plaza, near Spaceship Earth; on the far side of Innoventions East; on the far side of Innoventions West; and outside the Journey Into Imagination pavilion. For quieter, air-conditioned conversations, use the telephones at The AT&T Global Neighborhood, or slip into the Coral Reef Restaurant or The Garden Grill Restaurant, where phones are in an alcove at the entrance.

**MESSAGE CENTER:** Walt Disney World's computerized Message Center is located at Guest Relations in Innoventions East. Here, visitors can leave and retrieve messages for one another. The Message Center is on a network also shared by the Magic Kingdom and Disney-MGM Studios, so visitors at one park can exchange messages with companions visiting elsewhere.

**FILM AND TWO-HOUR EXPRESS DEVELOPING:** Film is available at most Future World shops. Drop-off points for express developing are at the Kodak Camera Center at Epcot Center's Entrance Plaza, and at the Cameras & Film shop in the Journey Into Imagination pavilion. Developed pictures can be picked up at the Kodak Camera Center at the Entrance Plaza or delivered to any WDW resort.

**CAMERA RENTAL:** Video camcorders, replacement batteries, and 35mm cameras are sold and rented at the Kodak Camera Center at Epcot's Entrance Plaza, and at Cameras & Film in the Journey Into Imagination pavilion. Rented equipment may be returned to a Kodak Camera Center in any major theme park.

**MAIL DROPS:** There are mail drops at the following locations in Future World: Epcot's Main Gate; the Guest Relations Window at Epcot's Entrance Plaza; and near the telephones on the far sides of Innoventions East and Innoventions West. A postage stamp machine is near the lockers at Epcot's Entrance Plaza.

**BANKING:** There is an automated teller machine (ATM) just outside Epcot Center's Main Gate, and one near the Showcase Plaza in the World Showcase. There is an American Express cash machine just outside Epcot's Main Gate, near the Guest Relations Window. Personal checks up to about $25 can be cashed at Guest Relations in Innoventions East.

**LOCKERS:** There are lockers located near the Kodak Camera Center at Epcot's Entrance Plaza; at the Bus Information Center in front of Epcot Center; and at the International Gateway in the World Showcase.

**PACKAGE PICKUP:** Visitors can forward purchases free of charge to Package Pickup, next to the Guest Relations Window at Epcot's Entrance Plaza, or to Showcase Gifts at the International Gateway in the World Showcase, and pick them up as they leave the park. Allow two to three hours between purchase and pickup. Guests at WDW resorts may have packages delivered to their hotel.

**FIRST AID:** The first-aid office is adjacent to the Odyssey Center. Aspirin and other first-aid needs are dispensed free of charge. Over-the-counter medications are available at the Centorium in Innoventions East and at the Stroller Shop in Epcot's Entrance Plaza. They are not on display and must be requested.

**VISITORS WITH DISABILITIES:** A complimentary guidebook for visitors with disabilities is available at Guest Relations in Innoventions East. All attractions in Future World have wheelchair access; however, visitors must leave their wheelchairs to board the ride vehicles at Journey Into Imagination, Body Wars, and Spaceship Earth.

**WHEELCHAIR RENTALS:** Wheelchairs can be rented outside the Main Gate at Epcot Center, near the handicap parking area; at Epcot's Entrance Plaza; and at the International Gateway in the World Showcase. Electric Convenience Vehicles can be rented at Epcot's Entrance Plaza, and should be reserved one day ahead (407 824-4321). Only a limited number of these vehicles is available, so reserve early (by 8 AM). Replacement batteries, if needed, will be brought to your vehicle if you alert a Cast Member.

**VISITORS WITH HEARING IMPAIRMENTS:** A written text of Epcot's attractions is available at Guest Relations in Innoventions East. Assistive listening devices are also available there for some attractions. A telecommunications device for the deaf (TDD) is available in The AT&T Global Neighborhood. Hearing aid–compatible and amplified telephones are located throughout Epcot Center.

**VISITORS WITH SIGHT IMPAIRMENTS:** Tape players, touring cassettes that describe the park, and guidebooks in Braille are available at Guest Relations in Innoventions East.

**FOREIGN LANGUAGE ASSISTANCE:** Personal translator units (PTUs) that offer French, Spanish, and German translations of some Epcot attractions and presentations are available at Guest Relations in Innoventions East. Park maps are also available in French, Spanish, German, and a few other languages. Spanish-, French-, or German-speaking visitors may request assistance from the Walt Disney World Foreign Language Center by calling 824-7900 between 8:30 AM and 9 PM.

## COMING ATTRACTIONS

*Walt Disney conceived of Future World as a technology-of-the-future showcase that would continually change. As a result, plans are always on the drawing board for new attractions, but until construction actually begins, these have a way of changing or becoming delayed. At the time of publication, a new attraction and the updating and expansion of several existing ones were in the works.*

**WORLD OF MOTION EXPANSION:** The World of Motion is undergoing a complete redesign. Its present attraction is being replaced with a new one that gives visitors the experience of putting a vehicle through the rigors of an automotive test track, from hot and cold chambers to check the effects of weather on paint, to skids on slick surfaces, speeds up to sixty miles per hour, sharp turns, and sudden braking effects, to test ease of handling and safety features. The attraction is expected to open in 1997.

**JOURNEYS IN SPACE:** In the planning stages for some time, this new attraction will replace Horizons and may involve NASA. High-tech systems and thrilling special effects will let visitors experience traveling through outer space to distant galaxies.

**UNIVERSE OF ENERGY UPDATE:** In early 1996, this pavilion is scheduled to revamp its dioramas and Audio-Animatronics, and to update its current attraction to reflect themes of the formation of the earth and new energy sources now in use and under development.

# Half-Day Tours at Future World

The morning and evening half-day tours that follow are designed to allow first-time visitors to experience the best of Future World in four to six hours, including lunch or dinner. Make your restaurant reservations well in advance of your tour, if possible.

The Morning Nature and Technology Tour, below, is designed for low-attendance times: October through March, excluding holidays. Be sure to enter Future World through Epcot Center's Main Gate for this tour, since the International Gateway in the World Showcase often opens one half hour later and is a short distance away. The Afternoon and Evening in the Future Tour may be used effectively year round, since attendance at Future World tends to drop significantly after 5 PM.

To create your own custom vacation at Walt Disney World, you can combine one of the half-day Future World tours with a half-day tour of any other theme park. For example, combine the Morning Nature and Technology Tour with an evening tour at the Magic Kingdom. The theme parks are most crowded in the afternoon, which is an ideal time to take advantage of the resort amenities at your hotel.

## MORNING NATURE AND TECHNOLOGY TOUR

*Five to six hours — October through March — including lunch.*
*Well in advance of your tour, reserve a late lunch (1 PM or later) at the Coral Reef Restaurant.*

✔ Eat a full breakfast before leaving your hotel.

✔ Arrive at Epcot's Entrance Plaza at least one half hour before the official opening time, and pick up an entertainment schedule at Guest Relations, located in Innoventions East. If you do not have a lunch reservation, go to the WorldKey Information Service at Innoventions East and reserve lunch for 1 PM or later at the Coral Reef Restaurant. If reservations are not available or if you prefer a light meal, plan on eating at the Sunshine Season Food Fair in The Land pavilion, the Electric Umbrella Restaurant in Innoventions East, or Pasta Piazza Ristorante in Innoventions West.

✔ While waiting for the rest of the park to open, ride SPACESHIP EARTH, which generally opens about one half hour earlier. The ride exits into THE AT&T GLOBAL NEIGHBORHOOD. Try out RIDE THE AT&T NETWORK, which is one of the attraction highlights of this area.

✔ When the park opens (sometime between 8 and 9 AM), visit, in the order listed below, those attractions that interest you:
  • Journey Into Imagination pavilion — MAGIC EYE THEATER (*Honey, I Shrunk the Audience*)
  • The Land pavilion — LIVING WITH THE LAND and HARVEST THEATER (*Circle of Life*)
  • The Living Seas pavilion — CARIBBEAN CORAL REEF RIDE
  • Wonders of Life pavilion — BODY WARS and/or CRANIUM COMMAND
  • Innoventions West — WALT DISNEY IMAGINEERING LABS and other exhibits.

✔ If you have a reservation, plan to arrive at the Coral Reef Restaurant ten minutes early. If you are lunching at one of the restaurants that does not take reservations, arrive at your leisure, the later the better for avoiding crowds.

✔ If you wish to continue your tour after lunch, visit attractions you missed earlier, tour pavilions that interest you, or try to catch some of the following:
- Universe of Energy pavilion — **UNIVERSE OF ENERGY**
- Innoventions East — exhibits and demonstrations.

## AFTERNOON AND EVENING IN THE FUTURE TOUR

*Four to five hours — year round — including dinner, on nights when IllumiNations is at 9 PM or later.*
*Well in advance of your tour, reserve a 7 PM dinner at the Coral Reef Restaurant.*
*If you do not have reservations on the day of your tour, at 10 AM call Same Day Reservations (939-3463).*

✔ Arrive at Epcot's Entrance Plaza at 3:30 PM. Pick up an entertainment schedule at Guest Relations in Innoventions East, which lists the show times for live performances and IllumiNations.

✔ If you do not have a dinner reservation or if you prefer a light meal, plan to eat at the Sunshine Season Food Fair in The Land pavilion, Pasta Piazza Ristorante in Innoventions West, or the Electric Umbrella Restaurant in Innoventions East.

✔ Visit, in the order listed below, those attractions that interest you:
- Universe of Energy pavilion — **UNIVERSE OF ENERGY** (if the wait is fifteen minutes or less)
- Wonders of Life pavilion — **BODY WARS** and/or **CRANIUM COMMAND** (skip if the wait is more than 20 minutes)
- The Living Seas pavilion — **CARIBBEAN CORAL REEF RIDE**
- The Land pavilion — **LIVING WITH THE LAND** and **HARVEST THEATER** (*Circle of Life*)
- Journey Into Imagination pavilion — **MAGIC EYE THEATER** (*Honey, I Shrunk the Audience*).

✔ Pause in your tour in order to arrive at the Coral Reef Restaurant about ten minutes early. If you are dining at one of the restaurants that does not take reservations, plan to arrive at least ninety minutes before IllumiNations is scheduled to begin.

✔ After dinner, if you still have time before IllumiNations begins and if Future World is open late, visit attractions you may have missed earlier. Other entertaining attractions include:
- **SPACESHIP EARTH** (which stays open late) and **THE AT&T GLOBAL NEIGHBORHOOD**
- Innoventions West — **WALT DISNEY IMAGINEERING LABS** and exhibits
- Innoventions East — exhibits and demonstrations
- Canada pavilion in the World Showcase — **O CANADA!**
- Mexico pavilion in the World Showcase — **EL RIO DEL TIEMPO**.

✔ About twenty minutes before **ILLUMINATIONS** is scheduled to begin (usually at 9 PM; at 10 PM June through August), position yourself along the World Showcase promenade. Good views of IllumiNations can be found at the following locations:
- Mexico (near Cantina de San Angel)
- United Kingdom (on either side of the pavilion)
- Along the promenade between the United Kingdom and France, and on the bridge near France.

✔ After IllumiNations ends and while the crowds rush out, you may want to linger in the World Showcase. In time, a bus will stop for you anywhere along the promenade and give you a lift to your exit. ◆

# THE WORLD SHOWCASE AT EPCOT

The World Showcase — occupying the back half of Epcot Center — is designed as a permanent and ever-expanding world's fair. Currently, eleven international pavilions encircle the forty-acre World Showcase Lagoon. Each pavilion features entertainment, restaurants, and shops, and each offers visitors a glimpse of its host country's history, architecture, clothing, horticulture, crafts, music, dance, and other fine arts.

**WHEN TO GO:** Although large crowds arrive here between lunch and dinner, the World Showcase rarely feels overcrowded because it is spread out over a very large area. The best time to visit is at opening, usually about 11 AM, and at night when the pavilions are strikingly lit. In the early evening, the World Showcase restaurants fill with diners, and crowds linger on the promenade to wait for the IllumiNations fireworks show held at closing time (generally about 9 or 10 PM). Opening and closing times vary throughout the year, so check ahead at Guest Services in your resort, or call 407 824-4321.

**HOW TO GET THERE:** Visitors customarily enter the World Showcase by walking through Epcot's Future World from the Main Gate toward the World Showcase Lagoon. The large Epcot parking lot is free to guests at WDW resorts (other visitors are charged about $7). The parking lot is serviced by trams. WDW buses travel between Epcot Center and all WDW resorts, theme parks, and the Transportation and Ticket Center (TTC). The monorail system services Epcot Center from the TTC, the Magic Kingdom, and the following resorts: Contemporary, Polynesian, and Grand Floridian. Visitors can also enter the World Showcase through the International Gateway. Water launches service the following resorts: Dolphin, Swan, Yacht Club, and BoardWalk. The Beach Club is within walking distance.

**IN-PARK TRANSPORTATION:** The promenade around the World Showcase Lagoon is $1\,^1/_4$ miles long. Several double-decker buses circle the promenade clockwise, stopping for passengers at bus stops at Norway, Canada, France, and Italy. Watercraft called FriendShips carry passengers back and forth across the lagoon, from Germany or Morocco to the Showcase Plaza near Future World.

✳

## ATTRACTIONS

✗✗✗ – Good entertainment.   ✗✗ – Enjoyable if you have the time and interest.   ✗ – Of limited appeal.

**MEXICO:** The Mexico pavilion is designed as a massive Mayan pyramid surrounded by lush tropical foliage. Inside the entrance of the pavilion, an exhibition of Mexican and pre-Columbian art is on display. The interior of the pavilion is fashioned after an open-air market in a Mexican village at twilight. Handicrafts, jewelry, and clothing are offered in an array of colorful shops housed in the colonial-style façades that encircle the town square. At the rear of the pavilion, a restaurant overlooks an indoor river and a smoking volcano in the distance.

✦ *El Rio del Tiempo* — This charming Mexican travelogue by boat lacks the sophisticated special effects of many Disney attractions, but its simplicity is refreshing. The ride provides a relaxing interlude after lunch or dinner. Duration: 7 minutes. ✗✗

**NORWAY:** As visitors enter this serene Old World pavilion, a fourteenth-century fortress and medieval church give way to the cobblestone courtyards and steep gabled rooftops of a traditional Norwegian town

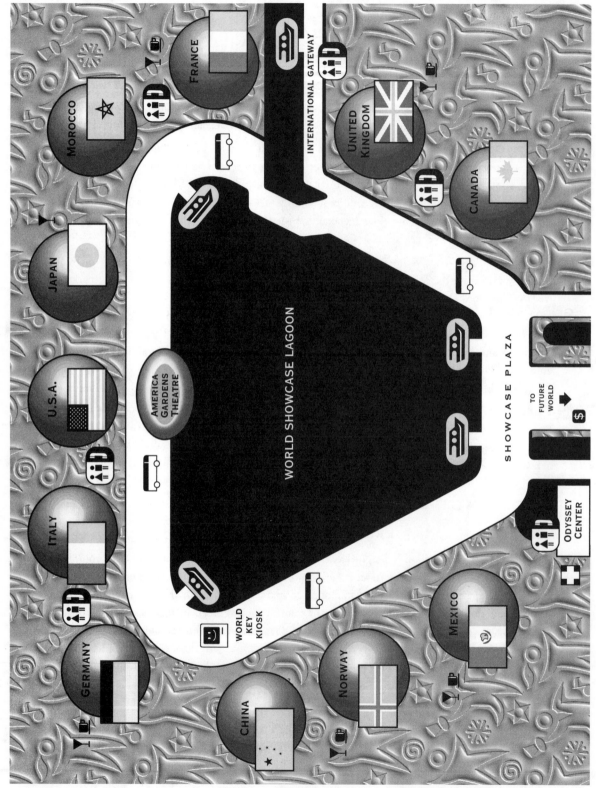

WORLD SHOWCASE

FRANCE

MOROCCO

INTERNATIONAL GATEWAY

UNITED KINGDOM

CANADA

JAPAN

WORLD SHOWCASE LAGOON

AMERICA GARDENS THEATRE

U.S.A.

SHOWCASE PLAZA

TO FUTURE WORLD

ITALY

ODYSSEY CENTER

MEXICO

WORLD KEY KIOSK

GERMANY

NORWAY

CHINA

square. Shops housed in the fortress offer Norwegian hand-knit woolens, wood carvings, and metal and glass artifacts.

✦ *Maelstrom* — Clever special effects and Audio-Animatronics enliven this dramatic shipboard passage through the era of Viking sea exploration. But take care: Visitors in the front of the boat may get splashed. Following the ride, a short film showcases the spirit of Norway. Duration: 15 minutes. ✖✖

CHINA: A colorful half-scale model of the Temple of Heaven is the centerpiece of this exotic pavilion. Traditional Chinese music accompanies strollers through charming Oriental gardens filled with roses, mulberry trees, water oaks, and pomegranates and accented with landscaped reflecting pools. The large shopping gallery offers a multitude of Chinese gifts and goods, including furniture and fine arts. The exhibition of Chinese art at the House of the Whispering Willows gallery is particularly impressive.

✦ *Wonders of China* — This vivid, fast-paced Circle-Vision 360 film portrays the people and culture of China narrated by a fancifully re-created Li Po, treasured poet of ancient China. Viewers are surrounded by a large circular screen and transported from the vast grasslands of Mongolia to modern-day Shanghai. No seating. Duration: 19 minutes. ✖✖✖

GERMANY: Fairy-tale Bavarian architecture surrounds the charming town square of the Germany pavilion. A statue of St. George and the dragon dominates the center of the square, which is ringed by a festive Biergarten restaurant and entertainment hall, plus several colorfully stocked shops offering wines, toys, glassware, and timepieces. At the rear of the square, a chiming glockenspiel rings the hour, and a strolling musician plays waltzes and polkas on the accordion.

ITALY: A scaled-down version of the Venetian Campanile and a faithful replica of the Doge's Palace dominate the piazza of the Italy pavilion. The fountain at the rear of the piazza is a lovely re-creation of the Fontana de Nettuno. Venetian bridges lead to a gondola landing at the edge of the World Showcase Lagoon. Live entertainment, ranging from operatic arias to street theater performances, is scheduled from time to time in the piazza. At Cucina Italiana, visitors can sample the foods and wines of Italy.

U.S.A.: The American Adventure pavilion is housed in a colonial-style red-brick mansion. Inside, the Heritage Manor gift shop sells glassware, toys, and hand-painted porcelain. The colorful gardens surrounding the pavilion are dotted with sycamore and magnolia trees, and a carefully tended rose garden at the side of the pavilion blooms with specimens named after U.S. presidents. At the edge of the World Showcase Lagoon, the America Gardens Theatre presents live entertainment throughout the day.

✦ *The American Adventure* — This recently updated Audio-Animatronic show is an outstanding example of Disney's entertainment technology. Mark Twain and Benjamin Franklin guide visitors on a patriotic multimedia trip through American history, including contributions from Susan B. Anthony, Andrew Carnegie, and others. The Disney genius for detail shines in every vignette, from Will Rogers' spinning lariat to Theodore Roosevelt's notoriously ruddy complexion. Duration: 29 minutes. ✖✖✖

JAPAN: In the garden of the Japanese pavilion, rocks, manicured trees, fish ponds, and wind chimes are carefully blended to create a mood of peaceful reflection. A scarlet *torii* gate, symbol of good luck, greets visitors arriving by way of the World Showcase Lagoon. The pavilion's prominent pagoda is a replica of the eighth-century Horyuji Temple of Nara. Throughout the day, classical Japanese music and dances are performed in the pavilion, and the Bijutsu-kan Gallery features traditional and modern Japanese art.

**MOROCCO:** This pavilion meticulously re-creates the architecture and mystery of North Africa. A replica of the Koutoubia Minaret of Marrakesh greets visitors at the entrance to a flower-filled courtyard, complete with a splashing fountain. The Bab Boujouloud gate leads into the Medina, a bazaar where rugs, jewelry, clothing, leather goods, brassware, and pottery spill out of shops into the narrow passageways. The exquisitely tiled Gallery of Arts and History exhibits examples of fine Moroccan craftsmanship.

**FRANCE:** The Belle Epoque reigns once more in the Parisian streets and gardens of the French pavilion. Models of the Eiffel Tower and the Galerie des Halles are reproduced here, along with mansard roofs, poster-covered kiosks, and sidewalk cafes. Quaint shops on the street offer perfumes, leather goods, jewelry, and crystal. Strolling street musicians sing familiar French ballads, an acting troupe stages comic skits, and talented French artists render portraits of visitors along the waterfront. The sweeping lawn and Lombardy poplars in the large park at the side of the pavilion are reminiscent of those in Georges Seurat's painting *A Sunday Afternoon on the Island of La Grande Jatte.*

✦ *Impressions de France* — Shown in the Palais du Cinema, this wide-screen travel film immerses viewers in the culture and landscapes of France. The soundtrack highlights France's contributions to the world of classical music. Duration: 18 minutes. ✗✗

**UNITED KINGDOM:** In this picturesque pavilion, visitors stroll from an elegant British town square through English gardens and down a street filled with small Tudor, Georgian, and Victorian buildings. A replica of Anne Hathaway's thatched-roof cottage adds special charm. London plane trees and box hedges line the sidewalks, and visitors can make calls from classic red phone booths, once hallmarks of the United Kingdom. Several lovely shops offer toys, cashmere sweaters, china, crystal, and fine teas. Of special interest are the hedged herb and perennial gardens behind the Tea Caddy, and the formal garden courtyard and gazebo at the rear of the pavilion.

**CANADA:** Magnificent towering totem poles frame the Northwest Mercantile trading post at the entrance to the Canada pavilion. The natural beauty of the Canadian Rockies, complete with a waterfall and a rushing stream, is impressively captured here. Northwest Mercantile sells Native American and Eskimo crafts and traditional trapper's clothing. The Caledonia Bagpipe Band can be heard by visitors walking under the birch, willow, maple, and plum trees in the pavilion's Victoria Gardens, where more than forty different flowering plants are always in bloom.

✦ *O Canada!* — This scenic film sweeps across Canada, from the Pacific Coast to the Rockies to the Arctic Ocean. The Circle-Vision 360 screen surrounds visitors with Canada's breathtaking natural wonders, along with scenes of its sporting events and urban and rural life. Visitors stand in the center of the theater during the show. Duration: 18 minutes. ✗✗✗

## SPECIAL EVENTS AND LIVE ENTERTAINMENT

*Live entertainment is scheduled daily in each international pavilion. In addition, guest artisans from the individual nations demonstrate their crafts throughout the day. As you enter the park, pick up an entertainment schedule in Guest Relations, located at Innoventions East in Future World, or at the International Gateway near the France pavilion. Schedules are also available at most World Showcase shops.*

**AMERICA GARDENS THEATRE:** This covered outdoor theater on the edge of the World Showcase Lagoon in front of the U.S.A. pavilion features regularly scheduled performances of concerts, folk dances, and themed events. On weekends during the summer and on holidays, guest celebrities make appearances. This is a good rest stop when you are ready to sit down and relax. Duration: 25 minutes. ✘

**ILLUMINATIONS:** This spectacular fireworks, laser, music, and water show bursts into action over the World Showcase Lagoon nightly at 9 and 10 PM, depending on the time of year. Arrive at the World Showcase early for a good viewing position along the promenade. Some of the best viewing locations are the Cantina de San Angel in Mexico; lagoonside at the Rose & Crown Dining Room in the United Kingdom; along the promenade between China, Germany, and Italy; and along the promenade between France, the United Kingdom, and Canada. There are somewhat limited but dramatic views at the gondola landing in front of Italy and on the upper deck in front of the Matsu No Ma Lounge in Japan. An update of the show is in the works. Duration: 20 minutes. ✘✘✘

**TOUR:** *Hidden Treasures of the World Showcase* — This walking tour explores the architecture and construction techniques of the international pavilions that make the World Showcase a renowned panorama of design. Tours depart at 9:30 AM from the Tour Garden in Epcot's Entrance Plaza on Wednesdays and Saturdays to visit the east side of the World Showcase (Mexico, Norway, China, Germany, Italy, and U.S.A.), and on Fridays and Sundays to visit the west side (Canada, United Kingdom, France, Morocco, Japan, and U.S.A.). Reservations are required (407 939-8687). Same-day reservations may be made at the Tour Garden; about $25. Duration: 3 hours. ✘✘

**TOUR:** *Gardens of the World* — This walking tour explains the horticultural efforts that created the unique, often sensational landscaping in the World Showcase. Many of the plants and care techniques were imported from the nations represented. Tours cover one side of the World Showcase, either Mexico, Norway, China, Germany, Italy, and U.S.A.; or Canada, United Kingdom, France, Morocco, Japan, and U.S.A. Tours depart at 9:30 AM from the Tour Garden in Epcot's Entrance Plaza on Mondays, Tuesdays, and Thursdays. Reservations are required (407 939-8687). Same-day reservations may be made at the Tour Garden; about $25. Duration: 3 hours. ✘✘

## FULL-SERVICE RESTAURANTS

*All WDW visitors can make restaurant reservations up to sixty days in advance (except for Bistro de Paris, where reservations can be made up to seven days in advance). Same-day reservations can be made at the WorldKey Information Service kiosk near the Germany pavilion; at the WorldKey Information Service at Innoventions East in Future World; or at the restaurant itself. Smoking is not permitted. See "Restaurants," page 163, for reviews and reservation information.*

**MEXICO:** *San Angel Inn Restaurante* — Mexican specialties are served at the edge of an indoor river, complete with a smoking volcano in the distance, under a cleverly simulated evening sky. The atmosphere is both romantic and entertaining. Beer (Dos Equis), wine, and spirits are served. Open for lunch and dinner; reservations necessary.

**NORWAY:** *Restaurant Akershus* — This all-you-can-eat Norwegian smorgasbord features a hot and cold buffet of fish, meats, salads, and cheeses. The interior is fashioned as a dining room in a medieval fortress. Beer (Ringnes), wine, and spirits are available. Open for lunch and dinner; reservations recommended.

**CHINA:** *Nine Dragons Restaurant* — Dishes in several traditional Chinese cooking styles are served in a formal Oriental dining room. Entrees are served as individual meals, not family-style dishes. Beer (Tsing Tao), wine, and spirits are available. Open for lunch and dinner; reservations necessary.

**GERMANY:** *Biergarten* — Diners seated at long communal tables enjoy a buffet of traditional German dishes in a huge Bavarian hall. German wines and beer (Beck's, in thirty-three-ounce steins) are served. Performances featuring musicians, yodelers, and folk dancers are scheduled throughout the day. Open for lunch and dinner; reservations necessary.

**ITALY:** *L'Originale Alfredo di Roma Ristorante* — This popular restaurant features Italian dishes, including the house specialty, fettuccine Alfredo. Musicians sing Italian ballads during dinner. Beer, wine, and spirits are served. Open for lunch and dinner; reservations necessary.

**JAPAN:** *Teppanyaki Dining* — In this large second-floor restaurant, guests can enjoy *teppanyaki*-style cooking. Seating is at large communal tables, each with its own grill, where a stir-fry chef prepares the meal — a show in itself. The menu includes beef, chicken, and seafood, accompanied with stir-fried vegetables. Beer, wine, and spirits are served. Open for lunch and dinner; reservations necessary.

*Tempura Kiku* — In this small restaurant adjacent to Teppanyaki Dining, guests are seated at a U-shaped counter surrounding a tempura bar and grill, where they dine on batter-fried chicken, seafood, and vegetables. Beer, wine, and spirits are served. Open for lunch and dinner; no reservations.

**MOROCCO:** *Restaurant Marrakesh* — Traditional Moroccan cuisine is featured in this exotic dining room. Beef, lamb, fish, and chicken are prepared with a variety of aromatic spices and served with couscous. Musicians and belly dancers entertain guests during lunch and dinner. Beer, wine, and spirits are served. Open for lunch and dinner; reservations recommended.

**FRANCE:** *Chefs de France* — Traditional French cuisine created by three of France's celebrated chefs is served in a small, busy, French-style dining room. The menu incorporates fresh seafood from Florida. The wine list is classically French, and beer and spirits are also served. Open for lunch and dinner; reservations necessary.

*Bistro de Paris* — Located above the Chefs de France, this restaurant serves French nouvelle cuisine in a romantic and intimate setting. French wines, beer, and spirits are served. Open for dinner only (lunch may be offered during peak attendance times); reservations necessary.

*Au Petit Café* — Light French entrees, salads, and sandwiches are served in this pleasant canopied outdoor cafe, which faces the promenade and affords many excellent people-watching opportunities. Beer, wine, and spirits are served. The restaurant has a smoking section. Open all day; no reservations.

**UNITED KINGDOM:** *Rose & Crown Dining Room* — This handsome lagoonside restaurant serves steak and kidney pie, roast prime rib, and very good fish and chips. Guests may sit outside on the terrace overlooking the lagoon, an especially good location for viewing the IllumiNations performance. Spirits, wine, and a selection of ales on tap are available. Open for lunch and dinner; reservations necessary.

**CANADA:** *Le Cellier* — In this large, but cozy restaurant with a wine-cellar atmosphere, guests select from hearty Canadian dishes such as Tortierre Pie (a traditional pork pie), chicken and meatball stew, and poached salmon. Cafeteria-style service with Canadian wine and beer (La Batt's). Open for lunch and dinner; no reservations. (Le Cellier may be closed seasonally during low-attendance times.)

✤

## COCKTAIL LOUNGES AND CAFES

*The international pavilions at the World Showcase have refreshment stands that serve snacks and fast food. Those listed below are especially pleasant and make ideal rendezvous spots. For before-dinner cocktails, try the restful Matsu No Ma Lounge in Japan or the lively Rose & Crown Pub in the United Kingdom.*

**MEXICO:** *Cantina de San Angel* — This outdoor cafe, overlooking the World Showcase Lagoon, serves Mexican snacks such as burritos and tostadas, frozen Margaritas, beer, coffee, and hot chocolate. ☕🍸

**NORWAY:** *Kringla Bakeri og Kafé* — This pleasant snack bar cafe offers open-face sandwiches, pastries, and beer. Its shaded outdoor location is perfect for an afternoon or evening rest stop. ☕🍸

**GERMANY:** *Sommerfest* — Cold German beers and wines, along with such traditional snacks as soft pretzels and bratwurst, are available at this outdoor cafe. ☕🍸

    *Weinkeller* — There's a wine-tasting bar in this lively shop. On a warm day, it is an ideal place to cool off while sampling the wines of Germany. No seating. 🍸

**JAPAN:** *Matsu No Ma Lounge* — This serene second-floor cocktail lounge has an excellent view of the World Showcase and is a great place to cool off on a hot day. The full bar serves hot sake, Japanese beer, and cocktails, as well as sashimi, sushi, and green tea. 🍸

**FRANCE:** *Boulangerie Pâtisserie* — This popular shop bakes its pastry on the premises and serves strong French-roast coffee that guests can enjoy at outdoor tables in a picturesque Parisian-style courtyard. ☕

    *La Maison du Vin* — Guests can sample and buy the fine wines of France in this handsome wine shop. No seating. 🍸

**UNITED KINGDOM:** *Rose & Crown Pub* — This busy public house, a beloved hangout of World Showcase veterans, has several fine ales on tap. Guests who order snacks or drinks at the bar can carry them to the outdoor terrace adjacent to the Rose & Crown Dining Room. At 3:30 PM, the pub serves a traditional high tea. It is popular with insiders and must be reserved early. Only same-day reservations are taken, which may be made through the WorldKey Information Service or at the restaurant itself. ☕🍸

✤

## SERVICES

**WORLDKEY INFORMATION SERVICE:** This interactive information and reservation system is head-quartered at Innoventions East in Future World, where visitors arrive early in the day to make restaurant reservations. There is also a WorldKey Information Service kiosk in front of the Germany pavilion. The system's simple-to-use touch-screen computer terminals offer detailed information about all of Epcot Center, including schedules for the day's events and shows. By touching the words *Call Attendant*, visitors can speak directly to a Guest Relations representative to make restaurant reservations.

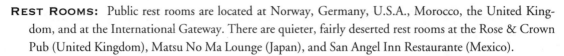

**REST ROOMS:** Public rest rooms are located at Norway, Germany, U.S.A., Morocco, the United Kingdom, and at the International Gateway. There are quieter, fairly deserted rest rooms at the Rose & Crown Pub (United Kingdom), Matsu No Ma Lounge (Japan), and San Angel Inn Restaurante (Mexico).

**TELEPHONES:** Public telephones are located near the rest rooms in Norway, Germany, U.S.A., Morocco, and the United Kingdom. Telephones are also located near the rest rooms in the cooler, quieter restaurants in Mexico, Japan, and Morocco.

**MESSAGE CENTER:** Walt Disney World's computerized Message Center is located at Guest Relations in Innoventions East in Future World. Here, visitors can leave and retrieve messages for one another. The Message Center is on a network shared by the Magic Kingdom and Disney-MGM Studios, so visitors at one park can exchange messages with companions visiting elsewhere.

**FILM AND TWO-HOUR EXPRESS DEVELOPING:** Film is available in at least one shop in every pavilion. Drop-off points for two-hour express developing are at Mexico (Artesanías Mexicanas), U.S.A. (Heritage Manor Gifts), and the International Gateway (World Traveler). Developed pictures can be picked up in the Kodak Camera Center at Epcot Center's Entrance Plaza or delivered to any WDW resort.

**CAMERA RENTAL:** Video camcorders, replacement batteries, and 35mm cameras are sold and rented in the World Traveler at the International Gateway and in the Kodak Camera Center at Epcot Center's Entrance Plaza. Replacement batteries for video cameras are also available at Die Weinachts Ecke in Germany. Rented equipment may be returned to a Kodak Camera Center in any major theme park.

**MAIL DROPS:** Mail drops are located at the following pavilions: Mexico, China, Germany, U.S.A., and the United Kingdom. A postage stamp machine is located near the lockers at Epcot's Entrance Plaza.

**BANKING:** There are automated teller machines (ATMs) near the Showcase Plaza and just outside Epcot Center's Main Gate. An American Express cash machine is outside Epcot Center's Main Gate, near the Guest Relations Window. Personal checks up to about $25 can be cashed at Guest Relations in Innoventions East at Future World.

**LOCKERS:** There are lockers at the International Gateway; near the Kodak Camera Center at Epcot's Entrance Plaza; and at the Bus Information Center, just outside Epcot's Entrance Plaza.

**PACKAGE PICKUP:** Visitors can forward purchases free of charge to Showcase Gifts at the International Gateway or to Package Pickup, next to the Guest Relations Window at Epcot's Entrance Plaza, and pick them up as they leave the park. Allow two to three hours between purchase and pickup. Guests at WDW resorts may have packages delivered to their hotel.

**FIRST AID:** The first-aid office is adjacent to the Odyssey Center, near the Mexico pavilion where Future World meets the World Showcase. Aspirin and other first-aid needs are dispensed free of charge. Over-the-counter medications are available at Disney Traders at Showcase Plaza. They are not on display and must be requested at the counter.

**VISITORS WITH DISABILITIES:** A complimentary guidebook for guests with disabilities is available at Guest Relations in Innoventions East in Future World. All attractions in the World Showcase have wheelchair access; however, visitors must leave their wheelchairs to ride Maelstrom in Norway.

**WHEELCHAIR RENTALS:** Wheelchairs can be rented at the International Gateway; outside Epcot Center's Main Gate, near the handicap parking area; and at Epcot's Entrance Plaza in Future World. Electric Convenience Vehicles can be rented at Epcot's Entrance Plaza, and should be reserved one day ahead (407 824-4321). Only a limited number of these vehicles is available, so reserve early (by 8 AM). Replacement batteries, if needed, will be brought to your vehicle if you alert a Cast Member.

**VISITORS WITH HEARING IMPAIRMENTS:** A written text of Epcot's attractions is available at Guest Relations in Innoventions East in Future World. Assistive listening devices are also available there for some attractions. A telecommunications device for the deaf (TDD) is available in The AT&T Global Neighborhood. Hearing aid–compatible and amplified telephones are located throughout Epcot Center.

**VISITORS WITH SIGHT IMPAIRMENTS:** Tape players, touring cassettes that describe the park, and guidebooks in Braille are available at Guest Relations in Innoventions East in Future World.

**FOREIGN LANGUAGE ASSISTANCE:** Personal translator units (PTUs) that offer French, Spanish, and German translations of some Epcot attractions and presentations are available at Guest Relations in Innoventions East in Future World. Park maps are also available in French, Spanish, German, and a few other languages. Spanish-, French-, or German-speaking visitors may request assistance from the Walt Disney World Foreign Language Center by calling 824-7900 between 8:30 AM and 9 PM.

## COMING ATTRACTIONS

*Plans are always on the drawing board for new attractions at Walt Disney World, but until construction actually begins, these plans have a way of changing or becoming delayed. Several changes and additions were rumored or in the works at the time of publication.*

**SWITZERLAND:** A new pavilion was proposed some time ago to be built near Norway, but the project's development has lagged. Design concepts for the pavilion include a chalet restaurant and a Matterhorn ride attraction.

**JAPAN:** An expansion of the Japanese pavilion is in the works that will give visitors a taste of modern Japan and the sophisticated, high-tech glitz and glamor of Tokyo's Ginza district. An exciting Mt. Fuji ride has been mentioned as an attraction expected to be included in the expansion.

**DENMARK:** A Danish pavilion evoking the ambience of Tivoli Gardens has been in discussion for some time, but seems to be on indefinite hold.

**RUSSIA:** An on-again, off-again Russian pavilion, featuring onion dome–spired buildings and attractions and exhibits centered around Russian folktales, is rumored to be on again. The currently projected date for the pavilion's opening is 1999.

**OTHERS:** Pavilions for Australia, Israel, the Ukraine, Austria, and various African nations, among others, have been discussed over the years. Some have even reached the stage where conceptual drawings have been developed. Many of these projects, however, may never go beyond the conceptual stage, and others have been placed on indefinite hold until a sponsor can be found to help underwrite the construction and maintenance costs of a pavilion.

# Half-Day Tours at the World Showcase

The afternoon and evening half-day tours that follow are designed to allow first-time visitors to experience the best of the World Showcase in four to six hours, including lunch or dinner in one of the World Showcase restaurants. If possible, make your restaurant reservation well in advance of your tour.

The Winter Afternoon Around-the-World Tour, below, is designed for low-attendance times: October through March, excluding holidays. The IllumiNations Evening Tour may be used effectively year round.

To create your own custom vacation at Walt Disney World, you can combine one of the half-day World Showcase tours with a half-day tour of any other theme park. For example, combine the Winter Afternoon Around-the-World Tour at the World Showcase with the evening tour at Pleasure Island.

## WINTER AFTERNOON AROUND-THE-WORLD TOUR

*Four to five hours — October through March — including lunch.*
*Well in advance of this tour, reserve a late lunch at 1 PM or later at a World Showcase restaurant.*
*If you do not have reservations on the day of your tour, call Same Day Reservations after 10 AM (939-3463).*

✔ Arrive at Epcot's Entrance Plaza or at the International Gateway at about 11 AM. As you enter, pick up an entertainment schedule.

✔ Proceed to the World Showcase Lagoon. If you do not have a lunch reservation or prefer a light meal, plan to eat at a restaurant that does not take reservations, such as Tempura Kiku in Japan and Au Petit Café in France, or Kringla Bakeri og Kafé in Norway or Cantina de San Angel in Mexico.

✔ Catch a double-decker bus at the nearest bus stop (located at Norway, Canada, France, or Italy). Ride the bus around the lagoon once or twice to get a complete overview of the World Showcase.

✔ Get off at a pavilion bus stop that is opposite the World Showcase Lagoon from the pavilion where you will be having lunch, and begin your walking tour of the World Showcase.

✔ Moving in a clockwise direction, tour the international pavilions, beginning anywhere on the list below. (Your tour will be interrupted when you reach your lunch destination.) As you visit the pavilions, try to take in some of the following highlights that interest you:
  - Mexico — shops and EL RIO DEL TIEMPO
  - Norway — MAELSTROM
  - China — WONDERS OF CHINA film presentation, shops, architecture, and gardens
  - Germany — shops and wine tasting at the Weinkeller
  - Italy — architecture and live music, theater, or other street entertainment
  - U.S.A. — crafts exhibit, THE AMERICAN ADVENTURE, and AMERICA GARDENS THEATRE (if time permits)
  - Japan — gardens, shops, and street entertainment
  - Morocco — shops, architecture, and courtyard musicians
  - France — IMPRESSIONS DE FRANCE film presentation, shops, and street entertainment
  - United Kingdom — shops, street theater, and Rose & Crown Pub for refreshments
  - Canada — Victoria Gardens and O CANADA! film presentation.

✔ Plan to arrive at your lunch destination ten minutes early.

✔ After lunch, continue your tour of the World Showcase.

## ILLUMINATIONS EVENING TOUR

*Four to five hours — year round — including dinner, on nights when IllumiNations is at 9 PM or later.*
*Make a dinner reservation well in advance of this tour at one of the World Showcase restaurants.*
*If you prefer an early dinner, reserve a table at 6 PM or before.*
*If you prefer a late dinner, reserve about ninety minutes before IllumiNations begins (at 9 or 10 PM).*
*If you do not have reservations on the day of your tour, call Same Day Reservations after 10 AM (939-3463).*

✔ Arrive at the World Showcase at 5 PM. Pick up an entertainment schedule, which lists the show times for live performances and IllumiNations.

✔ Catch a double-decker bus at the nearest bus stop, either at Norway, Canada, France, or Italy, and ride the bus around the lagoon once or twice to get a complete overview of the World Showcase.

✔ For your early dinner or to begin your tour, get off at the bus stop nearest your selected or reserved restaurant. If you do not have reservations or prefer a light meal, plan to eat at one of the restaurants that does not take reservations such as Tempura Kiku in Japan or Au Petit Café in France, or try one of the cafes such as Cantina de San Angel in Mexico, Kringla Bakeri og Kafé in Norway, or Yakatori House in Japan. (Restaurant Marrakesh in Morocco, Biergarten in Germany, and L'Originale Alfredo di Roma Ristorante in Italy all offer entertainment at dinner.)

✔ Before or after your meal, tour the World Showcase, walking in a clockwise direction. As you visit the international pavilions, try to take in some of the following highlights that interest you:
  - Mexico — shops and **EL RIO DEL TIEMPO** (if there is no line)
  - Norway — **MAELSTROM** (if the line is short)
  - China — shops, architecture, and **WONDERS OF CHINA** film presentation (if time permits)
  - Germany — street entertainment and wine tasting at the Weinkeller
  - Italy — shops and street theater performance
  - U.S.A. — **THE AMERICAN ADVENTURE** or **AMERICA GARDENS THEATRE** (if time permits)
  - Japan — shops, art exhibit, and before-dinner refreshments at the Matsu No Ma Lounge
  - Morocco — shops, architecture, and street entertainment
  - France — **IMPRESSIONS DE FRANCE** film presentation (if there is only a short wait)
  - United Kingdom — shops, street theater, and Rose & Crown Pub for refreshments
  - Canada — Victoria Gardens (if daylight) and **O CANADA!** film presentation (if time permits).

✔ One half hour before **ILLUMINATIONS** is scheduled to begin, find a viewing spot at the edge of the World Showcase Lagoon. The following locations offer some of the best views:
  - United Kingdom (on either side of the pavilion)
  - Along the promenade between Mexico and China, Germany and Italy
  - On the bridge or waterside in front of France.

✔ After IllumiNations, you may want to linger and browse while the crowds rush out. In time, a bus will stop for you anywhere along the promenade and give you a lift to your exit. ◆

WORLD SHOWCASE

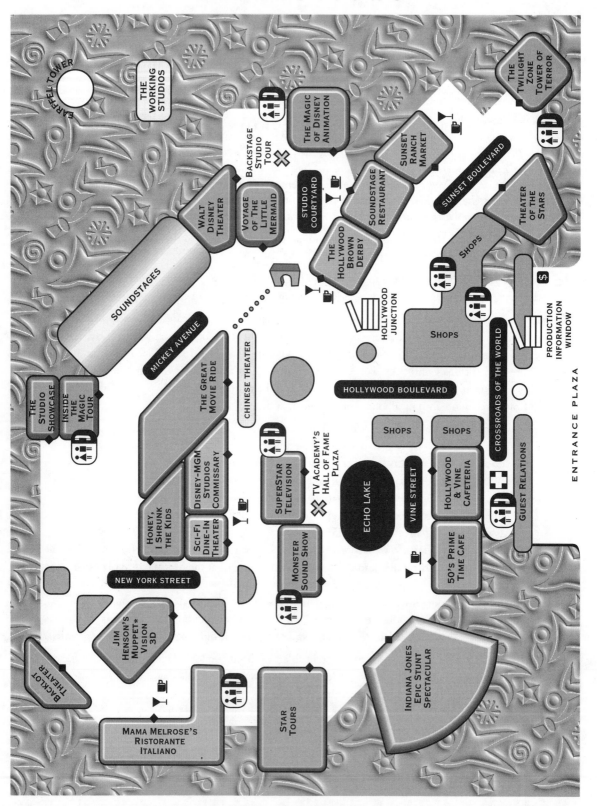

DISNEY-MGM STUDIOS

EARFFEL TOWER
THE WORKING STUDIOS
THE MAGIC OF DISNEY ANIMATION
THE TWILIGHT ZONE TOWER OF TERROR
BACKSTAGE STUDIO TOUR
SUNSET RANCH MARKET
SUNSET BOULEVARD
WALT DISNEY THEATER
VOYAGE OF THE LITTLE MERMAID
STUDIO COURTYARD
SOUNDSTAGE RESTAURANT
THEATER OF THE STARS
THE HOLLYWOOD BROWN DERBY
SOUNDSTAGES
SHOPS
MICKEY AVENUE
HOLLYWOOD JUNCTION
SHOPS
PRODUCTION INFORMATION WINDOW
THE STUDIO SHOWCASE
INSIDE THE MAGIC TOUR
THE GREAT MOVIE RIDE
CHINESE THEATER
HOLLYWOOD BOULEVARD
CROSSROADS OF THE WORLD
ENTRANCE PLAZA
SHOPS
SHOPS
SUPERSTAR TELEVISION
TV ACADEMY'S HALL OF FAME PLAZA
VINE STREET
HONEY, I SHRUNK THE KIDS
DISNEY-MGM STUDIOS COMMISSARY
ECHO LAKE
HOLLYWOOD & VINE CAFETERIA
GUEST RELATIONS
SCI-FI DINE-IN THEATER
MONSTER SOUND SHOW
50'S PRIME TIME CAFE
NEW YORK STREET
BACKLOT THEATER
JIM HENSON'S MUPPET*VISION 3D
INDIANA JONES EPIC STUNT SPECTACULAR
MAMA MELROSE'S RISTORANTE ITALIANO
STAR TOURS

# DISNEY-MGM STUDIOS

Disney-MGM Studios steeps visitors in the aura and ambience of Hollywood's most glamorous era and showcases the nuts-and-bolts aspects of film and television production. The park combines working production studios (accessible to visitors) with rides, live performances, shops, and restaurants that reflect the exciting world of television and motion picture entertainment. Sunset Boulevard was recently opened, featuring The Twilight Zone Tower of Terror attraction. The park's centerpiece, the elaborate Chinese Theater, is a full-scale copy of the Hollywood original, complete with movie star handprints in the forecourt's cement.

**WHEN TO GO:** The best times to visit are in the morning when the park opens, and at about 4 PM, when parents push a stroller brigade down Hollywood Boulevard in a mass exodus from the park. Television shows and movies are in production in the soundstages on weekdays, and fireworks displays are featured during peak seasons. Opening, closing, and event times vary throughout the year, so check ahead at Guest Services in your resort, or call 407 824-4321.

Visitors who would like to view a film production in progress or join a television show audience (or even appear as guests) should check at the Production Information Window at the Entrance Plaza. Tickets are available on a first-come, first-served basis; call 407 560-7299 for show times and information. As you enter the park, be sure to pick up an entertainment schedule at the Crossroads of the World kiosk. A Guest Information Board, located at the junction of Hollywood and Sunset Boulevards, lists attraction wait times and special events.

**HOW TO GET THERE:** The parking lot at Disney-MGM Studios is free to WDW resort guests (other visitors are charged about $7). The parking lot is serviced by trams. WDW buses travel between Disney-MGM Studios and all WDW resorts, theme parks, and the Transportation and Ticket Center. Water launches service the following resorts: Dolphin, Swan, Yacht Club, Beach Club, and BoardWalk.

## ATTRACTIONS

✗✗✗ – Solid Disney entertainment.   ✗✗ – A pleasant experience for most visitors.   ✗ – Of limited appeal.

**THE GREAT MOVIE RIDE:** Tucked into the Chinese Theater, this ride takes visitors on a multimedia journey through the history of the movies. In the theater lobby visitors see famous movie artifacts, including a carousel horse from *Mary Poppins* and one of the three pairs of ruby slippers made for *The Wizard of Oz*. A large tram then takes visitors past spectacular sets featuring live talent, Audio-Animatronic figures, and convincing special effects that re-create detailed scenes from such popular films as *The Wizard of Oz, Public Enemy, Alien,* and *Raiders of the Lost Ark*. The ride ends with a grand finale of clips from Academy Award–winning films. Duration: 20 minutes. ✗✗✗

**SUPERSTAR TELEVISION:** In this audience-participation show, visitors are selected in the preshow area to participate in the attraction. They perform on a stage with a special blue backdrop that allows a video editor to "key" them in as they become characters in popular shows such as "Home Improvement," "I Love Lucy," and "Cheers." The results, shown on huge overhead projection screens, can be hilarious. Duration: 30 minutes. ✗✗✗

**MONSTER SOUND SHOW:** Sound effects — the work of film crew members known as Foley artists — are the focus of this audience-participation show. After a preshow video featuring David Letterman, selected visitors are put to work as sound technicians on a short film starring Martin Short and Chevy Chase. The film is shown once with its original sound track, a second time to let the "technicians" put in their designated sound effects, then once again, this time with the new sound track, often with highly amusing results. After the show, visitors can try their skills in SoundWorks, a not-to-be-missed hands-on sound-effects gallery that can also be entered directly through the exit doors to the right of the Monster Sound Show entrance. Duration: 15 minutes. ✗✗

**THE TWILIGHT ZONE TOWER OF TERROR:** Visitors step into an abandoned, lightning-seared hotel and watch a video of Rod Serling relating a tale of guests who vanished from the hotel's elevator during a storm long ago. As visitors ride the elevator to investigate the mystery, another storm begins. Eerie scenes from another dimension, some with the missing guests, appear each time the elevator doors open. One startling scene, however, is real — visitors discover they are precariously suspended thirteen floors above the grounds. The lights flicker and the elevator, with its doors still open, plummets in the darkness, rises in a rush, and plummets again, giving visitors a free-fall experience they will not soon forget. Cutting-edge special effects and a programmable design make this a changeable, not-to-be-missed attraction. The thrill can be taxing, however, and health restrictions apply. Duration: 5 minutes. ✗✗✗

**STAR TOURS:** *Star Wars* robots R2D2 and C3PO beckon visitors into a futuristic, somewhat alien hangar where intergalactic craft are being serviced. The robots are employees of a travel agency booking visitors on a tour to the Moon of Endor. The spacecraft, which is actually a modified flight simulator, tilts and rocks dramatically during the show. With special effects and spectacular imagery, visitors are hurtled through space at the speed of light in a ship run amok, risking collisions with giant ice crystals and destruction by laser-wielding fighter ships. The seat belts provided are definitely required for this ride, which is not for those prone to motion sickness. A new simulator show may be introduced in 1997 to commemorate the twentieth anniversary of the first release of *Star Wars*. Duration: 6 minutes. ✗✗✗

**JIM HENSON'S MUPPET*VISION 3D:** This brilliantly conceived multimedia attraction, expected to undergo some changes in the near future, is one of those most often recommended by both visitors and insiders at Disney-MGM Studios. Visitors wear special glasses as they watch this a presentation that, at press time, revolves around the escapades at Muppet Labs when Waldo, a new character symbolizing 3-D, is unleashed. Combining an amusing 3-D film with live Muppets, pyrotechnics, bubbles, and a number of other special effects designed to evoke a you-are-there feeling, this attraction appeals to both young people and adults. Duration: 20 minutes. ✗✗✗

**HONEY, I SHRUNK THE KIDS MOVIE SET ADVENTURE:** This elaborate playground, based on the film *Honey, I Shrunk the Kids,* combines slides, rope ladders, and other equipment in a set that resembles a gigantic backyard filled with huge blades of grass and monstrously large ants. While the oversized props are interesting because of their scale, this playground was really designed for the children who pack the place. No time limit. ✗

**THE STUDIO SHOWCASE:** This gallery displays a frequently changing exhibit of some of the props, miniatures, and costumes used in many popular television shows and feature films. No time limit. ✗

**THE WALT DISNEY THEATER:** In this pleasant movie theater, visitors are presented with a short film exploring the behind-the-scenes work on recently released Disney movies such as *Pocahontas* and *Toy Story*. Although the air-conditioned theater is a nice break on a hot day, visitors anxious to see some of the more thrilling attractions may want to skip this one (and its long lines), since its "making-of" pieces tend to be the same as those presented on many cable channels. Shows change throughout the year. Duration: Approximately 20 minutes. ✘

**TV ACADEMY HALL OF FAME PLAZA:** This outdoor exhibit, located near SuperStar Television, is an adjunct to the Academy of Television Arts and Sciences Hall of Fame in North Hollywood, California. A giant Emmy statue stands among busts and bronze figures of inductees such as Rod Serling, Mary Tyler Moore, Bill Cosby, Carol Burnett, and, of course, Walt Disney. No time limit. ✘

## LIVE SHOWS AND SPECIAL EVENTS

*Live entertainment and extemporaneous happenings occur daily throughout Disney-MGM Studios. Along the Boulevards, visitors encounter zany Hollywood characters who involve them in movie-related antics. On certain afternoons, a street party may start up somewhere in the park or a Star Motorcade may carry one of Hollywood's greats to the Chinese Theater for a Handprint Ceremony and Star Interview.*

**INDIANA JONES EPIC STUNT SPECTACULAR:** This dramatic live-action show features the work of stunt designers and performers. A number of audience members are preselected to act as "extras." In reenactments of familiar scenes from the Indiana Jones movies, the professional stunt performers fall from buildings and dodge threatening boulders, fiery explosions, and out-of-control trucks. The fascinating explanation of the secrets behind the stunts does not seem to reduce their excitement or sense of realism. For the best view, arrive at least twenty minutes early and find a seat in the upper center. Shows are scheduled continuously throughout the day, but may be abbreviated if the weather looks threatening. Duration: 30 minutes. ✘✘

**THEATER OF THE STARS:** The famed Hollywood Bowl is fancifully reproduced in this shaded outdoor amphitheater on Sunset Boulevard. Here, talented singers and dancers, top-flight choreography and stage direction, elaborate sets, and imaginative costumes combine to create productions that are memorable for adults as well as children. The shows change periodically and are usually based on a recent Disney animated film. They are scheduled throughout the day, but the best time to see the show is late in the afternoon, when the crowds have thinned. Duration: Approximately 25 minutes. ✘✘✘

**VOYAGE OF THE LITTLE MERMAID:** This live performance of scenes from the Disney movie of the same name includes special effects that simulate rippling water overhead to evoke a sense of being under the sea. Families with young children find this attraction delightful. Visitors unfamiliar with the movie may wish to simply enjoy the show as song-and-dance numbers with colorful, cheerful denizens of the sea. On hot days, it's an ideal place to sit down and cool off — in fact, the audience is misted occasionally, in keeping with the watery theme. Shows are scheduled continuously. Duration: 15 minutes. ✘✘

**BACKLOT THEATER:** In this outdoor theater, visitors enjoy live productions that change periodically and are based on popular Disney feature films. The recent Spirit of Pocahontas show reweaves *Pocahontas* into a tale told by a tribal storyteller. Singing and dancing live performers, puppetry, distinctive special effects, elaborate costumes, and a novel animated set and proscenium enhance the tale, charming adults and children alike. The early performances and those late in the day are the best ones to catch, since the theater can become uncomfortably hot in the afternoon. Duration: Approximately 30 minutes. **✗✗✗**

**FEATURE PARADE:** Held once daily at 1 PM (twice in summer, at 11:30 AM and 3:30 PM), the Disney-MGM Studios parades are large-scale extravaganzas. They change from time to time to reflect the theme of a recently released Disney movie, such as *Aladdin* or *Toy Story*. Ornately designed floats, giant inflatable figures, live performers in elaborate costumes, and music and sound effects are just some features of this festive event. It is best viewed at the beginning of Hollywood Boulevard, near the Entrance Plaza. Duration: Approximately 15 minutes. **✗✗**

**NIGHTTIME FIREWORKS:** When the park stays open late, it presents fireworks shows considered by many to be the most dramatic at Walt Disney World. The pyrotechnics, mixed with music, special projection effects, and giant inflatable figures, light the sky over the park with multicolored bursts and dramatic fountains of glittering sparks, and leave visitors cheering for more. The best viewing spot is at the intersection of Hollywood and Sunset Boulevards. Sorcery in the Sky, the current show designed around Mickey Mouse's role as the Sorcerer's Apprentice in *Fantasia*, is expected to be replaced in the near future with Fantasmic Hollywood! (See "Coming Attractions," page 43.) Check the entertainment schedule for show times and dates. Duration for Sorcery in the Sky: Approximately 10 minutes. **✗✗✗**

# TOURS

**BACKSTAGE STUDIO TOUR:** Visitors get a truly informative behind-the-scenes look at motion picture production on this tram ride past the costume and scenic shops, lighting and camera departments, and residential street sets used in films and television shows. In the future, Disney may change the tour highlight, which is currently Catastrophe Canyon, where visitors feel the searing heat from an exploding tanker truck and, if sitting on the left side, are splashed by the waters of a flash flood. Tours are continuous. Duration: 25 minutes. **✗✗**

**INSIDE THE MAGIC — SPECIAL EFFECTS AND PRODUCTION TOUR:** This walking tour is an optional continuation of the Backstage Studio Tour and appeals to visitors who want a more in-depth view of motion picture production. The tour presents little opportunity to sit down and relies heavily on videos for explanatory narration. At a special-effects water tank, visitors learn how sea battles and storm sequences are created. They learn about "blue screen" techniques as an audience member, perched on a giant bee, is filmed against an already existing background scene. Visitors then tour the soundstages (empty, if no production is scheduled) and watch a short video featuring Bette Midler, followed by an explanation of how Midler's antics were filmed. The tour is much more interesting when productions are actually underway on the soundstages, so before signing up, check at the Production Information Window or Guest Relations. Tours are continuous. Duration: Approximately 45 minutes. **✗**

**THE MAGIC OF DISNEY ANIMATION:** After leaving the waiting area, which has displays of classic and current animation cels, visitors enter a theater for a highly entertaining and informative film about animation starring Robin Williams and Walter Cronkite, then tour Disney's working animation studio, where artists create future animated features. The various activities going on are explained on overhead monitors. Tours are continuous. Duration: Approximately 20 minutes. ✗✗

## FULL-SERVICE RESTAURANTS

*All WDW visitors can make restaurant reservations up to sixty days in advance. Same-day reservations may be made at Hollywood Junction, located at the intersection of Hollywood and Sunset Boulevards, or at the restaurant itself. Smoking is not permitted. See "Restaurants," page 163, for reviews and reservation information.*

**THE HOLLYWOOD BROWN DERBY:** Caricatures of famous personalities line the walls of this elegant, bustling restaurant. Steaks, seafood, pasta, and salads, including the house specialty, Cobb salad, are featured, along with a selection of specialty desserts. Beer, wine, and spirits are served, as are espresso and cappuccino. Open for lunch and dinner; reservations necessary.

**SCI-FI DINE-IN THEATER:** Under a twinkling night sky, rows of booths shaped like vintage convertibles create a drive-in movie setting, complete with car-side speakers and a big screen showing classic science fiction and horror film clips. This is a popular restaurant for families with young children. Burgers and specialty dishes such as They Called It Seafood — linguine topped with shrimp and other seafood — are the order of the day, along with the perfect movie appetizer, popcorn. Beer and wine are served. Open for lunch and dinner; reservations necessary.

**50'S PRIME TIME CAFE:** Decorated with fifties-style kitchens and dinette tables, this entertaining restaurant airs sitcoms of the period on black and white televisions, and serves such delectables as Aunt Selma's Lobster Salad and Granny's Pot Roast. Soda fountain treats are also featured. Beer, wine, and spirits are available. Open for lunch and dinner; reservations necessary.

**HOLLYWOOD & VINE CAFETERIA:** Located next door to the 50's Prime Time Cafe, this cafeteria-style restaurant is designed in a chromium blend of Art Deco and Diner Classic. Featured entrees include barbecued ribs, cold seafood and chicken, and a variety of salads. Beer and wine are available. Open for breakfast and lunch (and seasonally for dinner); no reservations.

**MAMA MELROSE'S RISTORANTE ITALIANO:** Loud good humor and basil-flavored olive oil for dipping bread create a trattoria ambience in this restaurant, which features Italian cuisine and thin-crust pizzas baked in brick ovens. Beer, wine, and spirits are served, as are espresso and cappuccino. Open for lunch (and seasonally for dinner); reservations necessary.

## COCKTAIL LOUNGES AND CAFES

*Refreshment stands that serve snacks and fast food all day are located throughout Disney-MGM Studios. Those listed below are especially pleasant and make ideal rendezvous spots. For before-dinner cocktails, try The Catwalk Bar or the lively and surreal Tune In Lounge next to the 50's Prime Time Cafe.*

**SUNSET RANCH MARKET:** This pleasant outdoor food court on Sunset Boulevard is designed as a farmer's market, with umbrella-shaded tables, a tiny victory garden, and a small stage with live musical performances at various times throughout the day. Fruit, snacks, specialty hot dogs, and frozen yogurt treats are available here, as are coffee, beer, and wine coolers. ▇Υ

**THE CATWALK BAR:** Filled with props, lights, and production equipment, this pleasant secluded bar is in the scaffolding above the Soundstage Restaurant and serves a limited selection of appetizers. Fine California wines, beer, and spirits are available, as are espresso and cappuccino. ▇Υ

**TUNE IN LOUNGE:** Located next to the 50's Prime Time Cafe, this bar serves up beer, wine, and spirits, along with appetizers and sitcoms, in a classic fifties environment, complete with black-and-white TVs and Naugahyde couches. ▇Υ

**SOUNDSTAGE RESTAURANT:** This food court resembling a massive production studio is decorated with props and sets from recent Disney films. Available at the counters are pizza, sandwiches, soup, and salad, as well as coffee, beer, and wine. ▇Υ

**DISNEY-MGM STUDIOS COMMISSARY:** Located next to the Chinese Theater, this large counter-service eatery has a streamlined contemporary decor and a display of Emmy awards earned by Disney productions. Snacks and fast food, including vegetarian chili, are served here, as are beer and coffee. ▇Υ

## SERVICES

**REST ROOMS:** Public rest rooms are located throughout Disney-MGM Studios. The rest rooms at the foot of Sunset Boulevard, between the Theater of the Stars and The Twilight Zone Tower of Terror, are rarely crowded. Visitors can also find cool and quiet rest rooms at the Disney-MGM Studios Commissary, the Tune In Lounge, The Hollywood Brown Derby, and The Catwalk Bar.

**TELEPHONES:** Public telephones are located throughout Disney-MGM Studios. The most secluded outdoor phones are those near the first-aid office in the Entrance Plaza and those by the rest rooms near The Twilight Zone Tower of Terror. The phones near the rest rooms at The Catwalk Bar, Mama Melrose's Ristorante Italiano, and the Disney-MGM Studios Commissary are not only quiet, but air-conditioned.

**MESSAGE CENTER:** Visitors can leave and retrieve messages for each other at the Message Center, located at Guest Relations. The Message Center is on a computer network also shared by Epcot Center and the Magic Kingdom, so visitors at one park can exchange messages with companions visiting elsewhere.

**FILM AND TWO-HOUR EXPRESS DEVELOPING:** Film is available at most Disney-MGM Studios shops. Drop-off points for express developing are at the Darkroom, on Hollywood Boulevard; at the Disney Studio Store, next to Voyage of The Little Mermaid; and at the Loony Bin, at the far end of Mickey Avenue. Developed film may be picked up at the Darkroom or delivered to any WDW resort. The Darkroom also offers one-hour developing.

**CAMERA RENTAL:** Video camcorders, replacement batteries, and 35mm cameras are available at the Darkroom, on Hollywood Boulevard. Rented equipment may be returned to the Kodak Camera Center in any major theme park.

**MAIL DROPS:** The mail-drop location at Disney-MGM Studios is just outside the Entrance Plaza. A stamp machine is located next to Oscar's Classic Car Souvenirs on Hollywood Boulevard.

**BANKING:** There is an automated teller machine (ATM) outside the Entrance Plaza, near the Production Information Window. Personal checks up to about $25 can be cashed at Guest Relations, located near the Entrance Plaza.

**LOCKERS:** Lockers are located at Oscar's Classic Car Souvenirs on Hollywood Boulevard.

**FIRST AID:** The first-aid office is at Disney-MGM Studios' Entrance Plaza, next to Guest Relations. Aspirin and other first-aid is dispensed free of charge. Over-the-counter medications are available at Golden Age Souvenirs, near SuperStar Television. They are not on display and must be requested at the counter.

**VISITORS WITH DISABILITIES:** A guidebook for guests with disabilities is available free of charge at Guest Relations, at Disney-MGM Studios' Entrance Plaza. Most attractions at Disney-MGM Studios have wheelchair access; however, visitors must leave their wheelchairs to ride Star Tours and The Twilight Zone Tower of Terror.

**WHEELCHAIR RENTALS:** Wheelchairs may be rented at Oscar's Classic Car Souvenirs on Hollywood Boulevard, just inside the Main Gate. Electric Convenience Vehicles can also be rented, and should be reserved one day ahead (407 824-4321). Only a limited number of these vehicles is available, so reserve early (by 8 AM). Replacement batteries, if needed, will be brought to your vehicle by a Cast Member.

**VISITORS WITH HEARING IMPAIRMENTS:** A written text of Disney-MGM Studios' attractions is available at Guest Relations, near the Entrance Plaza. Assistive listening devices are also available there for Muppet*Vision 3D, Voyage of The Little Mermaid, SuperStar Television, and the Sci-Fi Dine-In Theater Restaurant. A telecommunications device for the deaf (TDD) is also available at Guest Relations. Hearing aid–compatible and amplified telephones are available throughout the park.

**VISITORS WITH SIGHT IMPAIRMENTS:** Tape players and touring cassettes that describe the park are available at Guest Relations, at Disney-MGM Studios' Entrance Plaza. A Braille map of the park is located on a pedestal in front of Guest Relations.

**FOREIGN LANGUAGE ASSISTANCE:** Park maps in French, Spanish, German, Japanese, and a few other languages are available at Guest Relations, at Disney-MGM Studios' Entrance Plaza. Spanish-, French-, or German-speaking visitors may request assistance from the Walt Disney World Foreign Language Center by calling 824-7900 between 8:30 AM and 9 PM.

## COMING ATTRACTIONS

*Plans are always on the drawing board for new attractions throughout Walt Disney World, but until construction actually begins, these have a way of changing or stalling. At the time of publication, several new attractions and a revamping of currently existing ones were in the works.*

**BACKSTAGE STUDIO TOUR UPDATE:** A new thrill scene based on *Journey to the Center of the Earth* may replace Catastrophe Canyon in early 1996, when the tram tour is to be revamped and updated.

**DISNEY*VISION:** A new virtual reality attraction, based on riding the ornate flying carpet from *Aladdin*, is expected to open in 1997. The ride has been selectively tested in Innoventions West at Future World in Epcot Center. Rumors have it that this attraction may replace Jim Henson's Muppet*Vision 3D.

**FANTASMIC HOLLYWOOD!:** Similar to the attraction at California's Disneyland, but not as lengthy, this multimedia showcase of highlights from Disney classics mixes live performers, special effects, giant inflatables, colored mists, waterscreen projections, and pyrotechnics. The 1996 opening date rumored for this show may be delayed due to design and technical changes underway for the waterscreens.

**STAR TOURS UPDATE:** A new simulator-based adventure ride (which may also have a new name) is being designed to commemorate the twentieth anniversary of the beginning of the *Star Wars* film series. It is expected to premiere in 1997.

# Half-Day Tours at Disney-MGM Studios

The morning and evening half-day tours that follow are designed to allow first-time visitors to experience the best of Disney-MGM Studios in four to six hours, including a lunch or dinner in one of the park's restaurants. If possible, make your restaurant reservation in advance.

To create your own custom vacation at Walt Disney World, you can combine one of the half-day Disney-MGM Studios tours with a half-day tour at any other theme park. For example, combine the Morning in Movieland Tour at Disney-MGM Studios with an evening tour at the Magic Kingdom. The theme parks are most crowded in the afternoons, which is a good time for a relaxing break at your hotel.

## MORNING IN MOVIELAND TOUR

*Five to six hours — year round — including lunch.*
*Well in advance of your tour, reserve a late lunch (1:30 PM) at one of the Disney-MGM Studios restaurants.*

✔ Eat a full breakfast before leaving your hotel.

✔ Arrive at Disney-MGM Studios' Entrance Plaza at least one half hour before the scheduled opening time.

✔ When the park opens, proceed to the Crossroads of the World kiosk for an entertainment schedule.

✔ If you do not have a lunch reservation: Walk to Hollywood Junction, located at the intersection of Hollywood and Sunset Boulevards, and reserve lunch for 1:30 PM or later. (If you prefer a light meal, plan on eating at the Disney-MGM Studios Commissary or the Hollywood & Vine Cafeteria.)

✔ Begin your tour with a quick stroll along Hollywood and Sunset Boulevards. When you reach the end of Sunset Boulevard, visit any of the following attractions that interest you in this order:
- **THE TWILIGHT ZONE TOWER OF TERROR** (if you like one-of-a-kind thrill rides)
- **THE GREAT MOVIE RIDE**
- **STAR TOURS** (if you like thrill rides and are not prone to motion sickness)
- **JIM HENSON'S MUPPET*VISION 3D**
- **BACKSTAGE STUDIO TOUR** (tram portion only)
- If you still have an hour or so before your lunch reservation, see **SUPERSTAR TELEVISION** or catch the **FEATURE PARADE** (if it is scheduled at 11:30 AM).

✔ Plan to arrive at your lunch destination ten minutes early.

✔ If you wish to continue touring after lunch, take in the show at the THEATER OF THE STARS or BACKLOT THEATER, and see the INDIANA JONES EPIC STUNT SPECTACULAR and THE MAGIC OF DISNEY ANIMATION.

✔ Try to see the FEATURE PARADE on your way out of the park. (During peak seasons and on selected weekends, an afternoon parade is scheduled at about 3:30 PM.)

## NIGHT OF THE STARS AFTERNOON AND EVENING TOUR

*Five hours — June through August (and any day when the park is open late) — including dinner.*
*Make dinner reservations well in advance of this tour.*
*Book a seating no later than ninety minutes before the Nighttime Fireworks is scheduled to begin.*
*If you do not have reservations on the day of your tour, at 10 AM call Same Day Reservations (939-3463).*

✔ Arrive at Disney-MGM Studios' Entrance Plaza just before 4 PM.

✔ At the Crossroads of the World kiosk, pick up an entertainment schedule, which lists the show times for live performances and the Nighttime Fireworks show.

✔ Catch the second performance of the FEATURE PARADE at 3:30 PM (scheduled during peak seasons).

✔ If you do not have a dinner reservation: Proceed to Hollywood Junction, located at the intersection of Hollywood and Sunset Boulevards, and make a reservation that lets you finish your meal before the fireworks begin. (If you have difficulty making reservations, or would prefer a light meal, try the Disney-MGM Studios Commissary, which does not require reservations.)

✔ Visit, in the order listed below, those attractions that interest you. Skip those with long lines and pick them up later. Your tour will be temporarily interrupted for your dinner reservation.
   • THE TWILIGHT ZONE TOWER OF TERROR (if you like one-of-a-kind thrill rides)
   • THE MAGIC OF DISNEY ANIMATION
   • THE GREAT MOVIE RIDE
   • BACKSTAGE STUDIO TOUR (tram portion only)
   • JIM HENSON'S MUPPET*VISION 3D
   • STAR TOURS (if you like thrill rides, you're not prone to motion sickness, and the line is short)
   • INDIANA JONES EPIC STUNT SPECTACULAR.

✔ Pause in your tour in order to arrive at your dinner destination ten minutes early.

✔ After dinner, resume your tour. Check the entertainment schedule for special events, or visit attractions you may have missed earlier. Other entertaining attractions include:
   • SUPERSTAR TELEVISION
   • MONSTER SOUND SHOW (especially SoundWorks, which you can enter at the exit)
   • The performance at THEATER OF THE STARS.

✔ About fifteen minutes before the NIGHTTIME FIREWORKS show is scheduled to begin, find a viewing spot anywhere near the intersection of Hollywood and Sunset Boulevards.

✔ After the show, you may wish to browse through the shops along Hollywood Boulevard (they stay open late) or find an empty bench and people-watch while the crowds rush out. ◆

DISNEY-MGM STUDIOS

MAGIC KINGDOM

SPACE MOUNTAIN

SKYWAY

CAROUSEL OF PROGRESS

GRAND PRIX RACEWAY

TOMORROWLAND

GRANDMA DUCK'S FARM

MICKEY'S STARLAND SHOW

MICKEY'S HOLLYWOOD THEATRE

MICKEY'S STARLAND

MAD TEA PARTY

ASTRO ORBITER

TOMORROWLAND TRANSIT AUTHORITY

TOMORROWLAND

GALAXY PALACE THEATER AT ROCKETTOWER PLAZA

ExtraTERRORestrial Alien Encounter

MR. TOAD'S WILD RIDE

SNOW WHITE'S ADVENTURES

TRANS-PORTARIUM

DREAMFLIGHT

20,000 LEAGUES UNDER THE SEA

DUMBO THE FLYING ELEPHANT

MAIN STREET CINEMA

GOLDEN CARROUSEL CINDERELLA'S

CINDERELLA'S CASTLE

CASTLE FORECOURT STAGE

MAIN STREET, U.S.A.

FANTASY FAIRE

FANTASYLAND

IT'S A SMALL WORLD

SKY WAY

LEGEND OF THE LION KING

PETER PAN'S FLIGHT

THE HALL OF PRESIDENTS

CITY HALL

THE HAUNTED MANSION

MIKE FINK KEEL BOATS

DIAMOND HORSESHOE SALOON REVIEW

SWISS FAMILY TREEHOUSE

LIBERTY SQUARE RIVERBOAT

LIBERTY SQUARE

SHOOTIN' ARCADE

JUNGLE CRUISE

TOM SAWYER ISLAND

FRONTIERLAND

COUNTRY BEAR JAMBOREE

ENCHANTED TIKI BIRDS

ADVENTURELAND

PIRATES OF THE CARIBBEAN

BIG THUNDER MOUNTAIN RAILROAD

TOM SAWYER RAFTS

SPLASH MOUNTAIN

# MAGIC KINGDOM

The Magic Kingdom, a replica of California's Disneyland, was the first theme park built at Walt Disney World a quarter-century ago. Covering about one hundred acres (twenty more than Disneyland), the park opened with six theme lands: Adventureland, Frontierland, Liberty Square, Fantasyland, Tomorrowland, and Main Street, U.S.A. A seventh theme land, Mickey's Starland, was added in 1988, and in 1995, Tomorrowland was redesigned as an imaginary "city-of-the-future" based on visions from the past. The Magic Kingdom has many attractions similar to Disneyland's, plus several that are different. While Sleeping Beauty's Castle is Disneyland's centerpiece, Cinderella's Castle is the Magic Kingdom's. Designed to enchant children, the Magic Kingdom can trigger childhood nostalgia in adults, especially avid Disney fans.

**WHEN TO GO:** The best time to visit the Magic Kingdom is while schools are in session, certainly not during the summer months or holiday periods. Even during off-peak seasons, it's a good idea to arrive at the gates early in the morning, at least one half hour before the official opening time. It's even better to begin touring after 4 PM, when parents are herding their exhausted children toward the exit. Visitors should try to go on an evening when the Nighttime Electrical Parade and Fantasy in the Sky fireworks are scheduled. Opening, closing, and event times vary throughout the year, so check ahead at Guest Services in your resort, or call 407 824-4321.

**HOW TO GET THERE:** The vast Magic Kingdom parking lot is free to guests at WDW resorts (other visitors are charged about $7). The parking lot is serviced by trams that carry visitors to the Transportation and Ticket Center (TTC), the hub for all WDW transportation. Water launches and monorails transport visitors from the TTC to the park entrance. Water launches also service the Magic Kingdom from Discovery Island, River Country, and the following resorts: Fort Wilderness, Wilderness Lodge, Polynesian, and Grand Floridian. Sleek monorails, gliding on nearly fourteen miles of track, connect the Magic Kingdom and the TTC to Epcot Center and the following resorts: Contemporary, Polynesian, and Grand Floridian. (Visitors who want to make the most of the monorail ride should ask the driver if they can ride in front, where the view is great.) WDW buses travel between the Magic Kingdom and all Walt Disney World resorts and theme parks, and drop passengers at the park entrance.

**IN-PARK TRANSPORTATION:** Several transportation options are available in each part of the Magic Kingdom. Visitors can travel down Main Street in horse-drawn trolleys, jitneys, colorful double-decker buses, bell-clanging fire trucks, and purring antique cars. Between Fantasyland and Tomorrowland, visitors can ride the Skyway, an aerial gondola that provides a sweeping view of the Magic Kingdom. The Walt Disney World Railroad, with four authentic steam engine–powered trains, circles the park continuously, with stations at Main Street, U.S.A., Frontierland, and Mickey's Starland.

## ATTRACTIONS

**✗✗✗** – Solid Disney entertainment.  **✗✗** – Good fun if you're in the mood.  **✗** – For the very young at heart.
**👫** – Designed for small fry.

**MAIN STREET, U.S.A.:** From its entryway beneath the train station to its view of Cinderella's Castle in the distance, Main Street, U.S.A., is the first environment visitors encounter as they enter the Magic

Kingdom. It is a picture-perfect turn-of-the-century town. Visitors can take care of banking needs in a traditional setting; drop by City Hall for entertainment schedules; browse through a wide variety of specialty shops (including The Chapeau, featuring the monogrammed mouse ears made famous by the Mouseketeers); peer into the old-time Harmony Barber Shop or even get a haircut (call 407 824-6550 for an appointment); and take a break to people-watch in the Town Square, a pleasant plaza with benches, shade, and periodic live band concerts.

✦ *City Hall Information Center* — On arriving at the Magic Kingdom, visitors should make their first stop City Hall, located at the beginning of Main Street. A helpful staff provides maps and entertainment schedules; operates a Message Center for visitors; and makes resort, guided tour, and restaurant reservations. City Hall is also a good rendezvous point for visitors traveling in groups.

✦ *Main Street Cinema* — In this old-fashioned (and air-conditioned) movie house, visitors can watch *Mickey's Big Break,* a recent production that seamlessly mixes real-life footage with cartoon animation and features Mickey Mouse, Disney CEO Michael Eisner, and a host of big-screen stars. The theater has no seats and films run continuously. Duration: Approximately 15 minutes. ✗

✦ *Walt Disney World Railroad, Main Street Station* — Four open-air trains, pulled by whistle-blowing steam-puffing engines, travel the Walt Disney World Railroad on a mile-and-a-half tour of the park. Fans of the Grand-Canyon-and-dinosaur diorama for which California's Disneyland is noted will be disappointed, since it is absent here, but this leisurely trip through the lush foliage lining the track, coupled with views of most of the theme lands, is still worth the ride. Visitors can board and disembark at the Main Street, Frontierland, and Mickey's Starland stations. The trains run every four to seven minutes. Duration: Approximately 20 minutes for the entire circuit. ✗✗

**ADVENTURELAND:** At the end of Main Street, off to the left, Adventureland welcomes visitors into a tropical fantasy that is a blend of Africa, the Caribbean, Asia, the South Seas, and a bit of New Orleans. The dense foliage and mysterious rustles, squawks, and cries lend an exotic flavor. Adventureland is currently undergoing refurbishing and remodeling, and every day brings a change.

✦ *Jungle Cruise* — A lighthearted reminder of the Bogart-Hepburn classic film *The African Queen,* this recently revamped and expanded attraction takes visitors on a steamy adventure cruise down some of the world's great rivers — the Amazon, Congo, Nile, and Mekong — with a detour through the cavernous interior of a mysterious Asian temple. The guide delivers a witty, pun-laced narration about the rivers and their denizens, all the while protecting visitors from the clearly fake, yet entertaining local hostiles and wild animals along the riverbank. Exotic jungle plants, cascading waterfalls, updated Audio-Animatronic figures, and delightful special effects all add up to an ambience of comic adventure. There are always very long lines for this attraction. Duration: 9 minutes. ✗✗

✦ *Pirates of the Caribbean* — In the underground catacombs of a mysterious stone fortress, visitors board boats for a ride through a coastal settlement under attack by a band of raucous, rum-sotted pirates. After floating through dimly lit passages with unexpected drops, visitors are treated to humorous and, at times, disturbing vignettes of attacking ships with shots exploding overhead, high-spirited drunken debauchery, buildings on fire, and rooms heaped with treasure. While not as riveting (or romantic) as the same attraction at California's Disneyland, the elaborate sets, rich costuming, and sophisticated Audio-Animatronics still make this a must-see special-effects attraction. Duration: 9 minutes. ✗✗✗

MAGIC KINGDOM

✦ *Swiss Family Treehouse* — This walkthrough attraction invites visitors to tour the multilevel home of the famous shipwrecked family. Built into a giant replica of a banyan tree draped with real Spanish moss, it is the ultimate treehouse, with everything from cozy bedrooms to an intricate plumbing system — running water in every room! There are many stairs and almost always lots of kids enthusiastically exploring the novel rustic abode. Duration: Approximately 15 to 20 minutes. ✗

✦ *Enchanted Tiki Birds* — The dimly lit tropical lodge of the Enchanted Tiki Birds, filled with singing birds and flowers and chanting tikis, awaits visitors at the Tropical Serenade, a sing-along attraction. Visitors join in the familiar tunes, including the birds' "national" anthem, "Let's All Sing Like the Birdies Sing." It's a good place to relax and cool off, despite the groan-eliciting puns that lace the birds' chatter and the variable volume levels, sometimes piercing high notes, and overwhelming bass tones of the updated sound track and renovated sound system. There's an exit at the far side of the theater, and visitors may leave the show at any time. Duration: 25 minutes. ✗

**FRONTIERLAND:** Adjacent to Adventureland, visitors enter the American frontier of the nineteenth century, the world of Davy Crockett, Mark Twain, and the miners of the Gold Rush. Here, stone, clapboard, and split-log structures evoke the distinct frontiers of the East, the Midwest, and the Southwest. The Frontierland attractions have a rough-and-tumble quality to them, and two of the three Magic Kingdom roller-coaster rides are here.

✦ *Big Thunder Mountain Railroad* — On this roller-coaster ride, visitors travel through a Gold Rush–era mountain mining town on what soon becomes a runaway train. The roller coaster relies on side-to-side, rather than up-and-down, motion, but it's fast nonetheless and its creative special effects and scenery are great as they flash by. Crashing rocks, rushing waterfalls, flapping bats, braying donkeys, and a flooded mining town make for a lively experience. Many visitors consider this ride to be more fun and enchanting at night. Duration: 4 minutes. ✗✗✗

✦ *Country Bear Jamboree* — Almost two dozen whimsical Audio-Animatronic bears make for lively antics at this performance in Grizzly Hall. Henry, the show's emcee, introduces the bears, who tell tall tales, crack corny jokes, and perform musical numbers. Many of the show's players, including popular favorite Big Al, have been recently updated. The show and decor are changed throughout the year to reflect seasonal holidays. Duration: 15 minutes. ✗✗

✦ *Frontierland Shootin' Arcade* — This attraction puts an electronic spin on the traditional carnival shooting gallery. Using real buffalo rifles (fitted with infrared beams instead of bullets); visitors shoot at frontier-motif targets in a Tombstone Territory setting. Through the magic of special effects, "hit" targets twist, howl, or trigger a secondary humorous effect. Don't spend too long aiming; accuracy yields no prize and rifles are programmed to provide a specified number of either shots *or* minutes of service, whichever comes first. Kids flock to this arcade, which requires spending money in the form of small change. Duration: 2 minutes or 25 shots for 50 cents. 👫

✦ *Splash Mountain* — The Disney classic, *Song of the South,* sets the theme of this water-chute roller coaster. Amid the antics of Brer Rabbit, Brer Fox, Brer Bear, and their friends, visitors are swept along in log boats on a half-mile journey through bayous, gardens, swamps, and caves. Sudden unexpected drops and slow, lazy drifts alternately startle and lull visitors until they confront Brer Fox, in a quandary about throwing Brer Rabbit into the briar patch. From there, the ride goes downhill, literally, plunging almost five stories to splash into the giant briar patch below. The outstanding Audio-Animatronics and sets in this attraction, as well as the pacing and sound track, show Disney wizardry at its most creative. Expect to get fairly wet (you may want to take along a plastic poncho or large garbage bag). Duration: 11 minutes. ✖✖✖

✦ *Tom Sawyer Island* — This attraction evokes the adventuresome Missouri frontier of Mark Twain's famed character, and it appeals to youngsters with plenty of energy to burn. Ferried back and forth to the island on rafts, visitors can spelunk in a spooky cave, wobble across a barrel bridge, walk along mysterious winding paths, inspect a working windmill and waterwheel, and explore the Fort Sam Clemens stockade. Although the island can make a pleasant interlude for adults, it is overrun with free-wheeling children all day and closes at sundown. No time limit. 👫

✦ *Walt Disney World Railroad, Frontierland Station* — With its open, airy boarding platform and large wooden water tank, this atmospheric Old West railroad station artfully captures the mood of nineteenth-century train travel. Of the three stops on the Walt Disney World Railroad, this one is the busiest. Duration: Approximately 20 minutes for the entire circuit. ✖✖

**LIBERTY SQUARE:** Liberty Square captures the ambience of a town square at the time of the American Revolution. The buildings are accurate in their architectural styling and detail, right down to their leather-hinged shutters hanging slightly askew. A reproduction of the Liberty Bell, cast at the same foundry as the original, hangs in the square, and a huge one-hundred-year-old live oak nearby is hung with thirteen metal lanterns representing the light of freedom in each of the original thirteen colonies.

✦ *Liberty Square Riverboat* — Visitors board this steam-powered stern-wheeler, which actually rides on an underwater rail, for a sedate journey around Tom Sawyer Island. Sights en route include a burning cabin, Fort Sam Clemens, and a number of other props in woods and clearings along the shore. The boat leaves on the hour and the half hour. Duration: 15 minutes. ✖

✦ *Mike Fink Keel Boats* — The small, squat boats on this water ride evoke a backwoods mood. Like the Liberty Square Riverboat, the keelboats circle Tom Sawyer Island. Visitors glide by various river-bank sights, including a burning log cabin and Fort Sam Clemens. This warm-weather attraction operates seasonally and closes at sundown. (This attraction is closed seasonally.) Duration: 10 minutes. ✖

✦ *The Hall of Presidents* — Restyled in 1994, this attraction opens with a 70mm film (narrated by author Maya Angelou) showcasing the U.S. Constitution and selected historical events that shaped its amendments. As the film ends, a curtain rises to reveal Audio-Animatronic representation of all forty-two U.S. Presidents in a startlingly lifelike tableau. Rustles fill the air when a roll call begins and each figure responds to his name as the others nod, turn to look, or shift restlessly. Clinton checks his watch while Lincoln speaks and later gives a speech of his own, the show's first-ever by a living president. This attraction's tone is more serious than most at the Magic Kingdom, but its sophisticated Audio-Animatronics (plus the sit-down air-conditioned theater) make it very worthwhile. Duration: 23 minutes. ✖✖✖

✦ *The Haunted Mansion* — This creaking, groaning, and moaning eighteenth-century-style red-brick mansion with its eerie sounds is Liberty Square's most popular attraction. Visitors pass by a town graveyard with wretchedly punned tombstone epitaphs, to be welcomed into the house by a creepy, supercilious butler and led into a waiting area decorated with some very unusual family portraits. Visitors then board ride vehicles that carry them off on a dark and spooky tour of the mansion. Ghosts dance, and rattles, rustles, and screams fill the air, while quirky, ghastly humor permeates the ongoing narration. The clever sets, props, and visual effects make The Haunted Mansion an especially enjoyable attraction for adults. Duration: 9 minutes. ✗✗✗

FANTASYLAND: A potpourri of glittering carousel horses, colorful banners, wacky rides, and fairy-tale encounters, Fantasyland is the theme land that best reflects the light-hearted side of Walt Disney's imagination. The appealing Alpine-village setting with half-timbered buildings and festive tentlike structures spreads out behind Cinderella's Castle, the Magic Kingdom's beautiful centerpiece. Although most of the attractions are really designed with children in mind, adults will enjoy taking in the sights.

✦ *Cinderella's Golden Carrousel* — Sparkling with mirrors, gilded decorations, painted scenes from the movie Cinderella, and beautifully detailed horses, this elegant merry-go-round is a true classic. Its riders are carried back in time in leisurely, pleasant circles. No two horses are alike, and the carrousel is especially pretty and evocative at twilight. Duration: 2 minutes. 👫

✦ *Dumbo the Flying Elephant* — Appealing to the very young, this richly detailed version of the kiddie carnival attraction takes visitors in sixteen big-eared Dumbo-shaped gondolas on a slow ride with gentle lifts and drops around a golden crown. Adults can bypass this ride without missing out on anything special. Duration: 2 minutes. 👫

✦ *It's A Small World* — Visitors board boats for this whimsical water journey through a world populated by dolls representing children of every nationality. The moving dolls, dressed in elaborate folk costumes, sing the verses to "It's A Small World" in the language of the culture they represent. Although the tune is difficult to shake off, visitors seem to come away happy (or perhaps mesmerized by the repetitive expressions of the designers' good intentions). Long lines move quickly, and on a hot day, this ride can be a godsend — it's air-conditioned. Duration: 11 minutes. ✗✗

✦ *Mad Tea Party* — Drawing from the children's classic *Alice in Wonderland,* this attraction features giant, madly spinning pastel-painted teacups on a whirling ride that is not for the weak of stomach. The Mad Tea Party is really a fairly typical carnival ride that has been dressed up Disney style. Kids are its greatest fans. Duration: 2 minutes. 👫

✦ *Legend of the Lion King* — Visitors pass by some of the artwork used to create Disney's highly popular movie, *The Lion King.* They enter a room with a stage, where they meet a sleepy Rafiki (the baboon, played by a live performer) and watch the "Circle of Life" film clip on a giant screen. As the music fades, visitors proceed into a sit-down theater where Rafiki, large puppets, special effects, and animation clips projected on the screen at the rear of the stage mix together in a multimedia re-creation of selected scenes from the movie. Visitors should avoid seats at the sides of the theater or the first three rows, since the elevated stage and its proscenium can partially block views of some stage action and the film clips. Duration: Preshow 8 minutes; show 20 minutes. ✗✗

✦ *Mr. Toad's Wild Ride* — This wacky drive takes visitors through barn doors, chicken coops, a fireplace, and on a collision course with an oncoming train. Adults who expect the word *wild* to have a meaning other than "silly" will be disappointed, although the ride has its fans. Duration: 3 minutes. 👫

✦ *Peter Pan's Flight* — Set in Never-Never Land, this attraction takes visitors for a flight in miniature versions of Captain Hook's pirate ship. The ride starts high above the rooftops of London and dips down from time to time into settings that re-create scenes from *Peter Pan.* Although designed to amuse children, Peter Pan's Flight is actually surprisingly delightful and leaves adults as well as children with a happy glow. Duration: 4 minutes. ✖✖

✦ *Skyway to Tomorrowland* — An Alpine chalet houses this cable car ride to Tomorrowland. Open-air gondolas give visitors a spectacular bird's-eye view of the Magic Kingdom. Each car holds only a few people and no specific scenario demands attention, so visitors who are comfortable with heights can just relax and enjoy the view. Duration: 5 minutes. ✖✖

✦ *Snow White's Adventures* — This ride takes visitors in wooden mining cars past sets depicting scenes from the Disney animated classic (some enhanced with Audio-Animatronic figures). Originally designed to let visitors see the world through Snow White's terrified eyes, the attraction was toned down in 1994 to make the wicked witch less scary and include the heroine in some new, more colorful scenes. The attraction lacks the unique "you-are-there" feel of the original, and most adults will find little to enchant them. Duration: 2 minutes. ✖

✦ *20,000 Leagues Under the Sea* — This attraction, now closed, is scheduled to reopen in late 1996. No decision has been reached on whether it will be as a new and completely original attraction or as a new walkthrough attraction similar to *Les Mystères du Nautilus* at Disneyland Paris. There, visitors take a narrated tour through Captain Nemo's submarine, where special multimedia effects and an exciting escape from a "giant" squid attack enhance the tour.

**MICKEY'S STARLAND:** Opened in 1988 as Mickey's Birthdayland, a tribute to Mickey Mouse's sixtieth anniversary, Mickey's Starland is made up of brightly colored kid-sized buildings that look as though they were taken right out of a cartoon and set in the small country town of Duckburg. With a farm animal petting zoo, a live theater, Mickey's personal residence, and a large population of Disney characters, Mickey's Starland appeals primarily to small children and devoted Disney-character fans.

✦ *Grandma Duck's Farm* — In this barnyard petting zoo, complete with windmill and water tower, visitors can reach through the fence rails and pet Minnie Moo the cow and many of her animal friends, including ponies, ducks, rabbits, pigs, sheep, and roof-climbing goats. (Watch for the natural Mickey Mouse patterns in the markings on the cow, pigs, and other animals.) This attraction is rarely crowded, and animal lovers of all ages can enjoy it at any time of day. No time limitation. ✖

✦ *Mickey's Hollywood Theatre* — This large, round tentlike structure houses Mickey's dressing room, fitted with lighted mirrors and racks of costumes. Mickey Mouse fans have a chance to collect autographs and photographs here when they meet Mickey backstage between his many public appearances. No time limitation. ✖

✦ *Mickey's House and Starland Show* — Mickey's bright yellow house, decorated with furnishings and props familiar to Disney cartoon lovers, is always open. When visitors exit the house at the rear, they pass the residences of other Disney characters, including Donald Duck's houseboat and Goofy's sloppy bachelor pad. Just beyond is a yellow-and-white-striped tent, where Mickey and friends perform energetic live skits. Duration: Approximately 35 minutes. 🚶

✦ *Walt Disney World Railroad, Mickey's Starland Station* — The vividly painted train station at Mickey's Starland sets the cartoon-fantasy tone of the small, cheerful town of Duckburg. Disney characters can often be seen here greeting visitors or waving good-bye to them. Duration: Approximately 20 minutes for the entire circuit. ✘✘

**TOMORROWLAND:** Tomorrowland, which had a facelift in 1994, now represents a sci-fi city-of-the-future as envisioned by the machine-age dreamers of the past, evoking a sense of comic-book surrealism. Visitors strolling on the walkway from Main Street pass under an arch of rich-hued and jumbled metal rods, elements repeated in sculptures and building details. Sleek glass kiosks and oddly angular palm trees sprout out of the pavement; the architecture is retro-moderne, with an offbeat pastel color scheme accented by vividly colored graphics and neon lights. As part of the "modernization," almost all of Tomorrowland's attractions were revamped or replaced with new ones.

✦ *Transportarium* — In this stand-up theater, an intertemporal-tour planner named Timekeeper sends visitors on a wacky trip through time with his multiple-lensed assistant Nine-Eye. A Circle-Vision 360 film depicts Timekeeper's sloppy temporal technique, which has visitors ricocheting through the centuries, brings them face to face with Jules Verne, and swoops them off on time-travel adventures. This attraction is adapted from *Le Visionarium* at Disneyland Paris, with the addition of Audio-Animatronic figures. The attraction accommodates about three thousand visitors each hour, so Transportarium can be enjoyed at almost any time. Duration: 18 minutes. ✘✘✘

✦ *Carousel of Progress* — Visitors seated on a revolving turntable watch Audio-Animatronic figures depict lifestyles from the early 1900s through the not-too-distant future. In each humorous scene, the husband marvels at the age's technological advancements, while his family puts them to use with unexpected results. The 1994 update of this attraction adds a historical preshow film with Walt Disney and restores its original tune, "There's a Great Big Beautiful Tomorrow." Duration: 22 minutes. ✘✘

✦ *Dreamflight* — This attraction, which was also technically revamped for the new Tomorrow-land, takes visitors on a cheerful educational journey through the history of modern aviation. The attraction uses giant pop-up books as opening and closing motifs, and mixes three-dimensional sets and props with special you-are-there effects, 70mm film footage, video imagery, and creative computer graphics. Duration: 6 minutes. ✘✘

✦ *Grand Prix Raceway* — Visitors drive noisy miniature gasoline-powered cars at less than seven miles per hour along one of four parallel tracks. This attraction seems out of place in the new Tomorrow-land and will disappoint adults. Duration: Less than 5 minutes, depending on driving speed. 👫

✦ *The ExtraTERRORestrial Alien Encounter* — A video pitch for X-S Tech's new teletrans-porter greets visitors, who are then invited into a room for a demo of it in action. During the demo, however, a technical glitch slightly sizzles the fuzzy alien beamed from one cylinder to another. Then, visitors enter a theater, where they are firmly harnessed into seats to observe a real interplanetary teletransport. It, too, is botched, and circuits blow as it imports a frightful alien monster who breaks loose. In the darkness, frightening sounds and glimpses of horrifying events attest to the monster's destructiveness, but visitors can't escape their harnesses. As drops of warm wetness fall on them, they hear the monster move closer and closer, until it is so near they can smell its breath and feel it pulling at their harness. This scary attraction combines sophisticated Audio-Animatronics and special effects with the psychology of terror. The attraction is interactive, so if you want to keep a low-profile, don't scream. Duration: Preshows about 3 minutes each; show 9 minutes. ✘✘✘

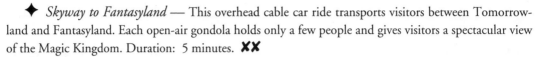
◆ *Skyway to Fantasyland* — This overhead cable car ride transports visitors between Tomorrowland and Fantasyland. Each open-air gondola holds only a few people and gives visitors a spectacular view of the Magic Kingdom. Duration: 5 minutes. ✗✗

◆ *Space Mountain* — This wild roller-coaster ride through the cosmos is housed in a huge, spired and domed structure visible throughout the Magic Kingdom and beyond. The moment they enter the sleek spaceport's futuristic environment, visitors are caught up in the excitement. Once on board, they are hurtled through mostly dark space, illuminated occasionally by flashing comets, colorful bursts, and whirling galaxies. Distinctive special effects, the creative use of darkness, and two roller coasters running concurrently make this attraction a must-try experience. The thrill can be taxing, however, and health restrictions apply. Duration: Preshow and post show 15 minutes; ride 3 minutes. ✗✗✗

◆ *Astro Orbiter* — Color-splashed rockets rapidly spin, dip, and lift riders in circles as they rush past giant planets. The new design is striking and imaginative, but most adult visitors will be disappointed by this spiffed-up version of the StarJets carnival ride. Duration: 2 minutes. 👥👤

◆ *Tomorrowland Transit Authority* — This updated version of the WEDway PeopleMover takes visitors aboard a pollution-free, elevated-track tram on a narrated tour that travels just about ten miles per hour above, alongside, and through several Tomorrowland attractions, including Space Mountain. Duration: 10 minutes. ✗✗

## SPECIAL EVENTS AND LIVE ENTERTAINMENT

*Live entertainment events are scheduled throughout the day at numerous locations in the Magic Kingdom. As you enter the park, pick up an entertainment schedule at City Hall, on Main Street.*

**DIAMOND HORSESHOE SALOON REVUE:** Songs and dances from the Gay Nineties entertain visitors of all ages in this Old West saloon in Frontierland. The lively and very popular production includes rollicking tunes, comic vignettes, energetic dance performances, and some skillful sleight-of-hand demonstrations. Visitors can lounge at the long bar or sit at tables scattered throughout the room to enjoy the show, which runs continuously from 10 AM until 6 PM. Counter-service snacks, sandwiches, and beverages are available for purchase to enjoy during the show. Duration: No set time. Good for about 30 minutes. ✗✗

**AFTERNOON PARADE:** This large-scale extravaganza changes themes from time to time and gives visitors in the Magic Kingdom a festive treat every afternoon at 3 PM. Elaborate floats, dancers and stiltwalkers in flashy costumes, and giant inflatables of Disney characters are just some of this grand parade's features. It is best watched from Frontierland or Liberty Square, where crowds are thinner than on Main Street. Duration: Approximately 15 minutes. ✗✗

**NIGHTTIME ELECTRICAL PARADE:** At selected times throughout the year, high-tech lighting and sound, fantastic set designs, and live performers create a magical nighttime parade of elaborate twinkling floats that wends its way through the Magic Kingdom. Check the entertainment schedule for show times. The parade attracts huge crowds, especially along Main Street, where viewers gather as much as an hour before the parade begins. A handy tip: Those who want to watch the parade on Main Street should try to find a spot by a trash container — there will rarely be someone standing in front of it, and you can set packages, beverages, and other items on top. Otherwise, the parade is best watched from Frontierland or Liberty Square, where the crowds are thinner. On nights when the parade is held twice, the later one attracts smaller crowds. Duration: Approximately 18 minutes. ✗✗✗

**FANTASY IN THE SKY FIREWORKS:** When Magic Kingdom hours are extended to 10 PM or later, fireworks explode above Cinderella's Castle, preceded by Tinker Bell's dramatic flight across the sky from a castle tower to Tomorrowland. The show is best watched from the walkway between Main Street and Tomorrowland, where crowds are thinner than on Main Street. Visitors interested in the fireworks only will find Mickey's Starland an ideal, uncrowded vantage point. Check the entertainment schedule for show times and dates. Duration: Approximately 7 minutes. ✗✗✗

**CASTLE FORECOURT STAGE:** At this outdoor gathering spot in front of Cinderella's Castle (the Main Street side), visitors can enjoy a variety of musical and theatrical shows featuring Disney characters from recent film releases. Check the entertainment schedule for show times. ✗✗

**FANTASY FAIRE:** When not in use as a dining pavilion, this giant striped tent in Fantasyland is the site of musical and theatrical performances featuring guest artists and Disney characters. Check the entertainment schedule for events and show times. ✗

**GALAXY PALACE THEATER AT ROCKETTOWER PLAZA:** Live music and dance performances with futuristic themes and intergalactic characters are staged in this large open-air theater in Tomorrowland. Check the entertainment schedule for events and show times. ✗

**TOUR:** *Keys to the Kingdom* — Departing daily from City Hall, this walking tour is an informative and hassle-free way for visitors to learn about the history of Walt Disney World, see highlights of the Magic Kingdom, and get a look at some of its backstage areas and lower-level "utilidors." Attractions visited may vary with the season, but often include the Tomorrowland Transit Authority, It's A Small World, The Haunted Mansion, Country Bear Jamboree, and Pirates of the Caribbean. Reservations for the 10:30 AM tour may be made up to forty-five days in advance. Call 407 939-8687. Visitors without advance reservations can take the 10 AM version of the tour, which fills quickly and is limited to the first fifteen people who sign up at City Hall; about $45, excluding food. Duration: Approximately 4 hours. ✗✗

## FULL-SERVICE RESTAURANTS

*Restaurant reservations may be made up to sixty days in advance by all visitors to WDW. Same-day reservations can be made at City Hall or at the restaurant itself. No alcohol is served in the Magic Kingdom. Smoking is not permitted. See "Restaurants," page 163, for reviews and reservation information.*

**MAIN STREET, U.S.A.:** *Tony's Town Square Restaurant* — Diners in this spacious restaurant with a sunny glassed-in patio and pleasant Victorian-style *Lady and the Tramp* decor enjoy waffles, eggs, and pancakes in the morning, and pasta, pizza, and other Italian dishes throughout the day. Espresso and cappuccino are served. Open for breakfast, lunch, and dinner; reservations suggested.

*The Plaza Restaurant* — This light and airy restaurant has a pleasant, fanciful Art Nouveau ambience. The menu features a selection of hot entrees, sandwiches, hamburgers, salads, and ice cream specialties. Espresso, cappuccino, and café mocha are served. Open for lunch and dinner; no reservations.

*The Crystal Palace* — This replica of a Victorian-era conservatory has a circular atrium and skylights throughout and offers cafeteria-style service in a spacious plant-filled environment. The menu features a full breakfast menu in the morning, and prime rib, roast chicken, seafood, and sandwiches during the day. Open for breakfast, lunch, and dinner; no reservations.

LIBERTY SQUARE: *Liberty Tree Tavern* — With its low lighting, plank floors, and giant fireplace, this friendly restaurant has a comfortable colonial ambience. The menu features New England clam chowder all day long, large salads and sandwiches at lunch. The Character Dinner includes chicken, steak, and special sausages. Open for lunch and dinner; reservations required.

FANTASYLAND: *King Stefan's Banquet Hall* — This restaurant high up in Cinderella's Castle has a medieval elegance and fantasy decor. Cinderella herself makes appearances here from time to time. At the Character Breakfast, waffles, pancakes, and egg dishes are featured. Salads, sandwiches, roast beef, seafood, and chicken dishes are served at lunch and dinner. Open all day; reservations required.

## CAFES

*There are refreshment stands that serve snacks and fast-food meals throughout the Magic Kingdom. A few, listed below, are pleasant rest stops and rendezvous spots. No alcohol is served in the Magic Kingdom.*

MAIN STREET, U.S.A.: *Main Street Bake Shop* — Freshly baked cookies, cakes, tarts, and pastries are available to eat at small, cozy tables tucked into a turn-of-the-century tearoom.

ADVENTURELAND: *El Pirata el Perico* — This fast-food stand serves sandwiches and the only tacos in the Magic Kingdom, which visitors can enjoy at umbrella-shaded tables located nearby.

LIBERTY SQUARE: *Sleepy Hollow* — This fast-food eatery offers vegetarian specialties, sandwiches, snacks, and a good view of the daily afternoon parade at the rail-side tables on its outdoor patio.

FANTASYLAND: *Pinocchio Village Haus* — This two-story Bavarian-styled restaurant features fast foods such as bratwurst, turkey sandwiches, and pasta salads.

TOMORROWLAND: *Cosmic Ray's Starlight Cafe* — Large open rooms decorated in bright contemporary colors and an outdoor terrace overlooking nearby gardens provide comfortable places to take a break and enjoy rotisserie chicken, hamburgers, sandwiches, pizza, pasta, and other fast food along with entertainment such as Sonny Eclipse's tunes on the Astro Organ.

## SERVICES

REST ROOMS: Public rest rooms are numerous throughout the Magic Kingdom. On Main Street, the rest rooms to the right of City Hall, although crowded in the morning and evening, are relatively empty in the afternoon. Despite large crowds, there are rarely waits in the rest rooms located across from the Swiss Family Treehouse, in the breezeway between Adventureland and Frontierland. In Fantasyland, the rest rooms behind the Enchanted Grove (near Mr. Toad's Wild Ride) usually do not attract large crowds. In Tomorrowland, the least crowded rest rooms are those by the Skyway to Fantasyland. For quieter accommodations, King Stefan's Banquet Hall in Cinderella's Castle has rest rooms halfway up the stairs, although most restaurant rest rooms are crowded during mealtimes.

**TELEPHONES:** Public telephones are located throughout the Magic Kingdom. The least busy are those near The Crystal Palace restaurant at the end of Main Street; at the exit to Pirates of the Caribbean in Adventureland; behind the Enchanted Grove (near Mr. Toad's Wild Ride) in Fantasyland; near the Skyway to Fantasyland in Tomorrowland; and at the Frontierland Railroad Station. To make calls in quieter, air-conditioned comfort, slip into a full-service restaurant (except Tony's Town Square Restaurant), where there are telephones near the rest rooms.

**MESSAGE CENTER:** At Walt Disney World's computerized Message Center, located at Guest Relations in City Hall on Main Street, visitors can leave and retrieve messages for one another. The Message Center is on a network also shared by Epcot Center and Disney-MGM Studios, so visitors at one park can exchange messages with companions visiting elsewhere.

**FILM AND TWO-HOUR EXPRESS DEVELOPING:** Film is available at shops and kiosks throughout the Magic Kingdom. Drop-off points for express developing are at the Newsstand and the Kodak Camera Center on Main Street; at the Crow's Nest in Adventureland; at the Kodak Kiosk in Fantasyland, across from Cinderella's Golden Carrousel; at Kodak's Funny Photos in Mickey's Starland; and at Geiger's Counter in Tomorrowland. Developed pictures may be picked up at the Kodak Camera Center on Main Street or delivered to any WDW resort.

**CAMERA RENTAL:** Video camcorders, replacement batteries, and 35mm cameras are available at the Kodak Camera Center on Main Street. Rented equipment may be returned to a Kodak Camera Center in any major theme park.

**MAIL DROPS:** Mail drops are located at the Newsstand, in front of City Hall and Tony's Town Square Restaurant, and here and there on both sides of Main Street; across from the Swiss Family Treehouse in Adventureland; across from the Country Bear Jamboree in Frontierland; near Tinker Bell's Treasures, across from Cinderella's Castle, in Fantasyland; and across from the Grand Prix Raceway in Tomorrowland. Stamps may be purchased at City Hall and the Emporium, both located on Main Street.

**BANKING:** The Sun Bank on Main Street, near the park entrance, provides full banking services and foreign currency exchange. An automated teller machine (ATM) is located at the bank and at the arcade next to Space Mountain in Tomorrowland. Personal checks up to about $25 can be cashed at Sun Bank and at Guest Relations at City Hall, on Main Street.

**LOCKERS:** Lockers are located on the lower level of the Main Street Railroad Station. Oversized packages may be left at City Hall, on Main Street.

**PACKAGE DELIVERY:** Guests staying at a Walt Disney World resort can have any merchandise they purchase at the Magic Kingdom shops delivered to their hotel free of charge.

**FIRST AID:** The first-aid station is located just past The Crystal Palace restaurant, at the end of Main Street. Aspirin and other first-aid needs are dispensed free of charge. Over-the-counter medications are available at the Emporium, on Main Street. They are not on display and must be requested at the counter.

MAGIC KINGDOM

**VISITORS WITH DISABILITIES:** A free guidebook for guests with disabilities is available at the Guest Relations Window in the Entrance Plaza and at City Hall, on Main Street. Visitors with disabilities should note that the monorail stop at the Contemporary resort is not accessible to wheelchairs. Most attractions at the Magic Kingdom have wheelchair access, but there are a number of exceptions. For these, special arrangements can usually be made to transfer visitors from wheelchairs into the ride vehicle. Ask at City Hall. Areas along the Magic Kingdom parade route are designated for visitors in wheelchairs. Ask at City Hall for these locations, available on a first-come, first-served basis.

**WHEELCHAIR RENTALS:** Wheelchairs can be rented at the Stroller Shop, in the Entrance Plaza. Electric Convenience Vehicles can also be rented and should be reserved one day ahead (407 824-4321). Only a limited number of these vehicles is available, so reserve early (by 8 AM). Replacement batteries, if needed, will be brought to your vehicle if you alert a Cast Member.

**VISITORS WITH HEARING IMPAIRMENTS:** A written description of the Magic Kingdom's attractions is available at City Hall, on Main Street. Hearing aid–compatible and amplified telephones can be found throughout the Magic Kingdom.

**VISITORS WITH SIGHT IMPAIRMENTS:** Tape players and touring cassettes describing the park are available at City Hall, on Main Street. Also available at City Hall are a Braille map and book describing the attractions.

**FOREIGN LANGUAGE ASSISTANCE:** Park maps in French, Spanish, German, Japanese, and a few other languages are available at City Hall, on Main Street. Spanish-, French-, or German-speaking visitors may request additional assistance by calling the Walt Disney World Foreign Language Center (824-7900) between 8:30 AM and 9 PM.

## COMING ATTRACTIONS

*There are always plans on the drawing board for new attractions throughout WDW, but until construction actually begins, these plans have a way of changing or becoming delayed. At the time of publication, an overall revamping of Adventureland was scheduled for 1996, as was an update of the Haunted Mansion, complete with new scenes and storyline.*

**FANTASYLAND:** *New 20,000 Leagues Under the Sea Attraction* — Closed in 1995 for revamping, this fantasy submarine ride, one of the Magic Kingdom's original attractions, may be converted into a sophisticated walkthrough attraction similar to *Les Mystères du Nautilus* at Disneyland Paris. Then again, it may be transformed into a completely different sort of attraction based on a *20,000 Leagues Under the Sea* theme. (We'll have to wait and see.)

**ADVENTURELAND:** *Adventureland Remodeling* — Portions of Adventureland are currently undergoing remodeling and are expected to be completed in early 1996. No details have been released, but rumor has it that a new ride will be built. The Jungle Cruise may be revamped yet again to tone down or eliminate some of the scenes that can be offensive to some visitors and to add new scenes, possibly including a crashed airplane (promised for many years). There is also speculation that a new attraction, Indiana Jones and the Temple of the Forbidden Eye, will begin construction in 1996.

# Half-Day Tours at the Magic Kingdom

The morning and evening half-day tours that follow are designed to allow first-time visitors to experience the best of the Magic Kingdom in four to five hours, including a lunch or dinner in one of the Magic Kingdom restaurants. If you wish to eat at King Stefan's Banquet Hall or Liberty Tree Tavern, make your restaurant reservation in advance, if possible. Otherwise, you will need to make same-day reservations in person at the restaurant's door, as there is no central reservations facility in the Magic Kingdom.

The Magic Kingdom Morning Tour, below, is designed for low-attendance times: September through March, excluding holidays. If you want to visit the Magic Kingdom in the morning during a crowded time, hurry first thing in the morning to some of the popular attractions that are not included on the Keys to the Kingdom tour, then join the tour, which leaves City Hall at 10 AM. Keys to the Kingdom may not always be offered, especially during peak periods in the summer. Make tour reservations ahead of time and ask which attractions will be visited (407 939-8687).

The Sparkling Lights Afternoon and Evening Tour is designed for peak-attendance times when the Magic Kingdom is open late and the Nighttime Electrical Parade and Fantasy in the Sky fireworks are scheduled (nightly from June through August and on Saturday nights and holidays throughout the year).

To create your own custom vacation at Walt Disney World, you can combine one of these half-day Magic Kingdom tours with a half-day tour of any other theme park. For example, combine the Magic Kingdom Morning Tour with an evening tour at the World Showcase. The theme parks are most crowded in the afternoons, which is an ideal time to relax or take advantage of the resort amenities at Walt Disney World.

## MAGIC KINGDOM MORNING TOUR

*Four to five hours — September through March (except holiday periods) — including lunch.*
*Reserve a late lunch in well advance (1 PM or later) at King Stefan's Banquet Hall or Liberty Tree Tavern,*
*or plan to have lunch at Tony's Town Square Restaurant or at your resort.*

✔ Eat a full breakfast before leaving your hotel.

✔ Arrive at the Magic Kingdom Entrance Plaza one half hour before the scheduled opening time.

✔ Take in the sights along Main Street, which opens before the rest of the park. If you do not have restaurant reservations, stop at Tony's Town Square Restaurant at the beginning of Main Street and book a table for 1 PM or later. Time your Main Street tour so you arrive at the walkway to Tomorrowland when the rest of the park opens (between 8 and 9 AM).

✔ Begin in Tomorrowland and visit, in the order below, any of the following attractions that interest you:
   • Tomorrowland — THE EXTRATERRORESTRIAL ALIEN ENCOUNTER (if scary attractions appeal to you), SPACE MOUNTAIN (if you like roller coasters), TRANSPORTARIUM, and TOMORROWLAND TRANSIT AUTHORITY
   • Mickey's Starland — for a quick stroll through Duckburg (no more than ten minutes)
   • Fantasyland — IT'S A SMALL WORLD (if you're feeling young at heart or want to cool off)
   • Liberty Square — THE HAUNTED MANSION and THE HALL OF PRESIDENTS (if U.S. history interests you)

- Frontierland — **SPLASH MOUNTAIN** and **BIG THUNDER MOUNTAIN RAILROAD** (if you like thrill rides)
- Adventureland — **JUNGLE CRUISE** and **PIRATES OF THE CARIBBEAN**.

✔ Plan to arrive at your lunch destination ten minutes early. If you did not visit all the attractions you wanted to see, return in the evening when the crowds are smaller.

## SPARKLING LIGHTS AFTERNOON AND EVENING TOUR

*Four to six hours — June through August (plus holidays and Saturday nights) — including dinner.*
*Reserve an early dinner well in advance of this tour at King Stefan's Banquet Hall or Liberty Tree Tavern.*
*If you prefer a late dinner, be sure to let the reservationist know that you want to see the Nighttime Electrical Parade and would like to finish dinner before the first parade begins (usually at 9 PM).*
*If you do not have reservations on the day of your tour, at 10 AM call Same Day Reservations (939-3463).*

✔ Arrive at the Magic Kingdom Entrance Plaza at 4 PM. Pick up an entertainment schedule, which lists the show times for live performances and the Nighttime Electrical Parade.

✔ If you do not have a dinner reservation, stop at Tony's Town Square Restaurant and book a table there for later, or plan to eat at The Crystal Palace or The Plaza Restaurant.

✔ As you make your way toward Adventureland, take in the sights along Main Street.

✔ Beginning in Adventureland, visit, in the order listed below, any of the following attractions that interest you (your tour will be interrupted at times for dinner and for the Nighttime Electrical Parade):
- Adventureland — **JUNGLE CRUISE** and **PIRATES OF THE CARIBBEAN**
- Frontierland — **SPLASH MOUNTAIN** and **BIG THUNDER MOUNTAIN RAILROAD** (if you like roller coasters)
- Liberty Square — **THE HAUNTED MANSION** and **THE HALL OF PRESIDENTS** (if U.S. history interests you)
- Frontierland — for a ride on the **WALT DISNEY WORLD RAILROAD** to Mickey's Starland
- Mickey's Starland — for a quick stroll through Duckburg on your way to Fantasyland
- Fantasyland — **IT'S A SMALL WORLD** (if you're feeling young at heart)
- Tomorrowland — **THE EXTRATERRORESTRIAL ALIEN ENCOUNTER** (if scary attractions appeal to you), **SPACE MOUNTAIN** (if you like roller coasters), **TRANSPORTARIUM**, and **TOMORROWLAND TRANSIT AUTHORITY**.

✔ Pause in the tour for your dinner reservation, then continue touring where you left off.

✔ Within one half hour before the start of the **NIGHTTIME ELECTRICAL PARADE**, secure a viewing spot along the parade route. Liberty Square and Frontierland are usually less crowded than Main Street.

✔ After the parade passes your viewing spot, pick up your tour where you left off in Tomorrowland. The lines will now be shorter.

✔ On nights when the park stays open late, be sure to stay for the **FANTASY IN THE SKY** fireworks show, which is scheduled about one hour after the Nighttime Electrical Parade. A good viewing location is from the walkway between Tomorrowland and Main Street, U.S.A. ◆

# PLEASURE ISLAND

Pleasure Island — with six acres of upbeat, sophisticated evening entertainment — was clearly designed for adults. During the day, visitors can shop the main street for trendy attire and contemporary gifts, have lunch, or catch a matinee at the Island's multiscreen movie theater complex. At night, however, Pleasure Island is transformed: Limousines line up at the entrances, the streets fill with party-goers, the nightclubs open their doors, and the outdoor stage comes alive with music and dance performances. There is a splashy New Year's Eve celebration, fireworks show, and street party every night on Pleasure Island. Over the next two years, Pleasure Island will expand its offerings to visitors in an area adjacent to the AMC Theatres, which will add fourteen more screens for a total of twenty-four. Other coming attractions include gourmet dining at Wolfgang Puck's Orlando Cafe, and two celebrity nightclubs: Lario's, established by pop superstar Gloria Estefan and her husband Emilio; and House of Blues, whose founders include Dan Ackroyd, Jim Belushi, David Geffen, and the rock group Aerosmith as partners, along with Isaac Tigrett (who also helped start the popular Hard Rock Cafe restaurant and entertainment chain).

**WHEN TO GO:** Pleasure Island's clubs are open from between 7 and 8 PM until 2 AM, the shops are open from 10 AM until 1 AM, and the AMC Theatres screen films from 10 AM until 1 AM (until 2 AM on weekends). The most crowded nights are Thursday (when WDW Cast Members receive discounts) and Friday and Saturday, when local residents join WDW visitors' ranks. To sample all of the Island's legendary nightlife, you'll need to get an early start; some clubs get rolling as early as 7:45 PM. Club entertainment changes frequently. The day you go, check the show time for the New Year's Eve show (934-7781) and plan accordingly. For performance times at the various clubs, pick up an entertainment schedule as you enter Pleasure Island. For information on featured films and show times at the AMC Pleasure Island Theatres, call 827-1300.

**HOW TO GET THERE:** Pleasure Island is located in the Disney Village Resorts Area. Free parking is available in the large lot at Pleasure Island and at the nearby Disney Village Marketplace and AMC Theatres. Starting at 5:30 PM, valet parking is offered. WDW buses travel at night between all WDW resorts and theme parks and Pleasure Island. Shuttle service is also available from most area hotels. Water launches service the following resorts: Vacation Club, Dixie Landings, Port Orleans, and Villas at the Disney Institute. Taxi service is available.

**ADMISSIONS AND RESTRICTIONS:** From 10 AM until 7 PM daily, admission to Pleasure Island is free and there are no age restrictions. After 7 PM, admission is about $18 for the evening, which covers admission to all clubs and entertainment. Admission to Pleasure Island is included with Length of Stay Passes and some Multiday Passes. Movie-Island combo tickets are also available. In addition, there are many discount passes to Pleasure Island available through hotels, restaurants, and merchants.

After 7 PM, no one under the age of eighteen is permitted on Pleasure Island or inside the clubs without an accompanying adult, except in Mannequins, which prohibits anyone under the age of twenty-one. All visitors over eighteen need a picture ID (valid passport, U.S. driver's license, or foreign driver's license with a back-up ID). Florida law prohibits serving alcohol to anyone under twenty-one. Alcoholic beverages may be consumed anywhere on Pleasure Island as long as they are carried in plastic cups, which are conveniently placed at club exits. Smoking is not permitted inside some clubs.

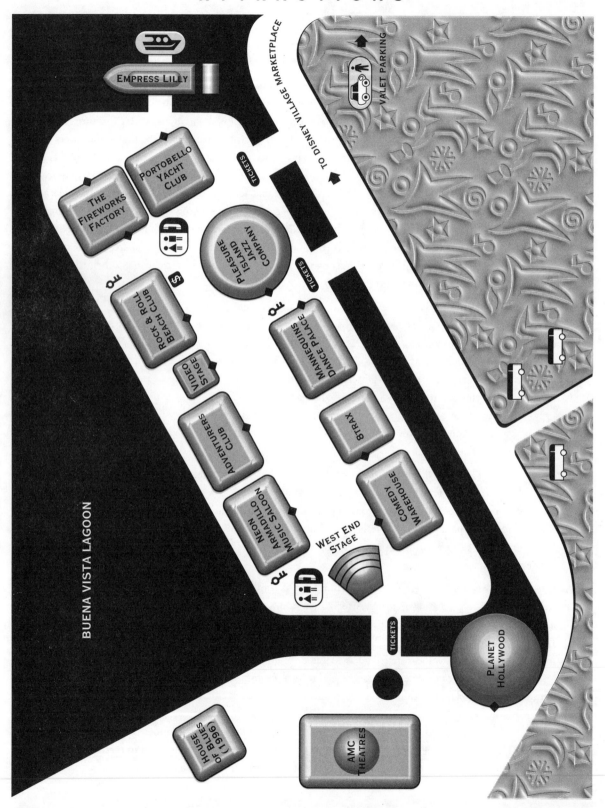

PLEASURE ISLAND

EMPRESS LILLY

THE FIREWORKS FACTORY

PORTOBELLO YACHT CLUB

PLEASURE ISLAND JAZZ COMPANY

TO DISNEY VILLAGE MARKETPLACE

VALET PARKING

TICKETS

TICKETS

ROCK & ROLL BEACH CLUB

VIDEO STAGE

ADVENTURERS CLUB

NEON ARMADILLO MUSIC SALOON

MANNEQUINS DANCE PALACE

8TRAX

COMEDY WAREHOUSE

WEST END STAGE

BUENA VISTA LAGOON

TICKETS

PLANET HOLLYWOOD

HOUSE OF BLUES (1996)

AMC THEATRES

62

## NIGHTCLUBS

✗✗✗ – Solid entertainment. ✗✗ – Good fun if you're in a party mood. ✗ – Worth a quick visit.

**MANNEQUINS DANCE PALACE:** Featuring dazzling light and sound shows, live on-stage dance performances, and mannequins dressed and posed to reflect myriad lifestyles, this club has been consistently rated the No. 1 dance club in the Southeast. The dance floor is a giant moving turntable that fills quickly as professional DJs work with high-tech sound equipment to spin contemporary music. Mannequins is the most popular gathering spot on Pleasure Island, and on weekends lines form at the club door around 8:30 PM. Beer, wine, and spirits are served, as are specialty drinks. Mannequins opens at 8 PM. No one under the age of twenty-one may enter. Themed special-effects, sound, laser, and dance performances are scheduled several times each night, and it's well worth the effort to catch one. Check the entertainment schedule for show times. ✗✗✗

**8TRAX:** This continually reinvented club has an urban-industrial ambience that makes it the most popular at Pleasure Island for visitors in their late teens and early twenties. The superior (and very loud) sound system pumps out disco hits from the seventies at the volume at which they were meant to be enjoyed. Visitors can perch on stools overlooking the pipe-railed dance floor or tucked into intimate alcoves created by black chain-link panels. 8TRAX opens at 8 PM. Beer, wine, and spirits are served, including specialty drinks. A limited selection of snacks and appetizers is also available. ✗✗

**COMEDY WAREHOUSE:** Every night, Pleasure Island visitors crowd into this large multilevel room decorated with movie props and settle onto its stools for some solid comedy entertainment. The talented house comedians, sometimes with a musician sidekick, expertly improvise hilarious skits and routines that play heavily off the audience — and the audience loves every minute of it. Celebrity comedians also make occasional appearances. Beer, wine, and spirits are served, including specialty drinks. On busy nights, lines form at the door up to an hour before the thirty-five-minute shows, which begin around 7:30 PM. The first show is the easiest to get into, and on weekends, the third show is timed to get guests back out on the street for the New Year's Eve show. Check the entertainment schedule for show times. Smoking is not permitted in this club. ✗✗

**NEON ARMADILLO MUSIC SALOON:** This high-energy country-western club has a dance floor, a huge chandelier in the shape of a spur, and live shows by well-known country-western performers. The club opens at 7 PM, with forty-five-minute sets of live music starting at around 8 PM, although visitors can come and go as they please. On some evenings, free dance classes teach visitors the latest country-western steps. Beer, wine, and spirits are served, including specialty drinks such as the Fuzzy Armadillo (peach schnapps, vodka, and rum) and the Neon Cactus (cactus juice, blue Curaçao, and gin). The Neon Armadillo also serves hamburgers, chili dogs, nachos, curly fries, and Buffalo Bill's Chicken Wings (with blue cheese dressing). Check the entertainment schedule for dance class and show times. ✗✗✗

**ADVENTURERS CLUB:** This take-off on a 1930s British explorers club is entered from an octagonal balcony that overlooks the main room below. The balcony, which houses a small bar and comfortable chairs, is filled with photos and other memorabilia from faraway and exotic places (including a must-see curio cabinet in the shape of a large zebra). The larger downstairs area is furnished with Victorian-style sofas and love seats, and at the long bar, the barstools may rise and lower subtly and unexpectedly at the whim of the bartender. The regular "club members," a group of slightly eccentric and delightfully self-centered performers, mingle with visitors, embroiling them in altercations, lectures, and a number of curious and inexplicable events that seem to happen every half hour or so in the club's library. Beer, wine, and spirits are served, including specialty drinks such as the Kungaloosh, a frozen blend of fruit juices laced with rum and blackberry brandy. The Adventurers Club opens at 7 PM, with shows presented periodically in the library, complete with haunted organ. Check the entertainment schedule for show times. Smoking is not permitted in this club. **XX**

**ROCK & ROLL BEACH CLUB:** To enter this dance club, visitors follow the surfboards lining the handrails up three flights of stairs. Below are two levels of bars, pool tables, and video games; the stage and dance floor are on the ground floor. Live bands perform contemporary and classic rock, and DJs spin a mean mix between sets. The atmosphere is relaxed, casual, and young (the music is very loud). Beer, wine, and spirits are served, including specialty drinks, and pizza is sold whole or by the slice. The Rock & Roll Beach Club opens at 7 PM, and the forty-five-minute live sets start at about 8 PM. Check the entertainment schedule for show times. **X**

**PLEASURE ISLAND JAZZ COMPANY:** In a cozy, casual circular room decorated with steamer trunks and the paraphernalia of traveling musicians, visitors can enjoy live jazz, blues, and classic jam sessions featuring local, national, and international performers. Beer, wine, and spirits are served, with a special focus on wines and champagnes by the glass. Snacks and appetizers are available, including "Grazing Samplers" such as Grilled Red Snapper with Green Peppercorn Sauce and Beef Tenderloin with Fried Onion Straws. The club also features an assortment of desserts and specialty coffee drinks. The Pleasure Island Jazz Company opens at 8 PM, and live sets start at about 8:30 PM. Check the entertainment schedule for show times. **XXX**

## EVENTS AND ENTERTAINMENT

**AMC PLEASURE ISLAND THEATRES:** The Pleasure Island movie theaters are located in a large industrial-style building with a soaring glass and steel atrium. Pleasure Island guests can cross the bridge behind the West End Stage to reach the theaters. Ten screens (soon to be expanded to twenty-four screens) show first-run movies, and all have Dolby stereo sound systems (currently, four have THX sound, and one has both THX and digital Surround Sound). All the modern comforts are present and accounted for, from the nifty decor to the comfortable seats with armrest drink holders, and the theaters are an achievement in spotlessness. The theaters are open to all WDW visitors, and guests at WDW resorts receive a discount with their resort ID. Low-attendance times are before 4 PM, and discount matinees are also available. To avoid lines, visitors can charge their tickets up to three days before the show (827-1311). Call 827-1300 for movie listings and show times. **XX**

**WEST END STAGE:** Framed by shiny high-tech lighting trusses and massive speakers, this huge outdoor performance platform presents live music that gets guests moving and keeps them jumping all night long, culminating with the spectacular New Year's Eve Street Party. Talented local bands and guest artists appear in concert nightly, with shows beginning around 7:30 PM. Check the entertainment schedule for show times and events. Visitors who wish to avoid the dense crowd near the stage can view the performances on the Hub Video Stage, an outdoor wall made up of twenty-five large video monitors located near Mannequins. The Hub Video Stage also features live performances from time to time. ✗✗

**NEW YEAR'S EVE STREET PARTY:** The New Year's Eve party of your dreams materializes every night at Pleasure Island. At the West End Stage, a laser-and-light show begins and professional dancers in sexy, eye-popping costumes work up a sweat as they power through their slick, complex, and fabulously choreographed routines. As the countdown to the New Year begins, around 10:45 PM (11:45 PM on Fridays and Saturdays), visitors add their voices, creating a street-party revelry that erupts — along with fireworks, confetti, and a sound and light show — into a frenetic, ecstatic dance party. Check the entertainment schedule for show times. ✗✗

**HOUSE OF BLUES:** At this combination restaurant and concert hall, performances by top-rated musicians are a nightly event. Visitors may either attend the featured performance (admission charged) or also enjoy dinner beforehand, featuring the Delta-region cuisine of Louisiana. Beer, wine, and spirits are served, as are espresso and cappuccino. Appetizers are available during the performances. The House of Blues also offers a Gospel Brunch, with live entertainment. Dinner begins at about 6:30 PM; the featured performance starts about 9 PM. Advance reservations are a must for both the show and dinner. (See "Dining Events," page 207.) ✗✗✗

## FULL-SERVICE RESTAURANTS

*The Pleasure Island restaurants are actually located outside of the entry gates and do not require a Pleasure Island admission ticket to enjoy. See "Restaurants," page 163, for reviews and reservation information.*

**THE FIREWORKS FACTORY:** "Dynamite" barbecued ribs and other applewood-smoked specialties are served in this lively open dining room decorated with pyrotechnic paraphernalia and powder burns. A late-night menu offers snacks, appetizers, and full dinners. Beer, wine, and spirits are served. The restaurant has a smoking section. Open all day until 2 AM; reservations recommended.

**PORTOBELLO YACHT CLUB:** Guests can enjoy Italian specialties, fresh seafood, and a variety of oven-fired thin-crust pizzas in one of several spacious dining areas featuring yachting trophies, photographs, and other maritime mementos. Beer, wine, and spirits are served, as are excellent espresso and cappuccino. The restaurant has a smoking section. Open all day until 1:30 AM; no reservations.

**PLANET HOLLYWOOD:** A razzle-dazzle, star-studded ambience greets guests as they enter this restaurant, where they can enjoy inventive New American cuisine and desserts, including a distinctive apple strudel made from a recipe used by Arnold Schwarzenegger's mother. Beer, wine, and spirits are served, as are excellent espresso and cappuccino. Smoking is permitted only at the bar. Open from 11 AM until 2 AM; no reservations.

**EMPRESS LILLY RIVERBOAT:** This huge crab-house-style restaurant opens in early 1996 aboard a detailed replica of a nineteenth-century stern-wheeler. Diners seated at tables on the riverboat's three decks enjoy pleasant views of Buena Vista Lagoon and the revolving paddle wheel. Beer, wine, and spirits are served. Open all day; no reservations.

## COCKTAIL LOUNGES AND CAFES

*A number of refreshment stands and shops scattered around Pleasure Island serve fast-food meals and snacks. The lounges listed below are the most pleasant for a sit-down respite from the clubs. They can also serve as rendezvous spots for visitors who want to club-hop separately and meet up later.*

**THE FIREWORKS FACTORY BAR:** This busy bar pours more than thirty-five domestic and imported beers, including ales, stouts, and micro-brews. "Explosive" specialty drinks are also offered, including Summer Sparklers (cranberry and apple juice with lemon-flavored vodka) and Bangmasters (lemonade laced with raspberry liqueur and vodka). Appetizers include Rock Shrimp Quesadillas, Fireworks Fried Onions, and Wild Mushroom Ravioli. This bar is popular with locals, and drink prices are reduced on weekday afternoons, from 3 until 7 PM.

**PORTOBELLO YACHT CLUB BAR:** Warm, dark mahogany paneling and polished brass fixtures create a pleasant, clubby atmosphere here. The full bar features an extensive array of grappas and good Italian wines. Appetizers include Quattro Formaggi Pizza, Antipasto Assortito, Calamaretti Fritti, and Carpaccio (thinly sliced raw sirloin with artichoke hearts and Parmigiano cheese, chives, and balsamic vinaigrette). WDW's most potent espresso and cappuccino can be found here.

**D-ZERTZ:** This small snack shop in the thick of Pleasure Island's action features pastries, candy, and ice cream, as well as coffee, espresso, and cappuccino. There is a small indoor seating area.

**PLANET HOLLYWOOD:** After an evening of club-hopping at Pleasure Island, dinner lines at this ultra-busy restaurant have disappeared, and visitors can take in the trendy scene from one of its two bars. After 10 PM, lines are gone and the lounges are available.

## SERVICES

**REST ROOMS:** All restaurants and clubs have rest rooms. An uncrowded public rest room is located between The Fireworks Factory and the Portobello Yacht Club. The rest rooms at the top of the stairs in The Fireworks Factory are quiet as well as uncrowded.

**TELEPHONES:** Outdoor public telephones are located near the rest rooms between The Fireworks Factory and the Portobello Yacht Club. There are telephones near the rest rooms in all restaurants and clubs, but the quietest phones are those at the Neon Armadillo, the Pleasure Island Jazz Company, or upstairs at The Fireworks Factory.

**BANKING:** An automatic teller machine (ATM) and a change machine are located under the stairs leading up to the Rock & Roll Beach Club.

**LOCKERS:** At the Rock & Roll Beach Club, there are lockers on the second level, near the elevator. At Mannequins Dance Palace, lockers are near the rest rooms on the ground level, inside the rest rooms, and next to the exit. The Neon Armadillo has a limited number of lockers in the hallway near the rest rooms.

**VISITORS WITH DISABILITIES:** All areas of Pleasure Island are wheelchair accessible, and all clubs have elevators.

# Evening Tour at Pleasure Island

*Five to six hours — year round — including dinner.*
*Make an early dinner reservation (about 6:30 PM) at The Fireworks Factory, or drop into the Portobello Yacht Club or the Empress Lilly Riverboat crab-house, where seating is usually available before 7 PM. If you wish to dine at Planet Hollywood, which does not take reservations, you will need to be in line no later than 5 PM.*

This tour is designed to allow first-time visitors to experience the best of Pleasure Island in a single evening. To create your own custom vacation at Walt Disney World, combine this tour with a morning tour at any other theme park. For example, combine the Evening Tour at Pleasure Island with a morning tour and lunch at Disney-MGM Studios. Use the afternoon to relax at a Walt Disney World resort.

✔ If you are dining at The Fireworks Factory or Portobello Yacht Club, enter Pleasure Island at 6 PM for a quick overview tour of the shops and attractions. At the entrance gate, pick up an entertainment schedule listing the evening's show times and events. Proceed to your selected restaurant for your 6:30 PM dinner.

✔ If you are dining at Planet Hollywood, you will need to be in line at the restaurant before 5 PM.

✔ After dinner, stroll through the nearest entrance to Pleasure Island. Buy a ticket if you need one.

✔ As you plan your early tour of the clubs, include some of the following entertainment:
  • **COMEDY WAREHOUSE** — for an improv comedy performance. (The first show of the evening starts around 7:30 PM.)
  • **MANNEQUINS DANCE PALACE** — for the not-to-be-missed high-energy light, sound, and dance show that begins around 9 PM. (Settle in upstairs at a spot with the stage platform clearly in view.)
  • **ADVENTURERS CLUB** — to eavesdrop on the club members' altercations or catch one of the bizarre performances in the adjacent library.
  • **NEON ARMADILLO MUSIC SALOON** — for live and lively country-western music and dancing, and perhaps even a chance to learn the latest dance steps.
  • **PLEASURE ISLAND JAZZ COMPANY** — to catch a set of live jazz and sample the outstanding appetizers.

✔ At about 10:30 PM (11:30 PM on Fridays and Saturdays), begin to work your way toward the West End Stage to enjoy the sizzling show that kicks off the **NEW YEAR'S EVE STREET PARTY**.

✔ If you plan to party on, return to your favorite club or try some of the following attractions:
  • **ROCK & ROLL BEACH CLUB** — to dance to R&R hits performed by a live band, or try your hand at a game of pool or pinball
  • **8TRAX** — for a "disco fever" experience with an eclectic mix of music from the seventies and the era's hottest dance styles
  • **PLANET HOLLYWOOD LOUNGES** — for a late-night tour of the spectacular movie-prop decor (bars are on the first and second floors)
  • **AMC PLEASURE ISLAND THEATRES** — for a late-night first-run feature. ◆

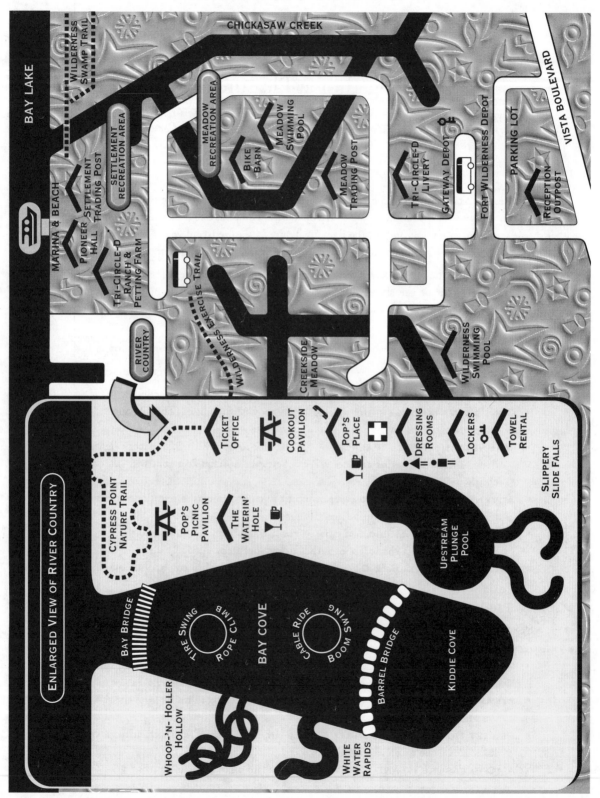

FORT WILDERNESS & RIVER COUNTRY

BAY LAKE

CHICKASAW CREEK

WILDERNESS SWAMP TRAIL

MARINA & BEACH

SETTLEMENT RECREATION AREA
PIONEER HALL
SETTLEMENT TRADING POST

TRI-CIRCLE-D RANCH & PETTING FARM

MEADOW RECREATION AREA
BIKE BARN
MEADOW SWIMMING POOL
MEADOW TRADING POST

TRI-CIRCLE-D LIVERY

GATEWAY DEPOT

FORT WILDERNESS DEPOT

PARKING LOT

RECEPTION OUTPOST

VISTA BOULEVARD

RIVER COUNTRY

WILDERNESS EXERCISE TRAIL

CREEKSIDE MEADOW

WILDERNESS SWIMMING POOL

ENLARGED VIEW OF RIVER COUNTRY

TICKET OFFICE

COOKOUT PAVILION

POP'S PLACE

DRESSING ROOMS

LOCKERS

TOWEL RENTAL

CYPRESS POINT NATURE TRAIL

POP'S PICNIC PAVILION

THE WATERIN' HOLE

SLIPPERY SLIDE FALLS

UPSTREAM PLUNGE POOL

BAY BRIDGE

WHOOP-'N-HOLLER HOLLOW

TIRE SWING
ROPE CLIMB

BAY COVE

CABLE RIDE
BOOM SWING

BARREL BRIDGE

KIDDIE COVE

WHITE WATER RAPIDS

# FORT WILDERNESS & RIVER COUNTRY

Fort Wilderness offers visitors an old-fashioned country getaway: swimming, boating, picnicking, hiking, horseback riding, fishing, and just kicking back in a 750-acre cypress- and pine-wooded recreation area and campground. This carefully preserved wilderness area is also a Walt Disney World resort, where guests can camp in tents, hook up RVs, or vacation in one of the resort's permanent trailer homes (see "Hotels," page 133). It is not unusual to spot native white-tailed deer, raccoons, opossums, and armadillos; the wetlands are home to numerous waterfowl.

Fort Wilderness has three main recreation complexes: MEADOW RECREATION AREA in the center of the park, where meandering canals attract both canoers and anglers and where bike paths lead off in every direction; SETTLEMENT RECREATION AREA at the edge of Bay Lake, with a busy marina and white sand beach, nature trails, staples, and restaurants; and RIVER COUNTRY at Bay Lake, a Disney-designed version of an old-fashioned swimming hole, complete with water slides and beaches. Throughout Fort Wilderness, visitors will find swimming pools, bicycle trails, volleyball nets, shuffleboard and tennis courts, fishing, water-skiing, horseback-riding, and live entertainment in the evenings.

WHEN TO GO: Fort Wilderness is open year round, and there are activities, attractions, and entertainment suitable to every type of weather. At the Fort Wilderness Marina, boats may be rented from 10 AM until sundown. At the Bike Barn, recreational equipment may be rented or borrowed from 8 AM until sundown. Closing times vary with the season.

River Country is open year round, except for October, when it is closed for maintenance. During holidays and peak-attendance months (April through September), the water park fills early with families and children, but during low-attendance periods (November through March), it can be a welcome escape from the crowded theme parks. Opening and closing times at River Country vary throughout the year, so check ahead at Guest Services in your resort or call River Country Information (407 824-2760). River Country may close on very cold days or during lightning storms. If the weather looks uncertain, call Disney Weather (824-4104) for details.

HOW TO GET THERE: Fort Wilderness is in the Magic Kingdom Resorts Area, adjacent to Bonnet Creek Golf Club, and extends from Vista Boulevard to the shores of Bay Lake. The Fort Wilderness Marina is serviced by ferry from the Magic Kingdom, Discovery Island, and the Contemporary resort. WDW shuttle buses service Fort Wilderness from the Wilderness Lodge resort, the theme parks, and the Transportation and Ticket Center. Visitors who are driving can reach Fort Wilderness by following the signs to the Magic Kingdom Resorts Area and then to Fort Wilderness — or they can take a shortcut and enter by way of Vista Boulevard. Parking in the Fort Wilderness Guest Parking Lot is free to guests at WDW resorts (other visitors are charged about $7).

IN-PARK TRANSPORTATION: The roads within Fort Wilderness are reserved for the Fort Wilderness internal bus transportation system, which operates daily from 7 AM until 2 AM. Bus routes are posted at all bus stops. (Passenger cars are allowed on the roads only to reach campsites, and there is no parking at the Fort Wilderness attractions.) After parking in the Fort Wilderness Guest Parking Lot, visitors should proceed to one of the two bus stops there, depending on their destination: The bus stop marked "Gateway Depot" is for the express bus to River Country; the smaller bus stop marked "Fort Wilderness

Depot" is for the buses to the Meadow Recreation Area and the Settlement Recreation Area, as well as to River Country. Guests who want to get around Fort Wilderness at their own pace can rent bicycles or electric carts at the Bike Barn, located in the Meadow Recreation Area. The electric carts hold up to four passengers and plug in for continuous recharging at scores of outlets throughout Fort Wilderness.

**ADMISSION:** Fort Wilderness is free to all visitors at Walt Disney World. Admission to River Country water park is about $17 for adults (about $14 for children). Admission to River Country is included with Length of Stay Passes and some Multiday Passes.

## SETTLEMENT RECREATION AREA

✖✖✖ – A memorable adventure.  ✖✖ – Good fun if you're in the mood.  ✖ – Strictly for the young at heart.

*The Settlement Recreation Area is nestled at the far end of Fort Wilderness, where it borders Bay Lake. The area itself encompasses the Fort Wilderness Marina and beach; Pioneer Hall, where the nightly Hoop-Dee-Doo Musical Revue dinner show is held; and the Tri-Circle-D Ranch exhibits. At the Settlement Trading Post, visitors can buy gifts, sundries, groceries, sandwiches, and beverages including beer and wine. They can also just come on in and cool off with a game of checkers. River Country is a short walk away.*

**FORT WILDERNESS MARINA:** The marina is situated on Bay Lake, in the center of Fort Wilderness' long, lovely white sand beach. Visitors can rent motorboats and sailboats or join waterskiing or fishing excursions. (See "Sports," page 213.) At the beach, visitors can swim or simply relax in lounge chairs under umbrellas or in the shade of the nearby trees. Lockers are available at the marina to store belongings, and the nearby Beach Shack provides refreshments and cold beer. The Fort Wilderness Marina is open every day from 10 AM until sundown. ✖✖

**WILDERNESS SWAMP TRAIL:** The 2.2-mile-long Wilderness Swamp Trail offers a beautiful nature hike among the local flora and fauna. Only the sounds of nature break the silence along the trail, which begins behind the Settlement Trading Post. The trail meanders into the forest, crosses the sun-drenched grassy banks of the Fort Wilderness waterways, and skirts the wetlands — populated by egrets, herons, and other native waterfowl — before plunging back into the deep shade of the overgrown forest canopy. The array of swamp ferns, saw palmetto, vine-covered cypress hung with Spanish moss, and rainbow-hued berries and flowers creates a semitropical paradise for nature-lovers. ✖✖✖

**WILDERNESS EXERCISE TRAIL:** This 1-mile (round trip) path begins across from the Tri-Circle-D Ranch and links Fort Wilderness to Disney's Wilderness Lodge. Self-guiding exercise stations along the way cue fitness enthusiasts through sit-ups, stretches, lunges, chin-ups, and other activities that add up to a serious workout. The trail winds through a deeply shaded pine forest, lush with ferns and palmettos. Twittering birds, shy marsh rabbits, deep shadows, and silence inspire a soothing sense of isolation and privacy. The trail turns back at Disney's Fort Wilderness Lodge Resort. ✖✖

**TRI-CIRCLE-D RANCH:** This stable and corral houses the horses used in Walt Disney World parades and the Blacksmith Shop where their hooves are tended. A small museum inside the Horse Barn displays photographs of Walt Disney and his beloved horses. Outside, the horses are bathed and groomed, much to their pleasure. Horse enthusiasts will enjoy close-up views of the beautiful Percherons that pull the trolleys along Main Street in the Magic Kingdom, and the elegant steeds with elaborately braided manes that are featured in the parades. At the Blacksmith Shop, visitors can watch the horses being shod and their hooves being dressed. ✖✖

**PETTING FARM:** This corral at the Tri-Circle-D Ranch is filled with chickens, turkeys, rabbits, goats, ducks, and some very beautiful and well-cared-for ponies. Interestingly, the Petting Farm, with its hands-on opportunities, attracts as many adults as children. ✖✖

## MEADOW RECREATION AREA

*The Meadow Recreation Area lies in the center of Fort Wilderness and offers access to the Fort Wilderness Waterways and bicycle trails. This area encompasses the Bike Barn, where visitors can rent bicycles, canoes, electric carts, fishing gear, and tennis equipment; and the Meadow Recreation Complex, which offers swimming, tennis, volleyball, and shuffleboard. (See "Sports," page 213.) The Meadow Trading Post sells gifts, sundries, groceries, sandwiches, and beverages, including beer and wine. On hot afternoons, visitors can spend time in the Meadow Trading Post cooling off and playing a game of checkers, or they can picnic by the creek at the tree-shaded tables out back.*

**CANOEING:** The grassy banks and tree-canopied waterways of Fort Wilderness are home to a variety of native waterfowl and fish. Visitors may tour the waterways by canoe or pedal boat and are welcome to fish for bass and bream. The Bike Barn rents canoes from 8 AM until sundown. Canoers are given a map of the waterway system and can bring a picnic lunch along on their adventure. ✖✖

**BICYCLING:** The nine miles of roads and trails in Fort Wilderness are ideal for bicycle tours. Bikers must contend with occasional traffic on the paved roads, but the extensive trail system was designed with bicycles in mind. The trails meander along waterways, past beaches and wetlands, through shady forests, and across bridges and boardwalks. The Bike Barn rents bicycles and tandem bikes from 8 AM until sundown and provides maps of the bike trails and roads of Fort Wilderness. ✖✖

**CANAL FISHING:** Fishing in the waterways at Fort Wilderness is one of Walt Disney World's hidden pleasures. Anglers can walk along the shores or rent canoes and paddle to any fishing spot that appeals to them. The Meadow Trading Post sells lures, and visitors who do not have their own gear can rent cane poles at the Bike Barn. Unless guests have their own kitchens, the fishing rule is catch and release. ✖✖

## RIVER COUNTRY ATTRACTIONS

*River Country, a water park located just a short walk from the Settlement Recreation Area, is modeled on a "swimming hole" that Huck Finn might have enjoyed. Visitors pay admission at the gate, and once inside, they can rent lockers and towels and settle into lounge chairs around the pool or on the sandy beach. There are a number of waterslides and water activities here, but River Country has a gentler, more nature-oriented atmosphere than either Typhoon Lagoon or Blizzard Beach. Two snack bars, Pop's Place and the smaller Waterin' Hole, offer hamburgers, hot dogs, sandwiches, salads, ice cream, beer, wine, and coffee. Generally, River Country is filled with kids, but it happens to be one of the most relaxing spots at Fort Wilderness, and it's great for people-watching.*

**BAY COVE:** Bay Cove, an inlet of Bay Lake, is bordered on one side by a large beach and the other by waterslides. It is the home of old-fashioned water play at River Country, complete with a Boom Swing, Rope Climb, Tire Swing, and Cable Ride. Two rickety bridges, Barrel Bridge and Bay Bridge, span the Cove and lead swimmers to the water-play equipment in the center and to the tube rides and body slides at Raft Rider Ridge on the far shore. ✗

**WHOOP-'N-HOLLER HOLLOW:** Across Bay Cove from the beach is Whoop-'n-Holler Hollow, where swimmers can climb to two thrilling, corkscrewing waterslides. One is longer than the other, but both are fast. The slides twist and turn and wind around each other, finally depositing riders, with a splash, into Bay Cove. This attraction is big with the kids. ✗

**WHITE WATER RAPIDS:** Despite its name, this is actually a slow inner-tube ride among gentle currents and calm pools. Riders cross Barrel Bridge and plop onto inner tubes atop Raft Rider Ridge. They meander down a 330-foot-long contoured chute, sometimes revolving in a slow whirlpool, before being gently washed into Bay Cove. ✗✗

**UPSTREAM PLUNGE POOL AND SLIPPERY SLIDES:** This crystal-clear 330,000-gallon swimming pool is heated in winter and is surrounded by lounge chairs, where most of the adults at River Country can be found relaxing. Slippery Slide Falls, at the back of the pool, offers two steeply angled waterslides for the adventurous youngsters who flock to them. The slides end with a free-fall splash landing. ✗✗

**CYPRESS POINT NATURE TRAIL:** This short but beautiful wooden boardwalk nature walk meanders through the wetlands at the edge of Bay Lake. Old-growth bald cypress trees provide shade, and egrets fish among the water reeds. Aviaries tucked into the moss-hung bayous house rehabilitated birds, including a red-tailed hawk, that are no longer able to survive in the wild. ✗✗✗

## EXCURSIONS AND TOURS

**WATERSKIING EXCURSION:** Waterskiers enjoy ideal conditions on the smooth surface of Bay Lake. Skiers can bring their own equipment or use the skis, Scurfers, or Hydraslides provided. Excursion boats carry up to five skiers and leave from the Fort Wilderness Marina throughout the day. Guides will also pick up skiers from other Magic Kingdom resorts. Waterskiing excursions must be booked in advance and cost about $80 per hour. (See "Waterskiing," page 242.) ✗✗

**FORT WILDERNESS TRAIL RIDE:** The Tri-Circle-D Livery maintains a herd of well-trained quarter-horses, paints, and Appaloosas for cowboy-guided trail rides. Groups of up to twenty take this gentle ride-at-a-walk through the shady pine forest. The Tri-Circle-D Livery is adjacent to the Fort Wilderness Guest Parking Lot. The trail ride leaves four times daily, and reservations are required (824-2832). Cost is about $20 for forty-five minutes. (See "Horseback Riding," page 231.) ✗✗

**FISHING EXCURSION:** Anglers can try their luck reeling in largemouth bass, bluegill, and other fish from Bay Lake. The Fort Wilderness Marina offers two-hour fishing excursions several times daily. Anglers can use their own equipment or that provided on the boat, but only guests staying in accommodations with kitchens are permitted to keep their catch. No license is required. Excursions must be booked in advance and cost about $130. (See "Fishing," page 221.) ✗✗

## EVENTS AND LIVE ENTERTAINMENT

*Many of the activities at Fort Wilderness, such as hayrides, Disney movies, and campfire entertainment, are presented with younger guests in mind. The events described below will also appeal to adults.*

**ELECTRICAL WATER PAGEANT:** This shimmering light show appears on Seven Seas Lagoon and Bay Lake every night. A thousand-foot-long string of barges transports an intricate and dynamic light and music show past the Polynesian, Grand Floridian, Contemporary, Wilderness Lodge, and Fort Wilderness resorts. King Neptune presides over the dancing images of sea life that come alive in animated lights and are reflected across the black waters of the Bay Lake. The show is brief, approximately seven minutes, but spectacular nonetheless. The Electrical Water Pageant reaches Fort Wilderness at about 9:45 PM. The best viewing location is at the Fort Wilderness Marina and beach. ✗✗✗

**HOOP-DEE-DOO MUSICAL REVUE:** This popular dinner show is held three times nightly in rustic, family-oriented Pioneer Hall. Colorfully dressed entertainers rely heavily on audience participation for a song-and-dance vaudeville performance laced with puns, broad humor, and groan-inducing punch lines. Reservations are difficult to get, so book well in advance. (See "Dining Events," page 206.) Same-day reservations are occasionally available (824-2858, between 8 AM and 6 PM), as is walk-up seating. ✗✗

## RESTAURANTS

*The restaurants below are located at Pioneer Hall in the Settlement Recreation Area. See "Restaurants," page 163, for reviews and reservation information. Smoking is not permitted in the restaurants.*

**TRAIL'S END BUFFETERIA:** Fried chicken, pizza, casseroles, soups, and a salad and fruit bar are offered in this casual cafeteria. A late-night pizza buffet and pizza to go are also featured. Beer and wine are served. Open for breakfast, lunch, and dinner; no reservations.

**CROCKETT'S TAVERN:** Frontier-style dinners are served in this log cabin bedecked with Davy Crockett memorabilia. Guests waiting for tables can sit in comfortable rockers on the large wraparound porch outside, or perch at the saloon-style bar. The menu features chicken, prime rib, seafood, Mexican food, and interestingly enough, buffalo burgers. At various times of the year, live entertainment is featured. Beer, wine, and spirits are served. Open for dinner; no reservations.

## SERVICES

**REST ROOMS:** Rest rooms are located at the Meadow Trading Post, Settlement Trading Post, Pioneer Hall, Reception Outpost in the Fort Wilderness Guest Parking Lot, and by the first-aid office in River Country. Air-conditioned comfort stations, complete with rest rooms, laundromats, showers, ice dispensers, and telephones, are located near all bus stops throughout the Fort Wilderness campsite locations.

**TELEPHONES:** Telephones can be found at the Gateway Depot bus stop in the Fort Wilderness Guest Parking Lot; at the comfort stations throughout the Fort Wilderness campsite locations; at Pioneer Hall and the Settlement Trading Post in the Settlement Recreation Area; and at the Meadow Trading Post in the Meadow Recreation Area.

**ELECTRIC CART RENTALS:** Visitors can rent electric carts by the day or hour for use in Fort Wilderness. The carts carry up to four passengers and cost about $25 per day. They run up to an hour (depending on the number of passengers) before needing a recharge at one of the plug-in recharging posts located throughout Fort Wilderness. Carts can be rented at the Bike Barn in the Meadow Recreation Area, which is open from 8 AM until sundown. Same-day reservations for carts are required and should be booked early in the morning (824-2742).

**LOCKERS:** Lockers are located at the Fort Wilderness Marina, River Country, Meadow Recreation Area, and at the Gateway Depot bus stop in the Fort Wilderness Guest Parking Lot.

**VISITORS WITH DISABILITIES:** Wheelchairs are available at the Reception Outpost in the Fort Wilderness Guest Parking Lot, but must be reserved in advance through Guest Services (407 824-2900). Guests can also rent electric carts for use in Fort Wilderness by making same-day reservations at the Bike Barn (824-2742).

# Getaway Tours at Fort Wilderness

The half-day and full-day tours that follow are designed to allow first-time visitors to experience the best of Fort Wilderness in four to seven hours, including lunch or dinner in one of the Fort Wilderness restaurants. To create your own custom vacation at Walt Disney World, you can combine a Fort Wilderness tour with a half-day tour from any other theme park. For example, combine a morning tour at Disney-MGM Studios with the Late Afternoon and Evening Wilderness Tour, or combine the Surf and Turf Day at Fort Wilderness with a late-evening visit to Pleasure Island or Disney's BoardWalk.

## LATE AFTERNOON AND EVENING WILDERNESS TOUR

*Four to five hours — year round — including the Hoop-Dee-Doo Musical Revue dinner show.*
*Well in advance of your trip, make reservations for the 7:15 PM Hoop-Dee-Doo Musical Revue dinner show.*
*(See "Dining Events," page 206.)*

✔ Park at the Contemporary resort and take the ferry to the Fort Wilderness Marina at about 3:30 PM.

✔ Rent a Water Sprite, sailboat, or canopy boat at the Fort Wilderness Marina for a relaxing hour-long boat tour of Bay Lake and Seven Seas Lagoon. Dock at any of the Disney resorts for a quick tour of their themed atmospheres.

✔ Return your boat to the Fort Wilderness Marina and stroll to the **TRI-CIRCLE-D RANCH.** Tour the Blacksmith Shop, the Petting Farm, and the small museum in the Horse Barn.

✔ If you have time and would enjoy a nature walk, follow the **WILDERNESS SWAMP TRAIL** behind the Settlement Trading Post. Or if you prefer, drop into Crockett's Tavern for a before-dinner cocktail or beverage. (Some visitors consider this a must to prepare for the entertainment that follows.)

✔ Plan to arrive at Pioneer Hall about fifteen minutes before the 7:15 PM **HOOP-DEE-DOO MUSICAL REVUE** dinner show.

✔ After dinner, you can catch the **ELECTRICAL WATER PAGEANT,** which cruises Bay Lake past the Fort Wilderness beach at about 9:45 PM. The last ferry leaves Fort Wilderness at 10 PM.

## SURF AND TURF DAY AT FORT WILDERNESS

*Five to seven hours — October through March — includes picnic lunch or lunch at Trail's End Buffeteria and (optional) the Hoop-Dee-Doo Musical Revue dinner show.*
*If you plan to attend the 5 PM Hoop-Dee-Doo Musical Revue,*
*make reservations well in advance of your trip (see "Dining Events," page 206).*
*If you are taking the Fort Wilderness Trail Ride, make advance reservations for the 2 PM ride.*
*(Same-day reservations are sometimes available. See "Horseback Riding," page 231.)*
*Early on the morning of your tour, reserve an electric cart for the day (824-2742).*

✔ Arrive at either the Fort Wilderness Guest Parking Lot or Fort Wilderness Marina at about 10 AM. Take a shuttle to the Bike Barn at the Meadow Recreation Area and rent an electric cart for the day.

✔ Drive your cart through Fort Wilderness, exploring the resort on your way to the **TRI-CIRCLE-D RANCH** in the Settlement Recreation Area. Find an electric hitching post for your cart (short posts with electrical outlets are located throughout Fort Wilderness). Plug the cart in before you tour the ranch. Drop into the Blacksmith Shop, the Petting Farm, and the small museum in the Horse Barn.

✔ If you are planning a picnic lunch, purchase picnic supplies at the Settlement Trading Post. Otherwise, head over to the Trail's End Buffeteria, nearby, for lunch. (Trail's End can also prepare food to go.)

✔ If you're picnicking, hike the **WILDERNESS SWAMP TRAIL,** which begins behind the Settlement Trading Post. There is a shady picnic spot near the bridge over Chickasaw Creek where the Wilderness Swamp Trail meets Bay Lake. If you're eating at Trail's End Buffeteria, take your nature walk on the Wilderness Swamp Trail after lunch.

✔ After your hike, choose between a boat tour of Bay Lake and Seven Seas Lagoon or a horseback trail ride through the forest.

  If you select the **BOAT TOUR,** walk to the Fort Wilderness Marina, nearby, and rent the boat of your choice. Explore the far reaches of Bay Lake and the adjacent wetlands, or dock at the resorts at Seven Seas Lagoon for a quick tour.

  If you have reserved the 2 PM **FORT WILDERNESS TRAIL RIDE,** drive your cart to the Tri-Circle-D Livery, adjacent to the Fort Wilderness Guest Parking Lot. Be sure to plug your cart in when you get there. The trail ride wanders through the forest and lasts about forty-five minutes.

✔ When you've finished your afternoon outing, return your cart to the Bike Barn. If you are not attending the Hoop-Dee-Doo Musical Revue dinner show, you can linger at the Meadow Recreation Area for a swim, tennis, shuffleboard, fishing, or any number of playful options before returning to your hotel.

  If you have reserved the 5 PM **HOOP-DEE-DOO MUSICAL REVUE,** take the shuttle bus back to Pioneer Hall. If you have time before the show, drop into Crockett's Tavern.

✔ Arrive about fifteen minutes early for the dinner show. ◆

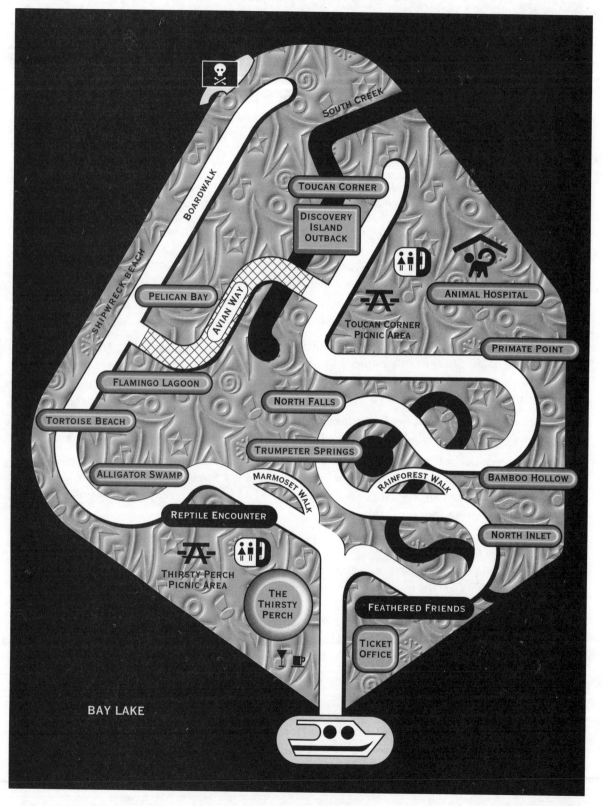

DISCOVERY ISLAND

SOUTH CREEK

BOARDWALK

TOUCAN CORNER

DISCOVERY ISLAND OUTBACK

SHIPWRECK BEACH

PELICAN BAY

AVIAN WAY

TOUCAN CORNER PICNIC AREA

ANIMAL HOSPITAL

PRIMATE POINT

FLAMINGO LAGOON

NORTH FALLS

TORTOISE BEACH

TRUMPETER SPRINGS

ALLIGATOR SWAMP

MARMOSET WALK

RAINFOREST WALK

BAMBOO HOLLOW

REPTILE ENCOUNTER

NORTH INLET

THIRSTY PERCH PICNIC AREA

THE THIRSTY PERCH

FEATHERED FRIENDS

TICKET OFFICE

BAY LAKE

# DISCOVERY ISLAND

Discovery Island is an idyllic escape into nature from the more structured entertainments at Walt Disney World. This natural eleven-acre island, in the middle of Bay Lake, was originally planned by Disney as a *Treasure Island* adventure. To create a lush forest environment, the island was landscaped with native trees, palms, and bamboo, along with hundreds of tropical specimen plants from around the world. A white sand beach was added, and a wrecked wooden sailing ship was transported here from the Florida coast to lend atmosphere. Aviaries were built and stocked with a wide variety of exotic birds, from elegant demoiselle cranes to flashy scarlet ibises. As the island ecology evolved and more wildlife arrived and thrived — both imported species and local volunteers — the *Treasure Island* concept was dropped and Discovery Island became a nature park. In 1979, it was accredited by the American Association of Zoological Parks and Aquariums, and it regularly exchanges animals with zoos throughout the world. Today, this sanctuary is home to more than 250 species of birds, reptiles, and mammals, including endangered species and disabled wildlife such as Galapagos tortoises, brown pelicans, and the American bald eagle.

At Discovery Island, visitors can stroll through the tropical foliage along a winding three-quarter-mile path, picnic on the white sand beach, pause beside a stream with gurgling cascades, and come face-to-face with a variety of birds and animals at almost every turn. Peacocks and rabbitlike Patagonian cavies, along with waterfowl native to the area, are among the many animals that roam freely on Discovery Island. Almost an acre of the island is enclosed in nearly invisible fine green netting, creating one of the largest walkthrough aviaries in the United States — so large that visitors often do not realize they are inside an enclosure. There are only a few places to sit down along the shady paths, so visitors should be comfortable with walking the three-quarter-mile distance.

**WHEN TO GO:** Discovery Island opens every day at 10 AM and closes between 5 PM and 7 PM, depending on the season. It is a delightful place to visit at any time of day. The best month to visit is November, before Thanksgiving, when the weather is cool and the island is virtually deserted. Discovery Island, however, is seldom crowded at any time. Nesting season lasts from February through September, and from about mid-February to mid-March, the island is closed for refurbishing (and perhaps to give the wildlife a people vacation). For up-to-the-minute information, call Walt Disney World Information (407 824-4321) or Discovery Island Information (407 824-2875). If the weather looks uncertain, call Disney Weather (824-4104) for details.

**HOW TO GET THERE:** The only way to reach Discovery Island is via the ferries that depart every twenty minutes from the Magic Kingdom Dock, the Fort Wilderness Marina, and the Marina Pavilion at the Contemporary Resort. The last ferries depart for Discovery Island at about 4 PM, although ferries do stop to pick up Discovery Island visitors until the park closes. Schedules vary with the season, so check ahead. Before boarding the ferries, hats should be held firmly or tied on, as the breezes can blow them overboard. Visitors are not permitted to dock rental boats at Discovery Island.

**ADMISSION:** Adult admission to Discovery Island is about $12 (about $7 for children). Discovery Island admission is included with Length of Stay Passes and some Multiday Passes. Tickets may be purchased at Guest Services in any Walt Disney World resort or at the Discovery Island ticket office. Ferries to Discovery Island are complimentary for all visitors.

## LIVE EXHIBITS

*Signs scattered around Discovery Island inform visitors about the specific kinds of animals they might see. Discovery Island changes from day to day as plants grow and bloom and birds and animals mature, breed, and give birth. Many island residents hide in the foliage, and visitors can find animals at almost every turn. Pick up a brochure, as you enter, which includes descriptions of some of the birds and animals, and a schedule of the animal shows. Follow the path to the right after you leave the Discovery Island Dock.*

**DISCOVERY ISLAND PATH:** This three-quarter-mile Discovery Island Path directs visitors in a roughly counter-clockwise direction around the island. It first enters an area known as Parrots Perch, where the island's bird shows are staged. This is the home of brightly plumaged macaws, cockatoos, and some of the other colorful birds that perform in the shows. The large trees here provide shade and nesting homes during mating season.

**NORTH INLET:** At the approach to North Inlet, visitors pass a wrinkled hornbill from Southeast Asia and palm cockatoos from New Guinea. The path crosses a flowing island stream where it empties into Bay Lake, then turns to enter a dense forest of tropical plants, palms, and flowering hibiscus. The path meanders back and forth across a series of footbridges, passing a stand of Senegal date palms and many other specimen plants along the way. North Inlet is home to marmosets and to laughing kookaburras from Australia, whose signature call can be heard at sundown as visitors are departing.

**TRUMPETER SPRINGS:** This area, which includes a small, tropically landscaped Rainforest Walk, is home to a pair of beautiful black-necked swans, as well as to the large white trumpeter swans, known for their distinctive call. These fairy-tale birds, the largest of the swans, have been nearly hunted out of existence. Discovery Island is hoping that they will breed successfully so they can supply other zoos. In spring, great white egrets nest in the treetops at Trumpeter Springs. The purple flowering princess shrub, native to Brazil, is among the plants that flourish here. Farther along the path is the Fishing Cat, a feline native of Southeast Asia that swims to catch its favorite food.

**NORTH FALLS:** At North Falls, visitors can enjoy cascading waterfalls and spot a variety of waterfowl fishing in the pools below. The flowing waterways on Discovery Island are actually an artificial water system, which is engineered to keep the water fresh and aerated. Water is pumped to a high level at North Falls, then drained through the lagoons and wetlands that are home to many species of waterfowl. Graceful Chilean flamingos occupy the lagoon at North Falls. They are lighter in color than the familiar bright orange Caribbean flamingos. Also nearby are yellow-billed hornbills from Ethiopia, who seem to spend the entire day grooming themselves.

**BAMBOO HOLLOW AND PRIMATE POINT:** This lovely grove is filled with fragrant flowering ginger and combines almost a dozen varieties of bamboo from many parts of the world, including vivid green golden bamboo. Primate Point is the home to beautiful golden conures from Brazil and a number of small mammals, including the endangered ring-tailed lemur from Madagascar, with a foxlike face and monkeylike body. Also in residence here are tree-dwelling, yellow-furred golden lion tamarins from the American tropics.

**ANIMAL HOSPITAL:** A recent addition to Discovery Island, the colorful wood-shingled Animal Hospital has walk-up windows where visitors can look into various animal-care facilities. In the nursery, animals orphaned in the wild are cared for around the clock until they can be released back into the wild or incorporated into exhibits. The operating room, also visible by window, is where animals undergo surgery for injuries. Visitors can watch the goings-on in the lab, too, where blood samples are studied to help diagnose animal diseases. The lab also houses an X-ray machine for diagnosing internal organ problems and bone fractures. This powerful machine is capable of X-raying a five-hundred-pound Galapagos tortoise. (You probably shouldn't stand too close to the window when one of those guys steps onto the table — the rays must be pretty intense.)

**TOUCAN CORNER:** Easily identified by their large beaks and distinctive squawking sounds, the colorful toucans that live here are native to the Western Hemisphere. The beautiful toto toucans reside in the large circular centerpiece aviary. Down the path leading to the beach are colorful keel-billed toucans from southern Mexico. In the other direction, a spacious aviary is home to the small, shy muntjac deer from Southeast Asia, who live companionably close to a flock of delicate demoiselle cranes. White-crested hornbills can also be found here, a species threatened by the destruction of its rain forests; and the tall birds with distinct red streaks above their eyes are federally protected sandhill cranes.

**AVIAN WAY:** Just beyond Toucan Corner, visitors can enter Avian Way, which is devoted to South American birds and waterfowl. Covering almost an acre, this huge walkthrough aviary is home to a colorful population, including one of the largest U.S. breeding colonies of the scarlet ibis. These birds, distinctively plumaged in an almost Day Glo red from a diet high in carotenes, were described by the early Spanish explorers as being covered in blood. Visitors pass through the aviary on elevated walkways high above the lagoons and nesting areas of the waterfowl. Tall trees reach through the top of the enclosure, creating the remarkable illusion of open sky. The aviary exits at the beach.

**PELICAN BAY:** The brown pelican is the state bird of Florida, and those that are sheltered here are among the permanently disabled birds on Discovery Island, unable to survive in the wild. Once threatened with extinction due to the effects of the pesticide DDT, the brown pelican is now protected by federal law and its population is slowly recovering. In the late afternoon, about 4 PM, animal caretakers feed the pelicans, which is an entertainment event in itself.

**BOARDWALK:** The Boardwalk skirts a lush tropical forest as it follows the island's white sand beach. Here, visitors have a chance to see many of the birds in the wild that are native to the area, including herring gulls, American coots, herons, egrets, and large turkey vultures. The path stops at the far end of the island where the *Hispaniola* is beached. This wrecked single-masted schooner was salvaged from the Florida Keys and offers a vivid example of the shipmaking craft of the eighteenth century. The waters of Bay Lake lap on the beach, and visitors may leave the path to lounge on the sand or walk barefoot at the water's edge.

**FLAMINGO LAGOON:** This shady lagoon across from the beach is home to a breeding colony of Caribbean flamingos, recognized by their distinctive bright pink plumage and awkward grace. The flamingos have adapted to the presence of humans, unlike their cousins, the Florida flamingos, which have not been seen in the wild since about 1920.

**TORTOISE BEACH:** Along the sandy beach of Discovery Island, Galapagos tortoises from the islands off the coast of Ecuador have found a new resort. These great lumbering beasts, weighing up to five hundred pounds and with lifespans of up to 150 years, are now a rare and endangered species.

**ALLIGATOR SWAMP:** Remodeled in 1992, this picturesque grotto is home to a number of American alligators. The population of these Florida natives, once declining because of the dictates of fashion and encroaching development, is now on the increase. The rare broadnose caiman, virtually extinct in the wild, can also be found at Alligator Swamp. As the path continues toward the dock it passes Marmoset Walk, a wood-chip path that loops past the Marmoset exhibit.

## EDUTAINMENT

**XXX** – A do-not-miss for animal-lovers. **XX** – An interesting diversion if you come upon it. **X** – Of limited appeal.

*Animal shows are scheduled several times daily at Discovery Island. Pick up an entertainment schedule at the Discovery Island ticket office for exact show times. Shows may be cancelled due to inclement weather.*

**FEATHERED FRIENDS SHOW:** Visitors sit on shaded benches to watch this pleasant, often funny show featuring the antics of tame macaws, cockatoos, and parrots. During the show, the parrot wranglers describe the special care and captive breeding programs for Discovery Island's many exotic, colorful birds. Next, the island's birds of prey are introduced, including a red-tailed hawk, a large owl, and a king vulture, and visitors have a chance to see these remarkable birds up close and learn about their feeding and mating habits. Visitors are encouraged to ask questions about the birds while learning more about the wildlife rehabilitation and protection programs at Discovery Island. Four shows daily, beginning at about 11:30 AM. Duration: Approximately 30 minutes. **XXX**

**REPTILE ENCOUNTER:** This informative reptile show is staged near Alligator Swamp, where visitors can sit in the shade on hand-hewn log benches or stand off to the side. An animal handler gives visitors a close-up look at a number of interesting reptiles and amphibians, including a small but toothy American alligator, a vivid green iguana from the treetops of the rain forest, and a gopher tortoise that burrows as deep as thirty feet underground. Other performers in the show include an indigo snake and a friendly Burmese python that literally hangs out with the crowd. Four shows daily, beginning at about 11 AM. Duration: Approximately 25 minutes. **XX**

## REFRESHMENTS AND PICNIC AREAS

*Two refreshment stands offer light meals and snacks, and Discovery Island has a number of picnic areas for those who bring their own food. The picnic spots are pleasant rest stops and rendezvous points.*

**THE THIRSTY PERCH:** The largest snack bar on Discovery Island, the Thirsty Perch offers sandwiches, snacks, soft drinks, coffee, and beer, as well as a selection of nature-oriented publications and souvenirs. It is located near the Discovery Island Dock. Visitors can purchase food and beverages at the Thirsty Perch, which they may consume anywhere on the island, provided they do not litter or offer food to the animals or birds, who are quite well fed.

**THIRSTY PERCH PICNIC AREA:** Located on the beach just beyond the Thirsty Perch, this area has a dozen or so picnic tables. To one side, a thick grove of bamboo provides shelter, and picnickers can watch the ferries dock as they eat. Egrets, cranes, peahens, and peacocks mingle with picnickers and provide entertainment. Don't miss the majestic American bald eagle behind the Thirsty Perch. Trash containers and rest rooms are nearby.

**DISCOVERY ISLAND OUTBACK:** This small snack stand is located at Toucan Corner, and offers a limited selection of soda, bottled water, chips, and candy. There are shaded tables across the path.

**TOUCAN CORNER PICNIC AREA:** Just across the path from Toucan Corner, this picnic area is tucked into a secluded glade. Several picnic tables are set on thick grass under the shade of tall palms. Toucan Corner Picnic Area is located in the center of the island and is filled with the sounds of birds. Trash containers and rest rooms are nearby.

**BOARDWALK AND SHIPWRECK BEACH:** Visitors who bring along a towel or ground cloth will find the white sands of Shipwreck Beach a fine spot for a beach picnic. Although swimming is not permitted, visitors may take off their shoes and walk along the water's edge. The Boardwalk divides the forest from the beach and leads to the shipwrecked *Hispaniola*. This area provides lovely views of Bay Lake and the resorts on the far shore. Trash containers are nearby; the nearest rest rooms are at Toucan Corner and the Thirsty Perch.

## SERVICES

**REST ROOMS:** Public rest rooms are located behind the Thirsty Perch and across from Toucan Corner in the Toucan Corner Picnic Area.

**TELEPHONES:** Public telephones are located behind the Thirsty Perch and next to the Toucan Corner Picnic Area.

**FILM:** A wide variety of film is available for sale at the Thirsty Perch.

**VISITORS WITH DISABILITIES:** All of Discovery Island is wheelchair accessible, and wheelchairs are available free of charge at the dock. Some, but not all of the ferries have wheelchair access, so visitors needing assistance may need to wait for a properly outfitted ferry.

## TOURING TIPS

✦ It is not a good idea to let any of the roaming birds or animals eat from your hand. They are not tame.

✦ The animal-caretakers are very knowledgeable and friendly, so ask questions when you spot them tending the animals. At 3:30 PM, head over to Pelican Bay for the birds' 4 PM feeding.

**ADULT EDUCATIONAL TOUR:** The Discovery Island Education Department arranges tours that focus on animal care and conservation, for groups of 15 to 20 adults. Visitors get to meet many of the island's residents and observe the behind-the-scenes operations at the zoo. The tour lasts approximately three hours; $25 per person. Reserve at least thirty days in advance (407 824-3784).

DISCOVERY ISLAND

# Getaway Tours at Discovery Island

The tours that follow are designed to allow first-time visitors to experience the best of Discovery Island in two to three hours; one tour includes a picnic lunch. To create your own custom vacation at Walt Disney World, you can combine the Mid-Morning Nature Walk and Picnic with an afternoon and evening tour at one of the theme parks. Or, you can use the Afternoon Nature-Break Tour as a midday getaway.

## AFTERNOON NATURE-BREAK TOUR

*Two to three hours — year round — does not include lunch.*

✔ After lunch, catch the ferry to Discovery Island. Schedule your arrival at about 1:30 PM. (Discovery Island ferries depart every twenty minutes from the Magic Kingdom Dock, the Fort Wilderness Marina, and Marina Pavilion at the Contemporary resort.)

✔ On arriving at Discovery Island, pick up an entertainment schedule at the ticket office.

✔ Stop by the Thirsty Perch, just ahead, and purchase a beverage to take along on your tour, if you wish. Step over to the path and bear left (clockwise), walking to the pleasant outdoor area where the Reptile Encounter show is staged.

✔ Catch the 2 PM performance of REPTILE ENCOUNTER, where you will meet a number of toothy creatures from around the world, some of which are endangered species.

✔ After the performance, you may want to stop at ALLIGATOR SWAMP for an up-close view of its many larger residents.

✔ Continue down the path to TORTOISE BEACH for a look at the huge, slow-moving Galapagos tortoises, then walk past FLAMINGO LAGOON on your right. Enjoy the distant view of Shipwreck Beach and the *Hispaniola*. Disney brought the wrecked sailing ship to the beach when the island was once known as Treasure Island, named after the Robert Louis Stevenson pirate novel.

✔ When you arrive at PELICAN BAY, turn right and enter the enormous aviary at AVIAN WAY. Stroll through and view the South American waterfowl far below the walkway. Exit at Toucan Corner.

✔ Explore the toucan aviaries at TOUCAN CORNER, then continue along the path toward the ANIMAL HOSPITAL. Take a brief tour of the facility, especially the nursery, before returning to the path.

✔ Continue down the path and enjoy the many sights and sounds as you walk past BAMBOO HOLLOW, NORTH FALLS, and TRUMPETER SPRINGS. As you stroll, keep an eye out for the unique Fishing Cat. In this area Discovery Island shows off its colorful flowers and lovely scents.

✔ Arrive at the Parrots Perch in time for the 3:30 PM performance of the FEATHERED FRIENDS SHOW. Here, you can experience the antics of the beautiful trained tropical birds and observe some of the remarkable birds of prey that live at Discovery Island.

✔ After the show, return to the Discovery Island Dock for your ferry back.

## MID-MORNING NATURE WALK AND PICNIC

*Three hours — year round — including a picnic lunch.*

✔ If you are planning to bring your own picnic lunch, ask your hotel coffee shop to pack one for you. You can buy beverages at Discovery Island. If you would like to picnic on the beach, you may want to bring along towels or a ground cloth.

✔ Catch the ferry to Discovery Island at about 11:45 AM. (Ferries depart every twenty minutes from the Magic Kingdom Dock, the Fort Wilderness Marina, and Marina Pavilion at the Contemporary resort.)

✔ On arriving at Discovery Island, pick up an entertainment schedule at the ticket office.

✔ If it is before 12:15 PM, stop by the Thirsty Perch, just ahead, and purchase beverages for your picnic (and food, if you did not bring your own). Step over to the path and bear to the right (counter-clockwise). Follow the path to Parrots Perch, an animal-show staging area.

✔ Grab a seat and catch the 12:30 PM performance of the **FEATHERED FRIENDS SHOW** to experience the antics of the beautiful trained tropical birds and meet some of the remarkable birds of prey that live at Discovery Island.

✔ When the show ends, continue down the path toward **NORTH INLET**. Enjoy the sights and sounds as you walk along past **TRUMPETER SPRINGS**, **NORTH FALLS**, and **BAMBOO HOLLOW**. On this part of the island there are many fascinating species of trees, shrubs, and tropical flowers.

✔ Stop at the **ANIMAL HOSPITAL** on your right and peek into the nursery and treatment rooms.

✔ Just ahead is **TOUCAN CORNER**. If you would like to picnic at a table in a secluded grassy glade, stop at the Toucan Corner Picnic Area for lunch. If you prefer to picnic on the beach in the sun, continue on.

✔ Just ahead on the path is **AVIAN WAY**. Enter the large enclosed aviary and stroll all the way through on the elevated walkways. Below you will see a variety of graceful South American waterfowl.

✔ Leave the aviary and turn right toward **PELICAN BAY** for a look at Florida's endangered state bird.

✔ If you're planning to picnic at the beach, you may want to continue up the **BOARDWALK**, which follows the shore toward the shipwrecked *Hispaniola*. Choose a sunny spot for your picnic anywhere on the sand.

✔ Turn around and follow the Boardwalk back toward **FLAMINGO LAGOON** and over to **TORTOISE BEACH**, on your right, for a look at the huge, slow-moving Galapagos tortoises. Some weigh as much as five hundred pounds.

✔ Continue on to **ALLIGATOR SWAMP**, where you can have an up-close, but quite safe view of its large and fearsome-looking residents.

✔ Stroll down the path to the rustic benches on your right for the 2 PM **REPTILE ENCOUNTER** show, where you will meet a number of engaging and toothsome creatures from around the world.

✔ After the show, return to the Discovery Island Dock for your ferry back. ◆

TYPHOON LAGOON

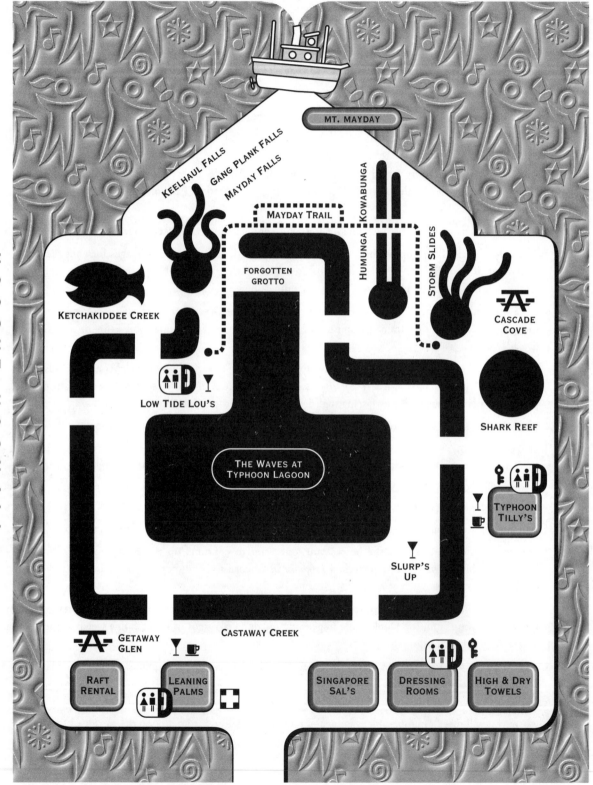

MT. MAYDAY

KEELHAUL FALLS
GANG PLANK FALLS
MAYDAY FALLS

MAYDAY TRAIL

HUMUNGA KOWABUNGA

STORM SLIDES

FORGOTTEN GROTTO

KETCHAKIDDEE CREEK

CASCADE COVE

LOW TIDE LOU'S

THE WAVES AT TYPHOON LAGOON

SHARK REEF

TYPHOON TILLY'S

SLURP'S UP

CASTAWAY CREEK

GETAWAY GLEN

RAFT RENTAL

LEANING PALMS

SINGAPORE SAL'S

DRESSING ROOMS

HIGH & DRY TOWELS

# TYPHOON LAGOON

Typhoon Lagoon is an imaginatively designed fifty-six-acre theme park devoted to water activities: whitewater rafting, snorkeling, waterslides, body surfing atop the largest machine-made waves in the world, and a long, lazy float down the meandering creek encircling the park. Depending on where their adventures take them, visitors can enjoy white sand beaches, shady coves, misty rain forests, and plunging waterfalls. According to Disney legend, the lagoon was once the site of a peaceful fishing village that was devastated by a raging typhoon. The *Miss Tilly* shrimp boat was neatly deposited on top of Mt. Mayday, the Placid Palms restaurant became the Leaning Palms, and the steamship at Shark Reef was permanently overturned. Part of the fun of Typhoon Lagoon is discovering other telltale signs of the storm.

WHEN TO GO: Typhoon Lagoon is open year round, except from mid-November through December when it is closed for refurbishing. Operating hours vary throughout the year, so check ahead at Guest Services in your resort or call Typhoon Lagoon Information (407 560-4141). During peak-attendance times (April through September) and weekends year round, it is essential to arrive before opening time (about 9 AM), since the park fills to capacity by about 10:30 AM and is closed to new arrivals until mid afternoon. During low-attendance times (October through March), mornings can be cool, so plan to visit in the afternoon, when Typhoon Lagoon provides a welcome contrast to the frenzied stimulation of the theme parks. The park closes about 6 PM in cool months and at 8 PM during the summer. Brief tropical rain showers are common in the summer months, usually in the late afternoon. During storms, swimmers are chased from the water to wait it out, and many simply leave for the day — especially families with children. Once the storm passes, the park empties significantly, making a post-storm visit highly desirable. If the weather looks uncertain, call Disney Weather (824-4104) for details.

HOW TO GET THERE: Typhoon Lagoon is in the Disney Village Resorts Area not far from the Disney Village Marketplace. Free parking is available in the Typhoon Lagoon parking lot. WDW buses service Typhoon Lagoon from the WDW resorts, the major theme parks, Disney Village Marketplace, and the Transportation and Ticket Center. Shuttle service is also available from most area hotels.

ADMISSION: Adult admission is about $26 per day (about $20 for children). Admission to Typhoon Lagoon is included with Length of Stay Passes and some Multiday Passes.

✳

## ATTRACTIONS

**✗✗✗** – A must for thrill seekers.  **✗✗** – Good fun for everyone.  **✗** – Of limited appeal.

THE WAVES AT TYPHOON LAGOON: The centerpiece of the park is the $2\frac{1}{2}$-acre lagoon and its famous wave maker, which creates impressive six-foot surfing waves. The machine also produces gentle bobbing waves perfect for floating on the inner tubes available for rent. The two types of waves alternate for an hour at a time all day long; surfing waves usually start on the even hours. Near the lagoon, a blackboard with the surf report gives information on the water temperature, weather, and alternating surf conditions. The *Miss Tilly,* a shrimp boat perched atop Mt. Mayday, gives a hoot and sprays a fifty-foot plume of water in the air every half hour, so visitors who are waiting for that first big curl can keep track of the time while experiencing other attractions. **✗✗✗**

**CASTAWAY CREEK:** Giant turquoise inner tubes draped with relaxed swimmers are swept along in the currents of Castaway Creek for a lazy thirty-minute float around the perimeter of the park. At the five entrances at different points along the fifteen-foot-wide creek, visitors can wait for an empty tube to float by or grab one of the tubes stacked nearby for the taking. Visitors may also simply swim with the currents of the creek if they wish. The currents are strong enough to keep floaters moving, and lifeguards along the way keep an eye on things. Rafters struggling to dodge flotsam and jetsam create laughing and bumping logjams. Where Castaway Creek passes through a misty rain forest, the going is slow enough to permit floaters-by to read the labels on the tropical trees and shrubs. A waterfall soaks all who pass under Mt. Mayday, so leave hats and cameras behind. ✗✗✗

**SHARK REEF:** Before entering the reef, be sure to visit the underwater viewing station. Fashioned as the boiler room of a half-sunken, overturned steamship, its windows reveal snorkelers swimming among the fish in the water above. The water in Shark Reef is salty and unheated to accommodate the Caribbean sea life. Those who wish to swim with the fish get life vests, snorkels and masks, and a five-minute lesson in using them. Then it's off for a shower and a brief swim across the lagoon, which has two islands, loads of interesting fish, and several small sharks. Since Shark Reef is kept cooler than the rest of Typhoon Lagoon, it's a great place to really chill out on hot days. ✗✗

**HUMUNGA KOWABUNGA:** Thrill-seeking waterslide enthusiasts will be thoroughly satisfied by the terrifyingly steep and fast descent on these two slides: about a fifty-foot drop in less than thirty seconds. Clothing with rivets or buckles is not allowed, and one-piece bathing suits are advised for women; sliding in thong-style suits may result in friction burns. Riders hit the water hard at the bottom, so nose plugs are also a good idea. The steepness of the slide is hidden from those in line by cleverly planted bushes. There are viewing bleachers at the bottom. You must be physically fit to ride. ✗✗

**STORM SLIDES:** These three body slides are tamer than those at Humunga Kowabunga, but still pretty exciting. Riders can choose from the Stern Burner, Jib Jammer, and Rudder Buster, all of which deliver more or less the same ride. Instead of a straight downward descent, these slides take riders on a circuitous corkscrew route through caves and waterfalls. The pool at the bottom is just deep enough to cushion landings. (Although they can be abrupt enough to wrench off the top of a two-piece bathing suit). There are viewing bleachers at the bottom. ✗✗

**MAYDAY FALLS:** Mayday Falls offers a twisty, speedy, bumps-and-ridges tube ride. The tubes are for single riders only, and riders are timed at the top and urged out at the bottom by lifeguards. Mayday Falls is slightly faster than Keelhaul Falls. ✗✗

**GANG PLANK FALLS:** Extra-large tubes that hold up to four people zip along speedily down the chute. Although this is the tamest of the three raft rides, in the process of shoving them off, the lifeguards duck every raft under a nearby waterfall, thoroughly soaking the occupants. ✗✗

**KEELHAUL FALLS:** The tube ride down Keelhaul Falls is slower than the one down Mayday Falls, but it plunges into a pitch-black tunnel about halfway down. This is a real thrill and completely unexpected, since riders are hurtling along with no clue as to what's coming next. Riders end up safely at the common landing pool, where they quickly exit. ✗✗

## TYPHOON LAGOON

**KETCHAKIDDEE CREEK:** This kids-only area is specially designed for small fry and their parents. An assortment of scaled-down water rides similar to those found throughout the park are offered here, along with floating toys and a little waterfall. It's happy but noisy, so those seeking relaxation should be sure to camp some distance away. ✗

## REFRESHMENT STANDS AND PICNIC AREAS

*The refreshment stands at Typhoon Lagoon serve snacks and fast-food meals all day, although the lines can be quite long. Beverage carts throughout the park sell beer and soft drinks, and guests may bring food and beverages into the park, but no glass containers or alcoholic beverages. There are no cooking facilities available in the park.*

**LEANING PALMS:** The largest refreshment stand, Leaning Palms, is to the left of the main entrance. Pizza, hamburgers, hot dogs, salads, and chicken and tuna sandwiches are sold here, along with soft drinks, beer, and coffee. Several large eating areas with shaded tables are nearby. 🍴🍸

**TYPHOON TILLY'S GALLEY & GROG:** Located on the far right side of the lagoon, this large refreshment stand has two separate walk-up counters. Both sides offer snacks, beverages, and ice cream, but the left counter, which opens earlier in the day, serves hot dogs and sandwiches, as well as beer and coffee. There are shaded tables nearby, or diners can picnic on the sand at Cascade Cove. Typhoon Tilly's may be closed during slow seasons. 🍴🍸

**SLURP'S UP:** This thatch-roofed beach shack serves a limited supply of snacks, as well as frozen fruit drinks, wine coolers, and beer. The small walk-up snack bar is located at the shoreline on the right side of Typhoon Lagoon. 🍸

**LOW TIDE LOU'S:** This small beach shack near the entrance to Gang Plank Falls sells the usual beach snacks plus soft drinks, wine coolers, and draft beer, which can be enjoyed in the quaint shelter nearby. Low Tide Lou's is near Ketchakiddee Creek, so the noise and activity level can be fairly high. 🍸

**GETAWAY GLEN PICNIC AREA:** This picnic area with many tables and play areas is on the left side of the lagoon near Leaning Palms. A volleyball net is permanently installed, but there is plenty of room for eating as well as playing. Overhanging shelters provide a shady break from the sun, and mist from the rain forest keeps things cool on windy days.

**CASCADE COVE PICNIC AREA:** Cascade Cove is located between Shark Reef and Castaway Creek on the right side of the lagoon. Chaise lounges, wooden tables, and shady overhangs create a welcome picnic spot. Cascade Cove is larger than Getaway Glen but fills up rapidly because of its proximity to Typhoon Tilly's.

## SERVICES

**REST ROOMS:** Public rest rooms are located near Typhoon Tilly's snack bar, the Leaning Palms snack bar, and at the base of Gang Plank Falls, close to Low Tide Lou's snack bar. All the rest rooms can get quite crowded in the afternoons. The rest rooms at the Dressing Rooms are the largest.

**TELEPHONES:** Public telephones are located outside the Dressing Rooms near Singapore Sal's and adjacent to all rest rooms. The phones inside the Dressing Rooms offer a shady spot for making calls. Those at Typhoon Tilly's are generally available.

**TOWELS:** Towels can be rented at High & Dry Towels, located to the right of the entrance walkway.

**CHANGING ROOMS & SHOWERS:** The Dressing Rooms, located next to Singapore Sal's, have many shower/changing rooms. Since all rest rooms in the park have shower cubicles, visitors can also use them to change, and most are less crowded than those at the Dressing Rooms.

**LOCKERS:** Keys to lockers near the Dressing Rooms or near Typhoon Tilly's can be rented at High & Dry Towels. Specify the location that you prefer.

**WATERTOYS:** Life vests are available free of charge at High & Dry Towels. Tubes for the bobbing waves in Typhoon Lagoon can be rented at Castaway Creek Raft Rentals. During busy times, tubes are also rented on the beach. Visitors are not permitted to bring their own equipment into the park.

**FIRST AID:** The first-aid station is located to the left of the main entrance, near the Leaning Palms snack bar. Aspirin and other first-aid needs are dispensed free of charge.

**VISITORS WITH DISABILITIES:** Wheelchairs may be rented just inside the entrance gate to Typhoon Lagoon, although only a limited number are available. All pathways are wheelchair accessible, and there is a ramp to the viewing station in Shark Reef. Most of the thrill rides are inappropriate for people with serious disabilities, but Castaway Creek and the bobbing waves in Typhoon Lagoon can be ideal.

## TOURING TIPS

✦ During high-attendance times, there is always a long line for rental towels and locker keys. If possible, bring your own towel and leave valuables behind. If you must have a locker, get in this line when the park first opens and ask for a key to the lockers near Typhoon Tilly's.

✦ Establish a "camp" by claiming a lounge chair and leaving your towels and belongings on top. At Typhoon Lagoon, this signals to all that the chair is occupied. Try to choose a site in the shade or under a shelter, which will keep your belongings dry in a sudden downpour and protect you against overexposure to the sun. If you want to work on your tan, you can always find a place in the sun.

✦ During the summer months, Typhoon Lagoon is a tempting destination, but the crowds can make it difficult. A good time to visit is after 4 PM, when parents are taking their tired kids back to their hotels and others are leaving to pursue dinner plans. Late afternoon is an enchanting time at Typhoon Lagoon, which often stays open until 8 PM. The park takes on a tropical remoteness, and lines to the attractions are short or nonexistent, so you can frolic to your heart's content or simply plop down in a lounge chair under the swaying palms with a wine cooler .

✦ Many WDW resort coffee shops will prepare a box lunch, so you can eat well and avoid the long lines at refreshment stands. Purchase drinks at one of the Typhoon Lagoon beverage carts.

# Half-Day Tour at Typhoon Lagoon

The half-day tour that follows is designed to allow first-time visitors to experience the best of Typhoon Lagoon in three to four hours. During peak seasons, this tour works best either in the early morning or late in the afternoon (3 or 4 PM). In cool seasons, the tour works best in the early afternoon (1 PM). Visitors on the Peak Season Morning Tour can buy a fast-food lunch inside the park, bring a box lunch from their hotel coffee shop, or plan to lunch at 1 PM or later at their hotel or a restaurant in nearby Disney Village Market-place. Visitors on the Peak Season Late Afternoon Tour may want to eat at the park and stay until closing (8 PM) or plan a late dinner elsewhere. Visitors on the Cool Season Early Afternoon Tour should eat lunch before they arrive.

✱

## THE MORNING AND AFTERNOON LAGOON TOURS

*Three to four hours.*
*Peak Season Morning Tour (9 AM) — April through September — lunch optional.*
*Peak Season Late Afternoon Tour (3 or 4 PM) — April through September — does not include dinner.*
*Cool Season Early Afternoon Tour (1 PM) — October through March — does not include lunch.*
*On the Peak Season Morning Tour, reverse the order of the numbered attractions to avoid long lines.*

✔ Pack a tote bag with sun block and a hat or visor. Wear your bathing suit under your clothes. If you have a towel, bring it rather than waste time in the towel line.

✔ If you are on the Morning Tour, arrive at the entrance to Typhoon Lagoon about twenty minutes before the park officially opens. Call 560-4141 or check with Guest Services in your resort for opening times.

✔ When you enter the park, get in the line to rent towels and a locker (if you need them) at High & Dry Towels. Request a locker near Typhoon Tilly's.

✔ Set up camp in one of the sheltered coves near Typhoon Tilly's. On the Afternoon Tours you may need to wait and watch for the perfect site to appear, as visitors begin to leave.

✔ Proceed to ❶ CASTAWAY CREEK. There is an entrance close to Typhoon Tilly's. Grab one of the extra tubes stacked here or look for an empty one floating by. Use the Water Tower as your exit landmark and take off down the creek for a revolution or two around the park.

✔ After you leave Castaway Creek, walk over to the ❷ SHARK REEF viewing station for an underwater view. Then go topside to gear up and join the snorkeling tour of Shark Reef.

✔ When you're done at Shark Reef, walk toward Mt. Mayday. Climb the stairs to Humunga Kowabunga, and turn off halfway up on MAYDAY TRAIL. Follow the trail across Mt. Mayday and behind Forgot-ten Grotto for a bird's-eye view of Typhoon Lagoon. Mayday Trail ends near ❸ KEELHAUL FALLS, where you can catch a white-water raft ride (or grab a beverage at Low Tide Lou's).

✔ If Keelhaul Falls whets your appetite for thrills, backtrack to ❹ STORM SLIDES for a ride down the spiraling water chutes. Daredevils can go on to the terrifying plunge at ❺ HUMUNGA KOWABUNGA.

✔ Relax and ride the bobbing waves or body surf in TYPHOON LAGOON (check the wave schedule in front of the Lagoon). The eruption of Mt. Mayday (every half hour) will tell you when surf's up. ◆

BLIZZARD BEACH

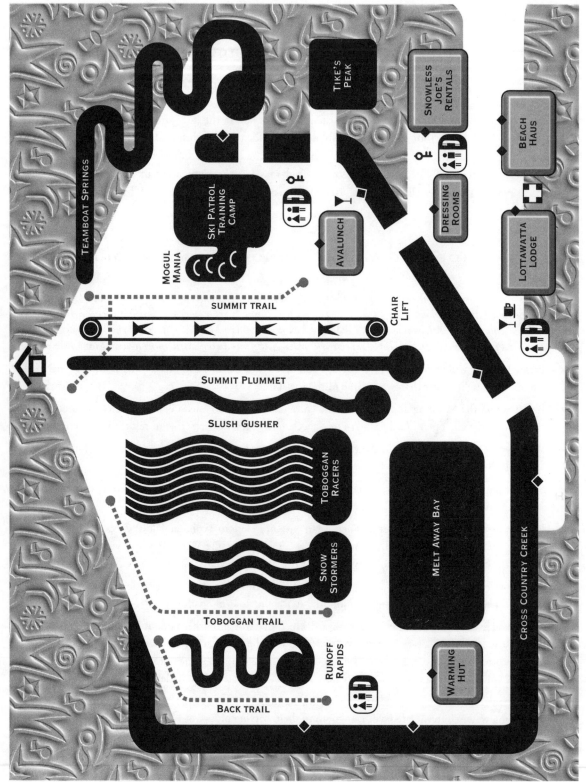

TEAMBOAT SPRINGS

TIKE'S PEAK

SNOWLESS JOE'S RENTALS

BEACH HAUS

MOGUL MANIA

SKI PATROL TRAINING CAMP

AVALUNCH

DRESSING ROOMS

LOTTAWATTA LODGE

SUMMIT TRAIL

CHAIR LIFT

SUMMIT PLUMMET

SLUSH GUSHER

TOBOGGAN RACERS

MELT AWAY BAY

SNOW STORMERS

CROSS COUNTRY CREEK

TOBOGGAN TRAIL

RUNOFF RAPIDS

WARMING HUT

BACK TRAIL

# BLIZZARD BEACH

Blizzard Beach, Walt Disney World's new water park, blends the wintery elements of a snowy landscape with the pleasures of frolicking under the warm Florida sun. Adventurous visitors can enjoy plunging waterslides and exciting tube and raft rides, while visitors with more sedate tastes can relax with around-the-park floats, beach picnics, and a bird's-eye view of the park from Mt. Gushmore's summit. The Disney yarn about Blizzard Beach is that a capricious Mother Nature set a snowstorm raging on Florida's Mt. Gushmore one day, inspiring developers to create an alpine snow park. When the climate returned to normal, however, the ice and snow began melting, and so did the developers' dreams. As they surveyed their dismal situation, they noticed an alligator having fun sliding down the mountain slopes in the slush. The 'gator's good time gave the developers a brilliant idea: Rather than offering visitors snow-based activities like skiing and sledding, why not use the snow-park equipment to take advantage of the melting ice and provide challenging water sports instead? Blizzard Beach was the result.

**WHEN TO GO:** Blizzard Beach is open all year, except from January to mid-February when it may be closed for maintenance. Operating hours vary throughout the year, so check ahead at Guest Services in your resort or call Blizzard Beach Information (407 560-3400). During peak attendance times (April through September), it is essential to arrive before opening time (about 9 AM), since the park restricts new arrivals when its parking lot fills, usually by 11 AM. During low-attendance times (October through March), mornings can be cool, so plan your visit to Blizzard Beach in the early afternoon as a relaxing break from the frenzy of the other theme parks. The park closes about 5 PM in the cool months, and about 8 PM during the summer. In the summer months, Florida has brief tropical rain showers, usually in the late afternoon. During storms, swimmers are chased from the water to wait it out, and many leave for the day — especially groups with children. After the storm passes, the park empties significantly, making a post-storm visit highly desirable. If the weather looks uncertain, call Disney Weather (824-4104) for details.

**HOW TO GET THERE:** Blizzard Beach is in the Disney-MGM Resorts area, not far from Disney-MGM Studios. Free parking is available in the Blizzard Beach parking lot. WDW buses service Blizzard Beach from the WDW resorts, the major theme parks, Disney Village Marketplace, and the Transportation and Ticket Center. Shuttle service is also available from most area hotels.

**ADMISSION:** Adult admission is about $26 per day (about $20 for children). Admission to Blizzard Beach is included with Length of Stay Passes and some Multiday Passes.

✳

## ATTRACTIONS

✘✘✘ – A must for thrill seekers.   ✘✘ – Good fun for water lovers.   ✘ – Of limited appeal.

**CROSS COUNTRY CREEK:** Relaxed riders on giant inner tubes drift along in the currents of Cross Country Creek for a pleasant thirty-minute float around the perimeter of Blizzard Beach. Cross Country Creek may seem like a dull ride on first glance, but the alpine landscaping, occasional fast-flowing waters, and a trip through a spooky cave of melting "ice" lend a bit of spice to the excursion. There are six entrances at different points along the creek where visitors can wait for an empty tube to float by or grab one of the tubes that stack up early or late in the day. Swimmers may also enter without tubes; the currents are strong enough to keep things moving. A complete trip takes about thirty minutes. ✗✗

CHAIR LIFT: Visitors can walk to the top of Mt. Gushmore or board the zany, colorful Chair Lift to travel to the following attractions: Summit Plummet, Slush Gusher, and Teamboat Springs. Riders on cable cars with mock skis attached beneath enjoy a sweeping view on their ascent. The trip up is very, very slow, and riders must exit quickly at the top. The Chair Lift is a one-way ride — the only way back down from the top of Mt. Gushmore is on the Summit Plummet Trail. ✗✗

SUMMIT PLUMMET: Billed as the fastest waterslide on earth, Summit Plummet will delight thrill-seeking enthusiasts. The one-tenth-mile course starts at the "ski jump" perched on Mt. Gushmore's summit. At speeds over fifty miles per hour, riders free fall more than one hundred feet into a pool at the foot of the mountain. Viewers looking up will also get a thrill as they watch riders vanish from the slopes into a cloud of mist. Only fit people are allowed on the ride, which is over in less than a minute. Women should wear one-piece bathing suits, as two-piece suits can lead to immodest exposure. ✗✗✗

SLUSH GUSHER: At ninety feet, Slush Gusher is touted as the world's tallest waterslide. Although not quite as daunting an experience as Summit Plummet, Slush Gusher takes riders on a roller-coaster-like descent through a wintery canyon landscape. Riders are positioned feet first, on their backs, with arms and legs crossed, and actually become airborne on parts of this ride. Only people in good physical condition are allowed on the ride, which should be avoided by those with back problems. ✗✗✗

TEAMBOAT SPRINGS: Extra-large inner tubes that hold up to five people zip over cascades down a twisting one-quarter-mile-long flume, the longest of its kind anywhere. ✗✗✗

SNOW STORMERS: Visitors pick up rafts at the bottom and ride them on one of three side-by-side slalom courses that zigzag down the mountainside. The challenge for rafters is to try to avoid bumping into the flags and "ski" gates as they speed down. ✗✗

TOBOGGAN RACER: Riders lie face down on toboggan-shaped rafts with front handles for a thrilling head-first descent down Mt. Gushmore on one of eight side-by-side waterslides. Lifting the handles speeds the descent; to maintain control, push down when approaching the bottom. ✗✗✗

RUNOFF RAPIDS: Runoff Rapids, on Mt. Gushmore's back face, offers three separate bumps-and-ridges inner tube rides for singles, doubles, and threesomes. One of the slides plunges riders into a twisty, pitch-black pipe slide. Riders are urged out of the way at the bottom by lifeguards. ✗✗

MELT AWAY BAY: Located at the bottom of Mt. Gushmore, Melt Away Bay is surrounded by a white sand beach and covers an area nearly the size of a football field. "Snow" from the mountain, "liquefied" by the warm Florida climate, cascades into the bay. The bay's wave-making machine, not nearly as dynamic as Typhoon Lagoon's, creates gentle Caribbean-style swells for swimmers, floaters, and splashers. The beach area is packed with lounge chairs, but the shade value of the covered picnic tables makes them the most coveted and convenient hangouts. ✗✗

BLIZZARD BEACH SKI PATROL TRAINING CAMP: Designed primarily for pre-teens, the Training Camp offers three separate activities:

- *Mogul Mania* — Mogul Mania offers a bumpy inner tube descent over a knobby water field in a "snowstorm." Friendly collisions are common. The tubes are for single riders only. ✘
- *Thin Ice Training Course* — The challenge here is to walk across a pool on floating, bobbing chunks of ersatz "ice" while holding onto a cargo net overhead. The pool is also a swimming area. ✘
- *Ski Patrol Shelter* — At this water-play area, riders hang on to a suspended T-bar at Fahrenheit Drop and glide out before dropping into an icy pool. The fast slide at Frozen Pipe Springs shoots riders into the same cold pool. ✘

**TIKE'S PEAK:** A specially designed area for small fry and their parents, this kids-only area offers a miniaturized Mt. Gushmore with selected scaled-down water rides similar to those found on the mountain. A castle made of "snow," cleverly transformed into a fountain, adds to the enchantment of this happy but noisy area. People seeking quiet relaxation should be sure to camp elsewhere. ✘

## REFRESHMENT STANDS AND PICNIC AREAS

*The refreshment stands at Blizzard Beach serve snacks and fast-food meals. A beverage cart (with a long line) near Snowless Joe's Tube and Towel Rentals sells ice cream, soft drinks, and beer. Visitors may bring food and beverages into the park, but no glass containers or alcoholic beverages. There are no cooking facilities.*

**LOTTAWATTA LODGE:** The largest refreshment stand, Lottawatta Lodge, is located near the park's main entrance. Designed with a ski lodge look, the walk-up counter offers salads, hamburgers, hot dogs, pizza, and sandwiches, along with soft drinks, beer, wine, and coffee. Tables are scattered on the partially shaded dining terrace, which offers great views of the park. 🍽🍸

**AVALUNCH:** Located near Tike's Peak, this food stand offers hot dogs, snacks, and ice cream, as well as soft drinks, beer, and wine coolers. There are shaded tables nearby. 🍸

**THE WARMING HUT:** This snow-covered snack shack on the far side of Melt Away Bay offers counter-service Italian sausages and snacks, along with soft drinks, frozen fruit drinks, strawberry wine coolers, and beer. There are shaded tables nearby. 🍸

**PICNIC SPOTS:** Unlike Typhoon Lagoon, picnic spots are hard to find at Blizzard Beach. The best bet is to arrive well before opening time and rush to stake a claim at one of the covered picnic tables surrounding Melt Away Bay. Do not pass Go: Do this first.

## SERVICES

**REST ROOMS:** Public rest rooms are located at the Dressing Rooms near the park's entrance, and near Lottawatta Lodge, Avalunch, and The Warming Hut. All the rest rooms can get quite crowded in the afternoons. The rest rooms at the Dressing Rooms are the largest; those at The Warming Hut are the least crowded.

**TELEPHONES:** Public telephones are located outside the Dressing Rooms near the park's entrance, and near all the rest rooms. The phones at Lottawatta Lodge are generally available. Those at The Warming Hut offer a quiet location for making calls.

**TOWELS:** Towels can be rented at Snowless Joe's Tube and Towel Rentals, near the entrance.

**SHOWER & CHANGING AREA:** The Dressing Rooms near the park's entrance have the only indoor showers at Blizzard Beach.

**LOCKERS:** Keys to the day lockers near the Dressing Rooms or near the rest rooms at Avalunch can be rented at Snowless Joe's Tube and Towel Rentals.

**WATERTOYS:** Life vests are available free of charge (with a deposit) at Snowless Joe's Tube and Towel Rentals. Visitors may bring flotation aids, such as water wings and flotation belts, but no masks or fins.

**FIRST AID:** The first-aid station is located near Lottawatta Lodge. Aspirin and other first-aid needs are dispensed free of charge.

**VISITORS WITH DISABILITIES:** A limited number of wheelchairs are available just inside the entrance gate to Blizzard Beach. Most pathways are wheelchair accessible. The Chair Lift has a wheelchair car, and wheelchairs are returned to the bottom by lifeguards. Most of the waterslides are off-limits to people with serious physical disabilities, but Teamboat Springs, Cross Country Creek, and the bobbing waves in Melt Away Bay are ideal for just about everyone.

## TOURING TIPS

✦ During high-attendance times in the warm months, a single long line for rental towels and locker keys will greet you. If you are planning to visit on a crowded day, wear your bathing suit under your clothes, bring your own towel, do not bring valuables you would want to store, and focus first on locating a place to "camp." If you *do* need a locker, make it a point to get to the park well before opening time and get into the locker line first thing.

✦ Establish a "camp" by claiming an umbrella-covered lounge chair or one of the shaded picnic tables. Leave your towels and belongings scattered on top; this signals to all that the chair or table is occupied. The picnic tables have shade covers, which will keep your towels and clothing dry in a sudden downpour (common in the warm months) and protect you against overexposure to the sun. You can always find a place in the sun to lounge and work on your tan.

✦ The Florida sun is very hot and can easily burn visitors, especially at Blizzard Beach, with its all-white, reflective "snow." To protect yourself, bring along a thin tee-shirt to wear over your bathing suit; you can wear the shirt on the slides and when swimming, as well.

✦ During the summer months, Blizzard Beach is a tempting destination, but crowds can make it difficult. A smart time to visit is after 3 PM when the park stays open until 7 or 8 PM. Families who arrived at opening time are taking their tired kids back to the hotel, and others are leaving to prepare for dinner. Summer afternoon downpours, which last only a half hour or so, also drive people away.

✦ Many of the coffee shops in the WDW resorts will prepare a box lunch for you to take into Blizzard Beach. This way, you can eat well and avoid the long lines at the refreshment stands. You can bring along beverages in a small cooler or purchase them at one of the beverage carts in the park.

BLIZZARD BEACH

# Half-Day Tour at Blizzard Beach

The half-day tour that follows is designed to allow first-time visitors to experience the best of Blizzard Beach in three to four hours. Depending on the time of year, this tour works best in the early morning during warm months and in the afternoon year round. This tour does not include meals. If you are visiting in the morning, you can purchase a fast-food lunch inside the park or bring a box lunch from the coffee shop in your resort. If you are touring in the afternoon, you may wish to eat lunch before you arrive.

## MORNING OR AFTERNOON AT BLIZZARD BEACH

*Three to four hours.*
*Peak Season Morning Tour (9 AM) — April through September — lunch optional.*
*Peak Season Late Afternoon Tour (3 or 4 PM) — April through September — does not include dinner.*
*Cool Season Early Afternoon Tour (1 PM) — October through March — does not include lunch.*
*On the Peak Season Morning Tour, reverse the order of the numbered attractions to avoid long lines.*

✔ Pack a tote bag with sun block and a hat or visor. Wear your bathing suit under your clothes. If you don't need a locker and have a towel, you might want to bring it and not waste time in line.

✔ If you are on the Morning Tour, arrive at the entrance to Blizzard Beach one half hour before the park officially opens (between 9 and 10 AM). Call 560-3400 or check with Guest Services in your resort for opening and closing times, which may vary with the season.

✔ As you enter the park, you can rent towels and lockers if you need them at Snowless Joe's Tube and Towel Rentals, located near the Dressing Rooms.

✔ Find a shady spot on the far side of Melt Away Bay, beyond The Warming Hut, and set up camp.

✔ Proceed to ❶ CROSS COUNTRY CREEK. There is an entrance close to The Warming Hut. Grab one of the extra tubes stacked here or look for an empty one floating by and take off down the creek for a revolution or two around the park. When you're ready for some action, exit where you entered.

✔ Climb the winding Back Trail to ❷ RUNOFF RAPIDS for a white-knuckle tube ride down the back side of Mt. Gushmore.

✔ Grab a raft at the Mat Pick-Up Station, and climb the Toboggan Trail to ❸ SNOW STORMERS to test your raft slalom skills, then ascend again for the downhill challenge at ❹ TOBOGGAN RACERS.

✔ Ride the Chair Lift to the summit of Mt. Gushmore — on busy days it may be faster to climb the steps of Summit Trail to the top — and take a wild tube ride down ❺ TEAMBOAT SPRINGS.

✔ Return to the top of Mt. Gushmore on the Chair Lift or the Summit Trail, where thrill seekers can head for ❻ SLUSH GUSHER to sample this very steep waterslide.

✔ If you are now ready for your big-time water adventure, head back to the top of Mt. Gushmore for the terrifying airborne plunge at ❼ SUMMIT PLUMMET.

✔ Take a well-deserved rest and ride the bobbing waves in MELT AWAY BAY or relax on the beach to work on your tan and watch all the goings-on. ◆

DISNEY'S BOARDWALK

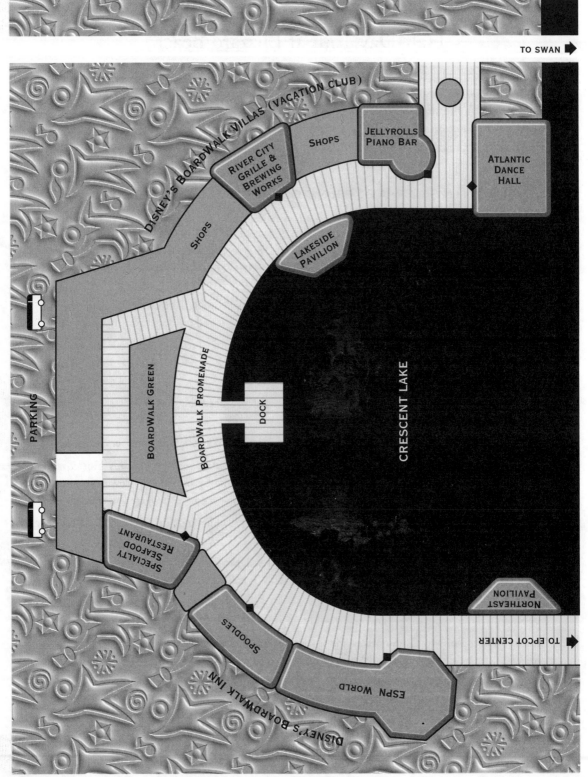

TO SWAN ➡

DISNEY'S BOARDWALK VILLAS (VACATION CLUB)

RIVER CITY GRILLE & BREWING WORKS

SHOPS

JELLYROLLS PIANO BAR

ATLANTIC DANCE HALL

SHOPS

LAKESIDE PAVILION

PARKING

BOARDWALK GREEN

BOARDWALK PROMENADE

DOCK

CRESCENT LAKE

SPECIALTY SEAFOOD RESTAURANT

SPOODLES

ESPN WORLD

NORTHEAST PAVILION

TO EPCOT CENTER ➡

DISNEY'S BOARDWALK INN

# DISNEY'S BOARDWALK

Disney's BoardWalk, opening mid-summer 1996, captures the turn-of-the-century ambience of Atlantic City's Boardwalk, the innovative amusement park that pioneered the concept of the shoreline promenade. Curving along a quarter-mile stretch of Crescent Lake, Disney's BoardWalk is a bustling waterfront complex where visitors can browse in specialty shops, dine overlooking the water or the BoardWalk Green, enjoy a variety of entertainment, and stroll along the wood-slatted BoardWalk Promenade, where artists sketch portraits and caricatures of visitors, performers entertain passersby, and colorful carts offer unique snacks and beverages. When the sun goes down and the midway lights come up, the BoardWalk is transformed into a re-creation of the amusement parks of the 1930s and 40s, which were designed for the pleasure of adults, rather than children. Along the Promenade, music spills from the clubs, aromas waft from the restaurants, and you hear the laughing voices of people out for a playful evening. With two hotels perched above the shops and restaurants — the informal yet elegant Disney's BoardWalk Inn and the cozy Disney's BoardWalk Villas (a Disney Vacation Club property) — Disney's BoardWalk is a combined attraction and destination vacation resort.

**WHEN TO GO:** The shops at Disney's BoardWalk are open from 10 AM until 1 AM. The sports clubs and arcade at ESPN World are open from 11 AM until 2 AM. The nightclubs at Disney's BoardWalk are open from 7 PM until 2 AM, and are usually in full swing by 8 PM. The most crowded times at the sports club are Mondays during football season and any time a major sports event is telecast. The most crowded times at the nightclubs are Friday and Saturday nights, when local residents join WDW visitors to enjoy the fun. For special-events schedules, check at Guest Services in your resort, or call 407 824-4321.

**HOW TO GET THERE:** Disney's BoardWalk is located in the Epcot Resorts Area. Parking is available at the BoardWalk's Guest Parking Lot on Epcot Resorts Boulevard, as well as at nearby resorts within walking distance: Beach Club, Yacht Club, Swan, and Dolphin. Valet parking is also available. WDW buses travel between Disney's BoardWalk and the WDW resorts and theme parks. The BoardWalk is within walking distance of Disney-MGM Studios and the International Gateway entrance to the World Show-case at Epcot Center. Water launches travel between Disney's BoardWalk and Disney-MGM Studios, as well as the following resorts: Swan, Dolphin, Yacht Club, and Beach Club. Taxi service is available.

**ADMISSIONS AND RESTRICTIONS:** Admission to Disney's BoardWalk is free. Florida law prohibits serving alcohol to anyone under twenty-one. Smoking is not permitted in restaurants.

✳

## ATTRACTIONS AND CLUBS

✗✗✗ – Solid entertainment.   ✗✗ – Good fun for most visitors.   ✗ – Worth a brief visit.

**ATLANTIC DANCE HALL:** Light-festooned terraces and a giant "DANCE HALL" sign glowing from its rooftop mark the Atlantic Dance Hall, a large two-story building that extends out over the waters of Crescent Lake. Inside, the ballroom captures the sleek elegance of the high-class casino dance clubs popular in the 1920s and '30s. A ten-piece band performs dance hits from the 1930s to the '90s that range from the zippy to the romantic, and lights sparkle across the dance floor, reflected from a large mirrored ball overhead. Stylish graphics adorn the glass in the mirrors that line the walls behind the club's four bars, and a sweeping staircase leads to a second-floor balcony that overlooks the dance floor and opens out onto the terraces. Beer, wine, and spirits are served. A selection of champagnes is offered, as are specialty drinks. Atlantic Dance Hall opens at about 8 PM. ✘✘✘

JELLYROLLS PIANO BAR: A rounded storefront with a striped awning and brightly lit windows welcomes guests to this rambunctious club. The large room has the look of an old warehouse, with old crates and bric-a-brac of uncertain origins cluttering the floor, hanging from the rafters, and jutting from the walls. Mismatched tables and chairs add to the visual chaos, and a wall of beer cans and bottles from around the world backs the bar tucked into one corner of the room. At a pair of battered pianos on a small stage, musicians put their flashiest playing styles to work as they try to outdo each other with their dancing digits, tossing out challenges and taking requests from the audience. Guests can see the nimble musicians' keyboard action reflected in the mirrors tilted crazily above the pianos. Beer, wine, and spirits are served, including such specialty drinks as Tickle the Ivories (vodka and Kahlúa floated with cream and served in a keyboard-decorated glass). Jellyrolls Piano Bar opens at about 7 PM. ✘✘✘

ESPN WORLD: This octagonal sports-poster-covered building with a giant arm and barbell above the door houses a complex of clubs that is the ultimate in entertainment for sports enthusiasts. In the evenings and any time that popular sports events are telecast, avid fans can be heard cheering on their favorites. The friendly exuberance is contagious, and even those with no interest in sports have a good time. ESPN World is open from about 11 AM until 2 AM.

✦ *Sports Central* — This live-action sports club is a large, tiered lounge featuring a wall of video monitors, the latest scores on a huge overhead scoreboard, and fully equipped television and radio broadcast studios. Live ESPN and ESPN2 programs such as "SportsCenter" and "SportsNight" are beamed by satellite from Sports Central to worldwide feeds, along with major league baseball spring-training reports, sports wrap-ups, interviews with sports figures and club visitors, and sports-oriented talk shows. Beer, wine, and spirits are served, including sports-themed specialty drinks, and baseball-park foods such as Dodger Dogs and Fenway Franks are featured. ✘✘✘

✦ *The Sidelines* — An impressive bank of overhead monitors offers guests a dazzling array of sports competitions at this club, which is modeled on the fifty-yard line of a football field and has servers costumed in uniforms patterned after those of referees. At the club's Penalty Box Bar, visitors seated at tables can switch on the sound for the sports event of their choice and, through a special audio feature, add their personal play-by-play commentaries. Beer, wine and spirits are also served, as are appetizers and a selection of hearty entrees. ✘✘

✦ *The Yard* — Chipped-brick walls, sports-related graffiti, and chain-link fencing create a gritty "urban schoolyard" atmosphere at this large arcade, which features the latest interactive and virtual-reality sports and adventure games. The Yard is a popular gathering spot for younger visitors bent on challenging themselves and each other. ✘

## FULL-SERVICE RESTAURANTS

*All WDW visitors can make restaurant reservations up to sixty days in advance. Same-day reservations may be made at the restaurant itself or by calling Same Day Reservations after 10 AM (939-3463).*

**BIG RIVER GRILLE & BREWING WORKS:** Making their way through piles of bags filled with hops, barley, and special ingredients, visitors find themselves in a fully operating microbrewery, complete with copper vats filled with fermenting mixtures. Guests can watch the brewmasters at work or settle in at the Brewer's Bar to enjoy the five private-label brews produced here, or purchase some to take along on their way out. The restaurant serves pub fare, such as pot roast, shepherd's pie, crab cakes, and meatloaf, as well as sandwiches. Entrees include prime rib, jerk chicken, and Porterhouse steak. Open for lunch and dinner; no reservations.

**SPOODLES:** At this family-style restaurant on the BoardWalk Promenade, piles of fresh produce and a hodgepodge decor of unmatched furniture and tableware create a comfortable, casual atmosphere. The restaurant has an open kitchen and features the cuisine of the Mediterranean. Guests seated indoors or at waterfront tables outdoors enjoy a view of Crescent Lake and the passersby strolling along the Promenade. Beer, wine, and spirits are served. Open all day until 10 PM; reservations recommended.

**SPECIALTY SEAFOOD RESTAURANT:** A large lobster is perched above the awning at this restaurant on the BoardWalk Green. Etched-glass mirrors, wood-paneled walls, fans in the high ceiling, and large windows that overlook the public square provide a casual, yet sophisticated ambience. Guests may dine at individual tables or, if they prefer, at the counter fronting the kitchen's gleaming copper hoods and open grill. Fresh seafood, steaks, and chicken are featured, along with grilled or sautéed vegetables. Beer, wine, and spirits served, as are espresso and cappuccino. Open for lunch and dinner; reservations recommended.

# Evening Tour at Disney's BoardWalk

*Four to five hours — year round — including dinner.*
*Make an early dinner reservation (about 6:30 PM) at one of the BoardWalk restaurants.*
*Disney's BoardWalk is within walking distance of nearby Epcot resorts, such as the Beach Club or Swan.*

✔ Arrive at **DISNEY'S BOARDWALK** around 5:30 PM. Stroll along the wood-slatted BoardWalk Promenade for a quick overview of entertainment sites and a browse through the shops.

✔ Proceed to your selected restaurant for your 6:30 PM dinner.

✔ After dinner, return to the BoardWalk Promenade and kick off the evening at **ESPN WORLD**. Even if you're not a sports fan, you'll want to check out the high-energy action at:
  • **SPORTS CENTRAL** — where you can watch, and maybe even participate in a live broadcast originating from the club's television and radio studios.
  • **THE SIDELINES** — where you can settle into the **PENALTY BOX BAR**, pick the event of your choice, tune in that audio at your table, and even add your own play-by-play commentary.

✔ Continue down the Promenade to the **BIG RIVER GRILLE & BREWING WORKS** to see how beer is made and, if you wish, sample some of the house brews.

✔ Head to **JELLYROLLS PIANO BAR** for a highly entertaining piano duel by very skilled musicians.

✔ Finally, cap off the night at the sophisticated **ATLANTIC DANCE HALL**, where you can watch the festive goings-on, sip champagne on the outdoor terrace, or dance the night away. ◆

DISNEY'S BOARDWALK

DISNEY VILLAGE MARKETPLACE

ART OF DISNEY · 2R'S READING AND RITING

MINNIE MIA'S

TEAM MICKEY'S ATHLETIC CLUB

GOURMET PANTRY

HARRINGTON BAY CLOTHIERS

CHEF MICKEY'S · VILLAGE LOUNGE · 24K PRECIOUS ADORNMENTS

RESORTWEAR UNLIMITED

THE CITY DISCOVER

CAPTAIN'S TOWER

MICKEY'S CHARACTER SHOP

CRISTAL ARTS

GOOFY'S GRILL

GREAT SOUTHERN CRAFT COMPANY

LANDING

CAP'N JACK'S MARINA

CAP'N JACK'S OYSTER BAR

BUENA VISTA LAGOON

DOCK STAGE

TOYS FANTASTIC · CHRISTMAS CHALET · YOU AND ME KID

GUEST SERVICES

EUROSPAIN

EMPRESS LILLY

TO PLEASURE ISLAND

VALET PARKING

# DISNEY VILLAGE MARKETPLACE

Disney Village Marketplace is a shopping and entertainment center with the atmosphere of a picturesque waterfront town. It is situated along the shore of Buena Vista Lagoon and adjacent to Pleasure Island. The complex was recently updated for its twenty-year anniversary with a pleasant waterfront promenade, fanciful gardens and topiaries, and entertaining "popjet" fountains. Continuing expansion will include a five-story Disney superstore that will replace the current Guest Services building. At the Marketplace, visitors can stroll along the waterfront, explore the shops, or relax in one of several restaurants or lounges. The many shops and boutiques in the Marketplace offer name-brand clothing, gourmet foods, special-interest gifts, and Disney collectibles. Disney Village Marketplace is also the site of seasonal outdoor entertainment, crafts demonstrations, and holiday celebrations, and it incorporates a large recreational marina for boating and fishing.

**WHEN TO GO:** Disney Village Marketplace shops are open every day of the year from 9:30 AM until about 11 PM. Unless you are going for a specific entertainment event, plan to visit first thing in the morning or in the evening after dinner, when crowds are smaller and parking places more abundant. For information on special events, call Disney Village Marketplace Guest Services (407 828-3058).

**HOW TO GET THERE:** Disney Village Marketplace is in the Disney Village Resorts Area. Free parking is available. The Marketplace is within walking distance of the Disney Institute and most of the Hotel Plaza resorts. WDW buses travel between all resorts and theme parks and Disney Village Marketplace. Water launches service the following resorts: Dixie Landings, Port Orleans, Vacation Club, and Villas at the Disney Institute. Valet parking is available near Pleasure Island starting at about 5:30 PM.

## SHOPS

**EUROSPAIN:** Eurospain offers a vast array of collectibles from all over the world, all displayed in uniquely designed showcases. The shop stocks selection of delicate floral ceramics from Italy, Austrian and Italian crystal, Goebels miniatures, ceramic masks, music boxes, porcelain figurines, and a variety of crystal and enameled jewelry. Crafts demonstrations include figurine painting and gold filigree work.

**TOYS FANTASTIC:** This Disney-Mattel collaboration stocks what is possibly the most complete selection of Barbie dolls and Barbie-doll paraphernalia in the world. The latest Disney character collectibles — such as Aladdin, Cinderella, and Pocahontas dolls — appear here first. Mattel's Hot Wheels and truckloads of accessories are also featured. For new arrivals, there's even a Disney Infant Department.

**CHRISTMAS CHALET:** Year round, the Christmas Chalet is the most popular shop at Disney Village Marketplace. One-of-a-kind Christmas ornaments, Nativity scenes, recordings of Christmas music, garlands, wreaths, and almost anything else required for the Christmas season is available here. Also offered are Mickey Mouse Christmas sweatshirts — a popular pick even in the middle of summer.

**YOU AND ME KID:** Designed to suggest a brightly colored toy box, the shop is filled to the brim with toys, games, electric trains, stuffed animals, and children's clothing. In the store's several annexes, visitors can have their pictures taken with Disney characters at Fototoons, and small children can play in an area designed especially for them.

**GREAT SOUTHERN CRAFT COMPANY:** In the outdoor area at the entrance to this shop, artisans demonstrate their craftmaking skills throughout the day. Inside, American crafts are featured, with a vast profusion of folk art, folk toys, handmade belts, quilts, dolls, stuffed animals, stained glass, ceramics, decoys, hand puppets, birdhouses, and baskets. Also on display are hand-dipped candles, scented oils and soaps, and a selection of toiletries. At the Lilly Langtry Photo Studio, tucked into an alcove, visitors can have themselves photographed in period costumes (some weigh as much as seventy-five pounds!). An expert stylist is on hand to outfit individuals or groups from a large rack of reproduction costumes.

**CRISTAL ARTS:** This shop, hung with magnificent crystal chandeliers, carries a large and sparkling selection of crystal jewelry, ornaments, vases, lamps, glasses, and bowls in all colors from all over the world. Also on view is a distinguished collection of Eastern European crystal goblets, bowls, and decanters. Throughout the day, glassblowers demonstrate their skills, creating tiny glass figurines for visitors, and custom crystal engraving is done on site.

**MICKEY'S CHARACTER SHOP:** This store is an emporium for all Disney merchandise: jewelry and watches, clothing, books, videos, music, collectible statuary, stuffed animals, notebooks, gift wrap, cards, and clothing. The centerpiece at Mickey's Character Shop is the Robomat, a spray-painting robot that paints Disney character art and the purchaser's name on clothing. With the ongoing demonstrations and the enormous collection of Disney merchandise for sale here, this shop is always crowded.

**HARRINGTON BAY CLOTHIERS:** With its pleasant masculine decor, this store provides a peaceful oasis for the shopping-weary. Men's casual and dress fashions are offered, including such brand names as Polo by Ralph Lauren, Boston Traders, Nautica, and Tommy Hilfiger. Also on display are accessories, tote bags, windbreakers, ties, and golf wear.

**CAPTAIN'S TOWER:** This octagonal shop, in a building that is open on all sides, is the site of special events and seasonal activities at Disney Village Marketplace, such as the Festival of the Masters art show. During those times, the Captain's Tower becomes a merchandising outlet for the featured event. The shop has several complete merchandise overhauls annually. At times, the store is dedicated exclusively to name-brand athletic shoes and sportswear. In the summer, fun-in-the-sun merchandise is featured.

**GOURMET PANTRY:** One side of this store, devoted to housewares, is a culinary collectors' paradise with a dizzying variety of gourmet cookware, utensils, cookbooks, and culinary gifts. The other half houses a deli counter stocked with cheese, salami, cold meats, quiches, salads, and Italian sandwiches sold by the inch; a liquor and wine shop; the Candy Shoppe; and a bakery that offers muffins, pastries, and cookies, and brews several gourmet coffees strong enough to get shoppers back on their feet. Shaded tables are scattered about outside. Gourmet Pantry provides free delivery service to the Walt Disney World resorts (828-3486, extension 3486). ☎

**DISCOVER:** Living topiary and bonsai, rocks and crystals, and nature-oriented books and gifts fill this pleasant natural wonders shop. Shoppers browse while listening to New Age music. Garden-lovers will find seeds and bulbs, birdhouses, gardening books and tools, sun hats, and an array of tee-shirts and tote bags with nature-themed designs. Also featured are herbal bathing products and cosmetics, and a large menagerie of exotic stuffed animals including giraffes, gorillas, lion cubs, and frogs.

DISNEY VILLAGE MARKETPLACE

**THE CITY:** Catering to a young adult crowd, this shop carries tee-shirts, miniskirts, designer blue jeans, leather jackets, and a few flashy outfits suitable for the nightclub scene at nearby Pleasure Island. Also offered are trendy sunglasses, belts, handbags, hats, and earrings.

**RESORTWEAR UNLIMITED:** In the summer months, this is the place to find women's casual wear, sun hats, sandals, sunglasses, and one of the largest selections of swimwear at Walt Disney World. During the winter months, jackets, slacks, and sweaters are also featured. Designers include Platinum, Liz Claiborne, and Peter Popovich. The shop also carries Keds sneakers, low-heeled dress shoes, and costume jewelry.

**24K PRECIOUS ADORNMENTS:** Here, shoppers can peruse fine gold jewelry and decorative gifts. The Mickey Mouse watches are designed by famous watchmakers, and some glitter with diamonds. In fact, many of the shop's finest pieces, including the exquisite cameos, incorporate Disney characters.

**ART OF DISNEY:** This is a not-to-be-missed gallery display of upscale Disney collectibles and original works of art based on Disney themes: sculptures, animation cels, mosaics, paintings, blown glass, and furniture. Prices above $10,000 are not unusual.

**2R's READING AND RITING:** Art of Disney opens onto this pleasant, busy bookstore, which features a range of books for children and adults, including current bestsellers. Also on display are stationery, magazines, videos, audiotapes and CDs, and Disney software and CD-ROMs. A walk-up coffee bar in the store serves espresso and cappuccino. 🍵

**TEAM MICKEY'S ATHLETIC CLUB:** This popular shop offers a huge selection of special-interest sportswear (most festooned with the Disney insignia), including bowling shirts and bags, baseball jerseys and jackets, golfing sweaters and bags, bicycling gear, rugby and polo shirts, aerobics outfits, and warm-up suits. In the athletic shoe department, a set of bleachers faces a wall where sixteen video monitors broadcast sporting events all day — a great spot for shopping-weary sports fans to cool off and relax.

## ACTIVITIES, EVENTS, AND LIVE ENTERTAINMENT

*Live entertainment and seasonal events are scheduled throughout the year at the Marketplace. These include a classic car show in June, a boat show in October, the Festival of the Masters art show in November, and a Nativity pageant at Christmas. Many of the shops feature daily demonstrations by guest artisans. Check with Disney Village Marketplace Guest Services for current entertainment schedules (407 828-3058).*

**DOCK STAGE:** The recently expanded Dock Stage is located in an open plaza at the edge of Buena Vista Lagoon. Throughout the year, it is the site of jazz concerts, high school band competitions, holiday celebrations, and other live entertainment.

**BOATING AT CAP'N JACK'S MARINA:** This busy and beautiful marina rents canopy boats, pontoon boats, and two-seater Water Sprites to visitors who would like to take a spin on Buena Vista Lagoon, explore the bayoulike Village Waterways, or tour the themed resorts in the Disney Village Resorts Area (see "Boating," page 216). Cap'n Jack's Marina is open daily from 10 AM until sundown.

**FISHING AT CAP'N JACK'S MARINA:** Guided fishing tours leave daily from Cap'n Jack's Marina in search of largemouth bass. The two-, three-, or four-hour fishing excursions should be booked in advance

(407 828-2461). Visitors who wish to test their fishing skills from the dock can rent old-fashioned cane poles at the Marina. Bait is provided, and there is a catch-and-release policy (see "Fishing," page 221).

## FULL-SERVICE RESTAURANTS

*All Walt Disney World visitors can make restaurant reservations up to sixty days in advance. Same-day reservations can be made at the restaurant itself, or by calling Same Day Reservations after 10 AM (939-3463). See "Restaurants," page 163, for reviews and reservation information. Unless otherwise noted, restaurants are nonsmoking.*

**CHEF MICKEY'S VILLAGE RESTAURANT:** This spacious family-oriented restaurant offers an American-style menu featuring Florida seafood, steak, and pasta dishes. Chef Mickey wanders through every evening during dinner, which thrills small fry. Beer, wine, and spirits are served, including their famous strawberry Margarita. Open for breakfast, lunch, and dinner; reservations suggested. (Chef Mickey's may be replaced soon by the Rainforest Cafe.)

**CAP'N JACK'S OYSTER BAR:** This octagonal restaurant is perched on a pier out in the lagoon. The unusual architecture offers diners a great view from any table, and the restaurant attracts a lively crowd for clams and oysters on the half shell, shrimp cocktails, crab cakes, lobster, and pasta. Beer, wine, and spirits are served. Open all day; no reservations. Visitors who just want to snack can walk in and seat themselves at the bar.

**THE FIREWORKS FACTORY:** "Dynamite" barbecued ribs and other applewood-smoked specialties are served in this lively open dining room decorated with pyrotechnic paraphernalia and powder burns. A late-night menu offers snacks, appetizers, and full dinners. Beer, wine, and spirits are served. The restaurant has a smoking section. Open all day until 2 to 3 AM; reservations recommended.

**PORTOBELLO YACHT CLUB:** Here, guests can enjoy Italian specialties, fresh seafood, and a variety of oven-fired thin-crust pizzas. Seating is available outdoors or inside one of several dining areas featuring yachting trophies and other maritime mementos. Beer, wine, and spirits are served, as are espresso and cappuccino. The restaurant has a smoking section. Open all day until 1:30 AM; no reservations.

***EMPRESS LILLY* RIVERBOAT:** This huge crabhouse-style restaurant opens in early 1996 aboard a detailed replica of a nineteenth-century stern-wheeler. Diners seated at tables on the riverboat's three decks enjoy pleasant views of Buena Vista Lagoon and the revolving paddle wheel in action. Beer, wine, and spirits are served. Open all day; no reservations.

## CAFES AND LOUNGES

*Several counter-service restaurants at Disney Village Marketplace serve fast-food meals and snacks. Those listed below are especially pleasant and make ideal rendezvous spots.*

**VILLAGE LOUNGE:** Adjacent to Chef Mickey's Village Restaurant, this large, comfortable lounge features two wide-screen TVs; the one at the bar generally broadcasts sports events. No snacks are served. (Chef Mickey's may be replaced soon by the Rainforest Cafe.)

## DISNEY VILLAGE MARKETPLACE

**CAP'N JACK'S OYSTER BAR:** The circular copper bar in this lively restaurant is known for its frozen strawberry Margaritas. This convivial bar is a great place for a quick pick-me-up or for a long, relaxing view of the sunset over Buena Vista Lagoon. Coffee and espresso are served as well.

**GOURMET PANTRY:** Step up to the bakery counter and check out the selection of freshly brewed gourmet coffees along the back wall. A long deli counter offers take-out snacks. There are shaded tables scattered outside the shop that offer pleasant views of the gardens, fountains, and shoppers.

**GOOFY'S GRILL:** The attraction at this counter-service restaurant is not the food — standard burgers and hot dogs — but its location facing the waterfront. This is the place to grab a beverage and sit out along the edge of Buena Vista Lagoon or stroll down the long dock. Milk shakes are served here, as are beer and coffee.

**MINNIE MIA'S ITALIAN EATERY:** This popular counter-service restaurant serves pizza, pasta, and submarine sandwiches, as well as sangría, wine, and coffee. Guests can sit inside the air-conditioned restaurant or outside at tables under the restaurant's large green-striped awning.

## SERVICES

**REST ROOMS:** Public rest rooms are located throughout Disney Village Marketplace. Those in Chef Mickey's Village Restaurant or Cap'n Jack's Oyster Bar are cool and quiet.

**TELEPHONES:** Outdoor public telephones can be found throughout Disney Village Marketplace, usually adjacent to the rest rooms. To make calls in air-conditioned comfort, try the phones in Chef Mickey's Village Restaurant or Cap'n Jack's Oyster Bar.

**GIFT WRAPPING:** Gift wrapping is available at Guest Services; prices average about $3.

**PACKAGE DELIVERY:** Guests staying at any Walt Disney World resort can drop purchases at Guest Services for free delivery to their hotel.

**FILM AND TWO-HOUR EXPRESS DEVELOPING:** A wide range of film may be purchased at Guest Services. Two-hour film processing is available at Guest Services, and developed film can be picked up there or delivered to any Walt Disney World resort.

**BANKING:** A branch of Sun Bank is located across the street from Disney Village Marketplace. There is an automatic teller machine (ATM) just outside Guest Services.

**MAIL DROP:** A mail box is located just outside Guest Services. Stamps are available inside.

**SHIPPING:** All shops in the Disney Village Marketplace will ship purchases.

**LOCKERS:** Coin lockers are located at Cap'n Jack's Marina.

**WHEELCHAIR RENTALS:** Wheelchairs are available for rent at Guest Services.

## HOT TIP

**THEME PARK TICKETS:** After 8 PM, Guest Services is the only location at WDW where late-arriving visitors can buy theme park tickets and avoid those long lines in the morning. Open until 10 PM. ◆

# 4-DAY VACATIONS

The unique touring itineraries that follow are designed to help both first-time and repeat visitors focus on their personal interests and streamline their vacation planning. Many visitors prefer to let serendipity and instinct guide them, which can certainly be an adventure in this highly complex playground. Experienced WDW visitors, however, are aware of the many entertainment choices they have, and carefully pre-plan their vacation schedule, especially during peak seasons when restaurants and entertainment events are booked far in advance. The 4-Day Vacations employ the same sophisticated pre-planning touring strategies.

## CHOOSING AND USING A 4-DAY VACATION

Each of the three vacation itineraries that follow addresses a special interest: The Romantic Adventure is designed for couples and private celebrations; the Disney Discovery Tour is the ideal learning adventure and samples a little of everything that WDW has to offer; and the Singles Safari is designed for singles, active vacationers, and the young at heart.

The 4-Day Vacations have an intense pace, and during peak seasons they can be difficult to accomplish. You can modify an itinerary to your own pace by skipping attractions or any activities marked "optional" in the schedule that you don't find absolutely irresistible. If you are like three out of four visitors to Walt Disney World, you'll be back, and you can catch those attractions next time. If you are planning to stay longer than four days, why not take a day off in the middle or at the end of the vacation tour, and luxuriate at your resort? You are, after all, *on vacation!* If you would rather fill those empty days with activities, you will find a number of options to extend your 4-Day Vacation listed on the next page.

The 4-Day Vacations work best when you have your own car or a rental car. WDW transportation can also be used, but you may not be able to travel easily or quickly to some destinations, especially during peak seasons or when visiting other resorts, unless you rely on taxis. If you do not have a car, be sure to use a taxi when it is specified in the text (which will save hours of your precious vacation time) and choose a resort location that offers many transportation options (see "Hotels," page 133). Whether you drive or not, it's a good idea to stay at a WDW resort, since the transportation privileges available to WDW resort guests are important to some of the logistics involved.

Each 4-Day Vacation begins on the afternoon that you arrive at Walt Disney World. As with any other vacation, the planning begins months earlier, so each vacation schedule includes a handy checklist of the reservations you will need to make and when you need to make them. On the day you arrive, all your decisions and reservations will have been made, and your most difficult task will be showing up for each event.

The first page of each 4-Day Vacation suggests the best time of year to use it and the best arrival days, which correspond to WDW events and schedules. You will also find a list of the resorts in keeping with the vacation's theme. The second page presents a vacation-at-a-glance overview of the experience you will have. The next four pages are the schedule you will follow, including a checklist of the advance reservations you need to make. Jot your travel dates in the spaces provided — this will be helpful when you are making your reservations. You may also want to copy the pages and carry them with you as you tour.

EXPANDING A 4-DAY VACATION

## DISCOUNTS & BUDGETING STRATEGIES

Although a stay at Walt Disney World is not inexpensive, there are a number of budget considerations built into the itineraries, such as a choice of resorts spanning a range of prices and budget dining options in the theme parks. (See also "Travel Discounts," page 244.) In addition, many of the activities suggested in the 4-Day Vacations take advantage of the Vacation Discount Coupons listed on page 272.

## EXPANDING YOUR 4-DAY VACATION

If you are staying longer than four days, you may wish to choose from some of the activities listed below to expand your selected 4-Day Vacation. Add these activities at the end of your four-day tour, but remember to make any necessary advance reservations for those you select:

DISNEY WORLD DISCOVERY: *Additional Days* — ❶ Join the studio audience for a television production at Disney-MGM Studios, then drop by the Casting Center to see how potential Disney Cast Members learn about Walt Disney World. In the evening take in the Hoop-Dee-Doo Musical Revue dinner show (for Disney-MGM production information, call 407 560-7299; see "Dining Events," page 205). ❷ Sign up for the Backstage Magic tour, an eight-hour exploration of the behind-the-scenes action at Walt Disney World; in the evening, dine at The Outback at Buena Vista Palace Resort and Spa, then drop into the Laughing Kookaburra for live music and dancing. (To reserve the tour, call 407 939-8687; to reserve The Outback, call 407 827-3430.) ❸ Spend the day at Typhoon Lagoon or Blizzard Beach, then catch an early dinner at Planet Hollywood and a first-run movie at the AMC Pleasure Island Theatres (for movie schedules, call 407 827-1300).

ROMANTIC ADVENTURE: *Additional Days* — ❶ Follow the Surf and Turf Day at Fort Wilderness tour and take in the Hoop-Dee-Doo Musical Revue in the evening (see "Fort Wilderness & River Country," page 75, and "Dining Events," page 206). ❷ Experience serious and thrilling water play at Blizzard Beach during the day and spend the evening at the Magic Kingdom for the Evening Parade and Fireworks Show (for Disney-MGM production information, call 407 560-7299). ❸ Enjoy an active day outdoors, bicycling, golfing, waterskiing, or fishing; in the evening join the MurderWatch Mystery Dinner Theater (see "Sports," page 213, and "Dining Events," page 209). ❹ Indulge in a spa experience at The Spa at Buena Vista Palace, then spend the evening exploring the nightclubs and entertainment at Disney's BoardWalk (for spa appointments, call 407 827-2727).

SINGLES SAFARI: *Additional Days* — ❶ Join the Hidden Treasures of the World Showcase tour at Epcot Center, then spend the late afternoon at Typhoon Lagoon or Blizzard Beach. In the evening, cruise the shops at Disney Village Marketplace and drop into the congenial Cap'n Jack's Oyster Bar or the *Empress Lilly* riverboat for a late dinner (for tour reservations, call 407 939-8687). ❷ Follow the Surf and Turf Day at Fort Wilderness tour and take in the Hoop-Dee-Doo Musical Revue dinner show (see "Fort Wilderness & River Country," page 75, and "Dining Events," page 206). ❸ Bicycle through the Village Resorts Area on the Country Club and Old Key West Ride, then catch dinner and performance at House of Blues in the evening (see "Bicycle Paths," page 214, and "Dining Events," page 207). ◆

# ROMANTIC ADVENTURE

*An Around-the-World Honeymoon Tour of International Cultures, Outdoor Adventures, Luxury Dining, and Nonstop Entertainment*

**BEST TIME OF YEAR FOR THIS ITINERARY**
*April through August; October and November*

**LEAST CROWDED TIMES FOR THIS ITINERARY**
*April, May, October, and November (except holidays)*

**BEST ARRIVAL DAY FOR THIS ITINERARY**
*Any Day (during June, July, and August)*
*Wednesday (during April, May, October, and November)*

**BEST BUDGET HOTELS FOR THIS ITINERARY**
*Disney's Dixie Landings Resort (river view)*
★ *DoubleTree Guest Suites Resort (WDW view)*

**BEST MODERATE HOTELS FOR THIS ITINERARY**
*Buena Vista Palace Resort and Spa (tower room)*
*Disney Vacation Club (upper-floor studio, forest view)*

**BEST DELUXE HOTELS FOR THIS ITINERARY**
*Disney's Wilderness Lodge (main lodge)*
*Disney's Polynesian Resort (lagoon or garden view)*

**ULTIMATE HOTEL EXPERIENCES FOR THIS ITINERARY**
*Disney's Grand Floridian Beach Resort (concierge room)*
*Disney's BoardWalk Inn (honeymoon cottage)*

**LOCAL TRANSPORTATION**
*For this itinerary, it is best to rent a car or use taxis when specified.*

**PACKING**
*Bring along clothes for the nightclubs, bathing suits, and water shoes.*
*Summer travelers will need umbrellas and walking shoes, not sandals.*

**TIPS**
*When making reservations, inquire whether the hotel has a honeymoon package.*

The Romantic Adventure itinerary combines intimate vacation experiences with theme park attractions that hold the most appeal for couples. Designed for private celebrations and memorable moments, this tour features waterway cruises, sophisticated dining events, whimsical parades, a New Year's Eve celebration, exotic wildlife and interplanetary encounters, dazzling light shows and colorful fireworks, travel through the past and fantasies of the future, the allure of Hollywood with a behind-the-scenes glimpse at moviemaking, sizzling nightclub entertainment, and cultural events and cuisines from around the world — all the elements that can create an unforgettable vacation and a wealth of shared adventures. ➤

# ROMANTIC ADVENTURE OVERVIEW

♥

## DAY ONE

- **EARLY EVENING AT THE MAGIC KINGDOM:** You begin your tour sampling adventures in exotic locales.
- **DINNER IN POLYNESIA:** Your arrival evening features the Polynesian Luau dinner show.

## DAY TWO

- **MORNING AT THE MAGIC KINGDOM:** This morning you time-travel into the future, and experience a close encounter with interplanetary travelers.
- **LUNCH AT THE MAGIC KINGDOM:** You'll lunch at King Stefan's Banquet Hall in Cinderella's Castle.
- **OPTIONAL AFTERNOON SAFARI AT DISCOVERY ISLAND:** After lunch, you can ferry across Bay Lake for a tour of a tropical zoological park.
- **EVENING IN THE WORLD SHOWCASE AT EPCOT:** Tonight you'll tour the pavilions at France, Morocco, Japan, U.S.A., Italy, Germany, China, and Norway, and enjoy the spectacular IllumiNations show.
- **DINNER IN THE WORLD SHOWCASE AT EPCOT:** You'll dine at the romantic San Angel Inn Restaurante, perched on a river inside the massive Mayan pyramid of the Mexico pavilion.

## DAY THREE

- **MORNING AT DISNEY-MGM STUDIOS:** This morning your tour takes you to Disney-MGM Studios and the glamor of early- and present-day Hollywood.
- **LUNCH AT DISNEY-MGM STUDIOS:** Your lunch destination is The Hollywood Brown Derby.
- **OPTIONAL AFTERNOON WATER ADVENTURE:** After lunch, you can rent a canopy boat for a cruise through the bayoulike Disney Village Waterways.
- **DINNER AT PLEASURE ISLAND:** This evening you will dine Italian-style at Portobello Yacht Club.
- **EVENING AT PLEASURE ISLAND:** Tonight you'll club-hop at Pleasure Island and take in the revelry and fireworks at Pleasure Island's nightly New Year's Eve Street Party.

## DAY FOUR

- **MORNING IN FUTURE WORLD AT EPCOT:** You return to Epcot Center this morning to explore the land, the sea, and the world of ideas and imagination.
- **LUNCH IN FUTURE WORLD AT EPCOT:** Your lunch destination is the Coral Reef Restaurant.
- **OPTIONAL AFTERNOON WATER ADVENTURE:** After lunch, you can venture to Typhoon Lagoon for thrilling water play and relaxation.
- **OPTIONAL AFTERNOON TEA:** If you decide to continue your tour of Epcot Center, you'll visit attractions at Canada and France in the World Showcase, then relax and take high tea at the Rose & Crown Dining Room in the United Kingdom.
- **ROMANTIC DINNER OF YOUR CHOICE:** Tonight you'll enjoy a romantic and unforgettable dining event, either at California Grill, with its celebrated New American cuisine and its spectacular view from the fifteenth floor of Disney's Contemporary Resort; or you'll have a private dinner on the Starlight Cruise, while touring Seven Seas Lagoon and Bay Lake. From either dinner location, you'll see the shimmering lights of the Electrical Water Pageant and the Fantasy in the Sky fireworks at the Magic Kingdom. ➤

# Romantic Adventure Schedule

*The next four pages show the schedule you will follow and the arrangements and reservations you must make to organize the Romantic Adventure. You may want to copy these pages and carry them with you.*

♥

## BEFORE YOU GO

**AT THE TIME YOU MAKE YOUR HOTEL RESERVATIONS:** Make dinner reservations for **DAY ONE** at the 9:30 PM **POLYNESIAN LUAU** dinner show (407 939-3463).

**UP TO SIXTY DAYS BEFORE YOU LEAVE:** Call Disney Dining Reservations (407 939-3463) and make the following reservations (restaurant reservations can be made up to sixty days in advance):

❏ **DAY TWO** — 1 PM lunch at **KING STEFAN'S BANQUET HALL** in the Magic Kingdom.

❏ **DAY TWO** — 7:30 PM dinner at **SAN ANGEL INN RESTAURANTE** at the Mexico pavilion in the World Showcase at Epcot Center. (If you prefer another restaurant, consider one in China or Italy. Be sure your seating is no later than ninety minutes before IllumiNations is scheduled.)

❏ **DAY THREE** — 1:30 PM lunch at **THE HOLLYWOOD BROWN DERBY** at Disney-MGM Studios.

❏ **DAY FOUR** — 11:30 AM lunch at **CORAL REEF RESTAURANT** in Future World at Epcot Center.

❏ **DAY FOUR (VISITOR'S CHOICE)** — 8 PM dinner at **CALIFORNIA GRILL** at Disney's Contemporary Resort.

    ❏ Or, book a private **STARLIGHT CRUISE** and dinner for two on the Seven Seas Lagoon. Ten days before you leave, call Captain's Shipyard at Disney's Grand Floridian Beach Resort (407 824-2439) and reserve the Starlight Cruise for two hours, beginning at 8 PM. Then call Private Dining at the resort (407 824-2474) and order your on-board dinner. (See "Excursion Cruises," page 220.)

♥

## DAY ONE: THE EVENING OF ARRIVAL

DAY / DATE

**AFTER YOU CHECK INTO YOUR HOTEL:** Stop at Guest Services, and if you do not have admission tickets, purchase a Multiday Pass that includes Discovery Island, Pleasure Island, and Typhoon Lagoon. Pick up a *Times and Information* pamphlet showing operating hours at the theme parks.

**6 PM OR EARLIER:** Drive, taxi, or ride the monorail to Disney's Polynesian Resort (do not take a bus). Stop at Guest Services and purchase your tickets for the **POLYNESIAN LUAU**. Hop the monorail from the Polynesian resort to the **MAGIC KINGDOM** (if the park is open late) and visit the following attractions that interest you: ❶ **JUNGLE CRUISE** and ❷ **PIRATES OF THE CARIBBEAN** in Adventureland; ❸ **THE HAUNTED MANSION** in Liberty Square; and ❹ **BIG THUNDER MOUNTAIN RAILROAD** in Frontierland (if you like thrill rides and the lines are not long).

**DINNER IN POLYNESIA:** Exit the park at 8:30 PM and monorail back to the Polynesian resort. If you have time, follow the torchlit path to the Seven Seas Lagoon and catch the **ELECTRICAL WATER PAGEANT** as it cruises by at about 9 PM, then proceed to Luau Cove for the POLYNESIAN LUAU dinner show. If you arrived at Walt Disney World late in the day and get to the Polynesian resort around 8 PM, order a Polynesian-style cocktail and enjoy the bartenders' skilled juggling antics at the hotel's Tambu Lounge. Then, beverage in hand, stroll out to the Seven Seas Lagoon for the 9 PM ELECTRICAL WATER PAGEANT.

BEFORE YOU RETIRE: You may want to leave a wake-up call tonight and order a room-service breakfast for tomorrow morning. You'll leave your hotel one hour before the Magic Kingdom opens.

## DAY TWO

DAY / DATE

ONE HOUR BEFORE THE MAGIC KINGDOM OPENS: Drive or take WDW transportation to the Magic Kingdom. If you are driving, park at the Contemporary resort and ride the monorail to the Magic Kingdom. Enter the park and walk to the end of Main Street to Tomorrowland. When the ropes are dropped, walk quickly to the following attractions that interest you: ❶ THE EXTRATERRORESTRIAL ALIEN ENCOUNTER; ❷ TRANSPORTARIUM; ❸ SPACE MOUNTAIN (if you like thrill rides and the lines are not long); ❹ DREAMFLIGHT; and ❺ CAROUSEL OF PROGRESS. Stroll to Fantasyland or ride the ❻ SKYWAY TO FANTASYLAND and, if you have time before lunch, take in ❼ LEGEND OF THE LION KING and ❽ THE HALL OF PRESIDENTS at Liberty Square.

1 PM LUNCH: King Stefan's Banquet Hall is located in Cinderella's Castle, at the center of the Magic Kingdom. (Light eaters and budget diners may wish to try The Crystal Palace restaurant on the other side of the Castle, at the end of Main Street.) After lunch, you can continue touring the Magic Kingdom, return to your resort to relax, or go on the Optional Afternoon Safari at Discovery Island.

OPTIONAL AFTERNOON SAFARI AT DISCOVERY ISLAND: Exit the Magic Kingdom and catch the monorail to the Contemporary resort. Take the short ferry ride across Bay Lake from the Contemporary's Marina Pavilion to Discovery Island. Tour the zoological park, talk to the animal-caretakers, visit the ANIMAL HOSPITAL, and catch the FEATHERED FRIENDS SHOW or REPTILE ENCOUNTER show, if you can. When you're ready to leave, ferry back to the Contemporary resort.

5 PM: Drive or taxi to the Beach Club resort. Walk through the hotel to the waterfront, stroll to the International Gateway, and enter the WORLD SHOWCASE AT EPCOT CENTER. Walk counter-clockwise around the lagoon, beginning at FRANCE, and tour the pavilions and shops (but not the attractions, which you'll see later). Catch some of the street entertainment as you tour the pavilions on your way toward MEXICO.

7:30 PM DINNER: San Angel Inn Restaurante is located inside the Mexico pavilion at the World Showcase. If you arrive early, there is a small lounge inside the pavilion, adjacent to the restaurant.

AFTER DINNER: If you have time, take the short EL RIO DEL TIEMPO boat ride through Mexico, which can be a fun and romantic finish to dinner. If ILLUMINATIONS begins at 9 PM tonight, view the show from the Cantina de San Angel on the edge of the lagoon, just outside the Mexico pavilion, or along the lagoon between Mexico and China. If IllumiNations begins at 10 PM, backtrack to NORWAY for the MAELSTROM attraction, then proceed to CHINA for the film WONDERS OF CHINA.

**BEFORE YOU RETIRE:** You may again wish to order a wake-up call and breakfast for tomorrow morning. You'll leave your hotel forty-five minutes before Disney-MGM Studios opens.

## DAY THREE

DAY / DATE

**BEFORE YOU LEAVE YOUR HOTEL:** You will be lunching late today, so be sure to have breakfast before heading to Disney-MGM Studios.

**FORTY-FIVE MINUTES BEFORE DISNEY-MGM STUDIOS OPENS:** Drive, taxi, or take WDW transportation to Disney-MGM Studios. As you enter, pick up an entertainment schedule at the Crossroads of the World kiosk. Stroll down Hollywood and Sunset Boulevards (which generally open early). Visit the following attractions in this order: ❶ THE TWILIGHT ZONE TOWER OF TERROR (if you like one-of-a-kind thrill rides); ❷ THE GREAT MOVIE RIDE; ❸ BACKSTAGE STUDIO TOUR (the tram portion only); ❹ JIM HENSON'S MUPPET*VISION 3D; ❺ STAR TOURS (if you like thrill rides); and ❻ INDIANA JONES EPIC STUNT SPECTACULAR. Try to catch the ❼ FEATURE PARADE on Hollywood Boulevard at about 11:30 AM (1 PM during nonpeak seasons). If you have time before or after lunch, take in a performance at ❽ THEATER OF THE STARS, and browse through any of the shops that interest you.

**1:30 PM LUNCH:** The Hollywood Brown Derby is located at the end of Hollywood Boulevard. (Light eaters and budget diners may wish to try the Disney-MGM Studios Commissary, next to the Chinese Theater.) After lunch, you can continue touring Disney-MGM Studios, proceed on to the Optional Afternoon Water Adventure, or return to your resort to relax.

**OPTIONAL AFTERNOON WATER ADVENTURE:** Exit the park and drive or take WDW transportation to Disney Village Marketplace to explore the DISNEY VILLAGE WATERWAYS. (If you are staying at a resort on the Waterways, you can rent a boat there.) Rent a canopy boat at Cap'n Jack's Marina, take off across Buena Vista Lagoon, and navigate the tree-lined waterways on the following course: ❶ Cruise past the small-town-America-style learning center and amphitheater of the new DISNEY INSTITUTE. ❷ Follow the Sassagoula River past Port Orleans to DIXIE LANDINGS for a look at the grand plantation mansions and rustic bayou lodges of the Old South. ❸ Backtrack and dock at PORT ORLEANS, where you can tour the streets of New Orleans' French Quarter as it prepares for Mardi Gras, and check out the decor at the Sassagoula Floatworks and Food Factory. ❹ Continue downstream and follow the Trumbo Canal to Old Key West at the VACATION CLUB. If it's a hot day, pull up at the dock and cool off with a relaxing poolside beverage at the Gurgling Suitcase before heading back.

**7 PM:** Drive or taxi to Pleasure Island. This evening you may want to dress for club-hopping.

**7:30 PM DINNER:** Enjoy an Italian dinner at Portobello Yacht Club, or stroll over to the waterfront where the *Empress Lilly* riverboat is docked, and have dinner at the crab house. (Neither takes reservations.)

**AFTER DINNER:** Enter PLEASURE ISLAND and stop at MANNEQUINS for the dazzling dance performance that begins about 9:30 PM, then drop into the ADVENTURERS CLUB and NEON ARMADILLO. Catch an improv performance at COMEDY WAREHOUSE, or enjoy a live set at PLEASURE ISLAND JAZZ COMPANY.

About 10:45 PM (11:45 PM on weekends), make sure you're outside at the West End Stage to celebrate at Pleasure Island's spectacular NEW YEAR'S EVE STREET PARTY, complete with fireworks and confetti.

BEFORE YOU RETIRE: You may want to leave a wake-up call and order a room-service breakfast for tomorrow. You'll be leaving your hotel forty-five minutes before Epcot Center opens.

# DAY FOUR

DAY / DATE

BEFORE YOU LEAVE YOUR HOTEL: Pack your tote bag with an umbrella, optional bathing suits, towels, and sun block. Be sure to wear your sunglasses and a hat or visor.

FORTY-FIVE MINUTES BEFORE EPCOT CENTER OPENS: Drive or take WDW transportation to the Main Gate at Epcot Center. (If you're having the Optional Afternoon Tea, go to WorldKey Information Service in Innoventions East and reserve a 3:30 PM seating at the Rose & Crown Dining Room.) Visit any of the following attractions that interest you, in this order: ❶ SPACESHIP EARTH (which generally opens early), then ❷ THE AT&T GLOBAL NEIGHBORHOOD; at the Wonders of Life pavilion, ❸ BODY WARS and ❹ THE MAKING OF ME; at Innoventions West, ❺ WALT DISNEY IMAGINEERING LABS and technology exhibits; at the Journey Into Imagination pavilion, ❻ MAGIC EYE THEATER (*Honey, I Shrunk the Audience*); at The Land pavilion, ❼ LIVING WITH THE LAND and ❽ HARVEST THEATER (*Circle of Life*); and at The Living Seas pavilion, ❾ CARIBBEAN CORAL REEF RIDE.

11:30 AM LUNCH: The Coral Reef Restaurant is located in The Living Seas pavilion at Future World. (Light eaters and budget diners may wish to try Pasta Piazza Ristorante in Innoventions West.) After lunch, you can continue your tour of Future World, go on to the Optional Afternoon Water Adventure or Optional Afternoon Tea, or return to your hotel to relax.

OPTIONAL AFTERNOON WATER ADVENTURE: Get to TYPHOON LAGOON by car or WDW bus. Set up camp in the shade near Typhoon Tilly's or at Cascade Cove, nearby, then spend the afternoon exploring the park (see "Half-Day Tour at Typhoon Lagoon," page 89, for touring strategies).

OPTIONAL AFTERNOON TEA: After lunch, continue touring Future World, or enter the World Showcase and see ❶ O CANADA!, ❷ IMPRESSIONS DE FRANCE, and ❸ THE AMERICAN ADVENTURE. At 3:30 PM, proceed to the United Kingdom pavilion for high tea at the Rose & Crown Dining Room.

8 PM ROMANTIC DINNER (VISITOR'S CHOICE): If you're dining at CALIFORNIA GRILL, drive, taxi, or monorail to the Contemporary resort about 7:30 PM. California Grill is located on the resort's fifteenth floor. The restaurant has a pleasant lounge and a great view of the ELECTRICAL WATER PAGEANT and the fireworks shows at the parks. If you wish, carry your drinks or dessert along and enjoy the shows outside.

If you choose the private STARLIGHT CRUISE and dinner for two on the Seven Seas Lagoon, drive, taxi, or monorail to the Grand Floridian resort at 7:30 PM. Your boat will be waiting at Captain's Shipyard Marina, behind the hotel. Tour the Seven Seas Lagoon and Bay Lake, dine on board, and enjoy the sights and sounds of the ELECTRICAL WATER PAGEANT, which cruises the area beginning at 9 PM. As you return, watch for the FANTASY IN THE SKY fireworks above the Magic Kingdom at 10 PM. ◆

# DISNEY WORLD DISCOVERY

*A Vacation Trek Through International Cultures, Space-Age Discovery,
Time-Travel Adventures, Tropical Wilderness Areas, and Nighttime Entertainment Events*

**BEST TIME OF YEAR FOR THIS ITINERARY**
*From mid-March through May and from October through mid-February*

**LEAST CROWDED TIMES FOR THIS ITINERARY**
*October through December (except holidays)*

**BEST ARRIVAL DAY FOR THIS ITINERARY**
*Wednesday*

**BEST BUDGET HOTELS FOR THIS ITINERARY**
★ *DoubleTree Guest Suites Resort (WDW view)*
*Disney's Dixie Landings Resort (Alligator Bayou, near lobby)*
*Disney's Port Orleans Resort (river view)*

**BEST MODERATE HOTELS FOR THIS ITINERARY**
*Disney Vacation Club (studio, near lobby)*
*Disney's Wilderness Lodge (standard room)*
*Walt Disney World Dolphin (standard balcony room)*

**BEST DELUXE HOTELS FOR THIS ITINERARY**
*Disney's Grand Floridian Beach Resort (courtyard view)*
*Disney's Polynesian Resort (lagoon view)*
*Disney's Contemporary Resort (tower room, WDW view)*

**ULTIMATE HOTEL EXPERIENCE FOR THIS ITINERARY**
*Disney's Yacht Club Resort (concierge room)*

**LOCAL TRANSPORTATION**
*For this itinerary, it is best to rent a car or use taxis when specified.*

**PACKING**
*Much of this itinerary is spent outside, so winter travelers should bring warm
clothing (it can get cold in Orlando). An umbrella may come in handy.*

**TIPS**
*Stand-out exhibits occur during the Epcot International Flower and Garden Festival
in late spring and during the holiday festivities from Thanksgiving through New Year's.*

Disney World Discovery combines the theme park attractions that excite curiosity with a glimpse of the imagination and technology behind their creation. From undersea worlds to outer space, this tour explores the past and the future, untamed wilderness areas, high-tech lifestyles, international architecture and culture, outdoor adventures, live entertainment events, and an unusual island retreat for endangered species — a stimulating vacation that samples the full spectrum of all that Walt Disney World has to offer. ➤

# DISNEY WORLD DISCOVERY OVERVIEW

## DAY ONE

- **EARLY EVENING IN THE TROPICS:** Your tour begins in the tropical gardens at Disney's Polynesian Resort.
- **DINNER IN POLYNESIA:** Your arrival evening features the 'Ohana dinner show.

## DAY TWO

- **MORNING IN THE WORLD SHOWCASE AT EPCOT:** This morning you'll visit Epcot Center to explore the history of communication and join your selected guided tour of international landscapes or architecture.
- **LUNCH IN THE WORLD SHOWCASE AT EPCOT:** You'll lunch at the Chefs de France on celebrated French cuisine in the France pavilion.
- **OPTIONAL AFTERNOON TEA:** After lunch, you visit Canada and France. Afterward, you can monorail to Disney's Grand Floridian Beach Resort to tour its Victorian gardens and architecture and take tea.
- **EARLY EVENING IN THE MAGIC KINGDOM:** This evening you'll explore equatorial jungles of Africa, Asia, and South America, and time-travel through the United States, past and future.
- **LAGOONSIDE DINNER:** Your dinner destination is Narcoossee's, overlooking the Seven Seas Lagoon at Disney's Grand Floridian Beach Resort.

## DAY THREE

- **MORNING AT DISCOVERY ISLAND:** This morning you ferry across Bay Lake for a tour of a wildlife refuge and tropical zoological park.
- **OPTIONAL FORT WILDERNESS PICNIC AND NATURE WALK:** You can ferry to Fort Wilderness across Bay Lake for a walk and a picnic lunch in the natural beauty of the Wilderness Swamp Trail.
- **AFTERNOON IN FUTURE WORLD AT EPCOT:** You return to Epcot Center this afternoon to explore the land, the sea, and the world of imagination and ideas.
- **DINNER IN THE WORLD SHOWCASE AT EPCOT:** You'll dine at San Angel Inn Restaurante, perched near a smoking volcano on a river inside the massive Mayan pyramid of the Mexico pavilion.
- **EVENING IN THE WORLD SHOWCASE AT EPCOT:** After dinner, you'll tour the pavilions and attractions at Mexico, Norway, and China, and enjoy the spectacular IllumiNations show.

## DAY FOUR

- **MORNING ON THE DISNEY VILLAGE WATERWAYS:** This morning you rent a canopy boat and cruise the bayoulike Disney Village Waterways for a tour of the landscapes and architecture of the Old South.
- **MIDDAY AT DISNEY VILLAGE MARKETPLACE:** You'll tour the shops and lunch at Cap'n Jack's Oyster Bar.
- **AFTERNOON AT DISNEY-MGM STUDIOS:** This afternoon you'll enjoy the glamor of early- and present-day Hollywood and get a behind-the-scenes look at motion picture production.
- **DISCOVERY DINNER OF YOUR CHOICE:** You'll either stay at Disney-MGM Studios to dine at The Hollywood Brown Derby and catch the Nighttime Fireworks show; or head to Baskervilles at the Grosvenor Resort for an evening of sleuthing at the MurderWatch Mystery Dinner Theatre.
- **OPTIONAL NIGHTLIFE TOUR:** After dinner, you can explore the nightclub scene at Pleasure Island and join the celebration at the nightly New Year's Eve Street Party. ➡

DISNEY WORLD DISCOVERY

# Disney World Discovery Schedule

*The next four pages show the schedule you will follow and the arrangements and reservations you must make to organize the Disney World Discovery tour. You may want to copy these pages and carry them with you.*

## BEFORE YOU GO

**AT THE TIME YOU MAKE YOUR HOTEL RESERVATIONS:** Make tour reservations on **DAY TWO** for either Gardens of the World or Hidden Treasures of the World Showcase (407 939-8687).

**UP TO SIXTY DAYS BEFORE YOU LEAVE:** Call Disney Dining Reservations (407 939-3463) and make the following reservations (restaurant reservations can be made up to sixty days in advance):

❑ **DAY ONE** — 7:30 PM dinner at **'OHANA** restaurant at Disney's Polynesian Resort.

❑ **DAY TWO** — 1:30 PM lunch at **CHEFS DE FRANCE** in the France pavilion in the World Showcase at Epcot Center. (If you prefer another restaurant, consider one in the United Kingdom or Morocco.)

❑ **DAY TWO** — 8:30 PM dinner at **NARCOOSSEE'S** at Disney's Grand Floridian Beach Resort.

❑ **DAY THREE** — 6:30 PM dinner at **SAN ANGEL INN RESTAURANTE** in the Mexico pavilion in the World Showcase at Epcot Center. (If you prefer another restaurant, consider one in Norway, China, or Germany.)

❑ **DAY FOUR (VISITOR'S CHOICE)** — 7 PM dinner at **THE HOLLYWOOD BROWN DERBY** at Disney-MGM Studios (if the park stays open late).

    ❑ Or, 6 PM **MURDERWATCH MYSTERY DINNER THEATRE** at the Grosvenor Resort (800 624-4109).

## DAY ONE: THE EVENING OF ARRIVAL

_____
DAY / DATE

**AFTER YOU CHECK INTO YOUR HOTEL:** Stop at Guest Services and, if you do not have admission tickets, purchase a Multiday Pass that includes Discovery Island and Pleasure Island. Also pick up a *Times and Information* pamphlet showing the operating schedules at the theme parks.

**6:30 PM OR EARLIER:** Drive, taxi, or monorail to Disney's Polynesian Resort. If you have time on your hands before your dinner, check out the colorful parrots, blooming orchids, and bromeliads in the resort's atrium jungle garden and tour the resort's paths and outdoor tropical gardens.

**7:30 PM DINNER:** 'Ohana is on the second floor of the Great Ceremonial House at the Polynesian.

**AFTER DINNER:** Walk through the torchlit gardens behind the hotel to the Seven Seas Lagoon beach to catch the shimmering lights of the **ELECTRICAL WATER PAGEANT**, which floats by at 9 PM.

**BEFORE YOU RETIRE:** Leave a wake-up call and perhaps order a room-service breakfast to be delivered early in the morning. Plan to leave your hotel at least forty-five minutes before Epcot Center opens.

## DAY TWO

FORTY-FIVE MINUTES BEFORE EPCOT CENTER OPENS: Drive or take WDW transportation to the Main Gate at Epcot Center. Ride SPACESHIP EARTH (which generally opens early) and visit THE AT&T GLOBAL NEIGHBORHOOD, where you can experience the interactive attractions. At 9:15 AM, proceed to the Tour Garden, located in Epcot's Entrance Plaza, to join your tour.

9:30 AM: The GARDENS OF THE WORLD tour explores the horticulture of the World Showcase, while the HIDDEN TREASURES OF THE WORLD SHOWCASE tour explores the art and architecture of the pavilions. The tours last about three hours, and end back at Future World. As your tour ends, drop out before it returns to Future World and proceed to the FRANCE pavilion.

1:30 PM LUNCH: Chefs de France is located at the front of the France pavilion. (Light eaters and budget diners may wish to try Au Petit Café in the France pavilion, or Pasta Piazza Ristorante at Innoventions West in Future World.) After lunch, continue your tour of the World Showcase. Catch the film presentations IMPRESSIONS DE FRANCE and O CANADA!, then return to your resort to relax, or proceed to the Optional Afternoon Tea.

OPTIONAL AFTERNOON TEA: Drive, monorail, or bus to Disney's Grand Floridian Beach Resort. Tour the resort's Victorian gardens and take in its turn-of-the-century architectural details. Be seated at the Garden View Lounge for high tea, which is served from 3 until 6 PM.

4:30 PM: Drive, monorail, or bus to the MAGIC KINGDOM. (If you are driving, park at the Grand Floridian and continue by monorail.) Stroll down Main Street and note the clever landscaping and nineteenth-century architectural details, especially on the upper floors. Beginning in Adventureland, take in as many of the following attractions as you can, in this order: ❶ JUNGLE CRUISE; ❷ SPLASH MOUNTAIN in Frontierland (if you like thrill rides and the lines are not too long); and ❸ THE HALL OF PRESIDENTS and ❹ THE HAUNTED MANSION, both in Liberty Square. (Keep an eye out for the century-old Liberty Tree, hung with thirteen metal lanterns, representing the original colonies.) Ride the ❺ SKYWAY TO TOMORROWLAND (if it is open and heights do not disturb you), or stroll through Fantasyland to Tomorrowland, and take the time-travel tour at ❻ TRANSPORTARIUM and see ❼ THE EXTRATERRORESTRIAL ALIEN ENCOUNTER. Cross the bridge from Tomorrowland toward the centerpiece topiary in front of Cinderella's Castle on your way out. Notice the serpent topiary on your left, and the All-America Rose Selection Display Garden to your right.

8 PM: Monorail from the Magic Kingdom to the Grand Floridian resort. On your way to dinner, you may want to linger in the hotel's lobby if there is a live music performance.

8:30 PM LAGOONSIDE DINNER: Narcoossee's is located on the waterfront behind the resort, overlooking the Seven Seas Lagoon. (Watch for the ELECTRICAL WATER PAGEANT, which floats by on the lagoon at about 9:15 PM.) As you leave, catch the Magic Kingdom fireworks show, which goes off at about 10 PM on nights when the park stays open late.

## DAY THREE

DAY / DATE

**9:30 AM:** Drive, taxi, or monorail to the Contemporary resort. Take the ferry from the Contemporary's Marina Pavilion to DISCOVERY ISLAND and pick up an entertainment schedule as you enter. Follow the path to the right (counter-clockwise) and explore the landscaping and wildlife in the zoological park. (The animal-caretakers can answer all your questions.) Catch the FEATHERED FRIENDS SHOW and REPTILE ENCOUNTER show, if you can. When you're ready to leave, return to your resort for lunch and to relax for the afternoon and evening ahead, or continue on to the Optional Fort Wilderness Picnic and Nature Walk.

**OPTIONAL FORT WILDERNESS PICNIC AND NATURE WALK:** About noon, ferry from Discovery Island to FORT WILDERNESS. You can buy picnic supplies to take on your walk at the Settlement Trading Post, across from the Fort Wilderness Marina, or have lunch at Trail's End Buffeteria, nearby, which has a salad bar and hot entrees. (Trail's End can also prepare food to go.) The WILDERNESS SWAMP TRAIL begins behind the Settlement Trading Post and meanders through two miles of forests, wetlands, beaches, and meadows. If you brought along a picnic, you'll find a shady spot to eat near the bridge over Chickasaw Creek, where the Wilderness Swamp Trail meets Bay Lake. After your hike, ferry back to the Contemporary, or continue by bus to your next destination.

**3 PM:** Drive or take WDW transportation to FUTURE WORLD at Epcot Center. Proceed directly to The Land pavilion to take in ❶ LIVING WITH THE LAND, then go to The Living Seas pavilion for the ❷ CARIBBEAN CORAL REEF RIDE to Sea Base Alpha, and tour the huge saltwater aquarium and the kelp gardens. Stroll past the dynamic fountains at the Journey Into Imagination pavilion and, at the ❸ MAGIC EYE THEATER, take in a performance of *Honey, I Shrunk the Audience*. If you have about forty minutes before dinner, return to The Land pavilion to catch the film *Circle of Life* at the ❹ HARVEST THEATER, or head to Innoventions West to see what's going on at ❺ WALT DISNEY IMAGINEERING LABS and to tour the high-tech communications and entertainment exhibits.

**6:30 PM DINNER:** San Angel Inn Restaurante is located inside the Mexico pavilion at the World Show-case. (Light eaters and budget diners may wish to dine in Future World at Pasta Piazza Ristorante in Innoventions West, or in the World Showcase at Cantina de San Angel in Mexico or Kringla Bakeri og Kafé in Norway, both with outdoor seating.)

**AFTER DINNER:** Take a voyage on ❶ EL RIO DEL TIEMPO in MEXICO, then check out the ❷ MAELSTROM attraction in NORWAY. If you have about forty minutes before IllumiNations is scheduled to begin, proceed to CHINA for the film presentation ❸ WONDERS OF CHINA. About twenty minutes before ILLUMINATIONS begins, find a viewing spot for the show at the edge of the World Showcase Lagoon. Good views can be found along the promenade from Mexico to Norway, and on the bridges in front of Italy. (If IllumiNations begins at 10 PM tonight, tour some of the other World Showcase pavilions, which are enchantingly lit at night.)

## DAY FOUR

DAY / DATE

**9:30 AM:** Drive or take WDW transportation to Disney Village Marketplace. Rent a canopy boat at Cap'n Jack's Marina to cruise along the DISNEY VILLAGE WATERWAYS. (If you're staying at a resort on the waterways, you can rent a boat there.) You may dock where you wish on your voyage. Guide your boat across Buena Vista Lagoon, past the reproduction nineteenth-century *Empress Lilly* riverboat, and enter the tree-lined waterways. Cruise past the colorful Village Green at the DISNEY INSTITUTE. Set your course for a water tour of the following theme resorts: ❶ Follow the Sassagoula River to PORT ORLEANS, where the streets and buildings of New Orleans' French Quarter are artfully reproduced as it prepares for Mardi Gras. ❷ Continue upstream to DIXIE LANDINGS to see the architecture and landscaping of the Old South, from the elegant plantation mansions with grassy banks and weeping willows, to the rustic bayou lodges surrounded by untamed palmettos and pine forest. ❸ Follow the Trumbo Canal to the VACATION CLUB, a re-creation of Old Key West set in South Florida–style landscaping. ❹ Head back to Cap'n Jack's Marina and tour the shops at Disney Village Marketplace, especially Discover, Gourmet Pantry, Great Southern Craft Company, and 2R's Reading and Riting. When you're ready for lunch, try Cap'n Jack's Oyster Bar, which is perched over Buena Vista Lagoon. (Budget diners or light eaters may wish to try Minnie Mia's Italian Eatery.)

**2:30 PM:** Drive or take WDW transportation to DISNEY-MGM STUDIOS. Stroll down Hollywood Boulevard and take in as many of the following attractions as you can before your dinner reservation: ❶ BACKSTAGE STUDIO TOUR (tram portion only) through the backlot and prop rooms, a surprise special-effects event, and the landscaped motion picture sets; ❷ THE GREAT MOVIE RIDE through a multimedia history of the great movies; and ❸ THE TWILIGHT ZONE TOWER OF TERROR (if you enjoy one-of-a-kind thrill rides). Catch a live performance at ❹ THEATER OF THE STARS, then continue on to ❺ MONSTER SOUND SHOW, ❻ INDIANA JONES EPIC STUNT SPECTACULAR, ❼ STAR TOURS (if you enjoy thrill rides), and ❽ JIM HENSON'S MUPPET*VISION 3D.

**DISCOVERY DINNER** (VISITOR'S CHOICE): If Disney-MGM Studios is open late and you are dining here, pause in your tour for your 7 PM dinner reservation at The Hollywood Brown Derby (located on Hollywood Boulevard, across from the Chinese Theater). After dinner, continue your tour where you left off until the NIGHTTIME FIREWORKS show kicks off at closing time.

If you are attending the MURDERWATCH MYSTERY DINNER THEATRE instead, leave Disney-MGM Studios around 5:30 PM and drive or taxi to the Grosvenor Resort, located at Hotel Plaza at Disney Village. The show begins at 6 PM in Baskervilles restaurant.

**OPTIONAL NIGHTLIFE TOUR:** Drive, taxi, or bus to PLEASURE ISLAND for an evening of nightclub adventures. Check out the scene at the ADVENTURERS CLUB, take in some live entertainment at NEON ARMADILLO and COMEDY WAREHOUSE, and catch a set at the PLEASURE ISLAND JAZZ COMPANY. Be back outside at 10:45 PM (11:45 PM on weekends) for Pleasure Island's renowned NEW YEAR'S EVE STREET PARTY and fireworks show, a flashy finish to your Disney World Discovery tour. ◆

# SINGLES SAFARI

*A Peak-Season Safari through Sophisticated Playgrounds, Sporting Destinations, and Cosmopolitan Night Spots for Single Travelers and the Young at Heart*

**BEST TIME OF YEAR FOR THIS ITINERARY**
*April through August (and holidays throughout the year)*

**LEAST CROWDED TIMES FOR THIS ITINERARY**
*April and May (except holidays)*

**BEST ARRIVAL DAY FOR THIS ITINERARY**
*Thursday*

**BEST BUDGET HOTEL FOR THIS ITINERARY**
*Courtyard by Marriott (upper floor, WDW view)*
*Travelodge Hotel (upper floor, WDW view)*
★ *DoubleTree Guest Suites Resort (pool view)*

**BEST MODERATE HOTELS FOR THIS ITINERARY**
*Buena Vista Palace Resort and Spa (WDW view)*
*Disney's Port Orleans Resort (river view)*

**BEST DELUXE HOTELS FOR THIS ITINERARY**
*Walt Disney World Dolphin (balcony room)*
*Walt Disney World Swan (pool view)*
*Disney's Contemporary Resort (tower room)*

**ULTIMATE HOTEL EXPERIENCE FOR THIS ITINERARY**
*Buena Vista Palace Resort and Spa (concierge floor)*

**LOCAL TRANSPORTATION**
*For this itinerary, it is best to rent a car or use taxis when specified.*

**PACKING**
*Bring club-hopping clothes, bathing suits, walking shoes (not sandals),
water shoes, and sports equipment (if you plan to use your own).*

**TIPS**
*Buena Vista Palace Resort and Spa offers a reasonable vacation package that includes
accommodations, park admission, and rental car, as do other non-Disney-owned resorts.*

Singles Safari combines the theme park attractions that adults enjoy most with activities that give visitors a chance to meet and mingle with fellow travelers, local residents, and Disney Cast Members. Starting off at Pleasure Island's nightly New Year's Eve Street Party, where perfect strangers toast each other as newfound friends, this expedition features a shared behind-the-scenes look at the Magic Kingdom, the glamor of Hollywood, excursions into international cultures and cuisines, leisurely lounging, exhilarating recreation, festive parades, and spectacular fireworks shows — all in all, a perfect mix for a memorable vacation. ➡

# SINGLES SAFARI OVERVIEW

## DAY ONE

- **EARLY DINNER AT PLEASURE ISLAND:** Your arrival evening starts with dinner in the sizzling social scene at Planet Hollywood (or at The Fireworks Factory, if you arrive late in the day).
- **EVENING AT PLEASURE ISLAND:** After dinner, you'll dance and club-hop at Pleasure Island, and join the outdoor revelry to catch the fireworks show at the Island's nightly New Year's Eve Street Party.

## DAY TWO

- **MORNING AND LUNCH AT THE MAGIC KINGDOM:** This morning you'll join people from around the world on a guided tour through the Magic Kingdom's backstage areas and most popular attractions.
- **OPTIONAL AFTERNOON COOL-DOWN:** After your guided tour, you can go to the Contemporary resort to swim in Bay Lake, sunbathe on a white sand beach, or head out on a waterskiing excursion.
- **EARLY DINNER IN POLYNESIA:** Your evening features 'Ohana's dinner show.
- **EVENING AT THE MAGIC KINGDOM:** Tonight you return to the Magic Kingdom to check out additional attractions, the sparkling Nighttime Electrical Parade, and the Fantasy in the Sky fireworks show.

## DAY THREE

- **ACTIVE MORNING:** This morning you'll venture to Blizzard Beach or Typhoon Lagoon for thrilling water play and relaxation. Or, you'll join the Fort Wilderness Trail Ride for a pleasant horseback excursion.
- **AFTERNOON AT DISNEY-MGM STUDIOS:** This afternoon your tour takes you to Disney-MGM Studios and the glamor of early- and present-day Hollywood.
- **DINNER AT DISNEY-MGM STUDIOS:** Your dinner destination is the 50's Prime Time Cafe.
- **EVENING AT DISNEY-MGM STUDIOS:** After dinner, your tour of the attractions and entertainment events at Disney-MGM Studios continues, capped by the park's Nighttime Fireworks show.

## DAY FOUR

- **MORNING IN FUTURE WORLD AT EPCOT:** This morning your tour takes you to Future World to explore the land, the sea, and the realm of imagination and ideas.
- **LUNCH IN THE WORLD SHOWCASE AT EPCOT:** You'll lunch at the Rose & Crown Dining Room, a comfortable pub–style restaurant in the United Kingdom pavilion and a favorite with locals and visitors.
- **OPTIONAL AFTERNOON ON THE WATERFRONT:** After lunch, you can either stroll along the BoardWalk and check out the entertainment and shops, or lounge at the Beach Club in a cabana on white sands.
- **EVENING IN THE WORLD SHOWCASE AT EPCOT:** Tonight you'll tour the World Showcase to explore the pavilions at France, Morocco, Japan, U.S.A., Italy, Germany, China, Norway, Mexico, and Canada, and enjoy the spectacular IllumiNations laser and fireworks show.
- **DINNER IN THE WORLD SHOWCASE AT EPCOT:** You'll dine communally at Teppanyaki Dining, on the second floor of the Japan pavilion, as entertaining chefs prepare your meal at the table.
- **OPTIONAL NIGHT OWL EVENT:** You can either dance and carouse until the wee hours at the BoardWalk's waterfront nightclubs, or at the Laughing Kookaburra, the popular club at the Buena Vista Palace Resort and Spa. Both entertainment destinations are frequented by local residents and visitors alike. ➧

SINGLES SAFARI

# Singles Safari Schedule

*The next four pages show the schedule you will follow and the arrangements and reservations you must make to organize the Singles Safari, a peak-attendance tour. You may want to copy these pages and carry them with you.*

## BEFORE YOU GO

**AT THE TIME YOU MAKE YOUR HOTEL RESERVATIONS:** Try to schedule your stay so that DAY ONE falls on a Thursday, to take advantage of the weekend activities.

**UP TO SIXTY DAYS BEFORE YOU LEAVE:** Call Disney Dining Reservations (407 939-3463), or call the restaurant directly, and make the following reservations:

❑ DAY ONE — 7:30 PM dinner at THE FIREWORKS FACTORY at Pleasure Island, if you will be arriving at Walt Disney World after 4 PM (407 934-8989). Early arrivals will eat at Planet Hollywood.

❑ DAY TWO — 6:15 PM dinner at 'OHANA restaurant at Disney's Polynesian Resort.

❑ DAY THREE — 7 PM dinner at the 50'S PRIME TIME CAFE at Disney-MGM Studios.

❑ DAY FOUR — 1 PM lunch at the ROSE & CROWN DINING ROOM in the United Kingdom pavilion in the World Showcase at Epcot Center. (If you prefer another restaurant, consider one in Future World.)

❑ DAY FOUR — 6:30 PM dinner at TEPPANYAKI DINING in the Japan pavilion in the World Showcase at Epcot Center. (If you prefer another restaurant, consider one in Germany or Norway.)

**UP TO FORTY DAYS BEFORE YOU LEAVE:** Make reservations for the KEYS TO THE KINGDOM tour at the Magic Kingdom for DAY TWO (407 939-8687).

**TEN DAYS BEFORE YOU LEAVE:** If you wish to waterski on DAY TWO, make 4 PM reservations for the excursion departing from the Contemporary resort (407 824-2621). If you wish to join the Fort Wilderness Trail Ride on DAY THREE, make 10:30 AM reservations (407 824-2832).

## DAY ONE: THE EVENING OF ARRIVAL

---
DAY / DATE

---

**AFTER YOU CHECK INTO YOUR HOTEL:** Stop at Guest Services and, if you do not have admission tickets, purchase a Multiday Pass that includes Pleasure Island and Blizzard Beach or Typhoon Lagoon. Also, pick up a *Times and Information* pamphlet showing the operating schedules at the theme parks.

**EARLY DINNER:** If you arrive at WDW early in the day, drive or take WDW transportation to PLEASURE ISLAND around 4 PM and head to Planet Hollywood for an early dinner, before the serious lines form.

**LATE ARRIVALS:** If you arrive at WDW after 4 PM, drive or take WDW transportation to the DISNEY VILLAGE MARKETPLACE at around 6 PM. If you wish, browse the shops and boutiques (check out The City for trendy attire). Then, head over to Pleasure Island for your 7:30 PM dinner reservation at The Fireworks Factory. If you are early, you can catch the last part of Happy Hour in the bar.

SINGLES SAFARI

**AFTER DINNER:** Enter PLEASURE ISLAND. Tour the island, then head to MANNEQUINS at 9 PM for the 9:30 PM light show and dance performance. Afterward, drop into NEON ARMADILLO for live country-western music, ADVENTURERS CLUB for some eccentric story-swapping, COMEDY WAREHOUSE for an improv performance, and 8TRAX for seventies-style dance music. Join the crowd at the West End Stage at 10:45 PM (11:45 PM on weekends) for the NEW YEAR'S EVE STREET PARTY, then party on.

**BEFORE YOU RETIRE:** If you play until the wee hours, you may want to leave a wake-up call and order a room-service breakfast for tomorrow. You'll leave for the Magic Kingdom at 8:30 AM.

## DAY TWO

DAY / DATE

**BEFORE YOU LEAVE YOUR HOTEL:** If you are planning to go for the Optional Afternoon Cool-Down, pack your tote bag with your bathing suit, towel (if you have one), and plastic bags for wet items.

**8:30 AM:** Drive or take WDW transportation to the MAGIC KINGDOM. (If you drive, park at the Polynesian resort and take the monorail to the Magic Kingdom.) Enter the park and proceed directly to Tomorrowland for THE EXTRATERRORESTRIAL ALIEN ENCOUNTER and, if you have time, take in TRANSPORTARIUM. Return to City Hall on Main Street for the guided tour.

**10:30 AM:** The KEYS TO THE KINGDOM tour lasts about four hours and includes backstage areas and lower-level "utilidors," as well as the following attractions: TOMORROWLAND TRANSPORTATION AUTHORITY, IT'S A SMALL WORLD, THE HAUNTED MANSION, COUNTRY BEAR JAMBOREE, and PIRATES OF THE CARIBBEAN. (The attractions visited may vary.) The tour breaks for lunch and is a great way to meet a variety of people from around the world. When the guided tour ends, you can return to your resort to relax, or go for the Optional Afternoon Cool-Down. (You'll return to the Magic Kingdom later tonight.)

**OPTIONAL AFTERNOON COOL-DOWN:** Exit the park and take the monorail to the Contemporary resort. Check out the pool and head for the beach, where you can sunbathe or go for a dip in Bay Lake (there are changing rooms and lockers at the resort's marina). If you have a 4 PM waterskiing reservation, your speedboat will be waiting for you at the Contemporary resort's Marina Pavilion.

**5:30 PM:** Drive, taxi, or monorail to the Polynesian resort for your 6 PM dinner reservation at 'Ohana.

**6:15 PM DINNER:** 'Ohana is located upstairs in the Great Ceremonial House. If you're early, check out the hotel's Tambu Lounge for Polynesian-style cocktails and the bartenders' skilled juggling antics.

**AFTER DINNER:** Monorail from the Polynesian to the MAGIC KINGDOM. Walk to Frontierland or ride the WALT DISNEY WORLD RAILROAD from the Main Street Station to the Frontierland Station. Proceed to ❶ BIG THUNDER MOUNTAIN RAILROAD and ❷ SPLASH MOUNTAIN. Watch the NIGHTTIME ELECTRICAL PARADE as it passes through Frontierland about 9 PM, then head to Tomorrowland. Catch the attractions you missed this morning, including: ❸ TRANSPORTARIUM, ❹ THE EXTRATERRORESTRIAL ALIEN ENCOUNTER, and ❺ SPACE MOUNTAIN. About 9:45 PM, find a spot on Tomorrowland's bridge to Main Street to view the FANTASY IN THE SKY fireworks show (about 10 PM). Afterward, continue your tour.

**BEFORE YOU RETIRE:** You may want to leave a wake-up call and order a room-service breakfast for tomorrow. You will be leaving your hotel one hour before your scheduled activity.

## DAY THREE

DAY / DATE

**BEFORE YOU LEAVE YOUR HOTEL:** For Blizzard Beach or Typhoon Lagoon, wear a bathing suit under your clothing, pack your tote bag with sun block, towel, and water shoes (the cement walkways get hot), and do not take anything requiring a locker. For the trail ride, wear long pants and shoes, not sandals.

**ACTIVE MORNING:** This morning, choose from an intense Blizzard Beach water-thrills experience, a tropical Typhoon Lagoon expedition, or a horseback riding adventure at Fort Wilderness.

• For **BLIZZARD BEACH,** drive or bus to the park forty-five minutes before it opens. Set up camp in the shade on the far side of Melt Away Bay, then plunge into the park's unique "winter" attractions (see "Half-Day Tour at Blizzard Beach," page 95, for touring strategies).

• For **TYPHOON LAGOON,** drive or bus to the park forty-five minutes before it opens. Set up camp in the shade near Cascade Cove, then explore the park's tropical fresh- and saltwater attractions (see "Half-Day Tour at Typhoon Lagoon," page 89, for touring strategies).

• For **HORSEBACK RIDING,** drive or taxi (do not take WDW transportation) to the Fort Wilderness Guest Parking Lot forty-five minutes before your scheduled trail ride. Head to the Trail Blaze Corral at Tri-Circle-D Livery, behind the parking lot, and mount up for the **FORT WILDERNESS TRAIL RIDE.** Afterward, you may wish to explore Fort Wilderness (see "Fort Wilderness & River Country," page 68, for touring options).

**LUNCH:** Have lunch at your Active Morning destination or return to your resort to relax.

**3 PM:** Drive, taxi, or take WDW transportation to **DISNEY-MGM STUDIOS.** As you arrive, watch for the the **FEATURE PARADE** that travels down Hollywood Boulevard about 3:30 PM (during peak seasons). Stroll down Hollywood Boulevard and visit the following attractions that interest you: ❶ **STAR TOURS** (if lines are too long, return after dinner); ❷ **JIM HENSON'S MUPPET*VISION 3D;** the performance at the ❸ **BACKLOT THEATER;** and the ❹ **BACKSTAGE STUDIO TOUR** (the tram portion only). If you have time before dinner, see ❺ **THE GREAT MOVIE RIDE** and ❻ **MONSTER SOUND SHOW,** and check out any scheduled entertainment events, such as the show at ❼ **THEATER OF THE STARS.** Plan to arrive at your dinner destination ten minutes early.

**7 PM DINNER:** The 50's Prime Time Cafe is located on Vine Street, near Echo Lake. (Light eaters and budget diners may wish to try Disney-MGM Studios Commissary, next to the Chinese Theater.)

**AFTER DINNER:** Continue touring the attractions, including ❽ **THE TWILIGHT ZONE TOWER OF TERROR** and ❾ **INDIANA JONES EPIC STUNT SPECTACULAR.** Be sure to catch the **NIGHTTIME FIREWORKS** show (about 9 or 10 PM). You'll find a good viewing spot near the Hollywood Brown Derby.

**BEFORE YOU RETIRE:** You may want to leave a wake-up call tonight and order a room-service breakfast for tomorrow. You'll be leaving for Future World at Epcot Center at 8:30 AM.

SINGLES SAFARI

## DAY FOUR

DAY / DATE

**BEFORE YOU LEAVE YOUR HOTEL:** You'll be touring all day, so pack a tote bag with whatever you'll need. Include a bathing suit, towel, and plastic bags for wet items if you're going to the Beach Club.

**8:30 AM:** Drive or taxi to the Beach Club, or take WDW transportation to the Main Gate at Epcot Center. (From the Beach Club, enter at the International Gateway.) Visit as many of the **FUTURE WORLD** attractions as you can, in this order: at the Journey Into Imagination pavilion, ❶ **MAGIC EYE THEATER** (*Honey, I Shrunk the Audience*); at the Wonders of Life pavilion, ❷ **BODY WARS** and ❸ **CRANIUM COMMAND**; at Innoventions West, ❹ **WALT DISNEY IMAGINEERING LABS**; at The Living Seas pavilion, ❺ **CARIBBEAN CORAL REEF RIDE**; and at The Land pavilion, ❻ **LIVING WITH THE LAND**. If you have time before lunch, take in ❼ **SPACESHIP EARTH** and ❽ **THE AT&T GLOBAL NEIGHBORHOOD**.

**1 PM LUNCH:** The Rose & Crown Dining Room is located at the United Kingdom pavilion in the World Showcase. If you arrive early, enjoy a beverage with the friendly people in the Pub. (Light eaters and budget diners may wish to dine in Future World at Pasta Piazza Ristorante in Innoventions West.) After lunch, continue touring Future World, or go on to the Optional Afternoon on the Waterfront.

**OPTIONAL AFTERNOON ON THE WATERFRONT:** Exit at the International Gateway. At Disney's Board-Walk, check out the entertainment and shops. Drop into **ESPN SPORTS WORLD**, where you can relax while soaking up some high-tech sports action. If you'd like to soak up some sun instead, head over to the Beach Club resort and settle into a cabana on the white sands (changing rooms and lockers are nearby).

**4 PM:** Return to the International Gateway and enter the **WORLD SHOWCASE**. Moving counter-clockwise, tour the pavilions and take in any of the attractions that interest you. Start with **FRANCE** and the film ❶ **IMPRESSIONS DE FRANCE**, then explore **MOROCCO** and **JAPAN**. Go on to the **U.S.A.** and ❷ **THE AMERICAN ADVENTURE**, then tour **ITALY** and **GERMANY**. Visit **CHINA** for the film ❸ **WONDERS OF CHINA**, then **NORWAY** for the ❹ **MAELSTROM** attraction. Stop in **MEXICO** to ride ❺ **EL RIO DEL TIEMPO**, then head over to **CANADA** for the film ❻ **O CANADA!** (Pause in your tour for your dinner reservation.)

**6:30 PM DINNER:** Teppanyaki Dining is located on the second floor of the Japan pavilion in the World Showcase. (Light eaters and budget diners may wish to try Sommerfest in Germany, Kringla Bakeri og Kafé in Norway, or Cantina de San Angel in Mexico.)

**AFTER DINNER:** Continue your tour. About thirty minutes before **ILLUMINATIONS** is scheduled to begin (at 9 or 10 PM), find a spot along the lagoon to view it. If you are going on to the Optional Night Owl Event, exit at the International Gateway when the show ends.

**OPTIONAL NIGHT OWL EVENT:** Enjoy an evening of late-night dancing and carousing either at Disney's BoardWalk or at the Laughing Kookaburra, a club located in the Buena Vista Palace Resort and Spa.

From the International Gateway, stroll along **DISNEY'S BOARDWALK**. Check out the action at the clubs, especially the **ATLANTIC BALLROOM**, where the spirited band will get you out onto the dance floor.

Or, drive or taxi from the Beach Club to the **LAUGHING KOOKABURRA**. The club features live dance music and deejays, and attracts local residents, Cast Members, and travelers from around the world. ◆

# TICKETS & TIMING

## ADMISSIONS

Walt Disney World theme park admissions come in a variety of prices and touring styles. Determine what you would like to see and do during your visit and purchase tickets in advance, if possible, to avoid long lines and to lock in prices. Keep in mind that it can take more than one day to see a single park, particularly during peak seasons. Ticket prices tend to increase about twice each year; however, once purchased, tickets are always valid. Magic Kingdom Club members receive the best discounts on tickets (see "Travel Discounts," page 244).

**ONE-DAY ONE-PARK TICKET:** One day's admission to a single theme park, either the Magic Kingdom, Disney-MGM Studios, or Epcot Center. About $42 (about $34 for children), including tax.

**FOUR-DAY VALUE PASS:** Four days' admission to a different theme park each day — Magic Kingdom, Disney-MGM Studios, and Epcot Center. The fourth day can be used to revisit any single park. The Four-Day Value Pass has no expiration date. The drawback to this pass is that visitors cannot split their visit between different parks on the same day and cannot choose to skip a park in order to spend more time in one of the other parks. About $138 (about $108 for children), including tax.

**FOUR-DAY PARK-HOPPER PASS:** Four days' unlimited admission to the Magic Kingdom, Disney-MGM Studios, and Epcot Center, including the use of WDW transportation linking the parks. Visitors can hop between the theme parks each day. The Four-Day Park-Hopper Pass has no expiration date. Passholders' photos are printed on each pass. About $153 (about $122 for children), including tax.

**FIVE-DAY WORLD-HOPPER PASS:** Five days' admission to the Magic Kingdom, Disney-MGM Studios, and Epcot Center, including the use of WDW transportation. After the first day the pass is used, it is good for seven consecutive days for visits to Typhoon Lagoon, Blizzard Beach, Pleasure Island, River Country, and Discovery Island. The Five-Day World-Hopper Pass has no expiration date. A passholder's photo is printed on each pass. About $207 (about $165 for children), including tax.

**LENGTH OF STAY PASS:** Guests staying at WDW resorts can purchase a Length of Stay Pass for a slight discount over comparable admission prices. Known also as the "Be Our Guest Pass," it includes admission to the Magic Kingdom, Disney-MGM Studios, Epcot Center, Typhoon Lagoon, Blizzard Beach, Pleasure Island, River Country, and Discovery Island. The pass must be purchased for the entire length of stay, can be used only during one stay, and cannot be saved for future visits. Length of Stay Passes are purchased upon check-in, and prices vary according to number of days covered. For example, a three-day Length of Stay Pass is about $135 (about $107 for children), and a five-day Length of Stay Pass (identical to a Five-Day World-Hopper Pass) is about $204 (about $162 for children), including tax.

**ONE-DAY ADMISSION TO ALL OTHER PARKS:** Visitors who do not have a Five-Day World-Hopper Pass or a Length of Stay Pass are charged admission at the following parks: Typhoon Lagoon, about $26 (about $20 for children); Blizzard Beach, about $26 (about $20 for children); River Country, about $17 (about $14 for children); Discovery Island, about $12 (about $7 for children); and Pleasure Island, about $18 for entry after 7 PM. All prices include tax.

**ANNUAL PASSPORTS:** Visitors who plan to visit for seven days or longer or who plan to return within the year should consider buying an Annual Passport. The basic Annual Passport, which includes one year of

CROWDS & WEATHER

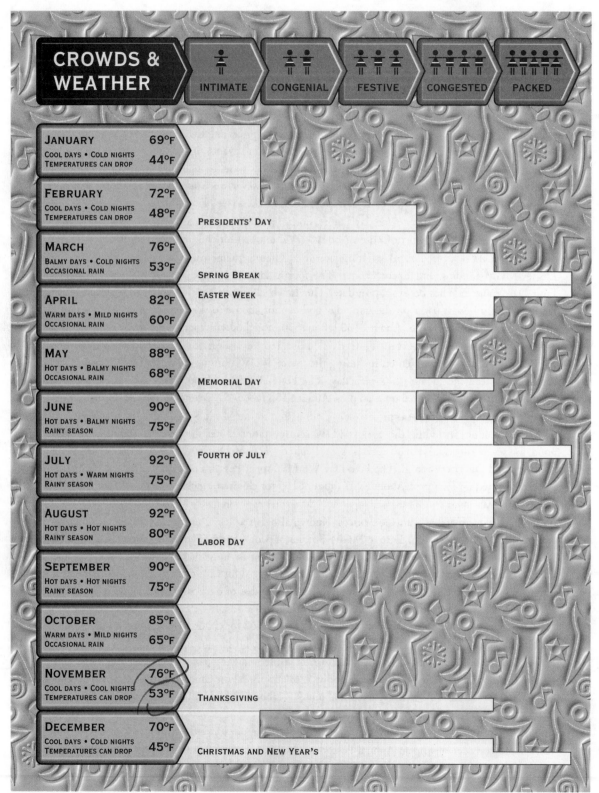

| CROWDS & WEATHER | INTIMATE | CONGENIAL | FESTIVE | CONGESTED | PACKED |
|---|---|---|---|---|---|

**JANUARY** 69°F
COOL DAYS • COLD NIGHTS 44°F
TEMPERATURES CAN DROP

**FEBRUARY** 72°F
COOL DAYS • COLD NIGHTS 48°F
TEMPERATURES CAN DROP
PRESIDENTS' DAY

**MARCH** 76°F
BALMY DAYS • COLD NIGHTS 53°F
OCCASIONAL RAIN
SPRING BREAK

**APRIL** 82°F
WARM DAYS • MILD NIGHTS 60°F
OCCASIONAL RAIN
EASTER WEEK

**MAY** 88°F
HOT DAYS • BALMY NIGHTS 68°F
OCCASIONAL RAIN
MEMORIAL DAY

**JUNE** 90°F
HOT DAYS • BALMY NIGHTS 75°F
RAINY SEASON

**JULY** 92°F
HOT DAYS • WARM NIGHTS 75°F
RAINY SEASON
FOURTH OF JULY

**AUGUST** 92°F
HOT DAYS • HOT NIGHTS 80°F
RAINY SEASON
LABOR DAY

**SEPTEMBER** 90°F
HOT DAYS • HOT NIGHTS 75°F
RAINY SEASON

**OCTOBER** 85°F
WARM DAYS • MILD NIGHTS 65°F
OCCASIONAL RAIN

**NOVEMBER** 76°F
COOL DAYS • COOL NIGHTS 53°F
TEMPERATURES CAN DROP
THANKSGIVING

**DECEMBER** 70°F
COOL DAYS • COLD NIGHTS 45°F
TEMPERATURES CAN DROP
CHRISTMAS AND NEW YEAR'S

unlimited admission to the Magic Kingdom, Disney-MGM Studios, and Epcot Center, as well as free parking and the use of WDW transportation, is about $255. The Premium Annual Passport, which has all the features of the basic one, but also includes unlimited admission to Typhoon Lagoon, Blizzard Beach, Pleasure Island, River Country, and Discovery Island, is about $355. Both prices include tax.

**PURCHASING TICKETS IN ADVANCE:** When purchasing tickets in advance, call ahead for current prices and ask about discounts that may be available during your visit (see also "Travel Discounts," page 244). Tickets can be purchased by telephone with a credit card (407 824-4321). Allow twenty-one days for delivery. Tickets can also be purchased by mail through Ticket Services, Walt Disney World Company, P.O. Box 10030, Lake Buena Vista, FL 32830. Allow six weeks for delivery. Walt Disney World accepts personal checks, money orders, traveler's checks, American Express, MasterCard, and Visa. Tickets can also be purchased at Disney Stores and at the Orlando International Airport. ◆

# CROWDS & WEATHER

As might be expected, crowd size is directly related to school vacations and national holidays. During peak-attendance times, the parks have extended hours with special parades and entertainment events. If possible, however, try to avoid these busy times. In summer, the parks are not only crowded with vacationing families, but uncomfortably hot. Fall and spring weather is ideal; winter can bring cold snaps, so pack accordingly (see "Packing," page 243). Call Disney Weather before you leave (407 824-4104).

**WINTER:** From Christmas week until New Year's Day, the crowds at Walt Disney World are awesome and the lines intimidating. During the three weeks preceding Christmas, however, the holiday decor and festivities are underway and attendance is sparse, making this an ideal time to visit. After New Year's Day, attendance drops dramatically and continues to be low until Presidents' Day, in mid-February. The temperature can dip to the mid-forties, even during the day, but there is little precipitation. Winter hours in the theme parks are shorter, but the smaller crowds make the attractions far more accessible.

**SPRING:** From early March until Easter and Spring Break, the crowds are light to moderate. After Easter and before the start of the summer season in early June, children are still in school and the weather is, for the most part, pleasant. There is little rain, and the temperatures range from the high sixties to the mid-eighties. During April, the days grow steadily warmer, although the nights remain balmy until June. This is an especially pleasant time for those interested in golf and other outdoor activities.

**SUMMER:** Summer brings vast crowds and long lines. The weather can be brutally hot as well, climbing into the nineties with high humidity and almost daily tropical showers in the afternoon. These brief storms tend to clear out the parks, so if you don't mind getting wet, it is a good time to tour. The first two weeks of June and last two weeks of August have lower attendance than the rest of the summer. Evenings can be balmy and delightful in June, but by August they are just plain hot.

**FALL:** In September, the weather is still quite hot, but from October on, the temperatures range from the fifties to mid-eighties, with little rain. The most pleasant vacation times at Walt Disney World are from the beginning of October through the weekend preceding Thanksgiving, and the week after Thanksgiving until the week before Christmas. The weather can get cold from after Thanksgiving, but the holiday decor, seasonal entertainment, and nearly deserted theme parks make for an ideal vacation. Although Thanksgiving week is busy, on Thanksgiving Day the crowd is almost always around the dinner table. ◆

# 12-MONTH SCHEDULE OF EVENTS

Walt Disney World presents a number of annual events and seasonal celebrations that can make your vacation memorable. From September through May, the theme parks close earlier, although Epcot Center is open until about 9 PM. The water parks close for refurbishing in fall or winter. Resort rates drop about 10 to 15 percent during value seasons in fall, winter, and spring, except holidays; and WDW offers special vacation packages throughout the year. For more information on schedules and events, call 407 824-4321.

**25TH ANNIVERSARY CELEBRATION:** *From October 1, 1996 through December 31, 1997 —* Make reservations now if you plan to arrive for the October kick-off of this once-in-a-lifetime event. Visitors can expect special parades and fireworks shows at the theme parks, an array of commemorative collectibles, special parties and festivities, surprise celebrity appearances, and contests and giveaways all year long. Special vacation packages will be offered at the Walt Disney World resorts, as well.

**JANUARY:** Special events include resort-wide New Year's Eve celebrations (see "Holidays at Walt Disney World," page 132), the Walt Disney World Indy 200, the month-long Fitness Festival, and the Walt Disney World Marathon (see "Sports," page 213). The Magic Kingdom and Disney-MGM Studios close early and do not offer fireworks shows or evening parades. Blizzard Beach is closed for refurbishing throughout the month. *Value-season resort rates begin on New Year's Day.*

**FEBRUARY:** Special celebrations include Valentine's Day at the Magic Kingdom, Mardi Gras at Pleasure Island, and Chinese New Year at Pleasure Island and Epcot Center. The Magic Kingdom and Disney-MGM Studios are open late only on weekends and during Presidents' Day week, with fireworks shows and evening parades. Blizzard Beach remains closed for refurbishing until mid-February; Discovery Island closes for refurbishing in mid-February and remains closed the rest of the month. *Value-season resort rates continue until about a week before Presidents' Day, when peak season begins.*

**MARCH:** Special events include the Bryant Gumbel/Walt Disney World Celebrity–Am Golf Tournament (see "Sports," page 213). All theme parks stay open late one week before and after Easter. The Magic Kingdom has fireworks shows and evening parades on the weekends. Disney-MGM Studios has fireworks shows on Saturdays. Discovery Island remains closed for refurbishing until the second week in March. *Peak-season resort rates continue until after Easter, when value season begins.*

**APRIL:** Special events include Earth Day celebrations at Epcot Center and Disney Village Marketplace, and the Happy Easter Parade at the Magic Kingdom (see "Holidays at Walt Disney World," page 132). The International Garden and Flower Festival at Epcot Center begins in late April. All theme parks stay open late one week before and after Easter. The Magic Kingdom has fireworks shows and evening parades on the weekends. Disney-MGM Studios has fireworks shows on Saturday nights. *Peak-season resort rates continue until after Easter, when value season begins.*

**MAY:** Special events include Mother's Day festivities at the Magic Kingdom, Disney Village Marketplace, and other WDW locations. The International Garden and Flower Festival at Epcot Center continues throughout the month. The Magic Kingdom stays open late and has fireworks shows on Saturday nights and Memorial Day weekend. Disney-MGM Studios closes early and does not offer fireworks shows, except during Memorial Day weekend. *Value-season resort rates apply throughout May.*

**JUNE:** Special events include Father's Day festivities at Disney-MGM Studios and other WDW locations, and the Classic Car Show at Disney Village Marketplace. The theme parks stay open late with a full schedule of parades and fireworks shows. *Value-season resort rates continue for two weeks following Memorial Day, when peak season begins.*

**JULY:** Special events include extended Fourth of July fireworks shows in all theme parks (see "Holidays at Walt Disney World," page 132). The theme parks are open late with a full schedule of parades, special entertainment, and fireworks shows. *Peak-season resort rates apply throughout July.*

**AUGUST:** All theme parks are open late, with a full schedule of special entertainment, fireworks shows, and parades until the week preceding Labor Day. At the end of the month, the WDW resorts begin offering Disney's Fall Fantasy vacation package, which includes special events and ongoing entertainment. *Value-season resort rates begin in mid-August.*

**SEPTEMBER:** Special events include the Night of Joy Christian-music program at the Magic Kingdom and Disney's Tour "D" Fun Bike Trip (see "Sports," page 213). The Magic Kingdom has fireworks shows and evening parades only on Labor Day weekend. After Labor Day weekend, the Magic Kingdom, Disney-MGM Studios, and Future World at Epcot Center close early. Some theme park attractions are closed for refurbishing during the fall. Disney's Fall Fantasy vacation package continues throughout the month. *Value-season resort rates apply throughout September.*

**OCTOBER:** WDW's 25th Anniversary Celebration begins on October 1, 1996 (continuing through 1997); large crowds are expected. Other events include the Boat Show at Disney Village Marketplace, the Pleasure Island Jazz Festival, and the Walt Disney World/Oldsmobile Golf Classic (see "Sports," page 213). Halloween festivities are staged at most theme parks. The Magic Kingdom closes early. Disney-MGM Studios stays open late with fireworks shows on Saturdays only. Some theme park attractions are closed for refurbishing during the fall. River Country is closed for refurbishing. Disney's Fall Fantasy vacation package continues throughout the month. *Value-season resort rates apply throughout October.*

**NOVEMBER:** Special events include the Festival of the Masters art show at Disney Village Marketplace, and the Walt Disney World Doll and Teddy Bear Convention. Resort-wide Christmas events begin after Thanksgiving (see "Holidays at Walt Disney World," page 132). The Magic Kingdom and Disney-MGM Studios close early; Magic Kingdom fireworks shows and evening parades occur on Saturdays only. Some theme park attractions are closed for refurbishing during the fall. Typhoon Lagoon closes for refurbishing in early November and remains closed the rest of the month. Disney's Fall Fantasy vacation package continues until Thanksgiving week. The resorts begin offering Disney's Magical Holidays vacation packages the week after Thanksgiving. *Value-season resort rates apply throughout November.*

**DECEMBER:** Christmas events and New Year's Eve celebrations are featured at the theme parks and at selected resorts (see "Holidays at Walt Disney World," page 132). The Magic Kingdom and Disney-MGM Studios close early until mid-December. Christmas ceremonies and celebrations occur daily until Christmas Eve. Mickey's Very Merry Christmas Party is held on selected evenings at the Magic Kingdom. From the week before Christmas through New Year's Eve, the theme parks are open late with a full schedule of parades and fireworks shows. Typhoon Lagoon remains closed for refurbishing until the end of December. Disney's Magical Holidays vacation packages continue until Christmas. *Value-season resort rates continue until the week before Christmas, when peak season begins.* ◆

# HOLIDAYS AT WALT DISNEY WORLD

Any holiday is fair game for the entertainment designers at Walt Disney World, and just about every holiday is celebrated. The holiday events and special festivities that may appeal to adult visitors include the following:

**EASTER:** The Magic Kingdom celebrates Easter with egg-decorating contests, but the draw is its nationally televised Happy Easter Parade of singers and dancers, remarkable Easter bonnets, and giant Easter egg and Easter basket floats. Disney Village Marketplace and many resorts hold egg hunts and other holiday events, and selected restaurants throughout WDW offer special Easter dinners.

**JULY FOURTH:** Flags are raised and bunting draped for Independence Day celebrations at WDW. Pleasure Island starts the festivities July third with an expanded midnight fireworks show. Marching bands parade through the Magic Kingdom and Epcot Center, and on the night of the Fourth, the fireworks shows at the Magic Kingdom, Disney-MGM Studios, and at IllumiNations in the World Showcase are the longest and most spectacular of the summer.

**THANKSGIVING:** Over the long Thanksgiving weekend, Walt Disney World offers two holidays in one. On Thanksgiving Day, selected full-service restaurants in the theme parks and resorts offer traditional Thanksgiving dinners. (Make your reservations early.) Late Thursday night, Disney Cast Members work overtime to transform all of WDW into a Christmas wonderland. When the parks open on Friday, they are decked in full Christmas regalia and feature special holiday entertainment and ceremonies.

**CHRISTMAS:** It's Christmas from Thanksgiving Day on at Walt Disney World. The theme parks sport towering decorated fir trees that come alive in nightly tree-lighting ceremonies. At the Magic Kingdom, Mickey's Very Merry Christmas Parade travels down Main Street on the weekends. On selected evenings, the Magic Kingdom reopens at 8 PM to celebrate Mickey's Very Merry Christmas Party with holiday food, carolers, special entertainment, and a fireworks show (admission is charged). Traditionally, Disney-MGM Studios re-creates Christmas in New York, with carolers, chestnut vendors, and strolling musicians. In the World Showcase at Epcot Center, the pavilions present Holidays Around the World, and choral groups in the nightly Christmas Candlelight Processional carol as they parade from Germany to the America Gardens Theatre for the Story of Christmas show. IllumiNations bursts forth with a special holiday theme, as well. Every night, Disney Village Marketplace lights its forty-foot fir tree and presents the Glory and Pageantry of Christmas, a living Nativity pageant. The Contemporary resort hosts the popular Jolly Holidays dinner show (see "Jolly Holidays," page 210). The resorts offer Disney's Magical Holidays vacation packages, which include accommodations at theme-decorated resorts and park admissions, and may include the Jolly Holidays dinner show. Call 407 827-7200 for information.

**NEW YEAR'S EVE:** On New Year's Eve, the theme parks stay open into the wee hours with park-wide celebrations and midnight fireworks shows. Pleasure Island stages a special-admission "REAL New Year's Eve" party with food, favors, and celebrity performers. At Fort Wilderness, a country music band creates a down-home New Year's celebration at the Hoop-Dee-Doo Musical Revue. The Yacht and Beach Club, Wilderness Lodge, and several Walt Disney World resorts offer cocktails in their lobby areas. The Grand Floridian, Contemporary, and Grosvenor resorts, among others, stage themed festivities that range from fifties dance parties to elegant balls. Guests at Arthur's 27, at the Buena Vista Palace Resort and Spa, celebrate with gourmet cuisine, champagne, and great views of the WDW fireworks shows. To free parents to celebrate at these events, many of the child care centers at Walt Disney World will keep children until about 2 AM (see "Babysitting & Day Camps," page 256). ◆

# HOTELS

Orlando has the highest concentration of hotel rooms in the U.S., and one out of seven of those rooms is located in Walt Disney World. There are also many hotels nearby that offer spacious accommodations and resort amenities at very good prices (see "Off-Site Hotels," page 159). Walt Disney World resort guests, however, can take advantage of a number of exclusive privileges, including versatile Length of Stay Passes priced at some savings over comparable admission tickets (see "Admissions," page 123). Other privileges include:

**TRANSPORTATION AND PARK ACCESS:** Resort guests can use the WDW transportation system to travel between the resorts and theme parks, making driving unnecessary. The WDW parking lots are free to resort guests who do drive. Guests can enter certain theme parks an hour before they open to the public, and resort guests are guaranteed entry, even if the park has exceeded visitor capacity.

**INFORMATION ACCESS:** Every hotel room provides the Disney Events Channel on television, an up-to-the-minute listing of shows, coming attractions, and special events. The Walt Disney World Switchboard connects guest rooms to every telephone on WDW property free of charge, and Guest Services at the resorts offers a wide range of services including restaurant and dinner show reservations and ticket sales.

**RESERVATION PRIVILEGES:** Any visitor to Walt Disney World can book restaurant reservations up to sixty days in advance; however, Walt Disney World resort guests receive discounts and preferred or advance tee times along with free taxi shuttles to the golf courses.

**RESORT IDENTIFICATION CARD:** This card acts as a pass for the WDW transportation system and allows guests to charge purchases and meals in most of the full-service restaurants. (Charging privileges are not available to guests at the privately run Dolphin, Swan, Shades of Green, and Hotel Plaza resorts.)

**THE WALT DISNEY WORLD RESORT EXPERIENCE:** The WDW resorts are a total-immersion experience, so guests never feel they've left the "magic" at the end of the day. This is due to the carefully crafted atmosphere of each resort and to the Disney Cast Members, who strive to offer the best possible vacation experience. Ratings in the hotel reviews are based on four criteria: Vacation **ATMOSPHERE**, **ATTITUDE** of the staff, **QUALITY** of the rooms, and **TRUE VALUE**, or vacation-bang-for-the-buck, as follows:

**XXXX**–SUPERIOR IN EVERY WAY    **XXX**–BETTER THAN MOST    **XX**–ADEQUATE    **X**–SUB-STANDARD.

**PRICES:** The WDW resorts offer a wide range of rates, depending on their amenities and location (see the "Walt Disney World Overview" map, page 10, for resort locations). Prices at most resorts differ in peak and value seasons (see "12-Month Schedule of Events," page 126, for seasons). The hotel reviews indicate the average starting price of a standard room or suite, before taxes (about 11 percent), as follows:

$ – UNDER $89
$$ – $90 TO $139
$$$ – $140 TO $199
$$$$ – $200 TO $299
$$$$$ – OVER $300
$$$$$$ – OVER $500

**RESERVATIONS:** Reservations for all resorts at Walt Disney World can be made through the WDW Central Reservations Office (407 934-7639). Reservations at the privately run WDW resorts can be made directly, as well; many have toll-free numbers. Vacation packages are available at most resorts. ◆

# BUENA VISTA PALACE RESORT AND SPA

**LOCATION:** Buena Vista Palace Resort and Spa is one of seven independently owned Hotel Plaza Resorts located on Walt Disney World property near Disney Village Marketplace. Guests are provided with shuttle service to the major WDW attractions and are offered special discounts at area shops and restaurants.

**AMBIENCE:** Large fountains mark the entrance to this imposing and majestic mirror-paneled high-rise hotel. The Buena Vista Palace is situated on twenty-seven acres of open land and pine forest and boasts its own private lagoon. Extensive spa facilities, about nine thousand luxurious square feet, offer guests a complete spa experience during their vacation. The elegant multilevel lobby encircles a narrow twenty-seven-story atrium. The guest rooms are tastefully furnished, and all rooms have private balconies. The Palace Suites, in an adjacent low-rise building, offer spacious living rooms and mini kitchens. The Buena Vista Palace Resort and Spa ranks as one of the top five resorts in the United States.

**RATES:** Standard rooms **$$$**. Crown-level concierge rooms **$$$$** (including Continental breakfast, appetizers, beverages, no-host cocktails, and special room amenities). Palace Suites **$$$$** (including separate bedroom, wet bar, refrigerator, two baths, and in-room coffeemaker). Rates vary with the season.

**AMENITIES:** Twenty-four-hour room service, mini bar, in-room safe, hair dryer, turndown service, voice mail, pay-per-view movies, and valet parking.

**RESTAURANTS:** *Watercress Cafe & Bake Shop* — Breakfast, lunch, and dinner, with soup and salad bar.
*Arthur's 27* — Elegant Continental dining in an award-winning rooftop restaurant.
*Outback* — Steak and seafood dinners, Australian style.

**RECREATION:** Two pools, lap pool, marina, tennis, volleyball, jogging path, full-service spa and fitness center, fitness training, exercise classes, steam room, sauna, massage, and whirlpools.

**HOTEL TRANSPORTATION:** Walk to Disney Village Marketplace and Pleasure Island. Shuttle bus to Epcot Center, Disney-MGM Studios, the Magic Kingdom, and Typhoon Lagoon. For transportation to other attractions, consult hotel Guest Services. Taxi service available.

**FEATURES:** The Buena Vista Palace Resort is ideal for the traveler looking for a complete spa experience. The resort's nightclub, Laughing Kookaburra, features a happy hour, live entertainment, and dancing.

**DRAWBACKS:** Guests relying on hotel buses to reach attractions may find them inconvenient.

**TIPS:** The resort offers a number of vacation packages that include accommodations, some meals, WDW admission, and other amenities. To receive a brochure, call the hotel directly (800 327-2990).
The Buena Vista Palace offers discounts to members of several travel clubs, including Meritz Exclusively Yours and Orlando Magicard.
A rental car can save considerable commuting time from this location.

**MAKING RESERVATIONS:** Call the Buena Vista Palace Resort and Spa toll-free number (800 327-2990) and inquire about special promotional rates or corporate rates. Reservations may also be made through WDW Central Reservations Office (407 934-7639).

**XXX** ATMOSPHERE. **XXX** ATTITUDE. **XXX** QUALITY. **XXXX** TRUE VALUE

**BUENA VISTA PALACE RESORT AND SPA**
**A PRIVATELY OWNED HOTEL**
**1900 BUENA VISTA DRIVE, LAKE BUENA VISTA, FLORIDA 32830**
**TELEPHONE (407) 827-2727 • FAX (407) 827-6034**

# COURTYARD BY MARRIOTT

**LOCATION:** Courtyard by Marriott is one of seven independently owned Hotel Plaza Resorts located on Walt Disney World property near Disney Village Marketplace. Guests are provided with shuttle service to the major WDW attractions and offered special discounts at area shops and restaurants.

**AMBIENCE:** This completely renovated high-rise hotel with a six-story garden wing has a modern white-stuccoed exterior, roofed with traditional terra-cotta mission tile. Inside, the fourteen-story atrium lobby has glass elevators that transport guests to the upper floors. A thatch-roofed bar at the back of the lobby, umbrella-shaded tables, and a small fountain to one side evoke a cool Caribbean mood. The turquoise-, coral-, and sand-colored guest rooms have standard but comfortable hotel-style furnishings with tropical accents. All rooms have balconies, many with views of Walt Disney World.

**RATES:** Standard rooms $. Rates vary with the season.

**AMENITIES:** Room service, in-room safe, coffeemaker, newspaper delivery, pay-per-view movies, on-line video library, and in-room Nintendo. Refrigerator available on request.

**RESTAURANTS:** *Courtyard Cafe & Grille* — Buffet and a la carte breakfast, lunch, and dinner.
*Village Deli* — New York–style deli sandwiches, pizza, frozen yogurt, and take-out menu for lunch, dinner, and late-night snacks.

**RECREATION:** Two pools, jogging path, fitness center, and whirlpool.

**HOTEL TRANSPORTATION:** Walk to Disney Village Marketplace and Pleasure Island. Shuttle bus to Epcot Center, Disney-MGM Studios, the Magic Kingdom, and Typhoon Lagoon. For transportation to other attractions, consult hotel Guest Services. Taxi service available.

**FEATURES:** Courtyard Club members earn points, have free local phone calls, and receive room discounts.
Visitors planning to tour the parks early in the morning can order pastries, espresso, or cappuccino from the lobby coffee bar to take along.

**DRAWBACKS:** Guests relying on hotel buses to reach attractions may find them inconvenient.
The parking lot can be overcrowded during peak seasons.

**TIPS:** Higher floors offer sweeping views. Request a room with a view of Pleasure Island and its nightly New Year's Eve fireworks display.
Courtyard by Marriott offers discounts to members of many travel clubs, including the American Automobile Association, the American Association of Retired Persons, and Orlando Magicard.
Courtyard by Marriott offers vacation packages that include accommodations, WDW admission, some meals, and other amenities. To receive a brochure, call (800 223-9930).
A rental car can save considerable commuting time from this location.

**MAKING RESERVATIONS:** First call Courtyard Central Reservations (800 321-2211), then call the hotel directly and compare rates (800 223-9930). Inquire about promotional rates or corporate rates. Reservations may also be made through WDW Central Reservations Office (407 934-7639).

**XX** ATMOSPHERE. **XX** ATTITUDE. **XX** QUALITY. **XXX** TRUE VALUE.

**COURTYARD BY MARRIOTT**
**A MARRIOTT HOTEL**
**1805 HOTEL PLAZA BOULEVARD, LAKE BUENA VISTA, FLORIDA 32830**
**TELEPHONE (407) 828-8888 • FAX (407) 827-4623**

# DISNEY VACATION CLUB

**LOCATION:** Disney Vacation Club is one of four hotels in the Disney Village Resorts Area. The Vacation Club is connected by waterway to Disney Village Marketplace and Pleasure Island. A new addition, the Vacation Club Suites, is slated to open mid 1996 at Disney's BoardWalk.

**AMBIENCE:** The village atmosphere of Key West with a dash of Caribbean flair is the theme here, complete with a landmark lighthouse at the edge of the resort's private lagoon. Charming tinned-roofed two- and three-story buildings, in pastel-colored clapboard with ornate white trim and picket fences, line the winding streets of the village. The accommodations feel like vacation homes and are furnished in shades of apricot, aqua, and celadon, colors used throughout the resort exteriors. All rooms have balconies that overlook waterways, golf greens, or woodlands. Clustered around the lagoon at the center of the resort is a small lobby, an inviting library, and recreational facilities and services.

**RATES:** Studios **$$$** (including wet bar, refrigerator, microwave, and coffeemaker). One-bedroom units **$$$$**. Two-bedroom units **$$$$$**. Three-bedroom units **$$$$$$**. All vacation homes except studios have wide-screen televisions, fully equipped kitchens, and laundry facilities. Rates vary with the season.

**AMENITIES:** Voice mail, in-room safe, VCR, and videocassette library.

**RESTAURANTS:** *Olivia's Cafe* — Breakfast, lunch, and dinner, featuring Florida and Caribbean cuisine.

**RECREATION:** Two pools, small beach, tennis, volleyball, shuffleboard, marina, bicycling, jogging path, fitness center, sauna, whirlpool, fitness training, and massage.

**WDW PUBLIC TRANSPORTATION:** Water launch or bus to Disney Village Marketplace and Pleasure Island. Bus to all theme parks, including the Magic Kingdom, Epcot Center, Blizzard Beach, Disney-MGM Studios, and Typhoon Lagoon. To reach other destinations, bus to the Transportation and Ticket Center (TTC) or Disney Village Marketplace and connect to destination buses. Taxi service available.

**FEATURES:** The resort is conveniently located for guests interested in golfing at WDW.

Guests may rent their own boats and commute by water to Disney Village Marketplace, Pleasure Island, and other Disney Village Resorts.

**DRAWBACKS:** WDW buses operate within the resort, but it is quite spread out. Guests relying on WDW buses to reach attractions may find them inconvenient or overcrowded.

**TIPS:** A rental car is a must for guests who want to see it all in a short amount of time.

Room locations that are close to the recreation area and lobby are in buildings 12, 13, and 14. Buildings 11 and 15 are secluded, but still close to the common areas. Building 23 is near the quiet pool.

Disney Vacation Club is actually a time-share and a member of Resort Condominiums International. RCI members can exchange time at Disney Vacation Club. Units not used by time-share owners are available to guests as full-service hotel accommodations.

**MAKING RESERVATIONS:** Call WDW Central Reservations Office (407 934-7639). Inquire about special promotional rates and vacation packages.

**XXX** ATMOSPHERE. **XXX** ATTITUDE. **XXXX** QUALITY. **XXX** TRUE VALUE.

**DISNEY VACATION CLUB**
**A DISNEY-OWNED HOTEL**
**1510 NORTH COVE ROAD, LAKE BUENA VISTA, FLORIDA 32830**
**TELEPHONE (407) 827-7700 • FAX (407) 827-7710**

# DISNEY'S ALL-STAR RESORTS

**LOCATION:** Disney's All-Star Resorts are located in the Disney-MGM Resorts Area. They are southwest of Disney-MGM Studios, near Blizzard Beach. There are three distinct resorts in the complex: Disney's All-Star Sports Resort, Disney's All-Star Music Resort, and Disney's All-Star Movies Resort, which is scheduled to open in 1998.

**AMBIENCE:** Each resort complex has five themed hotel buildings that are distinguished by massive three-dimensional entertainment-related architecture. Disney's All-Star Sports Resort, for example, has surfboards and shark fins at the Surf's Up building, and football helmets at Touchdown. Disney's All-Star Music Resort has trombones at the Jazz Inn building, top hats and white gloves at Broadway Hotel, and jukeboxes and electric guitars at Rock Inn. The theme of each building cluster is carried over to its lobby and rooms. The hotel rooms are small and simply furnished.

**RATES:** Standard rooms **$**.

**AMENITIES:** Voice mail, in-room safe, pizza delivery to rooms. Refrigerator on request for a fee.

**RESTAURANTS:** *All-Star Sports: End Zone Food Court* — Counter-service restaurants; open all day.
*All-Star Music: Intermission Food Court* — Counter-service restaurants; open all day.

**RECREATION:** Two pools at each resort complex.

**WDW PUBLIC TRANSPORTATION:** Bus to all theme parks, including the Magic Kingdom, Epcot Center, Disney-MGM Studios, Blizzard Beach, Typhoon Lagoon, Pleasure Island, and Disney Village Marketplace. To reach other destinations, bus to the Transportation and Ticket Center (TTC) and connect to destination buses. Taxi service available.

**FEATURES:** Pools are open twenty-four hours a day and designed to reflect the resort's theme. For example, at Disney's All-Star Sports Resort the pools are shaped like a baseball diamond and an ocean wave. At Disney's All-Star Music Resort, the pools are shaped like a grand piano and a guitar.

**DRAWBACKS:** WDW buses to most attractions are generally inconvenient and overcrowded due to the location of the resorts and their large number of rooms. The Magic Kingdom commute can be tedious.

The resorts are quite spread out, so it can be a very long trek from the guest rooms to the food courts — some rooms are more than a half-mile away.

The All-Star Resorts have no full-service restaurants and attract mainly families with young children.

**TIPS:** For locations near the bus stops and food courts, request a room in Surf's Up! at the All-Star Sports resort, and in Calypso at the All-Star Music resort. For the quietest, most secluded rooms, request an upper-floor room with a forest view in Country Fair at the All-Star Music resort.

A rental car at this location is essential to see all of WDW in a reasonable amount of time.

**MAKING RESERVATIONS:** Call WDW Central Reservations Office (407 934-7639). Inquire about special promotional rates and vacation packages.

✗ ATMOSPHERE. ✗✗ ATTITUDE. ✗✗ QUALITY. ✗ TRUE VALUE.

DISNEY'S ALL-STAR SPORTS RESORT      DISNEY'S ALL-STAR MUSIC RESORT
1701 WEST LAKE BUENA VISTA DRIVE      1801 WEST LAKE BUENA VISTA DRIVE
LAKE BUENA VISTA, FLORIDA 32830       LAKE BUENA VISTA, FLORIDA 32830
TELEPHONE (407) 939-5000              TELEPHONE (407) 939-6000
FAX (407) 939-7333                    FAX (407) 939-7222

# DISNEY'S BEACH CLUB RESORT

**LOCATION:** Disney's Beach Club Resort is one of six hotels in the Epcot Resorts Area. It is located within walking distance of the International Gateway to the World Showcase at Epcot Center. It faces Stormalong Bay and shares a white sand beach and harbor waterfront with Disney's Yacht Club Resort.

**AMBIENCE:** This sky blue multilevel resort was designed by architect Robert Stern and shares resort amenities with the more formal Yacht Club located next to it. The New England seacoast–style resort is beach oriented and has a sporty, casual decor, from the 1927 Chevrolet taxi parked in front to the pink marble floor tiles, striped wicker furnishings, and caged finches in the pastel-infused lobby. Guest rooms are cheerful and light, furnished with pink and white cabana-striped curtains and verdigris-finished wrought-iron bedsteads. Many rooms have verandas or small balconies.

**RATES:** Standard rooms **$$$$**.

**AMENITIES:** Twenty-four-hour room service, mini bar, hair dryer, in-room safe, newspaper delivery, turndown service, voice mail, and valet parking.

**RESTAURANTS:** *Cape May Cafe* — Breakfast buffet and clambake dinner buffet featuring lobster.
*Ariel's Restaurant* — Dinner featuring fresh seafood in an aquarium-themed dining room.
*Beaches and Cream* — Breakfast and all-day hamburgers with soda fountain specialties.

**RECREATION:** Pool, white sand beach, mini water park, marina, tennis, jogging path, volleyball, bocce ball (lawn bowling), croquet, fitness center, sauna, steam room, fitness classes, fitness training, whirlpool, and massage.

**WDW PUBLIC TRANSPORTATION:** Walk or water launch to the World Showcase at Epcot Center. Water launch to Disney-MGM Studios. Bus to the Magic Kingdom, Blizzard Beach, Pleasure Island, Disney Village Marketplace, and Typhoon Lagoon. To reach other destinations, bus to the Transportation and Ticket Center (TTC) and connect to destination buses. Taxi service available.

**FEATURES:** This full-amenity resort is conveniently located for guests primarily interested in Future World and the World Showcase at Epcot Center, and Disney-MGM Studios.

**DRAWBACKS:** WDW buses to the Magic Kingdom can be overcrowded during peak seasons.
  Although the more expensive lagoon-view rooms do have lovely water views, they can be noisy since Stormalong Bay water park is filled with children late into the night.

**TIPS:** The rooms on the fourth floor were originally designated as concierge rooms, so they are more spacious and more generous in comforts. The rooms on the second and fourth floors have balconies.
  Standard rooms that face the canal in front, but that are not above the parking portico, are a good value, while rooms located at the far end of the hotel facing the forest, although a bit of a trek from the lobby, offer pleasant views, quiet isolation, and fast access to the International Gateway at Epcot.

**MAKING RESERVATIONS:** Call WDW Central Reservations Office (407 934-7639). Inquire about special promotional rates and vacation packages.

**XXX** ATMOSPHERE. **XXXX** ATTITUDE. **XXXX** QUALITY. **XXX** TRUE VALUE.

**DISNEY'S BEACH CLUB RESORT**
**A DISNEY-OWNED HOTEL**
**1800 EPCOT RESORTS BOULEVARD, LAKE BUENA VISTA, FLORIDA 32830**
**TELEPHONE (407) 934-8000 • FAX (407) 934-3850**

# DISNEY'S BOARDWALK INN

**LOCATION:** Disney's BoardWalk Inn is one of six hotels in the Epcot Resorts Area. It is located at Disney's BoardWalk, a short distance from Disney-MGM Studios and within walking distance of the International Gateway to the World Showcase at Epcot Center. The Inn overlooks Crescent Lake and shares this waterfront location with another new resort, Disney Vacation Club Villas at the BoardWalk (see "New Hotels at WDW," page 158).

**AMBIENCE:** Opening in July 1996, the hotel is built on several levels behind Disney's BoardWalk, a new resort and entertainment complex fashioned after the festive Atlantic City Boardwalk of the 1920s and '30s. Its design recalls the cheerful, casual luxury of turn-of-the-century Eastern Seaboard hotels. Many of the rooms have French doors, and are decorated with rosebud-patterned rugs, comfortable and deliberately mismatched beach house–style furnishings, white marble baths, and curtains with soft images of vintage picture postcards. The hotel also has a number of two-story "honeymoon cottages" with intimate gardens, picket fences, and private entrances. All guests are provided with concierge-style services and have access to a private lounge.

**RATES:** Standard rooms $$$. One-bedroom cottages $$$$. Rates vary with the season.

**AMENITIES:** Twenty-four-hour room service, mini bar, coffeemaker, in-room safe, robe, hair dryer, newspaper delivery, turndown service, voice mail, and valet parking.

**RESTAURANTS:** The restaurants along the BoardWalk Promenade are adjacent to the hotel (see "Disney's BoardWalk," page 96). A private guest lounge serves Continental breakfast, snacks, and beverages. A concierge is on duty to take care of guests' additional needs.

**RECREATION:** Quiet pool, mini water park, tennis, jogging, croquet, fitness center, sauna, steam room, whirlpool, and massage.

**WDW PUBLIC TRANSPORTATION:** Walk to the World Showcase at Epcot Center. Walk or water launch to Disney-MGM Studios. Bus to the Magic Kingdom, Blizzard Beach, Typhoon Lagoon, Pleasure Island, and Disney Village Marketplace. To reach other destinations, bus to the Transportation and Ticket Center (TTC) and connect to destination buses. Taxi service available.

**FEATURES:** This full-amenity resort is conveniently located for guests primarily interested in Epcot Center and Disney-MGM Studios.

For the young-at-heart visitor, the resort's carnival-themed pool area, Luna Park, has a roller-coaster-style waterslide, giant spraying elephants, and a whimsical poolside bar.

**DRAWBACKS:** The Luna Park mini water park is very popular with children, and may not provide the serene poolside experience that some adults seek.

WDW buses to the Magic Kingdom can be overcrowded during peak seasons.

**TIPS:** The rooms overlooking the BoardWalk Promenade and Crescent Lake offer a bustling, brightly lit view. If that's not what you are looking for, request a room overlooking the quiet-pool area.

**MAKING RESERVATIONS:** Call WDW Central Reservations Office (407 934-7639). Inquire about special promotional rates and vacation packages.

**DISNEY'S BOARDWALK INN**
**A DISNEY-OWNED HOTEL**
**2101 EPCOT RESORTS BOULEVARD, LAKE BUENA VISTA, FLORIDA 32830**
**TELEPHONE (407) 934-7639**

# DISNEY'S CARIBBEAN BEACH RESORT

**LOCATION:** Disney's Caribbean Beach Resort is one of six hotels in the Epcot Resorts Area. The buildings of the resort encircle forty-acre Barefoot Bay, a series of three lakes created for the resort's exclusive use. From Disney's Caribbean Beach Resort it is a short drive to Epcot Center, Disney-MGM Studios, Typhoon Lagoon, Pleasure Island, and Disney Village Marketplace.

**AMBIENCE:** Built as Disney's first budget resort, the sprawling Caribbean Beach resort consists of clusters of pitched-roof two-story buildings painted in somewhat jarring colors and set in expertly designed tropical landscaping. Instead of a formal lobby, the resort welcomes guests at its modest freestanding Customs House, where overhead fans and wicker settees set a tropical note. The limited-amenity guest rooms, with subdued colors and wood furnishings, are functional and cozy. All resort activities are centered at Old Port Royale, on one side of Barefoot Bay.

**RATES:** Standard rooms $$. Rates remain the same year round.

**AMENITIES:** Mini bar, coffeemaker, voice mail, and pizza delivery to rooms.

**RESTAURANTS:** *Old Port Royale* — Food court with six counter-service restaurants.
*Captain's Tavern* — Dinner featuring prime rib and American cuisine.

**RECREATION:** Six pools, white sand beach, marina, bicycling, jogging path, nature walk, and whirlpool.

**WDW PUBLIC TRANSPORTATION:** Disney's Caribbean Beach Resort has its own internal bus system. WDW buses service to all theme parks, including the Magic Kingdom, Epcot Center, Blizzard Beach, Disney-MGM Studios, Pleasure Island, Disney Village Marketplace, and Typhoon Lagoon. To reach other destinations, bus to the Transportation and Ticket Center (TTC) or Disney Village Marketplace and connect to destination buses. Taxi service available.

**FEATURES:** Parrot Cay, a small island in the middle of Barefoot Bay, has a fantasy Spanish-fort playground, a tropical nature walk, and an aviary stocked with colorful birds.

**DRAWBACKS:** The resort is especially popular with families with young children, making it an all-day noisy experience at the pools and beaches.
   Because the resort sprawls over two hundred acres, it can be a long trek from guest rooms to the food court at Old Port Royale.
   WDW buses to attractions can be inconvenient and overcrowded from this location during peak seasons. Guests primarily interested in the Magic Kingdom will find the commute long and tedious.

**TIPS:** To select a room close to Old Port Royale, request Trinidad North, next door, or Jamaica, just across the bridge. For isolation, request Trinidad South, which has its own private beach and pool.
   The rooms on the second floor afford the most privacy.
   A rental car can speed commuting time from this location, especially when visiting other resorts.

**MAKING RESERVATIONS:** Call WDW Central Reservations Office (407 934-7639). Inquire about special promotional rates and vacation packages.

**XX** ATMOSPHERE. **XX** ATTITUDE. **XXX** QUALITY. **XXX** TRUE VALUE.

**DISNEY'S CARIBBEAN BEACH RESORT**
**A DISNEY-OWNED HOTEL**
**900 CAYMAN WAY, LAKE BUENA VISTA, FLORIDA 32830**
**TELEPHONE (407) 934-3400 • FAX (407) 934-3288**

# DISNEY'S CONTEMPORARY RESORT

**LOCATION:** Disney's Contemporary Resort is one of six hotels in the Magic Kingdom Resorts Area. It is conveniently located on the monorail line that serves the Magic Kingdom and Epcot Center, and has a long white sand beach that fronts Bay Lake.

**AMBIENCE:** The elongated pyramidal structure of this resort has an overall futuristic look. The minimalist-style first-floor lobby is strictly functional, with stylish, brightly colored angular furniture and pieces of sleek modern art. Most lobby amenities are actually located on the Concourse level, where the monorail glides through the glass-and-steel atrium. The resort's pool areas have been recently enlarged and a waterslide added. Tower rooms and suites are decorated in sophisticated neutrals, geometric-patterned fabrics, and streamlined furniture. The garden wing rooms are spacious, but set at some distance from the lobby. All rooms have a balcony or patio.

**RATES:** Garden wing rooms **$$$$**. Tower rooms **$$$$**. Tower concierge suites **$$$$$$** (including Continental breakfast, evening wine and cheese, and special room amenities). Rates vary with the season.

**AMENITIES:** Twenty-four-hour room service, in-room safe (tower rooms), newspaper delivery, voice mail, and valet parking.

**RESTAURANTS:** *California Grill* — Dinner West-Coast style, with the menu changing daily to accommodate market fresh foods. Preparing the dishes is part of the show in this dramatic exhibition kitchen.
*Contemporary Cafe* — Breakfast buffet and nightly dinner buffet.
*Concourse Steakhouse* — Breakfast, lunch, and dinner featuring steak and prime rib.

**RECREATION:** Two pools, white sand beach, marina, waterskiing, parasailing, tennis, volleyball, shuffleboard, jogging path, fitness center, sauna, whirlpool, fitness training, and massage.

**WDW PUBLIC TRANSPORTATION:** Walk to the Magic Kingdom. Monorail to the Magic Kingdom, the Transportation and Ticket Center (TTC), and Epcot Center. Water launch to Discovery Island, Fort Wilderness, and River Country. Bus to all other theme parks. Taxi service available.

**FEATURES:** In this most tennis-oriented of the WDW resorts, the Racquet Club offers practice courts and personal instruction.

**DRAWBACKS:** WDW buses to theme parks can be inconvenient or overcrowded during peak seasons. Guests must change trains at the TTC for monorails to Epcot Center.

**TIPS:** Tower rooms are the most popular, convenient, and expensive. Higher-floor rooms facing the Magic Kingdom have a view of the fireworks show.
Garden wing rooms, although less expensive, are some distance from the lobby. However, those on the first floor facing Bay Lake are popular, because they have glass doors that open onto small patios.

**MAKING RESERVATIONS:** Call WDW Central Reservations Office (407 934-7639). Inquire about special promotional rates and vacation packages.

**XXX** ATMOSPHERE. **XXX** ATTITUDE. **XXX** QUALITY. **XX** TRUE VALUE.

**DISNEY'S CONTEMPORARY RESORT**
**A DISNEY-OWNED HOTEL**
**4600 NORTH WORLD DRIVE, LAKE BUENA VISTA, FLORIDA 32830**
**TELEPHONE (407) 824-1000 • FAX (407) 824-3539**

# DISNEY'S DIXIE LANDINGS RESORT

**LOCATION:** Disney's Dixie Landings Resort is one of four hotels in the Disney Village Resorts Area. It is connected by carriage path and waterway to nearby Port Orleans resort and by waterway to Disney Village Marketplace and Pleasure Island.

**AMBIENCE:** The rustic bayous and antebellum mansions of the Old South are re-created at Dixie Landings. The large, sprawling resort has two sections. On one side is Alligator Bayou, with its two-story Cajun-style brick or stucco lodges sporting wide front porches and rough-hewn railings, all set in a dense moss-hung pine forest. On the other side is Magnolia Bend, with an array of elegant three-story plantation manors set apart by fountains, sweeping lawns, and weeping willows. The Sassagoula River loops through the resort, and in the center is the reception area, designed as a riverboat depot, circa 1880. The rooms in this limited-amenity resort are decorated simply in soft neutral colors; furnishings in the Bayou rooms are more rustic than in the Magnolia rooms. All rooms have a vanity-dressing area with two pedestal sinks.

**RATES:** Standard rooms $$. Rates remain the same year round.

**AMENITIES:** Voice mail, pizza delivery to rooms, and refrigerator on request for a fee; some room safes.

**RESTAURANTS:** *Boatwright's Dining Hall* — Breakfast and dinner featuring Cajun specialties.
*Colonel's Cotton Mill* — Food court with five counter-service restaurants for breakfast, lunch, and dinner, housed in an old cotton mill.

**RECREATION:** Five pools, theme pool, marina, bicycling, jogging path, whirlpool, and fishing hole.

**WDW PUBLIC TRANSPORTATION:** Water launch or bus to Disney Village Marketplace and Pleasure Island. Bus to all theme parks, including the Magic Kingdom, Epcot Center, Blizzard Beach, Disney-MGM Studios, and Typhoon Lagoon. To reach other destinations, bus to the Transportation and Ticket Center (TTC) or Disney Village Marketplace and connect to destination buses. Taxi service available.

**FEATURES:** The resort is conveniently located for guests interested in golfing at WDW.
Guests may rent their own boats and commute by water to Disney Village Marketplace, Pleasure Island, and other Disney Village Resorts.

**DRAWBACKS:** WDW buses to attractions can be inconvenient or overcrowded during peak seasons.
This budget-priced hotel is popular with young families; however, the buildings are very spread out and offer a great deal of privacy.

**TIPS:** This limited-amenity resort offers an excellent value for the price. Upgrade to a river-view room and you'll have a luxury setting for a fraction of the cost of WDW's premier resorts.
The most popular locations are those close to the common areas and lobby. If you prefer a plantation home, request a room in Oak Manor; for a more rustic setting, request lodges 14, 18, or 27.
A rental car can save commuting time from this location, especially when visiting other resorts.

**MAKING RESERVATIONS:** Call WDW Central Reservations Office (407 934-7639). Inquire about special promotional rates and vacation packages.

**XXX** ATMOSPHERE. **XXX** ATTITUDE. **XXX** QUALITY. **XXXX** TRUE VALUE.

**DISNEY'S DIXIE LANDINGS RESORT**
**A DISNEY-OWNED HOTEL**
**1251 DIXIE DRIVE, LAKE BUENA VISTA, FLORIDA 32830**
**TELEPHONE (407) 934-6000 • FAX (407) 934-5777**

# DISNEY'S FORT WILDERNESS RESORT AND CAMPGROUND

**LOCATION:** Disney's Fort Wilderness Resort and Campground is one of six hotels in the Magic Kingdom Resorts Area. It stretches from Vista Boulevard to the shores of Bay Lake.

**AMBIENCE:** This is not a hotel but a seven-hundred-acre full-amenity forested campground. Here, guests may rent campsites for tents, hookups for recreational vehicles, or one of the resort's permanent fully appointed trailers. Fort Wilderness offers a natural setting to return to after a hectic day at the theme parks and is itself a Disney World attraction (see "Fort Wilderness & River Country," page 68).

**RATES:** Wilderness homes (one-bedroom trailer homes) **$$$**. Campsites with full hookups **$**. Campsites with partial hookups **$**. Rates vary with the season.

**AMENITIES:** Wilderness homes include kitchen, cable TV, voice mail, housekeeping services, and outdoor grill. Full-hookup campsites include sanitary disposal, water, cable TV, electricity, and outdoor grill. Partial-hookup campsites include water, electricity, and outdoor grill. All campsite loops have air-conditioned rest rooms, showers, ice makers, laundry facilities, and telephones.

**RESTAURANTS:** *Trail's End Buffeteria* — Cafeteria-style breakfast, lunch, dinner, and late-night buffet. *Crockett's Tavern* — Dinner featuring steak and seafood in a Wild West setting.

**RECREATION:** Pool, lap pool, white sand beach, marina, tennis, bicycling, volleyball, basketball, tetherball, shuffleboard, jogging path, nature trail, horseback riding, canoeing, waterskiing, and fishing.

**WDW PUBLIC TRANSPORTATION:** Fort Wilderness has its own internal bus system to all campsites, Fort Wilderness attractions, and River Country (where there is no parking). Bikes and electric carts can also be rented for use within the resort. Water launch to the Magic Kingdom, Discovery Island, and the Contemporary resort. Bus from the Fort Wilderness Guest Parking Lot to other theme parks.

**FEATURES:** Fort Wilderness offers several entertainment events daily, including the Hoop-Dee-Doo Musical Revue dinner show, hayrides, movies, and the nightly Electrical Water Pageant.

Two on-site convenience stores, Settlement Trading Post and Meadow Trading Post, carry a limited supply of groceries, prepared foods, and sundries.

**DRAWBACKS:** WDW buses to attractions can be overcrowded and infrequent.

In the summer months there are mosquitoes and afternoon downpours, and the weather is very hot.

**TIPS:** A car is essential at this location, especially during the summer rainy season. Guests may drive to and from their campsites to all WDW attractions.

The most desirable Wilderness Home locations are on loops 2500 and 2700 near the swimming pool. The most desirable campsites are on loop 400, near the marina and River Country.

**MAKING RESERVATIONS:** Call WDW Central Reservations Office (407 934-7639). Inquire about special promotional rates and vacation packages.

**XXX** ATMOSPHERE. **XXX** ATTITUDE. **XX** QUALITY. **XX** TRUE VALUE.

**DISNEY'S FORT WILDERNESS RESORT AND CAMPGROUND**
**A DISNEY-OWNED HOTEL**
**3500 N. FORT WILDERNESS, LAKE BUENA VISTA, FLORIDA 32830**
**TELEPHONE (407) 824-2900 • FAX (407) 824-3508**

# DISNEY'S GRAND FLORIDIAN BEACH RESORT

**LOCATION:** Disney's Grand Floridian Beach Resort is one of six hotels in the Magic Kingdom Resorts Area. It is conveniently located on the monorail line that serves the Magic Kingdom and Epcot Center, and it has a white sand beach that fronts Seven Seas Lagoon.

**AMBIENCE:** The most elegant and expensive of the WDW resorts, this rambling, romantic Victorian-style hotel is fashioned after the grand seaside resorts of the 1890s. With its white banisters and railings, paned glass windows, peaked red-shingled roofs, and formal flower and shrub gardens, this resort is a favorite with honeymooners. Its spacious and luxurious stained-glass-domed lobby has ornate wrought-iron elevators, potted trees, and clusters of intimately placed settees where guests can sit and enjoy the ongoing live music in the common areas. The guest rooms are handsomely decorated, and each has a patio or balcony.

**RATES:** Standard rooms **$$$$**. Concierge rooms **$$$$$** (including Continental breakfast, afternoon snacks, evening cordials and appetizers, and special room amenities). Rates vary with the season.

**AMENITIES:** Twenty-four-hour room service, mini bar, in-room safe, hair dryers, robes, newspaper delivery, voice mail, and valet parking.

**RESTAURANTS:** *Victoria & Albert's* — Elegant, award-winning candlelight dinner; prix-fixe menu.
*Flagler's* — Italian dinners with singing servers.
*Narcoossee's* — Lunch and dinner featuring steaks and Florida seafood on the waterfront.
*1900 Park Fare* — Buffet-style breakfast and dinner; Disney characters drop by.
*Grand Floridian Cafe* — Breakfast, lunch, and dinner featuring Florida-style cuisine.

**RECREATION:** Pool, white sand beach, marina, waterskiing, tennis, volleyball, jogging path, fitness center, sauna, steam room, whirlpool, fitness classes, fitness training, and massage.

**WDW PUBLIC TRANSPORTATION:** Monorail or water launch to the Magic Kingdom. Monorail to the Transportation and Ticket Center (TTC) and Epcot Center. Monorail or water launch to the Magic Kingdom to transfer to water launch to Discovery Island, Fort Wilderness, and River Country. Bus to Pleasure Island. Bus or monorail to the TTC to transfer to destination buses for all other theme parks. Taxi service available.

**FEATURES:** The resort has pleasantly appointed clay tennis courts for guests interested in tennis.
A very good high tea is served from 3 PM until 6 PM in the Garden View Lounge.

**DRAWBACKS:** WDW buses to attractions can be inconvenient or overcrowded during peak seasons.
Guests must change trains at the TTC for monorails to Epcot Center.

**TIPS:** While all the rooms are graciously appointed, the rooms on the upper floors are more private.
The lagoon-view rooms are the most popular, but the rooms overlooking the central courtyard help maintain the enchantment of the Victorian-themed architecture, especially at night.

**MAKING RESERVATIONS:** Call WDW Central Reservations Office (407 934-7639). Inquire about special promotional rates and vacation packages.

**XXXX** ATMOSPHERE. **XXXX** ATTITUDE. **XXXX** QUALITY. **XXX** TRUE VALUE.

**DISNEY'S GRAND FLORIDIAN BEACH RESORT**
**A DISNEY-OWNED HOTEL**
**4401 FLORIDIAN WAY, LAKE BUENA VISTA, FLORIDA 32830**
**TELEPHONE (407) 824-3000 • FAX (407) 824-3186**

# DISNEY'S POLYNESIAN RESORT

**LOCATION:** Disney's Polynesian Resort is one of six hotels in the Magic Kingdom Resorts Area. It is conveniently located on the monorail line that serves the Magic Kingdom and Epcot Center, and it has a white sand beach that fronts Seven Seas Lagoon.

**AMBIENCE:** This aptly named resort, situated in an extensive tropical garden, features South Pacific lodge architecture. The hotel is a cluster of two- and three-story dark-beamed buildings scattered throughout the expertly landscaped grounds. The lobby entrance and atrium have a lush garden with a carp pond, bamboo, and blooming orchids. Guest rooms have ceiling fans and canopied beds and are decorated with batik and tapa-cloth prints in shades of green and brown. Most upper-floor rooms have balconies.

**RATES:** Standard rooms **$$$$**. Royal Polynesian concierge-service rooms **$$$$$$** (including Continental breakfast, afternoon snacks, evening wine and appetizers, no-host cocktails, and other amenities). Rates vary with the season.

**AMENITIES:** Room service, in-room safe, voice mail, and valet parking.

**RESTAURANTS:** *'Ohana* — Hawaiian-themed dinner served family style, featuring open-hearth grilled meats and seafood. Entertainment nightly.

*Coral Isle Cafe* — Breakfast, lunch, and dinner featuring Polynesian and Asian selections.

*Tangaroa Terrace* — Polynesia-themed a la carte and buffet breakfast and Italian-style a la carte and buffet dinner.

*Polynesian Luau* — Nightly dinner show featuring Polynesian family-style cuisine.

**RECREATION:** Two pools, white sand beach, marina, waterskiing, volleyball, and jogging path.

**WDW PUBLIC TRANSPORTATION:** Monorail or water launch to the Magic Kingdom. Walk to the Transportation and Ticket Center (TTC) and monorail to Epcot Center or transfer to destination buses for all other theme parks. Monorail or water launch to the Magic Kingdom and transfer to the water launch to Discovery Island, Fort Wilderness, and River Country. Taxi service available.

**FEATURES:** Carefully landscaped gardens with tropical plant specimens and nighttime torch lighting create an enchanting island atmosphere.

There are great views of the Electric Water Pageant and the Magic Kingdom fireworks from the beach.

**DRAWBACKS:** WDW buses to theme parks can be inconvenient or overcrowded during peak seasons.

This is a very popular hotel for families and can be heavily populated with children.

**TIPS:** The Polynesian resort is a convincing ambience for a tropical-style vacation. The most popular rooms are those with a view of the lagoon or the pools. For an isolated location, request one of the rooms farthest out, on the newest side of the hotel, facing the lagoon. Garden-view rooms are a good value. Upper-floor rooms offer the most privacy.

**MAKING RESERVATIONS:** Call WDW Central Reservations Office (407 934-7639). Inquire about special promotional rates and vacation packages.

**XXX** ATMOSPHERE. **XX** ATTITUDE. **XX** QUALITY. **XXX** TRUE VALUE.

**DISNEY'S POLYNESIAN RESORT**
**A DISNEY-OWNED HOTEL**
**1600 SOUTH SEAS DRIVE, LAKE BUENA VISTA, FLORIDA 32830**
**TELEPHONE (407) 824-2000 • FAX (407) 824-3174**

# DISNEY'S PORT ORLEANS RESORT

**LOCATION:** Disney's Port Orleans Resort is one of four hotels in the Disney Village Resorts Area. It is connected by carriage path and waterway to nearby Dixie Landings resort and by waterway to Disney Village Marketplace and Pleasure Island.

**AMBIENCE:** Port Orleans is designed to capture the atmosphere of the New Orleans's French Quarter preparing for Mardi Gras. Beyond the large steel-and-glass atrium lobby is a courtyard where a Dixieland band entertains guests. The resort is arranged in a complex grid of cobblestone streets with names like Rue D'Baga and Reveler's Row. The three-story row house–style buildings, some in red brick and others painted shades of ocher, peach, aqua, and French blue, mimic the diverse architectural styles of New Orleans. Ornate wrought-iron railings, varying rooflines, louvered shutters, French doors, and small front-yard gardens all amplify the atmosphere. At night old-fashioned street lamps form atmospheric pools of light among the magnolia and willow trees. The rooms are decorated simply in soft neutral colors with ceiling fans. A small vanity area features two old-fashioned pedestal sinks.

**RATES:** Standard rooms **$$**. Rates remain the same year round.

**AMENITIES:** Voice mail, pizza delivery to rooms, and refrigerator upon request for a fee.

**RESTAURANTS:** *Bonfamille's Café* — Breakfast and dinner featuring Creole and American cuisine.
*Sassagoula Floatworks and Food Factory* — Mardi Gras–themed food court with four counter-service restaurants for breakfast, lunch, and dinner.

**RECREATION:** Theme pool, marina, bicycling, croquet, jogging path, and whirlpool.

**WDW PUBLIC TRANSPORTATION:** Water launch or bus to Disney Village Marketplace and Pleasure Island. Bus to all theme parks, including the Magic Kingdom, Epcot Center, Blizzard Beach, Disney-MGM Studios, and Typhoon Lagoon. To reach other destinations, bus to the Transportation and Ticket Center (TTC) or Disney Village Marketplace and connect to destination buses. Taxi service available.

**FEATURES:** The resort is conveniently located for guests interested in golfing at WDW.
Guests may rent their own boats and commute by water to Disney Village Marketplace, Pleasure Island, and other Disney Village Resorts.

**DRAWBACKS:** This budget-priced hotel is oriented to young families, although the resort layout does have areas of privacy and quiet. The fantasy-themed pool scene is designed primarily for the young at heart.
WDW buses to attractions can be inconvenient or overcrowded during peak seasons.

**TIPS:** This limited-amenity resort offers an excellent value for the price. Upgrade to a top-floor river-view room and you'll have a luxury view for a fraction of the cost of WDW's premier resorts.
A rental car will save commuting time from this location, especially when visiting other resorts.

**MAKING RESERVATIONS:** Call WDW Central Reservations Office (407 934-7639). Inquire about special promotional rates and vacation packages.

**XXX** ATMOSPHERE. **XXX** ATTITUDE. **XXX** QUALITY. **XXXX** TRUE VALUE.

**DISNEY'S PORT ORLEANS RESORT**
**A DISNEY-OWNED HOTEL**
**2201 ORLEANS DRIVE, LAKE BUENA VISTA, FLORIDA 32830**
**TELEPHONE (407) 934-5000 • FAX (407) 934-5353**

# DISNEY'S WILDERNESS LODGE

**LOCATION:** Disney's Wilderness Lodge is one of six hotels in the Magic Kingdom Resorts Area. The resort is located deep in the forested area on the southwest shore of Bay Lake between Disney's Contemporary Resort and Fort Wilderness.

**AMBIENCE:** Disney's Wilderness Lodge was inspired by the U.S. National Park lodges built in the early 1900s. The quarry-stone pine-beamed building, surrounded by forest and filled with natural light, has a comfortable lodge-retreat atmosphere. Dark wood furnishings and Native American design motifs add a rustic, cozy touch to the lodge, which has an atrium lobby featuring unusual chandeliers of striking design, a massive rock fireplace, and two gigantic totem poles from the Pacific Northwest. A warm spring bubbling in the lobby appears to flow to the outdoor courtyard, where it is transformed into a waterfall that cascades into the resort's rock-carved swimming pools and spas. Nearby, a geyser modeled on Yellowstone's Old Faithful erupts frequently and dramatically.

**RATES:** Standard rooms **$$$**. Rates vary with the season.

**AMENITIES:** Room service, in-room safe, voice mail, and valet parking.

**RESTAURANTS:** *Artist Point Dining Room* — Breakfast and dinner featuring Pacific Northwest cuisine, fresh seasonal seafood, smoked-on-premises meats, and selected game such as venison.
*Whispering Canyon Cafe* — Hearty family-style breakfast, lunch, and dinner prepared with a rustic air; meats are roasted, smoked, grilled, and barbecued.

**RECREATION:** Pool, hot and cold mineral pools, white sand beach, marina, boating, waterskiing, bicycling, and jogging path.

**WDW PUBLIC TRANSPORTATION:** Bus to all theme parks. Bus to the Transportation and Ticket Center and transfer to monorails to Epcot Center and the Magic Kingdom or to buses to reach other destinations. Water launch to the Magic Kingdom and Discovery Island. Walk or bus to Fort Wilderness and River Country. Taxi service available.

**FEATURES:** The resort is adjacent to Fort Wilderness, providing nature trails, bike paths, fishing, tennis, volleyball, horseback riding, and a particularly good jogging trail that meanders through a beautiful forested area, with exercise stations along the way.

**DRAWBACKS:** Self-parking lots are crowded, distant, and not very well lit. Valet park, take a flashlight, or ask for an escort to your car.

**TIPS:** Upper rooms in the main lodge area offer the most privacy. Rooms on the top floor have balconies with solid walls that ensure privacy, but block the view.

The lake view rooms offer an unparalleled vista of Bay Lake and Discovery Island. The forest view rooms provide peaceful seclusion.

**MAKING RESERVATIONS:** Call WDW Central Reservations Office (407 934-7639). Inquire about special promotional rates and vacation packages.

**XXXX** ATMOSPHERE. **XXX** ATTITUDE. **XXX** QUALITY. **XXX** TRUE VALUE.

**DISNEY'S WILDERNESS LODGE**
**A DISNEY-OWNED HOTEL**
**901 TIMBERLINE DRIVE, LAKE BUENA VISTA, FLORIDA 32830**
**TELEPHONE (407) 824-3200 • FAX (407) 824-3232**

# DISNEY'S YACHT CLUB RESORT

**LOCATION:** Disney's Yacht Club Resort is one of six hotels in the Epcot Resorts Area. It is located within walking distance of the International Gateway to the World Showcase at Epcot Center. It faces Stormalong Bay and shares a white sand beach and harbor waterfront with Disney's Beach Club Resort.

**AMBIENCE:** Designed by architect Robert Stern, the gray and white clapboard-sided Yacht Club has rope-slung boardwalks and a picturesque lighthouse on its waterfront. It has a decidedly nautical motif and shares resort amenities with the more casually decorated Beach Club, next door. The lobby has dark wood floors, polished brass details, and tufted leather couches — the feeling is sophisticated yet comfortable. Guest rooms, with their white furniture, old-fashioned armoires, ceiling fans, and large balconies, have a pleasant home-away-from-home feeling.

**RATES:** Standard rooms $$$$. Concierge rooms $$$$$ (including Continental breakfast, afternoon snacks, evening wine and appetizers, and special room amenities). Rates vary with the season.

**AMENITIES:** Twenty-four-hour room service, mini bar, in-room safe, hair dryer, turndown service, voice mail, and valet parking. In-room checkers and chess games available on request.

**RESTAURANTS:** *Yacht Club Galley* — Breakfast buffet or a la carte; lunch and dinner with emphasis on New England specialties.

*Yachtsman Steakhouse* — Dinner featuring prime-cut steaks and a small selection of seafood and poultry dishes.

**RECREATION:** Pool, white sand beach, mini water park, marina, tennis, jogging path, volleyball, bocce ball, croquet, fitness center, sauna, steam room, whirlpool, fitness classes, fitness training, and massage.

**WDW PUBLIC TRANSPORTATION:** Walk, water launch, or tram to the World Showcase at Epcot Center. Water launch to Disney-MGM Studios. Bus to the Magic Kingdom, Blizzard Beach, Pleasure Island, Disney Village Marketplace, and Typhoon Lagoon. To reach other destinations, bus to the Transportation and Ticket Center (TTC) and connect to destination buses. Taxi service available.

**FEATURES:** This full-amenity resort is conveniently located for guests primarily interested in Future World and the World Showcase at Epcot Center, and Disney-MGM Studios.

The Yacht Club's location between the Beach Club and the Dolphin hotel makes the amenities at either resort easily accessible.

**DRAWBACKS:** WDW buses to the Magic Kingdom can be infrequent or overcrowded during peak seasons. Although the more-expensive rooms have water views, they can be noisy since Stormalong Bay water park is filled with children late into the night.

**TIPS:** Rooms surrounding the "quiet pool" are popular for their seclusion. Upper-floor garden-view or standard rooms to either side of the entrance are a very good value.

**MAKING RESERVATIONS:** Call WDW Central Reservations Office (407 934-7639). Inquire about special promotional rates and vacation packages.

**XXXX** ATMOSPHERE. **XXXX** ATTITUDE. **XXXX** QUALITY. **XXX** TRUE VALUE.

**DISNEY'S YACHT CLUB RESORT**
**A DISNEY-OWNED HOTEL**
**1700 EPCOT RESORTS BOULEVARD, LAKE BUENA VISTA, FLORIDA 32830**
**TELEPHONE (407) 934-7000 • FAX (407) 934-3450**

# DOUBLETREE GUEST SUITES RESORT

**LOCATION:** The DoubleTree Guest Suites Resort is one of seven independently owned Hotel Plaza Resorts located on Walt Disney World property near Disney Village Marketplace. Guests are provided with shuttle service to the major WDW attractions and offered special discounts at area shops and restaurants.

**AMBIENCE:** This sleek, mirror-glassed hotel is a contemporary, quasi-pyramidal, seven-story building. Its modern, comfortable lobby is decorated with large murals and bright color accents. DoubleTree is the only all-suites hotel inside Walt Disney World. The guest suites are very generous in size, and have been handsomely refurbished in soft pastel shades. Each suite features a separate bedroom and kitchenette.

**RATES:** One-bedroom suites **$$$**. Two-bedroom suites **$$$$**. Rates vary with season.

**AMENITIES:** Room service, refrigerator (unstocked), coffeemaker, microwave, hair dryer, pay-per-view movies, and three televisions (two color, one black and white) in each suite.

**RESTAURANTS:** *Streamers* — Large restaurant for a la carte and buffet breakfast. A variety of American-style dishes are offered at lunch and dinner.

**RECREATION:** Pool, tennis, jogging path, fitness center, and whirlpool.

**HOTEL TRANSPORTATION:** Walk to Disney Village Marketplace and Pleasure Island. Shuttle bus to Epcot Center, Disney-MGM Studios, the Magic Kingdom, and Typhoon Lagoon. For transportation to other attractions, consult hotel Guest Services. Taxi service available.

**FEATURES:** DoubleTree Guest Suites participates in the American Express Membership Miles program.

DoubleTree Guest Suites has been recently remodeled and is an excellent value for a suite at Walt Disney World. Each suite has a spacious living room that includes a dining area and limited kitchen facilities. The resort has a convenience store that also prepares a selection of deli sandwiches. Gooding's Supermarket is within walking distance.

DoubleTree Guest Suites has a particularly pleasant free-form pool with a congenial poolside area with bar. The pool is large enough for swimming laps.

**DRAWBACKS:** Guests relying on hotel buses to reach attractions may find them crowded in peak seasons.

**TIPS:** Rooms with a pool view are especially pleasant. Ground-floor rooms have sliding glass doors that open onto small open patios. Disney-view rooms are the most frequently requested.

DoubleTree Guest Suites offers discounts to members of several travel clubs, including the American Automobile Association, the American Association of Retired Persons, and Orlando Magicard.

The hotel offers vacation packages that include accommodations, WDW admission, breakfast, and other amenities. To receive a brochure, call the hotel directly (407 934-1000).

A rental car can save considerable commuting time from this location.

**MAKING RESERVATIONS:** First call DoubleTree Central Reservations (800 222-8733), then call the hotel directly and compare rates (407 934-1000). Inquire about promotional rates or corporate rates. Reservations may also be made through WDW Central Reservations Office (407 934-7639).

**XXX** ATMOSPHERE. **XXX** ATTITUDE. **XXXX** QUALITY. **XXXX** TRUE VALUE.

DOUBLETREE GUEST SUITES RESORT
DOUBLETREE HOTELS CORPORATION
2305 HOTEL PLAZA BOULEVARD, LAKE BUENA VISTA, FLORIDA 32830
TELEPHONE (407) 934-1000 • FAX (407) 934-1011

# GROSVENOR RESORT

**LOCATION:** The Grosvenor Resort is one of seven independently owned Hotel Plaza Resorts located on Walt Disney World property near Disney Village Marketplace. Guests are provided with shuttle service to the major WDW attractions and offered special discounts at area shops and restaurants.

**AMBIENCE:** The resort's boxy exterior architecture belies the graceful interior of this high-rise hotel and its two low-rise garden wings. The decor is British Colonial, and the dark green carpets, soft peach walls, rattan furnishings, and understated chandeliers give the spacious lobby a clubby, comfortable feel. The Grosvenor features its own Sherlock Holmes Museum and is frequented by European travelers.

**RATES:** Standard rooms $$$. Rates vary with the season.

**AMENITIES:** Room service, refrigerator (unstocked), in-room safe, coffeemaker, hair dryer, robe, pay-per-view movies, VCR, videocassette rentals, video camcorder rentals, and valet parking.

**RESTAURANTS:** *Baskervilles Restaurant* — British-themed dining room serving buffet breakfast, a la carte lunch, and buffet dinner featuring all-you-can-eat prime rib.
*Crumpet's Cafe* — Lobby deli market for light snacks; open twenty-four hours daily.

**RECREATION:** Two pools, tennis, volleyball, basketball, handball, shuffleboard, croquet, jogging path, fitness center, whirlpool, and massage.

**HOTEL TRANSPORTATION:** Walk to Disney Village Marketplace and Pleasure Island. Shuttle bus to Epcot Center, Disney-MGM Studios, the Magic Kingdom, and Typhoon Lagoon. For transportation to other attractions, consult hotel Guest Services. Taxi service available.

**FEATURES:** In-room VCRs allow guests to relax in the afternoon with movies from the hotel's video library or their own videos taken during the day.

On Saturday nights, the Grosvenor presents MurderWatch Mystery Dinner Theatre, a very popular dinner show that involves guests in solving a murder mystery staged by professional actors. The drama occurs at Baskervilles Restaurant while you dine at a fairly good prime rib buffet.

**DRAWBACKS:** Guests relying on hotel buses to reach attractions may find them inconvenient.

**TIPS:** The garden-wing rooms have private balconies; tower rooms do not, but the higher floors offer sweeping views. The garden-wing rooms with a pool view (odd-numbered rooms) are the most popular.

The Grosvenor offers discounts to travel club members, including the American Automobile Association, the American Association of Retired Persons, Entertainment Publications, and Orlando Magicard.

The Grosvenor offers vacation packages that include room, meals, WDW admission, taxes, and tips. To receive a brochure, call (800 624-4109).

A rental car can save considerable commuting time from this location.

**MAKING RESERVATIONS:** First call Best Western Central Reservations (800 528-1234), then call the hotel directly and compare rates (800 624-4109). Inquire about promotional rates or corporate rates. Reservations may also be made through WDW Central Reservations Office (407 934-7639).

**XXX** ATMOSPHERE. **XXX** ATTITUDE. **XXX** QUALITY. **XXXX** TRUE VALUE.

**GROSVENOR RESORT**
**A BEST WESTERN HOTEL**
**1850 HOTEL PLAZA BOULEVARD, LAKE BUENA VISTA, FLORIDA 32830**
**TELEPHONE (407) 827-6500 • FAX (407) 827-6542**

# THE HILTON RESORT

**LOCATION:** The Hilton Resort is one of seven independently owned Hotel Plaza Resorts located on Walt Disney World property near Disney Village Marketplace. Guests are provided with shuttle service to the major WDW attractions and offered special discounts at area shops and restaurants.

**AMBIENCE:** This hotel, one of the largest in the Hotel Plaza area, is a sprawling medium high-rise with wings that angle off to each side of the central structure. The hotel is situated on several acres of open land, and has a duck pond and fountains in front. The angular lobby has a muted tropical decor, with brass-railed staircases, pink conch-shell wall sconces, and a fountain with long-legged birds made of sculptured metal. Saltwater fish swim in the large aquarium behind the long, rose-colored marble reception desk. The guest rooms are pleasantly decorated with peach and light yellow accents and sand-colored bedspreads. The hotel caters to business travelers and seminar attendees.

**RATES:** Standard rooms **$$$**. Tower concierge rooms **$$$$** (including Continental breakfast; all-day snacks, no-host cocktails, and appetizers; evening tea, coffee, and petits fours; and other amenities). Rates vary with the season.

**AMENITIES:** Room service, mini bar, voice mail, pay-per-view movies, and valet parking.

**RESTAURANTS:** *Finn's Grill* — Lunch and dinner featuring Florida-Caribbean-style seafood and steaks.
*Country Fair Restaurant* — Breakfast, lunch, and dinner buffet-style or a la carte, indoors or on the terrace.
*Benihana's* — Steak or seafood dinners grilled and served by Japanese teppan chefs at communal tables.

**RECREATION:** Two pools, jogging path, fitness center, and sauna.

**HOTEL TRANSPORTATION:** Walk to Disney Village Marketplace and Pleasure Island. Shuttle bus to Epcot Center, Disney-MGM Studios, the Magic Kingdom, and Typhoon Lagoon. For transportation to other attractions, consult hotel Guest Services. Taxi service available.

**FEATURES:** Hilton Honors members can earn points and upgrade rooms.

**DRAWBACKS:** Guests relying on hotel buses to reach attractions may find them inconvenient.

**TIPS:** Almost all rooms have nice views, but the most popular rooms are those with views of the pool or of Walt Disney World and the evening fireworks show at Pleasure Island.
   The Hilton offers vacation packages that include accommodations, daily breakfast, WDW admission, and other amenities. To receive a brochure, call the resort's toll-free number (800 782-4414).
   The Hilton offers discounts to members of the American Automobile Association.
   A rental car can save considerable commuting time from this location.

**MAKING RESERVATIONS:** First call Hilton Central Reservations (800 445-8667), then call the hotel directly and compare rates (800 782-4414). Inquire about promotional rates or corporate rates. Reservations may also be made through WDW Central Reservations Office (407 934-7639).

**XX** ATMOSPHERE. **X** ATTITUDE. **XX** QUALITY. **XX** TRUE VALUE.

THE HILTON RESORT
A HILTON HOTEL
1751 HOTEL PLAZA BOULEVARD, LAKE BUENA VISTA, FLORIDA 32830
TELEPHONE (407) 827-4000 • FAX (407) 827-6369

# HOTEL ROYAL PLAZA

**LOCATION:** Hotel Royal Plaza is one of seven independently owned Hotel Plaza Resorts located on Walt Disney World property near Disney Village Marketplace. Guests are provided with shuttle service to the major WDW attractions and offered special discounts at area shops and restaurants.

**AMBIENCE:** In late 1995, this hotel underwent an impressive multi-million dollar renovation to become a Holiday Inn Crowne Plaza resort. This high rise hotel, with its pagoda-style roof and garden wing, has been detailed in shades of rose and pure white. The lobby has a stylish Caribbean flair, and in the guest rooms, ceilings have been raised and the rooms enlarged. Rooms are tastefully furnished in pale pastels with brightly-printed bedspreads. All tower rooms and suites have small half-moon-shaped balconies, offering sweeping views of Walt Disney World. The ground-level garden wing rooms have been extended to provide private patios.

**RATES:** Standard room **$$**. Concierge rooms **$$$** (including private glass elevator for concierge guests, Continental breakfast, in-room Jacuzzi, evening cocktails, and special room and lounge amenities). Rates vary with the season.

**AMENITIES:** Room service, mini bar, in-room safe, hair dryer, coffeemaker, VCR, videocassette library, and video camcorder rentals.

**RESTAURANTS:** *The Plaza Diner* — Breakfast buffet, lunch, and dinner from 6:30 AM until midnight. *The Island Bar and Restaurant* — Dinner s prepared in an exhibition-style kitchen.

**RECREATION:** Pool, tennis, putting green, shuffleboard, jogging path, fitness center, sauna, and whirlpool.

**HOTEL TRANSPORTATION:** Walk to Disney Village Marketplace and Pleasure Island. Shuttle bus to Epcot Center, Disney-MGM Studios, the Magic Kingdom, and Typhoon Lagoon. For transportation to other attractions, consult hotel Guest Services. Taxi service available.

**FEATURES:** The hotel's Island Sports Bar offers wide-screen television sporting events and a Happy Hour. All tower rooms and suites have large, deep, corner style bathtubs.

**DRAWBACKS:** Guests relying on hotel buses to reach attractions may find them inconvenient.

**TIPS:** The most popular rooms are the higher floor tower rooms with a view of Walt Disney World and the evening fireworks show at Pleasure Island. Also popular are the ground-floor poolside garden rooms.

Hotel Royal Plaza honors many travel clubs, including the American Automobile Association, the American Association of Retired Persons, Entertainment Publications, and Orlando Magicard.

The Royal Plaza offers several vacation packages that include accommodations, daily breakfast, WDW admission, and other amenities. To receive a brochure, call the hotel directly (407 828-2828).

A rental car can save considerable commuting time from this location.

**MAKING RESERVATIONS:** Call the Hotel Royal Plaza toll-free number (800 248-7890) and inquire about special promotional rates or corporate rates. Reservations may also be made through the WDW Central Reservations Office (407 934-7639).

**XXX** ATMOSPHERE. **XX** ATTITUDE. **XXX** QUALITY. **XXX** TRUE VALUE.

HOTEL ROYAL PLAZA
A CROWNE PLAZA RESORT
1905 HOTEL PLAZA BOULEVARD, LAKE BUENA VISTA, FLORIDA 32830
TELEPHONE (407) 828-2828 • FAX (407) 827-3977

# SHADES OF GREEN

**LOCATION:** Shades of Green is one of six hotels in the Magic Kingdom Resorts Area. As an Armed Forces Recreational Center, its accommodations are available only to active and retired military personnel and their families; however, the restaurants and golf courses are open to all visitors. The resort is located adjacent to the Magnolia and Palm golf courses, in a quiet area a short drive from the Magic Kingdom.

**AMBIENCE:** This wood-shingled low-rise hotel is set apart from the rest of WDW. The long entrance road winds through the two golf courses that surround the hotel. The lobby is a comfortable ranch-style room with rock walls and windows overlooking the pool and golf courses. Guest rooms are spacious quasi suites with a country-inn atmosphere, pine furnishings, and light patterned details. All rooms feature balconies or patios with views of the pools, the golf courses, or the resort's lush landscaping. The resort is very low-key and could be located anywhere — although the unmistakable whistle of the Walt Disney World Railroad trains at the Magic Kingdom can be heard from the grounds.

**RATES:** Standard room **$**. Rates increase based on military rank.

**AMENITIES:** Room service, voice mail, and valet parking.

**RESTAURANTS:** *The Garden Gallery* — A la carte breakfast and a dinner buffet featuring varying cuisine themes that vary nightly.
*Evergreens Sports Bar* — Poolside restaurant serving light meals all day.
*Back Porch Lounge* — Serves lunch and caters to the golf crowd.

**RECREATION:** Two pools, tennis, nature walk, fitness center, two PGA golf courses, pro shop, putting greens, driving ranges, and golf clinics.

**HOTEL TRANSPORTATION:** Shuttle bus to the Transportation and Ticket Center (TTC) to catch monorails to the Magic Kingdom and Epcot Center or transfer to WDW buses for other destinations. Shuttle bus to Blizzard Beach and Disney-MGM Studios. Water launch from the Magic Kingdom to Discovery Island and Fort Wilderness & River Country. Taxi service available.

**FEATURES:** Discount ticket pricing is available to military personnel and their guests. Call Shades of Green Guest Services or the Attraction Ticket Sales Office (407 824-1403).
Guests interested in golf will find the top-rated PGA Magnolia and Palm golf courses here.

**DRAWBACKS:** Shades of Green shuttle buses to some attractions can be inconvenient and crowded.

**TIPS:** A rental car will come in handy for this out-of-the-way resort and can save considerable commuting time to Fort Wilderness & River Country, Disney Village Marketplace, and Pleasure Island.
Rooms No. 101 to 113 on the ground floor (or 301 to 313 on the top floor) surround the quiet pool and have sweeping fairway views.
When the hotel is fully booked, ask about overflow rooms. Military personnel are sometimes able to stay at other Disney-owned hotels for the same rates if there is availability.

**MAKING RESERVATIONS:** Military personnel can call Shades of Green Reservations (407 824-3600).

**XX** ATMOSPHERE. **XXX** ATTITUDE. **XXX** QUALITY. **XXXX** TRUE VALUE.

**SHADES OF GREEN
AN ARMED FORCES RECREATION CENTER
1950 WEST MAGNOLIA/PALM, LAKE BUENA VISTA, FLORIDA 32830
TELEPHONE (407) 824-3400 • FAX (407) 824-3460**

# TRAVELODGE HOTEL

**LOCATION:** Travelodge Hotel is one of seven independently owned Hotel Plaza Resorts located on Walt Disney World property near Disney Village Marketplace. Guests are provided with shuttle service to the major WDW attractions and offered special discounts at area shops and restaurants.

**AMBIENCE:** This single-tower high-rise hotel has pale salmon walls, bright blue balconies, and an entrance portico formed of large white disks supported on cement pillars. The interior theme of the hotel is vaguely Caribbean, with rattan furniture and green faux-marble pillars. In the center of the round lobby, a circular staircase leads up to the meeting rooms on the mezzanine level. The guest rooms are serene and pleasantly decorated, and all rooms have balconies. Most of the rooms, especially on the higher floors, have impressive views. The grounds are artfully landscaped with tropical foliage.

**RATES:** Standard rooms **$$**. Rates vary with the season.

**AMENITIES:** Room service, mini bar, in-room safe, hair dryer, coffeemaker, newspaper delivery, and pay-per-view movies.

**RESTAURANTS:** *Traders Restaurant* — Breakfast and dinner, a la carte or buffet, indoors or on the terrace. *Parakeet Cafe* — Lobby deli serving light meals all day.

**RECREATION:** Pool, jogging path.

**HOTEL TRANSPORTATION:** Walk to Disney Village Marketplace and Pleasure Island. Shuttle bus to Epcot Center, Disney-MGM Studios, the Magic Kingdom, and Typhoon Lagoon. For transportation to other attractions, consult hotel Guest Services. Taxi service available.

**FEATURES:** Toppers Nite Club on the eighteenth floor offers entertainment until 2 AM and has sweeping views of Walt Disney World and the evening fireworks shows at the World Showcase and Pleasure Island. The club is popular with Disney Cast Members.

Members of Travelodge Business Break Club and Classic Travel Club (for seniors) receive room and rental car discounts and additional amenities.

**DRAWBACKS:** Guests relying on hotel buses to reach attractions may find them inconvenient. Guests looking for the recreational features of a full-scale resort will be disappointed here.

**TIPS:** For the best room location, request a high floor with a Walt Disney World view.

Travelodge offers discounts to members of several travel clubs, including the American Automobile Association, Entertainment Publications, Encore, and the American Association of Retired Persons.

Travelodge offers a selection of vacation packages that include accommodations, WDW admission, some meals, and other amenities. To receive a brochure, call the hotel directly (800 348-3765).

A rental car can save considerable commuting time from this location.

**MAKING RESERVATIONS:** First call Travelodge Hotels central reservations (800 578-7878), then call the hotel directly and compare rates (800 348-3765). Inquire about promotional rates or corporate rates. Reservations may also be made through WDW Central Reservations Office (407 934-7639).

✗ ATMOSPHERE. ✗✗✗ ATTITUDE. ✗✗ QUALITY. ✗✗ TRUE VALUE.

**TRAVELODGE HOTEL**
**FORTE HOTELS, INC.**
**2000 HOTEL PLAZA BOULEVARD, LAKE BUENA VISTA, FLORIDA 32830**
**TELEPHONE (407) 828-2424 • FAX (407) 828-8933**

# THE VILLAS AT THE DISNEY INSTITUTE
## (FORMERLY DISNEY'S VILLAGE RESORT)

**LOCATION:** Once known as Disney's Village Resort, The Villas at the Disney Institute is one of four hotels in the Disney Village Resorts Area. Spread out across 250 acres of woodlands, waterways, and golf greens, the resort fronts Buena Vista Lagoon along with Disney Village Marketplace and Pleasure Island. Disney Institute is located here, a campus-style complex built along the waterfront. Disney Institute is a seminar center that offers unique educational vacation experiences. (See "Disney Institute," page 254.)

**AMBIENCE:** This resort resembles a large country club and encompasses the fairways of Lake Buena Vista Golf Course. The facility is very spread out, with four distinct resort areas and interconnecting roadways. The dark brown Fairway Villas and Grand Vista Suites are scattered along tree-lined lanes or perched at the edge of the golf course. The tall Treehouses are isolated in a forested area, and some overlook the bayoulike waterways. Disney Institute guests stay at the Townhouses, which are within walking distance of Disney Village Marketplace, or at the Club Suites, which circle a small lake. The rooms have been recently remodeled and floor plans vary, with an occasional skylight or loft.

**RATES:** Currently available to all visitors are the three-bedroom Treehouses **$$$$$**, the two-bedroom Fairway Villas **$$$$$**, and two- and three-bedroom Grand Vista Suites **$$$$$$** (all with fully equipped kitchens). Rates vary with the season. Guests attending Disney Institute can stay at the Club Suites or the one- and two-bedroom Townhouses (both with refrigerator, microwave, and coffeemaker). Accommodations are included; see "Disney Institute," page 254, for pricing and reservation information.

**AMENITIES:** Room service, refrigerator, microwave, coffeemaker, and voice mail.

**RESTAURANTS:** *Seasons* — Breakfast, lunch, and dinner are served in one of the four seasonally decorated areas, sometimes featuring the talents of visiting international chefs teaching at Disney Institute.

**RECREATION:** Five pools, nearby marina, bicycling, tennis, jogging path, nature walk, full-service spa and fitness center, PGA golf course, putting green, driving range, and pro shop.

**WDW PUBLIC TRANSPORTATION:** Walk, bus, water launch, or rent an electric cart to travel to Disney Village Marketplace and Pleasure Island. Bus to all theme parks, including the Magic Kingdom, Epcot Center, Disney-MGM Studios, Blizzard Beach, and Typhoon Lagoon. To reach other destinations, connect with destination buses at Disney Village Marketplace. Taxi service available.

**FEATURES:** Electric carts may be rented both for use within the resort and at Disney Village Marketplace.

**DRAWBACKS:** WDW buses to theme parks can be inconvenient from this location during peak seasons.

**TIPS:** The interesting circular Treehouse Villas are ideal for romantic getaways. Request a water view. The Grand Vista Suites are spaciously designed homes for large groups and longer stays.

Although WDW buses operate within the resort, a rental car is quite helpful from this location.

**MAKING RESERVATIONS:** Call WDW Central Reservations Office (407 934-7639). Inquire about special promotional rates and vacation packages. For Disney Institute packages, call 800 496-6337.

**XXX** ATMOSPHERE. **XXX** ATTITUDE. **XXX** QUALITY. **XXX** TRUE VALUE.

**THE VILLAS AT THE DISNEY INSTITUTE
A DISNEY-OWNED HOTEL
1901 BUENA VISTA DRIVE, LAKE BUENA VISTA, FLORIDA 32830
TELEPHONE (407) 827-1100 • FAX (407) 934-2741**

# WALT DISNEY WORLD DOLPHIN

**LOCATION:** The Dolphin is one of six hotels in the Epcot Resorts Area. It is located a short distance from the International Gateway to the World Showcase at Epcot Center. It faces Crescent Lake and shares a waterfront plaza and white sand beach with the Swan hotel.

**AMBIENCE:** Designed by architect Michael Graves, this strikingly colored postmodern high-rise hotel features a fanciful multistory fountain cascading into a giant clam shell. The lobby is a larger-than-life striped circus tent with a dolphin-motif fountain and islands of wicker seating. Guest rooms are entertainingly detailed with cabana-striped bedspreads and painted tropical headboards.

**RATES:** Standard rooms $$$$. Dolphin Towers concierge rooms $$$$$ (including Continental breakfast, no-host cocktails and appetizers, desserts, and special room amenities). Rates vary with the season.

**AMENITIES:** Twenty-four-hour room service, mini bar, in-room safe, hair dryer, coffeemaker, turndown service, newspaper delivery, voice mail, pay-per-view movies, and valet parking.

**RESTAURANTS:** *Juan & Only* — Dinner featuring Mexican cuisine.
*Sum Chows* — Elegant dinner with innovative Asian nouvelle cuisine.
*Harry's Safari Bar & Grille* — Sunday brunch, and dinner featuring grilled steaks and seafood in a Congo-adventure setting.
*Coral Cafe* — All-day dining and breakfast and dinner buffets.
*Tubbi's Buffeteria* — Twenty-four-hour cafeteria and convenience market.

**RECREATION:** Pool, grotto pool, small beach, marina, tennis, volleyball, jogging path, fitness center, sauna, steam room, whirlpool, fitness classes, fitness training, and massage.

**WDW PUBLIC TRANSPORTATION:** Walk or water launch to Disney-MGM Studios. Water launch or tram to the World Showcase at Epcot Center. Bus to the Magic Kingdom, Blizzard Beach, Pleasure Island, Disney Village Marketplace, and Typhoon Lagoon. To reach other destinations, bus to the Transportation and Ticket Center (TTC) and connect to destination buses. Taxi service available.

**FEATURES:** Members of the ITT Sheraton Club earn points and may upgrade rooms.
Conveniently located for guests primarily interested in Epcot Center and Disney-MGM Studios.
The Body By Jake Health Studio on premises is one of the best at Walt Disney World.

**DRAWBACKS:** WDW buses to the Magic Kingdom can be overcrowded during peak seasons.

**TIPS:** The Dolphin offers several vacation packages that include accommodations, WDW admission, some meals, car rental, and other amenities. To receive a brochure, call the hotel directly (800 227-1500).
The most popular room locations are those with a view of IllumiNations and the pool-view rooms. Only rooms with a balcony have windows that open.

**MAKING RESERVATIONS:** First call Sheraton central reservations (800 325-3535), then call the hotel directly and compare rates (800 227-1500). Inquire about special promotional rates or corporate rates. Reservations may also be made through WDW Central Reservations Office (407 934-7639).

**XXX** ATMOSPHERE. **XXX** ATTITUDE. **XXX** QUALITY. **XXX** TRUE VALUE.

**WALT DISNEY WORLD DOLPHIN**
**A SHERATON HOTEL**
**1500 EPCOT RESORTS BOULEVARD, LAKE BUENA VISTA, FLORIDA 32830**
**TELEPHONE (407) 934-4000 • FAX (407) 934-4099**

# WALT DISNEY WORLD SWAN

**LOCATION:** The Swan is one of six hotels in the Epcot Resorts Area. It is located a short distance from the International Gateway to the World Showcase at Epcot Center. It faces Crescent Lake and shares a waterfront plaza and white sand beach with the Dolphin hotel.

**AMBIENCE:** This contemporary high-rise hotel, designed by noted architect Michael Graves, is a standout example of entertainment architecture. The Swan's water-fantasy theme is expressed in soft shades of turquoise and coral, which extend to the guest rooms decorated with a pineapple motif. The large lobby is divided into smaller alcoves, giving an impression of privacy and sophistication. The Swan houses an extensive convention center and caters to business travelers and seminar attendees, rather than families.

**RATES:** Standard rooms **$$$$**. Royal Beach Club concierge rooms **$$$$$** (including Continental breakfast, evening cocktails, appetizers, and special room amenities). Rates vary with the season.

**AMENITIES:** Twenty-four-hour room service, mini bar, in-room safe, turndown service, bathrobes, newspaper delivery, voice mail, pay-per-view movies, and valet parking.

**RESTAURANTS:** *Palio* — Dinner with light entertainment in an Italian bistro.
*Garden Grove Cafe* — All-day dining with family-style breakfast and dinner, featuring Florida seafood.
*Kimonos* — Evening and late-night cocktails, sushi, and oriental hors d'oeuvre.
*Splash Grill & Deli* — Breakfast a la carte and buffet, and all-day light meals.

**RECREATION:** Lap pool, small beach, marina, tennis, jogging path, fitness center, whirlpool, sauna, and massage.

**WDW PUBLIC TRANSPORTATION:** Walk or water launch to Disney-MGM Studios. Water launch or tram to the World Showcase at Epcot Center. Bus to the Magic Kingdom, Blizzard Beach, Pleasure Island, Disney Village Marketplace, and Typhoon Lagoon. To reach other destinations, bus to the Transportation and Ticket Center (TTC) and connect to destination buses. Taxi service available.

**FEATURES:** The resort is conveniently located for guests who are primarily interested in Epcot Center and Disney-MGM Studios. An excellent tennis club is also on site.
Westin Premier members earn points and may upgrade rooms.

**DRAWBACKS:** WDW buses to the Magic Kingdom can be overcrowded during peak seasons.

**TIPS:** The Swan offers a selection of resort packages that include accommodations, WDW admission, some meals, and other amenities. Some packages include car rental. To receive a brochure, call the hotel directly (407 934-3000).
For the best room value, request a standard resort room with a balcony, facing the pool.

**MAKING RESERVATIONS:** First call Westin central reservations (800 228-3000), then call the hotel directly and compare rates (407 934-3000). Inquire about special promotional rates or corporate rates. Reservations may also be made through WDW Central Reservations Office (407 934-7639).

**XXX** ATMOSPHERE. **XXX** ATTITUDE. **XXXX** QUALITY. **XXX** TRUE VALUE.

**WALT DISNEY WORLD SWAN**
**A WESTIN HOTEL**
**1200 EPCOT RESORTS BOULEVARD, LAKE BUENA VISTA, FLORIDA 32830**
**TELEPHONE (407) 934-3000 • FAX (407) 934-4499**

# NEW HOTELS AT WDW

In keeping with Walt Disney World's unprecedented expansion, which will continue through 1999, a number of new resorts are in the final planning stages or currently under construction. Sometimes promotional rates are offered during the opening phase of a new resort, and reservations are taken up to six months before opening. If you would like to stay at one of these new resorts, check with WDW Central Reservations Office (407 934-7639).

**DISNEY'S BOARDWALK VILLAS:** Scheduled to open in July 1996 at Disney's BoardWalk in the Epcot Resorts Area, Disney's BoardWalk Villas feature studio units and cozy one-, two-, and three-bedroom "summer cottages," all with full kitchens or kitchenettes, VCRs, and in-room whirlpools. The new resort will share a lobby area with Disney's BoardWalk Inn, as well as a fitness center, tennis courts, child care center, and themed pool area. Disney's BoardWalk Villas are a Disney Vacation Club property and operate in the same way as other Disney Vacation Club facilities: About two thirds of the units will be available for time-share owners; the other third will welcome regular guests. The private Member's Attic lounge, which features a spectacular view of the fireworks shows at Epcot Center, will be set aside for Vacation Club members, who will also be able to enjoy special activities and events held at the hotel's Community Hall. Situated above and behind the shops on the west side of the BoardWalk Promenade, Disney's BoardWalk Villas has a romantic and intimate atmosphere, yet is close to many attractions.

**DISNEY'S CORONADO SPRINGS RESORT:** This new resort in the Disney-MGM Resorts Area is scheduled to open in 1997 as a moderately priced American Southwest–themed hotel and convention center. Ground was cleared and foundations were laid for the resort in late 1994, but construction was put on temporary hold while the first two All-Star resorts were being completed. The resort will feature a marina and white sand beach, four themed swimming pools, a health club, and a full-service restaurant. The convention center will have the largest ballroom of any hotel in the Southeast. Coronado Springs resort is located near Disney-MGM Studios; Blizzard Beach water park; Disney's International Sports Complex, opening in 1997; and Disney's Wild Animal Kingdom, planned for 1998.

**DISNEY'S WILDERNESS JUNCTION RESORT:** Wilderness Junction, scheduled to open in 1997, will be located at Disney's Fort Wilderness Resort and Campground, in the Magic Kingdom Resorts Area. The hotel is designed to look like a giant fantasy log cabin, with rooms and lobby areas that evoke a "rusticating in comfort" ambience similar to that found at Disney's Wilderness Lodge, but with budget-priced rooms.

**DISNEY'S ALL-STAR MOVIES RESORT:** This new resort planned for the Disney-MGM Resorts Area will be the third entertainment-themed All-Star resort. Like the other two resorts here, All-Star Movies will have nineteen-hundred rooms in five movie-themed buildings. A food court and two pools will also be part of this resort, which is projected to open in 1998.

**DISNEY'S MEDITERRANEAN RESORT:** This resort, long planned for the Magic Kingdom Resorts Area, will bring the sparkling warmth of the Greek isles to Walt Disney World. The huge premium-priced resort will have luxury rooms and suites, as well as a marina, a full range of recreational facilities, and a large meeting and convention facility. The resort site is on the shores of Seven Seas Lagoon, between Disney's Contemporary Resort and the Transportation and Ticket Center. A new monorail station is also planned, however, an opening date has not been announced. ◆

# OFF-SITE HOTELS

The are hundreds of hotels and resorts surrounding Walt Disney World, ranging from budget motels to deluxe resorts to vacation villas for families or groups. Visitors who choose to stay off site will find a wide range of options to meet their vacation needs. The hotels listed below offer exceptional value, resort-style amenities, and transportation to the theme parks (see "Walt Disney World Overview," page 10, for locations). They were selected based on the following criteria: size of accommodations (most are all-suites hotels), proximity to Walt Disney World (all are within a five-minute drive), and quality (standards that appeal to sophisticated travelers). Many of these hotels were suggested by readers, whose ratings were incorporated with those of the reviewers to indicate overall quality in relation to cost. The results are indicated as:

✗✗✗✗ – An excellent value overall. ✗✗✗ – Good quality; outstanding facilities. ✗✗ – Adequate and pleasant.

## Best Western Buena Vista Suites
### 14450 International Drive, Lake Buena Vista, FL 32830

Best Western Buena Vista Suites is an all-suites hotel in a new seven-story building with a central interior corridor. The suites are large, handsomely decorated, and feature a separate living room, VCR, coffeemaker, microwave, and refrigerator. Deluxe suites have a king-size bed and a large whirlpool bathtub. Hotel amenities include a complimentary full American buffet breakfast daily, evening room service, pool, whirlpool, exercise room, and transportation to the Magic Kingdom, Epcot Center, and Disney-MGM Studios. During busy times such as Spring Break, however, the clamor from the hallway can be heard in some of the suites.

**LOCATION:** Best Western Buena Vista Suites is located about 2.5 miles from the Epcot Center entrance to Walt Disney World.

**AVERAGE RATES:** Standard suite $$. Deluxe suite $$$. Rates vary with the season.

**OVERALL VALUE:** ✗✗

**TELEPHONE:** Hotel 407 239-8588. Hotel toll-free 800 537-7737. Central reservations 800 528-1234.

## Days Inn Lake Buena Vista Resort & Suites
### 12205 Apopka-Vineland Road, Orlando, FL 32836

The Days Inn Lake Buena Vista is a quartet of six-story buildings surrounding a central courtyard pool with tropical landscaping. This recently renovated budget-priced hotel offers moderate-sized suites complete with mini kitchen, sitting area, and separate bedroom. Simply furnished standard-sized rooms are also available. Resort amenities include an Olympic pool, room service, full-service restaurant, and transportation to the Magic Kingdom, Epcot Center, and Disney-MGM Studios. While lacking many of the amenities and recreational facilities of the more upscale resorts, the hotel is a good value for cost-conscious visitors.

**LOCATION:** Days Inn Lake Buena Vista is located one block from the Hotel Plaza and Disney Village entrance to Walt Disney World.

**AVERAGE RATES:** Standard room $. Suite $$. Rates vary with the season.

**OVERALL RATING:** ✗✗

**TELEPHONE:** Hotel 407 239-0444. Central reservations 800 329-7466.

## Embassy Grand Beach Vacation Resort at Lake Bryan
*8317 Lake Bryan Beach Boulevard, Orlando, FL 32821*

The new Embassy Grand Beach Vacation Resort offers some of the largest accommodations in the Walt Disney World area. This all-suites resort consists of several sparkling-white four-story buildings with red-shingled roofs and wide interior hallways. The buildings are located on the shore of a large lake, creating a beach resort atmosphere. All suites feature three bedrooms, three baths, a large kitchen and dining area, a large screened porch with exterior dining area, a VCR, a stereo system, and three televisions. Resort amenities include a pool, an exercise room, tennis, volleyball, and jet- and waterskiing. The resort is a time-share property that is being managed as a hotel over the next several years while the time-shares are sold. Visitors are *not* required to attend a sales presentation while staying at this resort.

**LOCATION:** Embassy Grand Beach Vacation Resort at Lake Bryan is located two miles from the Hotel Plaza and Disney Village entrance to Walt Disney World and 2.5 miles from the Epcot Center entrance.

**AVERAGE RATES:** Three-bedroom suite **$$$$**. Rates vary with the season.

**OVERALL VALUE: XXXX**

**TELEPHONE:** Hotel 407 238-2800. Hotel toll-free 800 341-4440.

## Embassy Suites Resort Lake Buena Vista
*8100 Lake Avenue, Orlando, FL 32836*

This all-suites hotel is a pastel-hued six-story building with an enclosed atrium. The comfortable and immaculate two-room suites feature a living room, microwave, refrigerator, coffeemaker, wet bar, and VCR. Resort amenities include a complimentary full buffet breakfast daily, complimentary cocktails and beverages in the evenings, indoor-outdoor pool, room service, exercise room, sauna, tennis, volleyball, fitness trail, shuffleboard, and transportation to the Magic Kingdom, Epcot Center, and Disney-MGM Studios. There is a child care center on the premises. The Embassy Suites Resort has been designed to provide exceptional accessibility, comfort, and safety for visitors with disabilities.

**LOCATION:** Embassy Suites Resort is located one mile from the Hotel Plaza and Disney Village entrance to Walt Disney World.

**AVERAGE RATES:** Suite **$$$**. Rates vary with the season.

**OVERALL RATING: XXX**

**TELEPHONE:** Hotel 407 239-1144. Hotel toll-free 800 257-8483. Central reservations 800 362-2779.

## Holiday Inn SunSpree Resort Lake Buena Vista
*13351 State Road 535, Lake Buena Vista, FL 32830*

Holiday Inn SunSpree Resort is a vivid pink exterior-corridor hotel. Three low-rise buildings enclose a tropically landscaped pool area. The rooms are spacious and feature a mini kitchen, refrigerator, microwave, wet bar, coffeemaker, and VCR. Hotel amenities include a fitness center, whirlpools, room service, full-service restaurant, and transportation to Magic Kingdom, Epcot Center, and Disney-MGM Studios. A fully licensed child care and activity center with a kids-only restaurant is open from 8 AM until midnight. This hotel is an exceptional value for families on vacation and single parents on business who are traveling with children. Since the hotel is a family-oriented resort, it is often filled with children.

**LOCATION:** Holiday Inn SunSpree Resort Lake Buena Vista is located less than one mile from the Hotel Plaza and Disney Village entrance to Walt Disney World.

**AVERAGE RATES:** Standard room $$. Rates vary with the season.

**OVERALL RATING:** ✗✗✗

**TELEPHONE:** Hotel 407 239-4500. Hotel toll-free 800 366-6299. Central reservations 800 465-4329.

## Homewood Suites
*3100 Parkway Boulevard, Kissimmee, FL 34746*

This inviting all-suites hotel consists of seven two- and three-story villa-style buildings, each set close to the main reception building. The suites include one-bedroom/one-bath, two-bedroom/one-bath, and two-bedroom/two-bath layouts. The suites offer plenty of sprawl space, with a separate living room and a fully equipped kitchen complete with dishwasher and full-size refrigerator. Hotel amenities include a complimentary Continental breakfast daily featuring muffins made on the premises; a pool, whirlpool, and fitness center; complimentary grocery shopping service; and transportation to the Magic Kingdom, Epcot Center, and Disney-MGM Studios.

**LOCATION:** Homewood Suites is located about two miles from the Magic Kingdom entrance to Walt Disney World.

**AVERAGE RATES:** One-bedroom suite $$. Two-bedroom suite $$$. Rates vary with the season.

**OVERALL VALUE:** ✗✗

**TELEPHONE:** Hotel 407 396-2229. Hotel toll-free 800 255-4543. Central reservations 800 225-5466.

## Howard Johnson Park Square Inn & Suites
*8501 Palm Parkway, Lake Buena Vista, FL 38330*

The Howard Johnson Park Square Inn & Suites is set in two 3-story buildings. The hotel features both moderate-sized suites and standard rooms. The suites include a separate sitting area, microwave, refrigerator, coffeemaker, and wet bar. Hotel amenities include two pools, a whirlpool, a full-service restaurant, and transportation to the Magic Kingdom, Epcot Center, and Disney-MGM Studios. This hotel is a family-oriented resort and is often filled with children.

**LOCATION:** The Howard Johnson Park Square Inn & Suites is located one block from the Hotel Plaza and Disney Village entrance to Walt Disney World.

**AVERAGE RATES:** Standard room $. Suite $$. Rates vary with the season.

**OVERALL VALUE:** ✗✗

**TELEPHONE:** Hotel 407 239-6900. Hotel toll-free 800 635-8684. Central reservations 800 654-2000.

OFF SITE HOTELS

## PREMIER DESTINATION RESORTS

*The Hyatt Regency Grand Cypress and Marriott's Orlando World Center are rated among the top destination resorts in the world. Both have full recreation facilities and are minutes away from Walt Disney World.*

## Hyatt Regency Grand Cypress
*One Grand Cypress Boulevard, Orlando, FL 32836*

The Hyatt Regency Grand Cypress is a dramatic eighteen-story atrium building situated on fifteen-hundred acres of forest and landscaped recreation areas. Even-numbered hotel rooms generally face Disney property and have views of the theme parks and fireworks; odd-numbered rooms overlook the forest and greenways. Standard guest rooms are very compact, yet pleasant, and each features a balcony, mini bar, and pay-per-view movies. This self-contained luxury resort has five full-service restaurants and twenty-four-hour room service. Recreational facilities include a huge, free-form grotto swimming pool; a full-service spa and health club; a day care center; and youth camps. At various locations on the resort's property, guests will find tennis and racquetball courts; an eighteen-hole PGA golf course; stables, corrals, and trails for horseback riding; and a lake with canoes, sailboats, and paddle boats. For an additional charge, the resort offers transportation to the Magic Kingdom, Epcot Center, Disney-MGM Studios, and other attraction destinations.

**LOCATION:** Hyatt Regency Grand Cypress is located less than one mile from the Hotel Plaza and Disney Village entrance to Walt Disney World.

**AVERAGE RATES:** Standard rooms $$$. Regency Club concierge rooms $$$$$ (including Continental breakfast, evening cocktails, health club membership, and other amenities). Rates vary with the season.

**OVERALL VALUE:** ✗✗✗✗

**TELEPHONE:** Hotel 407 239-1234. Central reservations 800 233-1234.

## Marriott's Orlando World Center
*World Center Drive, Orlando, FL 32821*

Marriott's Orlando World Center has over fifteen-hundred elegant rooms and suites in a twenty-seven-story central tower flanked by tiered wings. The hotel, situated on 205 landscaped acres, surrounds a tropical lagoon–themed pool complex. Rooms range in size from moderate to spacious and feature a balcony or patio, a mini bar, a coffeemaker, an in-room safe, and pay-per-view movies. Resort amenities include five full-service restaurants, twenty-four-hour room service, pools, whirlpools, health club, massage, child care center, volleyball, basketball, miniature golf, tennis, and eighteen-hole golf course. For an additional charge, the hotel offers transportation to Walt Disney World. The hotel is ideal for visitors who want to be near WDW, yet experience a resort vacation away from it all.

**LOCATION:** Marriott's Orlando World Center is located two miles from the Epcot Center entrance to Walt Disney World.

**AVERAGE RATES:** Standard room $$$. Rates vary with the season.

**OVERALL VALUE:** ✗✗✗✗

**TELEPHONE:** Hotel 407 239-4200. Hotel toll-free 800 621-0638. Central reservations 800 228-9290. ◆

# RESTAURANTS

Walt Disney World is one of the few places where guests can arrive at an elegant restaurant in tee-shirts, shorts, and tennis shoes and be treated like dignitaries; most theme park restaurants do not expect guests to return to their hotel rooms to change before dinner. The only exception to this casual dress code is at some of the better resort restaurants, where guests tend to dress up (see "Resort Dining," page 198).

## THEME PARK DINING

There are hundreds of restaurants, fast-food counters, and food vendors throughout the theme parks. The full-service theme park restaurants, however, have unique dining atmospheres and are designed to be an extension of the Walt Disney World experience. Some food may not be up to epicurean standards overall, and the prices tend to be higher than those at the resorts, but most visitors will enjoy memorable dining experiences. Alcohol is served in all theme park restaurants except those in the Magic Kingdom, and smoking is prohibited in full-service restaurants, except where noted in the restaurant reviews. Many restaurants offer low-fat selections, indicated by "Healthy-Choice Entrees" in the restaurant reviews. Vegetarians will find a selection of salads, vegetables, and pasta entrees on most menus. Kosher, vegan, or other special meals can be requested in advance through Disney Dining Reservations (407 939-3463).

**PRICES:** At the Walt Disney World restaurants, entrees average $8 to $17 for lunch and $15 to $25 for dinner. Each restaurant review includes the average price range for single entrees as follows:

$ – UNDER $7
$$ – $8 TO $14
$$$ – $15 TO $21
$$$$ – $22 TO $29
$$$$$ – $30 TO $39
$$$$$$ – $40 AND OVER

**RESTAURANT RESERVATIONS:** Most full-service restaurants at the theme parks accept reservations and are usually booked early, especially during peak seasons. All Walt Disney World visitors can make restaurant reservations up to sixty days in advance by calling Disney Dining Reservations (407 939-3463), open from 7 AM until 10 PM Monday through Friday and from 7 AM until 8 PM on Saturday and Sunday (EST). WDW resort guests can also make reservations through Guest Services at their resort. Guest Services can usually put you on a waiting list or find an alternative, if the restaurant is booked.

**SAME-DAY RESERVATIONS BY TELEPHONE:** All Walt Disney World visitors can make restaurant reservations on the day they are touring by calling Same Day Reservations after 10 AM (939-3463).

**SAME-DAY RESERVATIONS — EPCOT CENTER:** When the park opens, head quickly to the WorldKey Information Service at Innoventions East to make your reservations. If you are entering through the International Gateway, use the WorldKey Information Service kiosk at the Germany pavilion.

**SAME-DAY RESERVATIONS— DISNEY-MGM STUDIOS:** When the park opens, make your reservations at Hollywood Junction, located at the intersection of Hollywood and Sunset Boulevards.

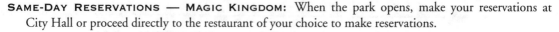

WALT DISNEY WORLD DINING

**SAME-DAY RESERVATIONS — MAGIC KINGDOM:** When the park opens, make your reservations at City Hall or proceed directly to the restaurant of your choice to make reservations.

**IF THE RESTAURANT IS ALREADY BOOKED:** Make backup reservations, then proceed to the restaurant of your choice and ask the host or hostess if seatings are available (some restaurants hold tables for walk-ins), or ask if you may put your name on a waiting list in the event of no-shows or a cancellation.

## GUIDE TO LOCATIONS OF WALT DISNEY WORLD'S FULL-SERVICE RESTAURANTS

*The guide below lists full-service restaurants (and dinner shows) both by location and by the type of cuisine served. Restaurants highlighted with ★ provide atmospheres that are ideal for adult relaxation.*

### WORLD SHOWCASE AT EPCOT

AU PETIT CAFÉ
BIERGARTEN
BISTRO DE PARIS ★
CHEFS DE FRANCE ★
LE CELLIER ★
L'ORIGINALE ALFREDO DI ROMA RISTORANTE ★
NINE DRAGONS RESTAURANT ★
RESTAURANT AKERSHUS
RESTAURANT MARRAKESH ★
ROSE & CROWN DINING ROOM ★
SAN ANGEL INN RESTAURANTE ★
TEMPURA KIKU
TEPPANYAKI DINING

### FUTURE WORLD AT EPCOT

CORAL REEF RESTAURANT ★
THE GARDEN GRILL RESTAURANT ★

### DISNEY-MGM STUDIOS

50's PRIME TIME CAFE
THE HOLLYWOOD BROWN DERBY ★
HOLLYWOOD & VINE CAFETERIA
MAMA MELROSE'S RISTORANTE ITALIANO
SCI-FI DINE-IN THEATER RESTAURANT

### MAGIC KINGDOM

THE CRYSTAL PALACE
KING STEFAN'S BANQUET HALL ★
LIBERTY TREE TAVERN
THE PLAZA RESTAURANT
TONY'S TOWN SQUARE RESTAURANT

### DISNEY VILLAGE MARKETPLACE

EMPRESS LILLY RIVERBOAT ★
CAP'N JACK'S OYSTER BAR ★
CHEF MICKEY'S VILLAGE RESTAURANT

### PLEASURE ISLAND

EMPRESS LILLY RIVERBOAT ★
THE FIREWORKS FACTORY
HOUSE OF BLUES
PORTOBELLO YACHT CLUB ★
PLANET HOLLYWOOD

### FORT WILDERNESS

CROCKETT'S TAVERN
HOOP-DEE-DOO MUSICAL REVUE
TRAIL'S END BUFFETERIA

### WDW RESORT RESTAURANTS

ARIEL'S ★
ARTIST POINT ★
ARTHUR'S 27 ★
BASKERVILLES ★
BOATWRIGHT'S DINING HALL
BONFAMILLE'S CAFE
CALIFORNIA GRILL ★
CAPE MAY CAFE
CONCOURSE STEAKHOUSE
FINN'S GRILL
FLAGLER'S ★
GRAND FLORIDIAN CAFE
HARRY'S SAFARI BAR & GRILLE ★
JUAN & ONLY'S
NARCOOSSEE'S ★
'OHANA
OLIVIA'S
THE OUTBACK ★
PALIO ★
POLYNESIAN LUAU
SEASONS ★
SUM CHOWS ★
VICTORIA & ALBERT'S ★
WHISPERING CANYON CAFE
YACHTSMAN STEAKHOUSE ★

WALT DISNEY WORLD DINING

## GUIDE TO CUISINE AT FULL-SERVICE RESTAURANTS

### AMERICAN

BASKERVILLES ★
CHEF MICKEY'S VILLAGE RESTAURANT
CROCKETT'S TAVERN
THE CRYSTAL PALACE
50'S PRIME TIME CAFE
THE FIREWORKS FACTORY
THE GARDEN GRILL RESTAURANT ★
GRAND FLORIDIAN CAFE
THE HOLLYWOOD BROWN DERBY ★
HOLLYWOOD & VINE CAFETERIA
HOOP-DEE-DOO MUSICAL REVUE
KING STEFAN'S BANQUET HALL ★
LIBERTY TREE TAVERN
PLANET HOLLYWOOD
THE PLAZA RESTAURANT
SCI-FI DINE-IN THEATER RESTAURANT
TRAIL'S END BUFFETERIA

### NEW AMERICAN CUISINE

ARTIST POINT ★
CALIFORNIA GRILL ★
PLANET HOLLYWOOD
SEASONS ★

### CONTINENTAL

ARTHUR'S 27 ★
VICTORIA & ALBERT'S ★

### SEAFOOD

ARIEL'S ★
ARTIST POINT ★
CALIFORNIA GRILL ★
CAPE MAY CAFE
CAP'N JACK'S OYSTER BAR ★
CORAL REEF RESTAURANT ★
EMPRESS LILY RIVERBOAT ★
FINN'S GRILL
HARRY'S SAFARI BAR & GRILLE ★
NARCOOSSEE'S ★
THE OUTBACK ★

### STEAK & PRIME RIB

BASKERVILLES ★
CONCOURSE STEAKHOUSE
CROCKETT'S TAVERN
HARRY'S SAFARI BAR & GRILLE ★
NARCOOSSEE'S ★
THE OUTBACK ★
YACHTSMAN STEAKHOUSE ★

### BARBECUE, CAJUN & CREOLE

BOATWRIGHT'S DINING HALL
BONFAMILLE'S CAFE
THE FIREWORKS FACTORY
HOUSE OF BLUES
WHISPERING CANYON CAFE

### MEXICAN

JUAN & ONLY'S
SAN ANGEL INN RESTAURANTE ★

### ITALIAN

FLAGLER'S ★
L'ORIGINALE ALFREDO DI ROMA RISTORANTE ★
MAMA MELROSE'S RISTORANTE ITALIANO
PALIO ★
PORTOBELLO YACHT CLUB ★
TONY'S TOWN SQUARE RESTAURANT

### FRENCH

AU PETIT CAFÉ
BISTRO DE PARIS ★
CHEFS DE FRANCE ★

### ASIAN & POLYNESIAN

NINE DRAGONS RESTAURANT (CHINESE) ★
'OHANA (POLYNESIAN)
POLYNESIAN LUAU (ASIAN/POLYNESIAN)
SUM CHOWS (ASIAN) ★
TEMPURA KIKU (JAPANESE)
TEPPANYAKI DINING (JAPANESE)

### INTERNATIONAL

BIERGARTEN (GERMAN)
LE CELLIER (CANADIAN) ★
RESTAURANT AKERSHUS (NORWEGIAN)
RESTAURANT MARRAKESH (MOROCCAN) ★
ROSE & CROWN DINING ROOM (BRITISH) ★

### CAFETERIAS & BUFFETS

BASKERVILLES ★
BIERGARTEN
CAPE MAY CAFE
LE CELLIER ★
THE CRYSTAL PALACE
HOLLYWOOD & VINE CAFETERIA
RESTAURANT AKERSHUS
TRAIL'S END BUFFETERIA
◆

# AU PETIT CAFÉ

**FOOD:** Au Petit Café serves light French-style a la carte dishes, including crepes, quiches, sandwiches served on croissants and French baguettes, and soups and salads.

**LOCATION:** Au Petit Café is an outdoor restaurant located at the Chefs de France building in front of the France pavilion in the World Showcase at Epcot Center. Look for the brick-red awning, under which diners are seated facing the promenade and the World Showcase Lagoon.

**DINING HOURS:** Open all day from 11:30 AM until park closing.

**AMBIENCE:** Guests enjoy outdoor dining Parisian style while sitting at small tables in this sidewalk cafe. White marble tables surrounded by delicate black iron chairs are situated under an open-sided awning supported by green pillars. Servers wear black bolero-style jackets and are wonderfully attentive. This cafe is an excellent spot from which to watch passersby and to view the FriendShip water launches plying the waters of the World Showcase Lagoon.

**SAMPLE ENTREES:** *Le Tartare de Saumon Légèrement Fumé aux Concombres Croquants Sauce Douce aux Herbes* (fresh and smoked salmon chopped and garnished with cucumbers, served with herb sauce and brioche); *La Salade de Blanc de Volaille aux Légumes Frais Sauce Curry* (sliced breast of chicken on bed of greens, with Gruyère cheese, fresh vegetables, and a light curry sauce, served chilled); *La Crêpe de Jambon Savoyarde* (a crepe filled with mushrooms and ham with a Gruyère cheese sauce).

**HEALTHY-CHOICE ENTREES:** *La Salade Niçoise* (mixed green salad arranged with white tuna, tomato, cucumber, potatoes, celery, and black olives, served with vinaigrette and tapenade); *L'Assiette Végétarienne* (vegetable plate).

**LUNCH:** The menu is the same for lunch and dinner.

**BEVERAGES:** French beer and wines are served, as are spirits. Soft drinks, mineral water, and café express, a hearty espressolike coffee, are offered. *Café Grand Marnier,* the restaurant's specialty drink, is made with café express, Grand Marnier liqueur, and whipped cream.

**AVERAGE PRICE RANGE:** Entrees $$.

**FEATURES:** One of the most popular dishes among frequent diners is *Le Sandwich de Saumon.*

The cafe dishes offered here were created by the celebrated chefs responsible for designing the menu at the Chefs de France restaurant. The desserts are fine examples of the art of Gaston Lenôtre, who is considered to be France's premier pastry and dessert chef.

On a beautiful day, outdoor dining along the World Showcase promenade can be an extraordinarily pleasant experience, especially during low-attendance times.

**DRAWBACKS:** Because of its outdoor location, Au Petit Café is not the best dining atmosphere on very hot or cold days, despite the view.

Since no reservations are taken, there can be a lengthy wait, especially during peak dining hours.

**RESERVATIONS:** No reservations are accepted; diners are seated on a first-come, first-served basis. Because the restaurant seating is outdoors, smoking is permitted.

### REVIEWERS' RATINGS

**XXXX** – As good as it gets. **XXX** – Better than most. **XX** – Adequate. **X** – Of limited appeal.

**XXX** FOOD *(Well-executed dishes and a good value for light eaters.)*

**XXX** SERVICE *(Friendly, helpful, and efficient.)*

**XXX** AMBIENCE *(Very pleasant outdoor dining, depending on the weather and the wait.)*

# BIERGARTEN

**FOOD:** The Biergarten serves a buffet of traditional German cuisine, including roasted meats, sauerbraten (a marinated beef dish), and German sausages (weisswurst, bratwurst, and knockwurst), along with red cabbage and potato salad.

**LOCATION:** The entrance to the restaurant is tucked in the back of the Germany pavilion in the World Showcase at Epcot Center. Guests can reach it by strolling through the *platz*, past St. George's fountain.

**DINING HOURS:** 11:30 AM for lunch, 4 PM for dinner.

**AMBIENCE:** The Biergarten is a spacious dining room fashioned after the famous beer halls of Munich. Ornate street lamps, balconies overflowing with geraniums, and water cascading from an old mill lend an outdoor air to the restaurant, creating an instant German vacation for guests. Bavarian-costumed servers carrying giant steins of beer add to the festivities. On the stage at the front of the hall, performances of German music, folk dancing, singing, and yodeling are featured throughout the day. The robust atmosphere of the Biergarten captures the essence of Oktoberfest, one of Germany's traditional celebrations.

**SAMPLE DINNER ENTREES:** Hot Selections — *Sauerbraten* (marinated beef), *Bratwurst* (pork sausage), *Knockwurst and Weisswurst* (sausages), *Kasseler* (smoked pork loin), *Wein Kraut* (wine kraut), *Spätzle* (noodles).

Cold Selections — *Rotkohl* (red cabbage), *Heringsalat* (herring and apple salad), *Kartoffelsalat* (potato salad), and a selection of cheese and bread.

**HEALTHY-CHOICE ENTREES:** Hot Selections — *Huhn* (roasted chicken), *Kartoffel* (roasted potatoes). Cold Selections — *Apfelmus* (applesauce), *Gurkensallat* (marinated cucumbers and onion).

**LUNCH:** Lunch and dinner menus are very similar, although prices are lower at lunch than at dinner.

**BEVERAGES:** A selection of fine wines from Germany is offered, along with Beck's beer on tap, served in thirty-three-ounce steins. Spirits, including German liqueurs such as Jägermeister and Kirschwasser, are available, as are soft drinks, coffee, and tea.

**AVERAGE PRICE RANGE:** Lunch buffet **$$**, dinner buffet **$$$**.

**FEATURES:** Buffet-style service at the Biergarten provides additional options for vegetarians.

Diners can enjoy a lively stage show of German music and dance at various times throughout the day. Check the entertainment schedule for show times.

For singles and those traveling solo, the Biergarten is a great place to meet fellow diners.

**DRAWBACKS:** Guests are seated communally at tables for eight or more, so an intimate conversation will have little privacy when the restaurant is busy. The large dining hall, when it is full, can be very noisy.

**RESERVATIONS:** All Walt Disney World visitors can make reservations up to sixty days in advance by calling Disney Dining Reservations (407 939-3463). Same-day reservations can be made through WorldKey Information Service at Epcot Center, at the restaurant itself, or by calling Same Day Reservations after 10 AM (939-3463).

### REVIEWERS' RATINGS

**✗✗✗✗** – As good as it gets. **✗✗✗** – Better than most. **✗✗** – Adequate. **✗** – Of limited appeal.

**✗** FOOD *(The German dishes are generally meat oriented, mostly sausage and kraut.)*

**✗✗** SERVICE *(Buffet style. Servers bring water and other beverages.)*

**✗✗✗** AMBIENCE *(A beautifully designed atmosphere, but the dining experience can be loud.)*

# BISTRO DE PARIS

**FOOD:** Bistro de Paris features French haute cuisine, including appetizers such as pâté de foie gras and smoked salmon, and entrees consisting of seafood, meats, and vegetables served with a variety of unique light sauces. Despite its name, which suggests casual food, Bistro de Paris is the most upscale of the restaurants in the France pavilion, with more refined selections than Chefs de France, downstairs.

**LOCATION:** The restaurant is located on the second floor of the Chefs de France building in the World Showcase at Epcot Center. Guests can find the restaurant by walking down the cobblestone street of the pavilion. The entrance is at the rear of the Chefs de France building.

**DINING HOURS:** 5:30 PM for dinner. The restaurant opens for lunch seasonally at noon, during peak-attendance times at the park.

**AMBIENCE:** Guests ascend a dramatic spiraling stairway to the restaurant. Hanging brass and milk glass chandeliers fill the dining room with soft, romantic light. Mirrors and artwork in ornate gold frames adorn the walls, giving the place a Parisian turn-of-the-century atmosphere. The bistro motif is reflected in the seating arrangements, with long banquettes and red upholstered chairs.

**SAMPLE DINNER ENTREES:** *La Bouillabaisse Marseillaise avec sa Rouille et ses Croûtons* (seafood casserole from the South of France, served with garlic sauce and croutons); *Le Suprême de Canard aux Griottes, Sauce Bigarade* (sautéed breast of duck garnished with French Griotte cherries and a red wine sauce); *Le Carré d'Agneau pour Deux à la Sariette en Persillade sur son Tian de Légumes Provençal* (rack of lamb for two, roasted and flavored with herb butter and served with vegetables).

**HEALTHY-CHOICE ENTREES:** *L'Espadon Grillé, Sauce Choron* (grilled swordfish with a tomato-béarnaise sauce and fresh vegetables). A vegetable plate is available on request.

**LUNCH:** Lunch is served seasonally, during peak attendance times. Lunch entrees are lighter, and prices are considerably lower than at dinner.

**BEVERAGES:** French wine and beer, as well as spirits, are served. Soft drinks, mineral water, tea, coffee, and café express are also available. The restaurant's popular after-dinner drink, *Café Grand Marnier,* is made with café express, Grand Marnier, and whipped cream.

**AVERAGE PRICE RANGE:** Lunch entrees $$, dinner entrees $$$$.

**FEATURES:** Three of France's premier *cuisiniers*, Paul Bocuse, Roger Vergé, and Gaston Lenôtre, created the dishes for Bistro de Paris.

With its intimate lighting and decor, the award-winning Bistro de Paris is especially romantic.

**DRAWBACKS:** Although very expensive, Bistro de Paris is one of the most popular of the World Showcase restaurants, and because it is very small, same-day reservations are difficult to secure.

**RESERVATIONS:** All Walt Disney World visitors can make reservations up to seven days in advance by calling Disney Dining Reservations (407 939-3463). Same-day reservations can be made through WorldKey Information Service at Epcot Center, at the restaurant itself, or by calling Same Day Reservations after 10 AM (939-3463).

### REVIEWERS' RATINGS

**XXXX** – As good as it gets.  **XXX** – Better than most.  **XX** – Adequate.  **X** – Of limited appeal.

**XXXX** FOOD *(Very good food beautifully presented — a fairly good overall value.)*
**XXXX** SERVICE *(Friendly and professional; more relaxed than Chefs de France, downstairs.)*
**XXXX** AMBIENCE *(Elegant, pretty, and very French.)*

# CAP'N JACK'S OYSTER BAR

**FOOD:** Cap'n Jack's serves an assortment of fresh seafood, including shrimp, oysters, crabmeat, clams, and scallops. The seafood is served fresh on the half shell, in salads, or cooked into crab cakes, seafood soups, and pasta dishes.

**LOCATION:** The restaurant is located at the end of a pier in the center of Disney Village Marketplace. It sits on Buena Vista Lagoon, and guests can reach it by walking along the waterfront.

**DINING HOURS:** Open all day from 11:30 AM.

**AMBIENCE:** The galley-style entrance at Cap'n Jack's has a glass-fronted display of the day's fresh seafood. The restaurant has two dining areas, one to the left of the galley and another surrounding the large hexagonal copper-topped bar in the middle of the restaurant. Both dining rooms are small, but offer delightful views of Buena Vista Lagoon and the *Empress Lilly* riverboat. A boathouse atmosphere has been achieved with plank-wood flooring, thickly varnished wooden tables, and leather-slung chairs.

**SAMPLE ENTREES:** *Jack's Shrimp Ziti* (baby shrimp and ziti tossed with garlic butter and topped with Parmesan cheese, served with garlic bread); *Zesty Crab Cakes* (crabmeat patties seasoned with onions and herbs, served with coleslaw and garlic bread); *Some Like It Cold* (oysters and clams on the half shell, peel-and-eat shrimp, and marinated scallops); *Some Like It Hot* (a cup of chowder, crab cakes, and smoked fish with garlic bread).

**HEALTHY-CHOICE ENTREES:** *Cap'n Sampler* (a salad plate of smoked fish, marinated scallops, and shrimp on assorted greens, served with house dressing and cocktail sauce).

**LUNCH:** The menu is the same for lunch and dinner.

**BEVERAGES:** Cold beer is served in Mason jars with handles. Wine and spirits are also offered, as are coffee, tea, and soft drinks. The restaurant is known for its fresh *Strawberry Margarita,* served in a large frosted glass.

**AVERAGE PRICE RANGE:** Entrees **$$**.

**FEATURES:** Cap'n Jack's is a casual, lively restaurant, with a friendly atmosphere. The circular bar is a great place to meet fellow vacationers while waiting for a table. Guests can also enjoy drinks and seafood delicacies at the bar.

The favorite entrees among regulars are the *Zesty Crab Cakes* and *Jack's Shrimp Ziti.*

If you are visiting at the right time of year, be sure to order stone crab from the Florida coast, which is wonderful and very hard to find.

The desserts at Cap'n Jack's, especially the *Key Lime Pie* and *Something Chocolate* (chocolate on chocolate cake), are superior.

**DRAWBACKS:** It is unclear from the signs in front of the restaurant how guests are seated. Guests must wait in line at the podium. If you just want to sit at the bar for a snack or beverage, bypass the line.

There can be a long wait for a table during peak dining times.

**RESERVATIONS:** No reservations are accepted; diners are seated on a first-come, first-served basis.

### REVIEWERS' RATINGS

**XXXX** – As good as it gets. **XXX** – Better than most. **XX** – Adequate. **X** – Of limited appeal.

**XXX** FOOD *(Good seafood at reasonable prices.)*

**XX** SERVICE *(Service is efficient, although servers can be indifferent at times.)*

**XXX** AMBIENCE *(Beautiful views and casual atmosphere, but it can get busy and loud.)*

# CHEF MICKEY'S VILLAGE RESTAURANT

**FOOD:** Chef Mickey's Village Restaurant serves up satisfying country-style cuisine. Breakfast entrees include eggs Benedict and corned beef hash. Lunch and dinner menus feature beef, chicken, seafood, and pasta as well as sandwiches and hamburgers.

**LOCATION:** The restaurant is currently located at the far end of Disney Village Marketplace, adjacent to Disney's Village Resort. (Chef Mickey's may be replaced soon by the Rainforest Cafe.)

**DINING HOURS:** Open all day from 9 AM. Lunch is served at 11:30 AM, dinner at 5:30 PM.

**AMBIENCE:** Chef Mickey's Village Restaurant is a two-tiered, light-filled modern dining room containing many flourishing plants and two immense ficus trees. The walls are covered with pictures of Mickey's friends, and Chef Mickey himself puts in an appearance at dinner time. The peaked ceilings and skylights allow sunshine to pour in, and the tall, slender windows provide a great view of Buena Vista Lagoon and the *Empress Lilly* riverboat. Servers wear white chef's jackets with Mickey Mouse bandanas.

**SAMPLE DINNER ENTREES:** *Smoked Baby Back Ribs* (barbecued ribs served with coleslaw, corn on the cob, and corn bread); *Steak Oscar* (twin broiled fillets topped with crabmeat, asparagus tips, béarnaise sauce, then glazed, and served with rice pilaf); *Chicken & Scampi Combo* (boneless chicken with Gulf shrimp, sautéed in garlic butter with herbs, served over rice pilaf); *Seafood Pasta Primavera* (pasta in a cream sauce, tossed with sea scallops and fresh vegetables); *Broiled Pork Chops* (with smothered red cabbage, mashed potatoes, and apple-flavored gravy).

**HEALTHY CHOICE ENTREES:** *Chicken Mediterranean* (boneless chunks of chicken stewed with tomatoes, onions, green peppers, and olives, served over rice pilaf); *Salmon Lasagna* (served with a spinach and pine nut sauce and fresh vegetables); *Captain's Catch* (selection of fresh seafood daily).

**BREAKFAST AND LUNCH:** Breakfasts feature egg dishes, waffles, and *Suns-Up* (a blend of fruit, fruit juice, and yogurt served as a breakfast drink). Lunch and dinner menus are similar, although the popular *Fajita Sizzler* (choice of beef or chicken with grilled peppers and onions, served with Cheddar cheese, guacamole, diced tomatoes, sour cream, and flour tortillas) is available only at lunch. Lunch prices are somewhat lower.

**BEVERAGES:** Wine, beer, and spirits are served, as are coffee, tea, and soft drinks. Specialty drinks include *Outrageous Fortune,* a combination of gin, peach schnapps, grenadine, and ginger ale.

**AVERAGE PRICE RANGE:** Breakfast entrees $, lunch entrees $$, dinner entrees $$$.

**FEATURES:** Guests waiting to dine can enjoy a before-dinner beverage and wide-screen TVs at the Village Lounge, adjoining Chef Mickey's Village Restaurant.

**DRAWBACKS:** Chef Mickey's presence every evening makes this restaurant a very popular place for families. Dinners can get quite noisy. Expect lots of kids.

**RESERVATIONS:** All Walt Disney World visitors can make reservations up to sixty days in advance by calling Disney Dining Reservations (407 939-3463). Same-day reservations can be made at the restaurant itself or by calling Same Day Reservations after 10 AM (939-3463).

**REVIEWERS' RATINGS**

**XXXX** – As good as it gets. **XXX** – Better than most. **XX** – Adequate. **X** – Of limited appeal.

**XXX** FOOD *(Classic American dishes; a favorite among frequent visitors.)*

**XXX** SERVICE *(Patient with kids; sometimes slow, sometimes frenzied, generally helpful.)*

**XX** AMBIENCE *(Homey, but crowded. Don't come here if you're avoiding Mickey.)*

# CHEFS DE FRANCE

**FOOD:** Chefs de France features French nouvelle cuisine: seafood, meat, poultry, and vegetable dishes accompanied by distinctive sauces created by three of France's premier chefs. One or two of the beautifully prepared appetizers and a salad, ordered together, can serve as a meal.

**LOCATION:** The mansard-roofed building housing Chefs de France stands on the corner at the entrance to the France pavilion in the World Showcase at Epcot Center. Diners pass under a brick-red awning across from the fountain to enter this restaurant.

**DINING HOURS:** 11:30 AM for lunch, 4:30 PM for dinner.

**AMBIENCE:** In this restaurant, accented with white linen tablecloths and fresh flowers on each table, guests can choose to dine in the formal dining room with its etched-glass partitions, wood-beamed ceilings, traditional patterned carpeting, and gilt-framed mirrors, or on the black and white tiled veranda, which is hung with pots of flowers and has tall arched windows overlooking the pavilion streets.

**SAMPLE DINNER ENTREES:** *Le vol au vent de rouget frais, les coquilles St-Jacques* (fillet of red snapper and fresh spinach baked in pastry, with sautéed scallops and crab dumplings with lobster cream sauce); *Le demi canard, sauce au chaud parfum et son gâteau de pomme de terre douce* (a half duck braised in red wine, served with cranberry and sweet potato mousse); *Le filet de boeuf mathurini* (tenderloin of beef sautéed with raisins in a brandy sauce); *Le saumon à l'oseille* (broiled fresh salmon with sorrel cream sauce, served with fresh vegetables); *Le soufflé léger saumon avec sauce homard à la façon de Gaston Lenôtre* (salmon soufflé served with lobster sauce) .

**HEALTHY-CHOICE ENTREES:** *L'assiette végétarienne* (vegetable plate).

**LUNCH:** Entree selections differ slightly at lunch, and prices are lower than at dinner.

**BEVERAGES:** French wine and beer are served, as are spirits, soft drinks, and mineral water. Thick and strong café express, very similar to espresso, is also offered. The comprehensive wine list includes vintages specially selected by the chefs who created the menu.

**AVERAGE PRICE RANGE:** Lunch entrees **$$**, dinner entrees **$$$**.

**FEATURES:** Three of France's premier *cuisiniers*, Paul Bocuse, Roger Vergé, and Gaston Lenôtre, created the dishes for Chefs de France.

A magnificent array of not-to-be-missed, reasonably priced desserts is offered.

The escargots with parsley and butter is a favorite appetizer among frequent diners here.

**DRAWBACKS:** Because this is one of the most popular restaurants at Epcot Center, it is difficult to get same-day reservations.

Tables are placed very close together, so be prepared to overhear conversations.

**RESERVATIONS:** All Walt Disney World visitors can make reservations up to sixty days in advance by calling Disney Dining Reservations (407 939-3463). Same-day reservations can be made through WorldKey Information Service at Epcot Center, at the restaurant itself, or by calling Same Day Reservations after 10 AM (939-3463).

### REVIEWERS' RATINGS
**XXXXX** – As good as it gets. **XXX** – Better than most. **XX** – Adequate. **X** – Of limited appeal.

**XXX** FOOD *(Fine cuisine incorporating fresh local ingredients. A very good food value.)*
**XXX** SERVICE *(Bustling and matter-of-fact, but efficient and ultimately professional.)*
**XXX** AMBIENCE *(Light, bright, and busy rather than romantic.)*

# CORAL REEF RESTAURANT

**FOOD:** The Coral Reef Restaurant serves an extensive array of seafood that is smoked, sautéed, or grilled. New American–style cuisine featuring chicken, beef, and pasta is also available.

**LOCATION:** The Coral Reef Restaurant is located in the Living Seas pavilion in Future World at Epcot Center. The restaurant has its own entrance at the side of the pavilion, where blue waves painted on the wall lead guests inside.

**DINING HOURS:** 11:30 AM for lunch, 4:30 PM for dinner.

**AMBIENCE:** The multitiered restaurant is adjacent to one of the largest saltwater aquariums in the world, holding more than 5.7 million gallons of sea water and nearly eight thousand underwater inhabitants. The coral reef sea life is visible to all diners through eight-foot-high acrylic windows, and diners are given a brochure as they enter to help them identify the fish. The undersea dining atmosphere is augmented by the dark blue walls, place mats, and carpeting, the dim lighting, and the fascinating view.

**SAMPLE DINNER ENTREES:** *Pan-smoked Grouper* (grouper marinated in lemon, cooked over hickory, and served with braised cabbage and a tomato-basil sauce); *Salmon Fillet* (salmon grilled with mesquite seasonings and topped with corn relish, or poached and topped with a light basil sauce); *Seafood Fettuccine* (shrimp and scallops served Alfredo style with butter and Parmesan cheese). All entrees served with soup or salad.

**HEALTHY-CHOICE ENTREES:** *Mixed Seafood Grill* (portions of grilled tuna, salmon, and shrimp); *Caribbean Tuna* (grilled tuna seasoned with Jamaican-jerk spices, served with a Caribbean coulis); *Woodsman Chicken* (boneless chicken breast, broiled and served with rice).

**LUNCH:** The lunch and dinner menus are very similar, and prices are only slightly lower at lunch. Neither soup nor salad is included with lunch.

**BEVERAGES:** Soft drinks, tea, coffee, and espresso are served. Selected beers from seven countries are offered, along with domestic and imported wines, spirits, and specialty drinks including the *Sea Star*, a blend of Chablis wine, strawberries, lime juice, banana, and club soda.

**AVERAGE PRICE RANGE:** Lunch entrees $$$, dinner entrees $$$$. 22-29

**FEATURES:** Diners sit eye to eye with an array of Caribbean reef fish, including sharks and barracuda. Keep an eye out for the grouper, weighing in at more than five hundred pounds. The best views are from tables in the middle of the third and fourth tiers.

**DRAWBACKS:** Coral Reef is a favorite among recent visitors. Dinner reservations fill well in advance, so it is difficult to get same-day reservations. Lunch is often easier to reserve.

The entrees are quite expensive, but of high quality. Skip the lobster.

**RESERVATIONS:** All Walt Disney World visitors can make reservations up to sixty days in advance by calling Disney Dining Reservations (407 939-3463). Same-day reservations can be made through WorldKey Information Service at Epcot Center, at the restaurant itself, or by calling Same Day Reservations after 10 AM (939-3463).

### REVIEWERS' RATINGS

**XXXX** – As good as it gets. **XXX** – Better than most. **XX** – Adequate. **X** – Of limited appeal.

**XXX** FOOD *(A wide variety of seafood, with interesting preparations and above-average prices.)*

**XXX** SERVICE *(Efficient and polite. Servers are occasionally uninformed about the entrees.)*

**XXXX** AMBIENCE *(Subdued lighting and great fish-watching — a memorable experience.)*

# CROCKETT'S TAVERN

**FOOD:** Crockett's Tavern serves frontier-style American cuisine and Mexican specialties. The menu features a large selection of hickory-smoked and charbroiled meats, including beef and beef ribs, chicken, fresh fish, and other seafood.

**LOCATION:** Crockett's Tavern is located in Pioneer Hall in the Settlement Recreation Area at Fort Wilderness. Guests can reach Pioneer Hall by ferrying to the Fort Wilderness Marina or by taking a bus from the Fort Wilderness Guest Parking Lot.

**DINING HOURS:** Dinner only from 5 PM.

**AMBIENCE:** A dozen rocking chairs, sure to be filled by evening, sit on the sturdy plank-wood front porch of Crockett's Tavern. After being greeted by the huge stuffed bear at the entrance, guests will notice that this log cabin restaurant overflows with the trappings of Davy Crockett. An Indian birch bark canoe is suspended from the ceiling, and Davy's rifle, coonskin hat, and an array of wilderness artifacts can be found throughout the restaurant. The dining room is furnished with wooden chairs, wide overhead fans, bright red tablecloths, and hurricane lanterns.

**SAMPLE DINNER ENTREES:** *The Alamo Entree* (beef and/or chicken fajitas, served with flour tortillas, guacamole, salsa, sour cream, and Cheddar cheese); *Georgie Russel's Bourbon Tenderloin* (fillet of beef tenderloin marinated in Tennessee sour mash, charbroiled and topped with mushrooms); *Mountain Top Rib and Chicken Dinner* (tangy barbecued beef ribs and crispy fried chicken); *Country Fried Chicken* (fresh chicken fried to crispy perfection). Entrees include salad, fresh baked bread, and two side dishes.

**HEALTHY-CHOICE ENTREES:** *Davy's Fresh Catch* (fresh catch of the day served with choice of two Side Fixin's).

**BEVERAGES:** Soft drinks, coffee, and tea are served, as are wine, beer, and spirits. The restaurant's specialty drinks include the *Gunslinger,* a blend of tropical fruit juices and rum, and *Davy's Lemonade,* made with Jack Daniels, Triple Sec, sour mix, half a lemon, and a touch of lime.

**PRICE RANGE:** Dinner entrees $$.

**FEATURES:** *Beulah Mae's Southern Shrimp* appetizer is generous in size and a great deal for the money.

Many of the beef dishes are less expensive versions of those served in the restaurants at the Wilderness Lodge resort.

Guests can unwind before or after dinner by soaking up the atmosphere at the saloon in Crockett's Tavern. This restaurant is especially convenient for Fort Wilderness Campground guests.

**DRAWBACKS:** The restaurant enjoys a reputation for a rowdy dinner atmosphere, filled with kids. If you're looking for a quiet evening, try another restaurant.

Due to the isolation of Pioneer Hall within Fort Wilderness, Crockett's Tavern can be difficult to reach from other locations in Walt Disney World.

**RESERVATIONS:** No reservations are accepted; diners are seated on a first-come, first-served basis.

### REVIEWERS' RATINGS

**XXXX** – As good as it gets.  **XXX** – Better than most.  **XX** – Adequate.  **X** – Of limited appeal.

**XXX** FOOD *(Good down-home American charbroiled meats with so-so accompaniments.)*

**XX** SERVICE *(Polite and very friendly, although sometimes harried. Food arrives quickly.)*

**XX** AMBIENCE *(Rustic cabin setting; probably not worth a special trip.)*

# THE CRYSTAL PALACE

**FOOD:** The Crystal Palace is a self-service restaurant that offers hot entrees incorporating beef, chicken, pasta, and fresh fish. Also available are a number of salads and sandwiches.

**LOCATION:** The Crystal Palace, a Magic Kingdom landmark, is located at the end of Main Street on the left, facing Cinderella's Castle. It can be approached from the bridge that leads into Adventureland.

**DINING HOURS:** Breakfast from park opening, lunch from 11:30 AM, dinner from 4:30 PM when park is open late.

**AMBIENCE:** This spacious, light-filled restaurant resembles the Victorian-era glass conservatory in San Francisco's Golden Gate Park, and gives guests the feeling that they're dining inside a giant greenhouse. In the gazebo atrium, an octagonal banquette surrounds a mass of greenery. A glass dome in the ceiling adds to the greenhouse experience. The food counter is located in the center of the restaurant, where guests order and pay for their meals before being seated in dining areas to either side. The tables along the window walls offer diners a view of the beautifully landscaped gardens and Cinderella's Castle beyond. The Victorian decor is enhanced with stained glass, latticework ceilings, ornate mirrors, and wrought-iron tables and chairs. In the afternoons, Dixieland jazz fills the air.

**SAMPLE DINNER ENTREES:** *Prime Rib* (a slice of prime rib served with fresh vegetables, rice or mashed potatoes, and a fresh-baked roll); *Beef Burgundy* (beef sautéed with mushrooms and wine, served in a pastry shell with fresh vegetables and a fresh-baked roll); *Italian Pasta Plate* (pasta with tomato sauce and meatballs, served with garlic bread); *Country Breaded Fish* (fresh fish lightly breaded and fried, served with fresh vegetables, rice or mashed potatoes, and a fresh-baked roll).

**HEALTHY-CHOICE ENTREES:** *Spit-Roasted Chicken* (a half chicken roasted and basted with rosemary and thyme, served with garden vegetables, rice or mashed potatoes, and a fresh-baked roll). A selection of salads and fresh fruit is also available.

**BREAKFAST AND LUNCH:** Breakfast entrees include eggs and hash brown potatoes, hotcakes, French toast, Danish pastry, and cereal. Lunch entrees are similar to those at dinner, although the lunch menu also features a selection of hot and cold sandwiches such as grilled turkey, barbecued pork, and a specialty club sandwich. A variety of large salads is also offered at lunch. Lunch prices are only slightly lower than dinner.

**BEVERAGES:** Coffee, tea, and soft drinks are served.

**AVERAGE PRICE RANGE:** Breakfast entrees $, lunch entrees $$, dinner entrees $$.

**FEATURES:** This restaurant has a wide selection of good desserts and is an excellent place for a midday break when the lunch crowd has thinned.

Health-conscious diners may order breakfast dishes made with EggBeaters.

**DRAWBACKS:** Because The Crystal Palace is very popular with families, there can be a long wait for tables during peak dining hours.

**RESERVATIONS:** No reservations are taken; diners are seated on a first-come, first-served basis.

### REVIEWERS' RATINGS
✗✗✗✗ – As good as it gets.  ✗✗✗ – Better than most.  ✗✗ – Adequate.  ✗ – Of limited appeal.

✗✗　**FOOD**　*(A good selection of standard dishes is offered here at reasonable prices.)*
✗✗　**SERVICE**　*(Self-service.)*
✗✗✗　**AMBIENCE**　*(Setting is a pleasant, light-filled turn-of-the-century solarium.)*

# 50'S PRIME TIME CAFE

**FOOD:** The 50's Prime Time Cafe serves cuisine popular in that era, such as pot roast, meat loaf, chicken, and lamb, prepared from family-style recipes and topped with lots of gravy. Steaks, seafood, hamburgers, and sandwiches are also available.

**LOCATION:** The restaurant is located on Vine Street across from Echo Lake at Disney-MGM Studios. Guests will find it by looking for the sign in the shape of a giant TV above it.

**DINING HOURS:** 11 AM for lunch, 4 PM for dinner.

**AMBIENCE:** Family-style dining in a unique mini-kitchenette is the feature at the 50's Prime Time Cafe. There are ruffled curtains, festive wallpaper, a black and white checkerboard tile floor, and plenty of plastic, vinyl, and chrome. Servers known as "Brother" or "Sis" act as bratty siblings and snitch to "Mom" about diners' manners or whether or not they clean their plates. Meals are served on dinner trays and colorful Fiestaware dishes. During meals, diners can watch "I Love Lucy" or "The Honeymooners," or a number of other period sitcoms on the old-fashioned black and white TVs that are scattered throughout the restaurant.

**SAMPLE DINNER ENTREES:** *Magnificent Meatloaf* (meat loaf prepared with mushrooms and peppers, served with mashed potatoes and mushroom gravy); *Granny's Pot Roast* (old-fashioned pot roast served with mashed potatoes); *Auntie's Roasted Lamb* (lamb shank served with mashed potatoes, garden vegetables, and special gravy).

**HEALTHY-CHOICE ENTREES:** *Mom's Shrimp or Chicken Spectacular* (shrimp, fresh chicken breast, or a combination of the two, grilled, seasoned with seven spices, and served with avocado salsa and rotini); *Dad's Fishin' Trip* (seasonal fresh fish, served with garden vegetables); *Aunt Selma's Lobster Salad* (fresh vegetable salad and lobster meat).

**LUNCH:** Lunch and dinner menus are similar, although prices are slightly lower at lunch.

**BEVERAGES:** Coffee, tea, and soft drinks are served, and refills are complimentary. The restaurant's soda fountain features such specialties as root beer floats, ice cream sodas, and milk shakes, including a peanut-butter-and-jelly-flavored shake. Beer, spirits, and wine are also available, and the wine list has a fairly good selection of Napa Valley and Sonoma County vintages.

**AVERAGE PRICE RANGE:** Lunch entrees $$, dinner entrees $$$.

**FEATURES:** The Prime Time Lounge, which can be entered from the restaurant, has a large wraparound bar decorated with black-and-white TVs. It's a unique setting for before-dinner cocktails.

**DRAWBACKS:** The 50's Prime Time Cafe is very popular during peak seasons, and same-day reservations can be difficult to secure.

**RESERVATIONS:** All Walt Disney World visitors can make reservations up to sixty days in advance by calling Disney Dining Reservations (407 939-3463). Same-day reservations can be made at Hollywood Junction (at the intersection of Hollywood and Sunset Boulevards) at Disney-MGM Studios, at the restaurant itself, or by calling Same Day Reservations after 10 AM (939-3463).

### REVIEWERS' RATINGS

**✗✗✗✗** – As good as it gets.  **✗✗✗** – Better than most.  **✗✗** – Adequate.  **✗** – Of limited appeal.

**✗✗** FOOD *(Hearty home cooking, but generally uninspired.)*

**✗✗✗** SERVICE *(Servers love role-playing with guests. Not a place for low-profile dining.)*

**✗✗✗** AMBIENCE *(A total fifties experience; good fun if you're in the mood.)*

# THE FIREWORKS FACTORY

**FOOD:** The Fireworks Factory is known for its "secret recipe" barbecue sauce used to flavor meats as they slowly cook on the apple-wood grill. The menu features smoked and grilled meats, seafood specialties, pasta dishes, and salads.

**LOCATION:** The restaurant is located on Pleasure Island, adjacent to Disney Village Marketplace.

**DINING HOURS:** Open all day. Lunch from 11:30 AM, dinner from 4 PM.

**AMBIENCE:** Signs of destruction are rampant at The Fireworks Factory, which looks like an ammunitions warehouse blown sky-high. All that's left standing is a marred steel substructure with partially blown-apart brick walls and corrugated tin siding. Stacked cases of beer partition off tables in alcoves, and scaffolding stairs lead to a second level that offers diners a view of Buena Vista Lagoon. This popular eatery attracts a lively crowd.

**SAMPLE DINNER ENTREES:** *Grilled Pork Chops* (thick-cut pork chops grilled with maple syrup and Pommery mustard, served with warm red cabbage slaw and horseradish mashed potatoes); *Black Angus Ribeye Steak* (tender rib-eye steak seasoned and grilled, served with horseradish mashed potatoes and tomato-cucumber slaw); *Mesquite Smoked Chicken* (a fresh half chicken seasoned and slow roasted over mesquite wood, blasted with Fireworks barbecue sauce, and served with a baked potato and seasonal vegetables); *Firecracker Platter* (a half pound of Dungeness crab clusters, a one-third slab of baby back ribs and a quarter of mesquite-smoked chicken served with sweet corn and baked potato).

**HEALTHY-CHOICE ENTREES:** *Roasted Garlic Chicken* (fresh breast of chicken marinated and grilled, topped with fresh herbs and fire roasted, with a smoked-tomato reduction, mashed Gruyère sweet potatoes and seasonal vegetables); *Oak Roasted Salmon* (fresh seasonal salmon, oak plank–roasted and served with a roasted-tomato and corn relish and angel hair sweet potatoes); *Seasonal Fruits* (a fresh selection served with berry yogurt).

**LUNCH:** Lunch and dinner menus are similar, although prices are slightly lower at lunch than at dinner.

**BEVERAGES:** Coffee, tea, and soft drinks are served, as well as a wide variety of domestic and imported beers, a reasonable selection of wines including some good California wines, and spirits. The Fireworks Factory offers a variety of specialty drinks such as the *21 Rum Salute*, consisting of Bacardi 151 rum, Bacardi dark rum, and a blend of secret ingredients.

**AVERAGE PRICE RANGE:** Lunch entrees $$, dinner entrees $$$.

**FEATURES:** The Fireworks Factory weekday Happy Hour offers drinks at reduced prices from 3 until 7 PM. This is one of the few late-night eating places at WDW, open until 2 AM or 3 AM (seasonally).

**DRAWBACKS:** Expect a noisy meal in this restaurant. Avoid the crush on Thursday nights (Cast Member discount night at Pleasure Island), unless that's the scene you're looking for.

**RESERVATIONS:** All Walt Disney World visitors can make reservations up to fourteen days in advance by calling the restaurant directly (407 934-8989) from 11:30 AM until 6 PM (EST). The Fireworks Factory has a smoking section.

### REVIEWERS' RATINGS

**XXXX** – As good as it gets. **XXX** – Better than most. **XX** – Adequate. **X** – Of limited appeal.

**XXX** FOOD *(A wide array of barbecue specialties; generous portions.)*
**XXX** SERVICE *(Cheerful and very efficient, given the crush.)*
**XXX** AMBIENCE *(Boisterous from Happy Hour well into the night. Appeals to a party crowd.)*

# THE GARDEN GRILL RESTAURANT

**FOOD:** The Garden Grill Restaurant serves all-you-can-eat traditional American cuisine family style. The menu offers seafood, meat, and poultry, prepared by smoking, grilling, and rotisserie. The fish and vegetables are actually grown in The Land pavilion gardens.

**LOCATION:** The restaurant is located inside The Land pavilion in Future World at Epcot Center. To reach it, guests walk to the back of the pavilion, along the balcony overlooking the attractions and the Sunshine Season Food Fair, below.

**DINING HOURS:** 8:30 AM for breakfast (7:30 AM on selected days), 11:15 AM for lunch, 4 PM for dinner.

**AMBIENCE:** This two-tiered revolving restaurant gives diners a chance to view the environmental exhibits in the Living with The Land attraction. The restaurant revolves past scenes of a rain forest, a desert, and a prairie complete with buffalo. Roomy upholstered booths make the excursion quite comfortable. Farmer Mickey and a cast of Disney characters drop by to greet diners.

**CHARACTER DINNER ENTREES:** *Roasted Chicken with Rocky Top Seasoning, Smoked Flank Steak*, and *Farm Fresh Catfish* are served family-style in sizzling skillets. The trio of entrees are accompanied by farm fresh salad, smashed potatoes, mushroom gravy, garden vegetables, smoked relish, squaw bread, biscuits, and apple butter.

**HEALTHY-CHOICE ENTREES:** *Farm Fresh Fish* and *Garden Pasta Primavera* (available as a special order for vegetarians).

**CHARACTER BREAKFAST AND CHARACTER LUNCH:** The family-style Character Breakfast entrees includes scrambled eggs, sausage, ham steak, and cheese grits. The lunch and dinner menus are the same.

**BEVERAGES:** Coffee, tea, and soft drinks are included in the price of the fixed-price meal. Regional American beers and wines from California vineyards are featured. The restaurant's full bar features specialty drinks such as the *Garden Grill Bloody Mary*, a popular house specialty that is garnished with celery from The Land's own greenhouses.

**AVERAGE PRICE RANGE:** Character Breakfast $$$; Character Lunch $$$; Character Dinner $$$.

**FEATURES:** The slowly revolving restaurant provides an entertaining atmosphere at meals. For the best view, request a table on the lower tier. It takes about thirty-five minutes to make a complete revolution.

**DRAWBACKS:** During peak attendance times, it is very difficult to get same-day reservations for lunch. Dinner reservations are sometimes easier to secure.

Guests holding reservations at The Garden Grill may bypass the occasional long lines waiting to enter The Land pavilion by notifying a Cast Member.

**RESERVATIONS:** All Walt Disney World visitors can make reservations for Character Meals up to seven days in advance by calling Disney Dining Reservations (407 939-3463). Same-day reservations can be made through WorldKey Information Service at Epcot Center, at the restaurant itself, or by calling Same Day Reservations after 10 AM (939-3463).

## REVIEWERS' RATINGS

**XXXX** – As good as it gets.   **XXX** – Better than most.   **XX** – Adequate.   **X** – Of limited appeal.

**XXX**   FOOD   *(Inventive and flavorful traditional American cuisine.)*

**XXX**   SERVICE   *(The servers here are always pleasant and professional.)*

**XXXX**   AMBIENCE   *(Visually stimulating, with ever-changing scenery and cast of characters.)*

# HOLLYWOOD & VINE CAFETERIA

**FOOD:** Hollywood & Vine Cafeteria serves American-style beef, chicken, veal, seafood, and pasta dishes, along with sandwiches, a variety of large salads, and desserts such as pastries and ice cream specialties.

**LOCATION:** The restaurant is located on Vine Street across from Echo Lake at Disney-MGM Studios, next door to the 50's Prime Time Cafe.

**DINING HOURS:** Open all day. Breakfast from park opening, lunch from 11 AM, dinner starting from 4 PM only during the summer and on holidays, when the park stays open late.

**AMBIENCE:** Hollywood & Vine "Cafeteria of the Stars" is a replica of a Tinseltown diner from the late 1940s. In one room, a sprawling forty-foot mural features famous landmarks from Hollywood and the San Fernando Valley. Another very vivid mural features a detailed nighttime view of Hollywood Boulevard. Black and white photographs with scenes of early Hollywood hang on the walls. The dining room, furnished with pink geometric-patterned carpeting and black Venetian blinds, is divided into two sections with a long chrome cafeteria counter center stage. Guests select their food at the cafeteria, pay the cashier, and dine in the restaurant's pale pink Naugahyde booths or at Formica-topped tables surrounded by heavy-duty padded dinette chairs.

**SAMPLE ENTREES:** *Back Lot Ribs* (baby back ribs with barbecue sauce, served with vegetables and rice); *Academy Special* (cheese-stuffed pasta shells with tomato-herb sauce, served with vegetables); *Sunset Steak* (tenderloin tips simmered in a mushroom sauce, served with rice); *Carved Sirloin* (beef sirloin served with green beans, rice, and horseradish sauce).

**HEALTHY-CHOICE ENTREES:** *Seafood and Chicken Platter* (cold salad of shrimp, grilled chicken breast, mixed greens, and fresh fruit); *Malibu Marina* (assorted seafood and vegetables in a tomato sauce, served with rice); *Cahuenga Chicken* (roasted half chicken, served with vegetables and rice).

**BREAKFAST AND LUNCH:** The breakfast menu includes egg dishes, pancakes, French toast, and the restaurant's special *Rodeo Drive Blintzes* (cheese-filled crepes served with a choice of strawberry, blueberry, or pineapple topping). Lunch and dinner entrees are identical, although more entrees are added in the evening. Prices are the same for lunch and dinner.

**BEVERAGES:** Wine and beer are available at the cafeteria, as are coffee, tea, and soft drinks.

**AVERAGE PRICE RANGE:** Breakfast entrees $, lunch and dinner entrees $$.

**FEATURES:** Hollywood & Vine Cafeteria is a good choice for a quick meal or for light eaters. The line usually moves quickly, even during busy times.

A selection of pastries and ice cream specialties is available from a front counter all afternoon.

The Tune In Lounge, which can be entered directly from within the Hollywood & Vine Cafeteria, is an entertaining and relaxing stop for a before- or after-dinner drink.

**DRAWBACKS:** Hollywood & Vine Cafeteria is very large and attracts families with young children, so it can get very crowded and noisy during busy mealtimes.

**RESERVATIONS:** Cafeteria service. No reservations.

### REVIEWERS' RATINGS

**XXXX** – As good as it gets.  **XXX** – Better than most.  **XX** – Adequate.  **X** – Of limited appeal.

**XX**  FOOD  *(Surprisingly good for cafeteria-style food.)*

**XXX**  SERVICE  *(Self-service, with an exceptionally friendly staff.)*

**XX**  AMBIENCE  *(Interesting decor, but it can be a madhouse during peak dining hours.)*

# THE HOLLYWOOD BROWN DERBY

**FOOD:** The Hollywood Brown Derby serves charbroiled beef, grilled lamb and pork, sautéed veal, roasted chicken, seafood, pasta, and the original restaurant's famous Cobb salad.

**LOCATION:** The restaurant is housed in a Los Angeles–style Mediterranean building at the end of Hollywood Boulevard in Disney-MGM Studios, next to the working soundstages. The entrance is under a long, brown awning.

**DINING HOURS:** 11 AM for lunch, 4:30 PM for dinner.

**AMBIENCE:** Red carpet paves the way through the two-tiered Hollywood Brown Derby. The main dining area has white linen–covered tables favored by visiting celebrities. Booths line the walls of the upper tier, and maroon umbrellas shade tables on the outdoor patio. The restaurant's interior is accented with mahogany wainscoting and hanging chandeliers. The front windows have airy lace curtains; windows in other sections have velvet drapes or dark wood shutters. The restaurant's signature collection of caricatures adorns the walls, and Streetmosphere performers playing characters such as Hedda Hopper seeking good gossip mingle with diners at times or provide musical interludes on the restaurant's piano.

**SAMPLE DINNER ENTREES:** *Pasta and Seafood* (pasta tossed with sea scallops and shrimp in a creamy feta cheese sauce, served with garlic bread sticks); *Stuffed Chicken Breast* (sautéed chicken breast stuffed with shrimp mousse, served with champagne sauce and fresh garden vegetables); *Mixed Grill* (grilled lamb, tenderloin of beef, pork, veal liver, and pork sausage, served with fresh garden vegetables).

**HEALTHY-CHOICE ENTREES:** *Vegetable Medley* (sautéed fresh vegetables and legumes, served with angel-hair pasta, finished with herbs and raspberry vinegar); *Roast Chicken* (rotisserie-roasted half-chicken served with wild rice and fresh garden vegetables); *Baked Grouper* (grouper fillet lightly egg battered and baked to perfection, topped with meunière butter and served with pasta).

**LUNCH:** The lunch and dinner menus are very similar, and prices are only slightly lower at lunch.

**BEVERAGES:** A large selection of California wines is featured at The Hollywood Brown Derby, along with beer and spirits. Coffee, tea, and soft drinks are available, as are espresso and cappuccino. The Hollywood Brown Derby features after-dinner drinks, including vintage port and its specialty drink *Cafe Henry III*, a blend of Kahlúa, brandy, Galliano, Grand Marnier, and coffee.

**AVERAGE PRICE RANGE:** Lunch entrees **$$**, dinner entrees **$$$$**.

**FEATURES:** The Hollywood Brown Derby does not have a lounge, but The Catwalk Bar, upstairs, is a great place for before-dinner cocktails. There is an elevator adjacent to the waiting area.

**DRAWBACKS:** The restaurant is extremely popular and usually very busy, especially during peak seasons, making it difficult to secure same-day reservations.

**RESERVATIONS:** All Walt Disney World visitors can make reservations up to sixty days in advance by calling Disney Dining Reservations (407 939-3463). Same-day reservations can be made at Hollywood Junction (at the intersection of Hollywood and Sunset Boulevards) at Disney-MGM Studios, at the restaurant itself, or by calling Same Day Reservations after 10 AM (939-3463).

### REVIEWERS' RATINGS

**XXXX** – As good as it gets. **XXX** – Better than most. **XX** – Adequate. **X** – Of limited appeal.

**XXXX** FOOD (*Usually very good. Try the Cobb salad.*)

**XXX** SERVICE (*Very fast, very efficient, always professional.*)

**XXXX** AMBIENCE (*Very Hollywood, very comfortable and adult. Ask for a booth.*)

# KING STEFAN'S BANQUET HALL

**FOOD:** King Stefan's Banquet Hall serves hearty portions of beef, chicken, and fish, prepared in a quasi British-American fashion. A variety of large salads is also on the menu.

**LOCATION:** The restaurant is perched high atop Cinderella's Castle in Fantasyland at the Magic Kingdom. Guests will find the entrance at the rear of the castle, facing Fantasyland.

**DINING HOURS:** Breakfast from park opening, lunch from 11:30 AM, dinner from 4 PM.

**AMBIENCE:** King Stefan's Banquet Hall recalls the medieval splendor of long ago. Wall torches light the stone archways, and shields, swords, and suits of armor glint near the fireplace. Burgundy-carpeted stairs lead up to the large two-tiered dining room, where cathedral ceilings, carved wooden beams, fleur-de-lys carpeting, and tapestry-covered chairs mimic a royal atmosphere. Tall, narrow arched windows inset with stained glass give guests an overview of Fantasyland. Servers are costumed in brocaded medieval attire.

**SAMPLE DINNER ENTREES:** *Grand Duke* (steak grilled with green peppercorn sauce, served with roasted potatoes and sautéed vegetables); *Queen's Cut* (roast prime rib served with a baked potato and sautéed fresh vegetables); *Friar's Fowl* (chicken breast stuffed with ham, spinach, and mozzarella cheese, breaded and sautéed, and served over fettuccine with fresh mushrooms, tomatoes, and cilantro). Dinner entrees include a choice of soup or salad.

**HEALTHY-CHOICE ENTREES:** *The Royal Mariner* (fresh fish of the day, served with parsley potatoes and sautéed fresh vegetables); *Cinderella Salad* (assorted salad greens and vegetables, topped with tomatoes, cheese, and sautéed chicken, served with a dill vinaigrette).

**CHARACTER BREAKFAST AND LUNCH:** The all-you-can-eat Character Breakfast entrees include eggs, waffles, and sausage. Lunch and dinner menus are similar; however, the lunch menu also features large salads and sandwiches, including *The Coachman* (sliced turkey, turkey ham, turkey bacon, and Swiss cheese, served with marinated fresh vegetables). Lunch entrees include soup, but not salad, and prices are considerably lower at lunch than at dinner.

**BEVERAGES:** Coffee, tea, and soft drinks are served. All chilled beverages except bottled water and orange juice may be ordered in a King Stefan's souvenir glass.

**AVERAGE PRICE RANGE:** Character Breakfast **$$$**, lunch entrees **$$**, dinner entrees **$$$$**.

**FEATURES:** Cinderella herself visits King Stefan's Banquet Hall periodically throughout the day.
King Stefan's Banquet Hall is the only restaurant with an elevated view in the Magic Kingdom.

**DRAWBACKS:** King Stefan's Banquet Hall is very popular with visitors of all ages, and families are especially attracted to this restaurant. Reservations, which are required for breakfast, lunch, and dinner, are difficult to get during peak seasons.

**RESERVATIONS:** All Walt Disney World visitors can make lunch and dinner reservations up to sixty days in advance and Character Breakfast reservations up to seven days in advance by calling Disney Dining Reservations (407 939-3463). Same-day reservations can be made at City Hall or at the restaurant itself, or by calling Same Day Reservations after 10 AM (939-3463).

### REVIEWERS' RATINGS

**XXXX** – As good as it gets. **XXX** – Better than most. **XX** – Adequate. **X** – Of limited appeal.

**XX** FOOD *(Expensive, unexceptional food. You're paying for the view.)*
**XXX** SERVICE *(Very polite and attentive; sometimes slow at busy times.)*
**XXXX** AMBIENCE *(A unique atmosphere that provides a memorable experience.)*

# LE CELLIER

**FOOD:** Le Cellier serves an assortment of regional specialties from various provinces of Canada. Cheddar cheese soup, meat pies, and poached fresh salmon are some of the staple offerings of this cafeteria-style restaurant.

**LOCATION:** The entrance to Le Cellier is at the side of the Canada pavilion in the World Showcase at Epcot Center. Guests can reach it by walking down the ramp along the river flowing through the flowering Victoria Gardens.

**DINING HOURS:** Lunch from 12 noon, dinner from 5 PM.

**AMBIENCE:** The cool, comfortable feeling of dining inside a giant wine cellar is conveyed to guests at Le Cellier restaurant. Thick stone walls are adorned with wrought-iron lanterns, and dramatic archways divide the dining room into smaller, more intimate areas. The dark wood panels that line the walls are topped here and there by ironwork fashioned into a Canadian maple leaf pattern. Guests serve themselves at the cafeteria-style food counter, pay the cashier, and seat themselves at pleasant wooden tables with elegant tapestry-upholstered high-back chairs.

**SAMPLE DINNER ENTREES:** *Prime Rib (*only available on the dinner menu), *Chicken & Meatball Stew, Tortierre Pie,* and *Carved Pemeal Bacon.* All entrees are served with Yukon Gold potatoes or rice and vegetables.

**HEALTHY-CHOICE ENTREES:** *Poached Salmon* and *Fresh Catch of the Day.*

**LUNCH:** Lunch and dinner menus are similar, and most entrees are available at both meals. However, the lunch menu also features a *Smoked Beef Brisket Sandwich* .

**BEVERAGES:** La Batt's and Molson's beer are served, along with a variety of Canadian wines. Coffee, tea, mineral water, and soft drinks are also offered.

**AVERAGE PRICE RANGE:** Lunch entrees **$$**, dinner entrees **$$$**.

**FEATURES:** The most popular dishes among frequent guests at Le Cellier are the *Chicken and Meatball Stew* and *Tortierre Pie.*

Le Cellier may have one of the best entrances in the World Showcase. To reach it, guests meander through gorgeous flowering gardens, often accompanied by the music of a bagpipe band.

On hot afternoons, this dimly lit self-serve restaurant is a great place to relax and cool off. Go after 2 PM, when the lunch crowd has thinned out. Try the *Maple Syrup Pie* or *Apple-Berry-Rhubarb Pie.*

The cafeteria format allows light eaters to create and enjoy smaller meals.

The restaurant's location makes it an excellent rendezvous spot for visitors who have been touring Epcot Center separately.

**DRAWBACKS:** Because no reservations are taken, lines can be long and slow during peak dining hours. Dinner is usually less crowded than lunch.

Vegetarians may find the entree selection limited at Le Cellier.

**RESERVATIONS:** Cafeteria-style service; no reservations are taken.

### REVIEWERS' RATINGS

**XXXX** – As good as it gets. **XXX** – Better than most. **XX** – Adequate. **X** – Of limited appeal.

**XX** FOOD *(Hearty and flavorful; a good menu for visitors on the go who want a hot meal.)*

**XX** SERVICE *(Self-service; servers bring water and clear tables.)*

**XXX** AMBIENCE *(The pleasant dining room feels more like a restaurant than a cafeteria.)*

# LIBERTY TREE TAVERN

**FOOD:** Liberty Tree Tavern features a Character Dinner with an Early American menu including chicken, steak, and sausage. Traditional roast turkey accompanied with all the trimmings is available on the lunch menu every day, as are several New England–style dishes.

**LOCATION:** The restaurant is located at Liberty Square in the Magic Kingdom. Guests will find it in a white-pillared colonial-style building across from the Liberty Square Riverboat landing.

**DINING HOURS:** 11:30 AM for lunch, 4 PM for Character Dinner.

**AMBIENCE:** The Liberty Square Tavern immerses guests in an authentic re-creation of an eighteenth-century Early American dining hall, with pegged wood flooring and sparkling paned windows. The restaurant is divided into six themed dining areas, each decorated with reproductions of items associated with a famous historical figure, such as Ben Franklin's printing press and Betsy Ross' eyeglasses. One wall is fashioned from rough-cut stone and features a massive fireplace with an oak mantel. Iron candelabra hang from the beamed ceilings, and pewter and copper artifacts decorate the walls and moldings. Servers wear Early American colonial garb.

**CHARACTER DINNER ENTREES:** The family-style all-you-can-eat menu includes roasted chicken, marinated flank steak, trail sausage, rice pilaf, mashed potatoes, sautéed garden vegetables, and salad with Tavern dressing. Beverages are included with the meal; dessert, however, is not.

**LUNCH:** *Chesapeake Cheddar* (a medley of seafood in white wine sauce, topped with Cheddar cheese and served in a pastry shell, accompanied with sautéed garden vegetables); *New England Pot Roast* (braised beef in a burgundy wine sauce, served with sautéed garden vegetables and mashed potatoes).

**HEALTHY-CHOICE LUNCH ENTREES:** *Cape Cod Pasta* (sautéed shrimp and garden vegetables tossed with spinach linguine); *Fresh from the Harbor* (grilled fresh fish served over cucumber relish with sautéed garden vegetables); *Capitol Idea* (a medley of vegetables and beans with rice and grilled potato).

**BEVERAGES:** Coffee, tea, soft drinks, juice, espresso, and cappuccino are served. The *Star-Spangled Sherbet Punch,* a special nonalcoholic thirst quencher, is served in a Liberty Tree Tavern souvenir glass.

**AVERAGE PRICE RANGE:** Lunch entrees $$, Character Dinner $$$.

**FEATURES:** On hot days, this dimly lit restaurant is a great place to relax and cool off. At about 2 PM, the lunch crowds have gone and seating is often available.

The *New England Clam Chowder* is a lunch favorite among frequent diners at Liberty Tree Tavern.

**DRAWBACKS:** The familiar American dishes here make this restaurant a Magic Kingdom favorite for guests of all ages, so same-day reservations can be very difficult to get during peak seasons.

The restaurant is especially popular with families, so noise levels at meals can be quite high.

**RESERVATIONS:** All Walt Disney World visitors can make lunch reservations up to sixty days in advance and Character Dinner reservations up to fourteen days in advance by calling Disney Dining Reservations (407 939-3463). Same-day reservations can be made at City Hall or at the restaurant itself, or by calling Same Day Reservations after 10 AM (939-3463).

### REVIEWERS' RATINGS

**XXXX** – As good as it gets. **XXX** – Better than most. **XX** – Adequate. **X** – Of limited appeal.

**XX** FOOD *(A classic American meal with some interesting touches.)*

**XX** SERVICE *(Polite, but can be rushed and abrupt at busy times.)*

**XX** AMBIENCE *(Pleasant, dimly lit decor, but packed with kids during peak meal times.)*

# L'ORIGINALE ALFREDO DI ROMA RISTORANTE

**FOOD:** L'Originale Alfredo di Roma serves Italian cuisine and freshly made pasta accompanied with a selection of sauces. The featured pasta is *Le Originali Fettuccine all'Alfredo,* a creation of the namesake restaurant in Rome. Also on the menu are chicken, veal, and seafood dishes prepared in regional styles.

**LOCATION:** The restaurant is located across from the cascading Fontana di Nettuno, at the back of the Italy pavilion in the World Showcase at Epcot Center. Guests pass under a white-pillared portico lit by hanging lanterns to enter the palatial pink-stuccoed building.

**DINING HOURS:** Noon for lunch, 4 PM for dinner.

**AMBIENCE:** Photographs of international celebrities cover the walls of the restaurant's spacious entry area, where waiting guests are seated beneath an elaborate crystal chandelier. The elegant dining area, with mauve velvet chairs and pink tablecloths, has large windows looking out onto the piazza. The walls are covered with masterful trompe l'oeil murals depicting scenes from Italian country estates. Strolling musicians create a festive dining experience as they wander the room singing and playing Italian ballads and operatic arias.

**SAMPLE DINNER ENTREES:** *Le Originali Fettuccine all'Alfredo* (wide-noodle pasta tossed with butter and Parmesan cheese); *Pollo alla Parmigiana* (boneless chicken breast breaded and pan-fried, topped with tomato sauce and mozzarella cheese, served with ziti); *Cotoletta di Vitello Alfredo* (veal chop sautéed in black truffles and wine, served with fresh asparagus and mushrooms); *Saltimbocca alla Romana* (veal and Italian-style ham, thinly sliced, seasoned with sage, and pan-fried).

**HEALTHY-CHOICE ENTREES:** *Pollo alla Cacciatora* (chicken breast simmered with tomatoes, mushrooms, and onions, served with ziti); *Scaloppine of Veal al Marsala* (sliced veal in a mushroom and Marsala wine sauce).

**LUNCH:** Lunch and dinner menus are similar, although there are many more veal dishes at dinner. Prices are only slightly lower at lunch than at dinner.

**BEVERAGES:** Wine, beer, spirits, soft drinks, tea, and coffee are served, along with espresso and cappuccino. The wine list includes selections from various regions of Italy. A special after-dinner drink, *Caffè Alfredo,* is made of espresso with Sambuca, brandy, and Amaretto, topped with whipped cream.

**AVERAGE PRICE RANGE:** Lunch entrees $$, dinner entrees $$$.

**FEATURES:** The restaurant's pasta is made fresh daily on the premises. Guests can watch the pasta-making process through the kitchen windows.

**DRAWBACKS:** Since this is one of the most popular restaurants in the World Showcase, it can be extremely difficult to book same-day reservations for dinner.

**RESERVATIONS:** All Walt Disney World visitors can make reservations up to sixty days in advance by calling Disney Dining Reservations (407 939-3463). Same-day reservations can be made through WorldKey Information Service at Epcot Center, at the restaurant itself, or by calling Same Day Reservations after 10 AM (939-3463).

### REVIEWERS' RATINGS

**XXXX** – As good as it gets.   **XXX** – Better than most.   **XX** – Adequate.   **X** – Of limited appeal.

**XX** FOOD *(The meat and fish dishes outshine the pasta, which is unexceptional.)*

**XXX** SERVICE *(Generally efficient, spirited, and helpful.)*

**XXX** AMBIENCE *(Beautiful decor, but the room can feel crowded during peak dining times.)*

# MAMA MELROSE'S RISTORANTE ITALIANO

**FOOD:** Mama Melrose's Ristorante Italiano serves Italian cuisine with California-style touches and thin-crust pizzas baked in a hickory wood–burning oven. Beef, veal, fresh fish, and chicken are prepared with a variety of Italian sauces. All-you-can-eat pasta is featured, topped with a choice of sauces.

**LOCATION:** The restaurant is tucked away in the New York Street Backlot, "behind" New York Street and around the corner from Jim Henson's Muppet*Vision 3D at Disney-MGM Studios.

**DINING HOURS:** 11:30 AM for lunch, 4 PM for dinner.

**AMBIENCE:** The small waiting area at Mama Melrose's is permeated with delicious smells from the wood-burning ovens. As they are led to their tables, guests can catch a view of the chefs preparing meals. The walls and rafters are festooned with grapevines, hanging wine bottles, tiny lights, and other paraphernalia. The dim lighting evokes the feeling of twilight. Hardwood floors, red-checked tablecloths, and loud good humor create an offbeat trattoria atmosphere.

**SAMPLE DINNER ENTREES:** *Pollo alla Melrose's* (two breaded chicken breasts with tomato-basil-garlic sauce, topped with mozzarella and Parmesan cheese); *Venice Beach Delight* (pasta with shrimp and scallops served in a cream sauce); *Sunset Grill* (grilled tenderloin of beef with pizzaiola sauce and provolone cheese, served with pasta); *4-Star Pizza* (individual-sized pizza topped with fresh tomato, Brie, romano, mozzarella, and Gorgonzola cheeses).

**HEALTHY-CHOICE ENTREES:** *Casting Call* (fresh fish of the day); *Farmer's Market Lasagna* (vegetable lasagna); *Celebrity Chicken* (chicken Marsala, served with pasta); *Premiere Pasta e Pollo* (pasta with assorted fresh vegetables and chicken in a tomato-herb sauce).

**LUNCH:** Lunch and dinner menus are similar, although prices are slightly lower at lunch.

**BEVERAGES:** Californian and Italian French wines are featured at Mama Melrose's. Coffee, tea, soft drinks, espresso, and cappuccino are offered, as are beer and spirits. *Bella Cappuccino,* a house favorite, consists of cappuccino with Frangelico and Bailey's Irish Cream, topped with a touch of cinnamon.

**AVERAGE PRICE RANGE:** Lunch entrees $$, dinner entrees $$$.

**FEATURES:** The hickory wood–burning brick ovens and a hardwood charbroiler enable chefs to produce top-quality pizzas and grilled meats.

Mama Melrose's is a pleasant place to drop in for a beverage in the afternoon, once the mealtime crowds have gone. Guests are seated at dinner tables and given fresh-baked bread and basil-flavored olive oil to snack on.

The dessert most popular with frequent diners here is *Tiramisu,* a layered Italian confection.

**DRAWBACKS:** The restaurant is very large and can get crowded and noisy during peak dining hours.

**RESERVATIONS:** All Walt Disney World visitors can make reservations up to sixty days in advance by calling Disney Dining Reservations (407 939-3463). Same-day reservations can be made at Hollywood Junction (at the intersection of Hollywood and Sunset Boulevards) at Disney-MGM Studios, at the restaurant itself, or by calling Same Day Reservations after 10 AM (939-3463).

### REVIEWERS' RATINGS

✗✗✗✗ – As good as it gets. ✗✗✗ – Better than most. ✗✗ – Adequate. ✗ – Of limited appeal.

✗✗✗ FOOD *(The Italian entrees appeal to most guests; the thin-crust pizzas are especially good.)*

✗✗✗ SERVICE *(Efficient for such a large restaurant. At times, the hostess can be quite brusque.)*

✗✗ AMBIENCE *(The large dining room can get very noisy during peak dining hours.)*

# NINE DRAGONS RESTAURANT

**FOOD:** Nine Dragons Restaurant serves several different styles of Chinese cuisine: Light and mild Mandarin, hot and spicy Szechuan and Hunan, subtly flavored Cantonese, and internationally inspired Kiangsu from Shanghai. Meats, poultry, seafood, and vegetables are prepared with a variety of seasonings and sauces. The menu was created by the chefs at the Beijing Hotel in China.

**LOCATION:** The restaurant, a reproduction of Beijing's Summer Palace, is located just past the Gate of the Golden Sun at the China pavilion in the World Showcase at Epcot Center. It is entered through an elaborately carved arched doorway.

**DINING HOURS:** Open all day. Lunch from 11 AM, dinner from 4 PM.

**AMBIENCE:** An elaborately carved rosewood partition dominates the entry to the large open dining room of the Nine Dragons Restaurant. Plush, dark cranberry-colored carpeting, black-lacquered chairs, intricately painted ceilings, and white linen tablecloths give the restaurant a very formal ambience. Ornate paper lanterns supplement the light that pours in from octagonally shaped windows. The tables in the front of the restaurant offer a good view of the World Showcase promenade.

**SAMPLE DINNER ENTREES:** *Beef in Spicy Sha Cha Sauce* (beef strips stir-fried with bamboo shoots and snow peas); *Kang Bao Chicken* (stir-fried chicken, peanuts, and dried hot peppers); *Baby Back Pork Ribs* (honey-roasted ribs, served with pork-and-shrimp fried rice); *Jasmine Duck* (steamed duck marinated in jasmine tea and fried); *Shrimp or Scallops Royale* (stir-fried shrimp or scallops, in a spicy black bean sauce with green peppers). All entrees are served with rice and tea.

**HEALTHY-CHOICE ENTREES:** *Stir-fried Grouper and Garden Vegetables* (fresh grouper stir-fried with vegetables); *Lemon Chicken* (chicken breast braised in a lemon sauce); *Imperial String Beans* (string beans cooked in a lightly oiled wok).

**LUNCH:** Lunch and dinner menus are similar, although prices of some dishes are quite a bit lower at lunch.

**BEVERAGES:** Wine, Tsing Tao beer, and spirits are served. Fresh melon juice is available, as are soft drinks, mineral water, coffee, and tea. The restaurant features several specialty drinks, including the *Shanghai Surprise,* made with ginseng brandy, rum, grapefruit, lemon, and orange juice; and the *Xian Quencher,* a mixture of fresh melon juice and rum or vodka.

**AVERAGE PRICE RANGE:** Lunch entrees $$, dinner entrees $$$.

**FEATURES:** It is fairly easy to secure last-minute reservations for lunch and dinner at Nine Dragons. Popular dishes among frequent diners are the *Beef in Spicy Sha Cha Sauce* and *Kang Bao Chicken.*

**DRAWBACKS:** Dishes are served as individual meals with rice, rather than family style as in most Chinese restaurants in the United States. Many visitors consider the restaurant overpriced.

**RESERVATIONS:** All Walt Disney World visitors can make reservations up to sixty days in advance by calling Disney Dining Reservations (407 939-3463). Same-day reservations can be made through WorldKey Information Service at Epcot Center, at the restaurant itself, or by calling Same Day Reservations after 10 AM (939-3463).

### REVIEWERS' RATINGS

**XXXX** – As good as it gets.  **XXX** – Better than most.  **XX** – Adequate.  **X** – Of limited appeal.

**XX** FOOD *(Consistently average-quality cuisine at disproportionately high prices.)*

**XX** SERVICE *(Efficient but indifferent, and sometimes intrusive.)*

**XX** AMBIENCE *(A formal setting in an elegant room, but unexceptional overall.)*

# PLANET HOLLYWOOD

**FOOD:** The food at Planet Hollywood is inspired by the best of New American cuisine. Most of the dishes were developed by the restaurant chain's highly skilled master chefs. Entrees include salads, burgers, pasta, fajitas, pizza, ribs, chicken, and steak, all served in generous portions.

**LOCATION:** Planet Hollywood is located at Pleasure Island, close to the AMC Pleasure Island Theatres. Constructed over the lagoon, inside a dramatic blue celestial sphere, the restaurant is impossible to miss.

**DINING HOURS:** Open for lunch and dinner daily, from 11 AM until 2 AM.

**AMBIENCE:** A long canopied stairway (perfect for that "Hollywood" entrance) leads up to the intricately designed tri-level restaurant. Each level reflects a different movie genre, such as science fiction or action-adventure, and props and memorabilia from famous films hang from the walls and ceilings. There are two bars, a gift shop is tucked behind the visiting stars' "handprint" wall, and enormous monitors show music videos, film clips, and scenes from Planet Hollywood grand openings around the world. There's an air of excitement here — the sense that a celebrity could show up at any moment. Planet Hollywood is always busy, its staff is upbeat, and its razzle-dazzle ambience is memorable.

**SAMPLE DINNER ENTREES:** *Thai Shrimp* (butterflied shrimp tossed with julienned vegetables, peanuts, green onions, cilantro, spicy sweet chili sauce, and linguine); *Fajitas* (choice of chicken, beef, shrimp, or a combination,with a traditional Mexican presentation of whole-wheat tortillas, guacamole, pico de gallo, sour cream and mixed cheeses, served with black beans and Mexican rice); *St. Louis Ribs* (smoked spare-ribs, served with Planet Hollywood's own barbecue sauce, French fries, and black bean relish).

**HEALTHY-CHOICE ENTREES:** *Margherita* (linguine sauteed with fresh garlic, fresh plum tomatoes, basil, oregano, white wine, and olive oil, topped with fresh grated Parmesan cheese); *Vegetable Burger* (an all-vegetable patty with a garlic-soy-butter glaze, grilled to order. Served on a poppy seed kaiser roll with lettuce, tomato, and red onions).

**LUNCH:** The menu is the same for lunch and dinner.

**BEVERAGES:** Along with beer, champagne, and wine, Planet Hollywood features a large selection of specialty drinks in souvenir glasses, including the *The Terminator* (a cyborg's mixture of vodka, rum, gin, Grand Marnier, Tia Maria, Kahlúa, and sweet and sour mix, splashed with cranberry, then topped with draught beer). Coffee, tea, and soft drinks are also served, as are espresso and cappuccino.

**AVERAGE PRICE RANGE:** Entrees $$.

**FEATURES:** Planet Hollywood features spectacular desserts such as *Hollywood Mousse Pie, Ebony and Ivory Brownie,* and *Apple Strudel* made from an original recipe of Arnold Schwarzenegger's mother. The *Chicken Crunch* appetizer and *Hamburger* are favorites among staff and regular guests.

Parties of six who want to experience the ambience without the noise can request a table in one of the two sound-suppressed booths on the first floor.

**DRAWBACKS:** The wait for seating can be well over an hour. Arrive before 11 AM or before 5 PM.

**RESERVATIONS:** No reservations are taken; diners are seated on a first-come, first-served basis.

### REVIEWERS' RATINGS

**XXXX** – As good as it gets.  **XXX** – Better than most.  **XX** – Adequate.  **X** – Of limited appeal.

**XXXX** FOOD *(Excellent and unique dishes that are well thought out and artfully presented.)*
**XXXX** SERVICE *(Perhaps the best at WDW, given the traffic. Always professional and upbeat.)*
**XXX** AMBIENCE *(A total immersion in Hollywood-style entertainment. The music can be loud.)*

# THE PLAZA RESTAURANT

**FOOD:** The Plaza Restaurant offers a typical American lunchroom menu of grilled and cold sandwiches and hamburgers. Its main bill of fare, however, is a whimsical selection of soda fountain treats, including the Magic Kingdom's largest ice cream sundae.

**LOCATION:** The restaurant is located at the end of Main Street to the right, facing Cinderella's Castle. It can also be reached from the walkway leading into Tomorrowland.

**DINING HOURS:** Open all day from 11 AM.

**AMBIENCE:** The Plaza Restaurant is housed in an ornate Victorian building with a light-filled atrium veranda off to the side. The interior has splendid Art Nouveau touches, with carved white wall panels, an array of gold-etched mirrors, and intricate brass and glass chandeliers. Marble-topped tables are scattered throughout the cheerful dining room, which has an abundance of windows topped with gauzy white valances. The view from the round veranda takes in Cinderella's Castle, lovely gardens, and the sci-fi archway leading into Tomorrowland. As a tribute to the turn-of-the-century atmosphere, waitresses wear long black Victorian dresses with crisp white aprons.

**SAMPLE ENTREES:** *Reuben Sandwich* (grilled sandwich with corned beef, Swiss cheese, sauerkraut, and Thousand Island dressing); *Pastrami Sandwich* (sliced pastrami on rye bread); *Hot Roast Beef Sandwich* (slices of roast beef with melted Muenster cheese, bacon, shredded lettuce, and Thousand Island dressing, served on rye bread); *Cold Roast Beef Sandwich* (sliced roast beef, lettuce, tomato, onion, and horseradish sauce on pumpernickel bread). Sandwiches are served with German potato salad.

**HEALTHY-CHOICE ENTREES:** *Fresh Vegetable Sandwich* (sliced cucumber, squash, alfalfa sprouts, tomato, and Swiss cheese on whole-wheat bread with dill spread); *Turkey Burger* (grilled ground turkey with mozzarella cheese); *Fruit Plate* (fresh seasonal fruits served with bread and strawberry cream cheese).

**LUNCH:** The same menu is offered throughout the day.

**BEVERAGES:** Coffee, tea, soft drinks, and juice are served, and espresso, cappuccino, and café mocha are also featured. *Creamy Hand-Dipped Milk Shakes,* the Plaza's signature specialties, come in vanilla, chocolate, and strawberry. Ice cream floats and sodas are also available.

**AVERAGE PRICE RANGE:** Entrees $$.

**FEATURES:** Ice cream–lovers will feel right at home in The Plaza Restaurant. In addition to the listed specialties, there is the *Bicycle Built for Two,* a create-your-own-fantasy ice cream treat.

The Plaza Restaurant is a great place to come in and cool off on hot afternoons, after the lunch crowd has thinned out. Ask for a table on the veranda.

For health-conscious diners, fountain specialties can be prepared with nonfat ice cream.

**DRAWBACKS:** The Plaza is very popular. Since no advance reservations are taken, there are sometimes long lines during peak dining times. Waits can be up to an hour.

**RESERVATIONS:** No reservations taken; diners are seated on a first-come, first-served basis.

### REVIEWERS' RATINGS
**XXXX** – As good as it gets.  **XXX** – Better than most.  **XX** – Adequate.  **X** – Of limited appeal.

**XX** FOOD *(Expensive lunchroom sandwiches and kid-pleasing specialties.)*

**XX** SERVICE *(Servers are efficient, but have an impersonal, seemingly memorized, politeness.)*

**XX** AMBIENCE *(Pretty dining areas, but at busy times they're noisy with hungry kids.)*

# PORTOBELLO YACHT CLUB

**FOOD:** The Portobello Yacht Club has an interesting menu featuring Northern Italian cuisine, including thin-crust pizzas, original pasta creations, and seafood flown in fresh daily. Also available are charcoal-grilled steaks, chicken, and pork chops flavored with fresh herbs and roasted in the restaurant's wood-burning oven.

**LOCATION:** The restaurant is located on Pleasure Island, adjacent to Disney Village Marketplace, and can be reached by walking along the waterfront.

**DINING HOURS:** Open all day. Lunch from 11:30 AM, dinner from 4 PM.

**AMBIENCE:** Despite its Italian name, the Portobello Yacht Club seems to capture the atmosphere of a New England yacht club. High-beamed ceilings shelter an array of nautical paraphernalia and an entire wall of yachting photos. The tables are covered in white and mint-green tablecloths, with a decorative Italian plate at each setting. The long, comfortable mahogany bar is accented with brass and surrounded with black leather stools.

**SAMPLE ENTREES:** *Costoletta di Maiale* (a center-cut pork chop marinated with fresh herbs, wood-burning-oven roasted, and served with oven-roasted potatoes and seasonal vegetables); *Spaghettini alla Portobello* (Alaskan crab legs, scallops, clams, shrimp, and mussels with tomatoes, garlic, olive oil, wine, and herbs, lightly tossed with spaghettini pasta); *Vitello Milanese* (breaded and sautéed veal with mixed greens of arugula, spinach, red onion, and tomato with balsamic vinaigrette); *Vitello con Granchio* (veal flank steak served over angel hair pasta with blue crabmeat, tossed with tomato-basil cream).

**HEALTHY-CHOICE ENTREES:** *Pollo alla Griglia* (a half chicken marinated in olive oil, garlic, and fresh rosemary charcoal grilled, and served with natural reduction, oven-roasted potatoes and seasonal vegetables); *Bucatini all'Amatriciana* (long pasta tubes with plum tomatoes, Italian bacon, garlic, and fresh basil); *Saltimbocca di Pollo* (boneless breast of chicken with prosciutto ham, fresh sage, lemon, and garlic, served with pasta and seasonal vegetables).

**LUNCH:** The lunch menu has a limited selection of entrees, and prices are quite a bit lower than at dinner.

**BEVERAGES:** Wine, beer, and spirits are served. The impressive wine selection features a number of fine California and Italian wines. Coffee, tea, and espresso are offered, as is a tempting choice of house cappuccinos. *Caesar's Secret,* a specialty of the house, is concocted with Amaretto and Frangelico.

**AVERAGE PRICE RANGE:** Lunch entrees **$$**, dinner entrees **$$$**.

**FEATURES:** The restaurant features one of Walt Disney World's most extensive selections of grappas, single-malt Scotches, Cognacs, and brandies.
    This is one of the few late-night full-service restaurants at Walt Disney World, open until 1:30 AM. Portobello features a number of interesting desserts; the espresso ice cream is especially popular.

**DRAWBACKS:** Tables for two are very hard to get when the restaurant is crowded, and there are long waits.

**RESERVATIONS:** No reservations are taken; diners are generally seated on a first-come, first-served basis. The restaurant has a smoking section.

### REVIEWERS' RATINGS
**XXXX** – As good as it gets. **XXX** – Better than most. **XX** – Adequate. **X** – Of limited appeal.

    **XXX**   FOOD   *(An ambitious array of Northern Italian dishes, creatively prepared.)*
  **XXXX**   SERVICE   *(Very friendly, helpful, and fast.)*
    **XXX**   AMBIENCE   *(Pleasant, but crowded at peak dining hours. Good for a quiet lunch.)*

# RESTAURANT AKERSHUS

**FOOD:** Restaurant Akershus features an all-you-can-eat Norwegian buffet known as a *koldtbord*. The cold selections include an array of Norwegian salads and smoked fish, and the hot dishes incorporate meat, poultry, seafood, and vegetables. Diners are encouraged to return to the buffet for separate courses, beginning with appetizers, continuing with the cold buffet, and ending with hot entrees and cheeses.

**LOCATION:** The restaurant is tucked inside the Norway pavilion in the World Showcase at Epcot Center. The entrance is located across the traditional town square from Kringla Bakeri og Kafé.

**DINING HOURS:** 11:30 AM for lunch, 4:30 PM for dinner.

**AMBIENCE:** Restaurant Akershus is fashioned after the medieval castle fortress that spans most of Oslo's harbor. Its four dining areas feature historical touches such as tall clerestory-style leaded-glass windows with lace curtains, walls of large whitewashed bricks, cathedral ceilings with wooden beams and iron chandeliers, and dramatic stone archways. Tables are set with red napkins and crisp white tablecloths.

**SAMPLE DINNER ENTREES:** Cold selections: *kyllingsalat* (chicken salad), *kjottsalat* (meat salad), *potetsalat* (potato salad), *egg og kinkesalat* (egg and ham salad), *karrisild* (curried herring), *glassmestersild* (glass master herring), *sildesalat* (herring salad), *tomatsilde* (tomato herring), *røkelaks og eggerøre* (smoked salmon and scrambled eggs), *fisketerrin* (fish mousse), *roastbiff* (roast beef), *ostefat* (cheese platter), *fylt svinekam* (stuffed pork loin). Vegetarian selections include mixed green salad, pasta salad, cucumber salad, cabbage salad, vegetable salad, and tomato salad.

Hot selections: *kjøttkaker* (meatballs), *få'r I Kål* (lamb and cabbage), *røke svinekam* (smoked pork), *skinkegrateng* (pork and noodles). Side dishes include mashed rutabaga, red cabbage, and potatoes.

**HEALTHY-CHOICE ENTREES:** *Røkt kalkun* (smoked turkey), *steinbit I dillsaus* (wolffish with dill sauce), and poached salmon.

**LUNCH:** The food selection available at lunch and dinner varies slightly, although the price is quite a bit lower at lunch.

**BEVERAGES:** Soft drinks, mineral water, coffee, and tea are available, as is Ringnes beer on tap. The wine list features a good selection from California vineyards, along with a more limited selection from France, Italy, and Portugal. Spirits are served, featuring Norway's Linie aquavit.

**AVERAGE PRICE RANGE:** Lunch buffet $$, dinner buffet $$$.

**FEATURES:** Norwegian cuisine is not widely known, so guests will find it easy to get same-day reservations. The food is served as an all-you-can-eat buffet, which diners can return to as often as they wish.

**DRAWBACKS:** The selection of heavy desserts, ordered a la carte from the servers, is disappointing. Vegetarian diners may find the variety of available hot selections quite limited.

**RESERVATIONS:** All Walt Disney World visitors can make reservations up to sixty days in advance by calling Disney Dining Reservations (407 939-3463). Same-day reservations can be made through WorldKey Information Service at Epcot Center, at the restaurant itself, or by calling Same Day Reservations after 10 AM (939-3463).

### REVIEWERS' RATINGS

**XXXX** – As good as it gets.  **XXX** – Better than most.  **XX** – Adequate.  **X** – Of limited appeal.

**XX** FOOD *(Good quality, but some foods may be unappealing to some diners. Skip the desserts.)*

**XX** SERVICE *(Informal and, at times, uneven. Drinks and desserts are served a la carte.)*

**XX** AMBIENCE *(Spacious medieval-style interior with lots of room between tables.)*

# RESTAURANT MARRAKESH

**FOOD:** Restaurant Marrakesh serves North African cuisine featuring meats and fish cooked with aromatic spices, as well as couscous, a light and flavorful steamed-grain dish that is generally regarded as the national dish of Morocco.

**LOCATION:** The restaurant is tucked away in the back of the Morocco pavilion in the World Showcase at Epcot Center. Guests can reach it by wandering through Morocco's fascinating shopping bazaar.

**DINING HOURS:** 11 AM for lunch, 5 PM for dinner.

**AMBIENCE:** The opulent multitiered Restaurant Marrakesh has slim carved pillars reaching up to the high ceiling, which is painted in colorful geometrics and hung with chandeliers. Red velvet banquettes against the tiled walls provide seating in the upper-tier dining areas, while the tables on the main floor, below, surround a small stage and tiled dance floor where belly dancers and musicians perform. The waiters wear *djellabas,* the traditional long robes of Morocco.

**SAMPLE DINNER ENTREES:** *Tagine of Chicken* (braised half chicken flavored with cumin, paprika, garlic, green olives, and preserved lemon, served with sliced potatoes); *Shish Kebab* (grilled brochettes of lamb flavored with Moroccan spices, served with rice with almonds and raisins); *Meshoui* (lamb roasted with almonds and raisins); *Couscous* (semolina steamed and served with garden vegetables and a choice of chicken or lamb).

**HEALTHY-CHOICE ENTREES:** *Tagine of Grouper* (fillet of grouper baked with green peppers and tomatoes, served with rice with almonds and raisins); *Vegetable Couscous* (semolina steamed and served with garden vegetables).

**LUNCH:** Lunch and dinner menus are similar, and prices are only slightly lower at lunch than at dinner.

**BEVERAGES:** Wine, beer, spirits, soft drinks, and mineral water are served. Besides coffee and espresso, *atai benna'na',* or fresh-brewed mint tea, is also offered. The restaurant features a special cocktail called *Marrakesh Express,* which contains gin, citrus juices, and orange-blossom water. The wine list offers an interesting selection of French and Moroccan wines.

**AVERAGE PRICE RANGE:** Lunch entrees $$, dinner entrees $$$.

**FEATURES:** Moroccan musicians and belly dancers entertain at both lunch and dinner. Entertainment begins twenty minutes after the hour, so schedule your meal accordingly.

Because many guests are unfamiliar with Moroccan cuisine, it is easier to secure reservations at the Restaurant Marrakesh or dine without a reservation.

**DRAWBACKS:** Service is much too fast and the meats are sometimes dry, suggesting that much of the food is precooked. Wait to place your order if you wish to settle in first.

**RESERVATIONS:** All Walt Disney World visitors can make reservations up to sixty days in advance by calling Disney Dining Reservations (407 939-3463). Same-day reservations can be made through WorldKey Information Service at Epcot Center, at the restaurant itself, or by calling Same Day Reservations after 10 AM (939-3463).

### REVIEWERS' RATINGS

**XXXX** – As good as it gets.  **XXX** – Better than most.  **XX** – Adequate.  **X** – Of limited appeal.

**XXX**  FOOD  *(Delicious flavors, surprisingly appealing to American palates.)*

**XX**  SERVICE  *(Polite and helpful, but sometimes a bit too fast.)*

**XXX**  AMBIENCE  *(Memorable surroundings and interesting entertainment.)*

# ROSE & CROWN DINING ROOM

**FOOD:** The Rose & Crown Dining Room serves traditional British fare, including steak and kidney pie, bangers and mash, prime rib, and London-style fish and chips wrapped in waxed newspaper.

**LOCATION:** The Rose & Crown Dining Room is the only full-service restaurant that sits on the edge of the World Showcase Lagoon. It is located directly across the promenade from the United Kingdom pavilion in the World Showcase at Epcot Center.

**DINING HOURS:** 11:30 AM for lunch, 4:30 PM for dinner.

**AMBIENCE:** The Rose & Crown Dining Room has a generous touch of neighborhood pub–style architecture, with wood-plank flooring, mahogany wainscoting, and hardwood tables and chairs. Hanging milk glass chandeliers, white pressed-tin ceilings, and stained-glass room dividers provide atmospheric highlights. The Rose & Crown Pub, in the front of the restaurant, has a stand-up wraparound mahogany bar with etched-glass paneling. The restaurant and its adjoining terrace overlook the World Showcase Lagoon.

**SAMPLE DINNER ENTREES:** *Cottage Pie* (spiced ground beef and carrots topped with mashed potato and Cheddar cheese); *London-Style Fish & Chips* (cod fried in ale batter, served with fried potatoes and malt vinegar); *Argyle Prime Rib* (served with Yorkshire pudding and garden vegetables); *Northern Irish–Styled Chicken* (breast of chicken sautéed and served with mushroom sauce, mashed potatoes, and garden vegetables). Traditional British pies are served with soup or salad.

**HEALTHY-CHOICE ENTREES:** *Traditional British Vegetarian Pie* (served with soup or salad); *Grimsby* (broiled fillet of fresh fish served with garden vegetables).

**LUNCH:** The lunch menu differs from dinner and includes the *Hampton Lighter Appetite* (chilled vegetables served with Stilton cheese and walnut dressing). At lunch, the British pies do not come with soup or salad, and prices are lower than at dinner.

**BEVERAGES:** Bass ale, Guinness stout, and lager are served chilled or at room temperature. Wine and spirits are offered, as are coffee, tea, and soft drinks. Specialty drinks include the *Shandy,* a concoction of Bass ale and ginger beer, and *Irish Coffee,* made with Irish whiskey, coffee, and whipped cream.

**AVERAGE PRICE RANGE:** Lunch entrees $$, dinner entrees $$$.

**FEATURES:** The Rose & Crown Pub, located in the front part of the restaurant, is a great spot to enjoy cocktails before dinner and soak up the convivial atmosphere.

    Dining tables on the outdoor terrace provide an excellent view of the World Showcase Lagoon.

    The Rose & Crown serves a very popular high tea at 3:30 PM. Reservations are recommended.

**DRAWBACKS:** The restaurant fills its reservations quickly during peak seasons, and it can be difficult to secure same-day reservations.

**RESERVATIONS:** All Walt Disney World visitors can make reservations up to sixty days in advance by calling Disney Dining Reservations (407 939-3463). Same-day reservations can be made through WorldKey Information Service at Epcot Center, at the restaurant itself, or by calling Same Day Reservations after 10 AM (939-3463).

### REVIEWERS' RATINGS

**XXXX** – As good as it gets. **XXX** – Better than most. **XX** – Adequate. **X** – Of limited appeal.

**XXX** FOOD *(Delightfully good food and value. Try the fish and chips.)*

**XXX** SERVICE *(Servers, wearing nineteenth-century pub costumes, are charming and efficient.)*

**XXX** AMBIENCE *(A lively crowd and comfortable, cozy decor.)*

# SAN ANGEL INN RESTAURANTE

**FOOD:** The San Angel Inn Restaurante specializes in regional Mexican dishes. Seafood, beef, and chicken are prepared in savory sauces enhanced with chilies and a wealth of Mexican spices. The original San Angel Inn is one of Mexico City's historic showplaces.

**LOCATION:** San Angel Inn Restaurante is located in the rear of the Mexico pavilion in the World Showcase at Epcot Center. The restaurant overlooks an indoor river.

**DINING HOURS:** 11:30 AM for lunch, 4:30 PM for dinner.

**AMBIENCE:** Entering the Mexico pavilion, guests walk through a Mexican village at twilight to reach the restaurant at the edge of the river. Red-sashed servers attend guests seated in colonial-style chairs at tables covered with pale pink cloths. The restaurant is very dark and lit with lanterns (bring a penlight to read the menus). A distant view of a smoking volcano and an exotic Mayan pyramid lend an aura of mystery to this romantic dining room.

**SAMPLE DINNER ENTREES:** *Filete Ranchero* (grilled beef tenderloin served over corn tortillas, topped with ranchero sauce, poblano chili strips, Mexican cheese, and onions, and served with refried beans); *Huachinango a la Veracruzana* (fillet of red snapper poached in wine with onions, tomatoes, and Mexican chilies); *Enchiladas de Pollo* (corn tortillas filled with chicken, topped with tomato-chili sauce, cheese, sour cream, onions, and tomatillo sauce or mole sauce). Entrees are served with Mexican rice and a choice of soup or salad.

**HEALTHY-CHOICE ENTREES:** *Pescado Dorado* (fillet of mahimahi marinated in chili sauce, grilled, and served with Mexican rice and vegetables); *Mole Poblano* (chicken simmered with Mexican spices and a hint of chocolate, served with refried beans).

**LUNCH:** Lunch and dinner menus are very similar, although lunch does not include soup or salad, and prices are much lower than at dinner.

**BEVERAGES:** Mexican beers such as Dos Equis, Bohemia, and Tecate are served, as are wine and spirits. After-dinner drinks include *Mexican Coffee* (Kahlúa, tequila, and cream) and *Café de Olla* (coffee with cinnamon and brown sugar). Juice, soft drinks, mineral water, coffee, and tea are also available.

**AVERAGE PRICE RANGE:** Lunch entrees **$$**, dinner entrees **$$$**.

**FEATURES:** The San Angel Inn Restaurante has a small adjacent lounge where diners can unwind, wait for a table, and enjoy a Margarita with chips and salsa.

Many visitors find the San Angel Inn Restaurante to be the most romantic in the World Showcase.

**DRAWBACKS:** Guests who love their salsa hot may be disappointed — request *salsa picante* (hot salsa). San Angel Inn Restaurante's reservations fill quickly, so it is difficult to make same-day reservations.

**RESERVATIONS:** All Walt Disney World visitors can make reservations up to sixty days in advance by calling Disney Dining Reservations (407 939-3463). Same-day reservations can be made through WorldKey Information Service at Epcot Center, at the restaurant itself, or by calling Same Day Reservations after 10 AM (939-3463).

## REVIEWERS' RATINGS

**XXXX** – As good as it gets.  **XXX** – Better than most.  **XX** – Adequate.  **X** – Of limited appeal.

**XXX** FOOD *(Flavorful and satisfying. On request, the chef will modify food to suit guests' tastes.)*

**XXX** SERVICE *(Polite, fast, and eager to please.)*

**XXXX** AMBIENCE *(Enchanting and romantic; a memorable dining atmosphere.)*

# SCI-FI DINE-IN THEATER RESTAURANT

**FOOD:** The Sci-Fi Dine-In Theater Restaurant features hot entrees such as prime rib, rib-eye steaks, oven-roasted turkey, smoked barbecued chicken, broiled fresh fish, and pasta, along with a selection of hot and cold sandwiches and large salads.

**LOCATION:** The restaurant is located adjacent to the Chinese Theater at Disney-MGM Studios. Guests can find it by looking for the restaurant's sign, which looks like a movie theater marquee.

**DINING HOURS:** 11 AM for lunch, 4 PM for dinner.

**AMBIENCE:** The waiting area of the Sci-Fi Dine-In Theater Restaurant resembles the back of a typical movie set, with exposed wall studs and bolts. Guests enter the large dining room through what looks like a movie ticket booth and are seated at tables built into fifties-style convertibles. It's always evening at the Sci Fi Dine-In Theater Restaurant, and make-believe stars glisten in the sky against a moonlit Hollywood Hills mural. Clips from campy science fiction films and cartoons play continuously on the giant movie screen; sound is provided through drive-in speakers mounted at each car. All cars and most seats face forward. The drive-in snack bar–style kitchen is located in the back of the fenced-in theater, where servers dressed as carhops pick up the food and deliver it to the cars.

**SAMPLE DINNER ENTREES:** *The Towering Terror* (prime rib of beef au jus, served with green beans and a choice of potato); *They Called It Seafood* (linguine with crab and shrimp in a tomato-herb sauce, served with garlic bread sticks); *Saucer Sightings* (rib-eye steak served with green beans and a choice of potato); *Journey to the Center of the Pasta* (vegetable lasagna with tomato sauce, served with garlic bread sticks).

**HEALTHY-CHOICE ENTREES:** *Cosmic Creation* (roasted barbecue chicken, served with corn on the cob and a choice of potato); *Monster Mash* (roasted turkey served with dressing, mashed potatoes, green beans, and cranberry relish); *Terror of the Tides* (broiled fresh fish fillet with orange-tamarind sauce, served with green beans and a choice of potato).

**LUNCH:** The lunch menu has fewer hot entrees and features lower-priced sandwiches and salads.

**BEVERAGES:** Coffee, tea, juice, soft drinks, and milk shakes are served, as are beer and wine. The wine list includes a surprisingly good selection of California vintages.

**AVERAGE PRICE RANGE:** Lunch entrees **$$**, dinner entrees **$$**.

**FEATURES:** Dining here can be a memorable experience for those who enjoy unique environments.

**DRAWBACKS:** Dining entertainment is the featured attraction here, not the food, which is standard at best. Watching science fiction and horror films while eating is literally out of this world, but forget social conversation; most guests face forward except for a few cars with seats that face each other. The atmosphere is somewhat eerie and quiet because of the attention paid to the flicks on-screen.

**RESERVATIONS:** All Walt Disney World visitors can make reservations up to sixty days in advance by calling Disney Dining Reservations (407 939-3463). Same-day reservations can be made at Hollywood Junction (at the intersection of Hollywood and Sunset Boulevards) at Disney-MGM Studios, at the restaurant itself, or by calling Same Day Reservations after 10 AM (939-3463).

### REVIEWERS' RATINGS

**✗✗✗✗** – As good as it gets. **✗✗✗** – Better than most. **✗✗** – Adequate. **✗** – Of limited appeal.

**✗✗✗** FOOD *(Many dishes are favorites of frequent guests; the desserts can be quite good.)*

**✗✗✗** SERVICE *(Carhop servers do their best to serve efficiently while staying down in front.)*

**✗✗✗** AMBIENCE *(An eat-in-your-car experience. Strange, but fun if you're in the mood.)*

# TEMPURA KIKU

**FOOD:** Tempura Kiku features seafood, chicken, beef, and vegetables dipped in a light batter, deep-fried, and served with a dipping sauce. While tempura is considered by many to be a traditional Japanese dish, it actually originated with the Portuguese, who opened Western trade with Japan. Sushi and sashimi are also available.

**LOCATION:** Tempura Kiku is located in the Japan pavilion in the World Showcase at Epcot Center. The restaurant is on the second floor, above the Mitsukoshi Department Store.

**DINING HOURS:** 11:30 AM for lunch, 5 PM for dinner. Closed between 3 and 4:30 PM.

**AMBIENCE:** This small dining room is just off the waiting room for Teppanyaki Dining, the larger restaurant next door. Warm gold-toned walls, traditional wood detailing, and short blue-gray doorway curtains contrast pleasantly with high-tech cookware in the center of this sushi bar–style restaurant. Guests are seated at the counter surrounding the cooking area, where they can enjoy the personal attention of their own white-hatted chef. Questions regarding ingredients and cooking styles are welcomed, and chefs will gladly suggest meals for newcomers to Japanese cuisine.

**SAMPLE DINNER ENTREES:** *Tori* (deep-fried chicken strips and fresh vegetables); *Sakana* (deep-fried shrimp, scallop, lobster, fish, and fresh vegetables); *Ume* (deep-fried shrimp, chicken strips, and fresh vegetables); *Take* (shrimp, skewered beef, and chicken strips with fresh vegetables); *Ebi* (shrimp with fresh vegetables). Soup, salad, and rice are included with the meal.

**HEALTHY-CHOICE ENTREES:** Although most Japanese foods are low in fat, several of the accompaniments make an excellent choice for light eaters. *Sashimi* (assorted raw fish); *Nigiri-zushi* (assorted raw fish on seasoned rice; tuna rolled in rice and seaweed); *Gosho-maki* (crabmeat, avocado, cucumber, and smelt roe rolled in seasoned rice with sesame seeds and seaweed).

**LUNCH:** Lunch and dinner menus are very similar, although lunch does not include a salad and prices are much lower than at dinner.

**BEVERAGES:** Wine, plum wine, sake, Kirin beer, and soft drinks are served, along with coffee and traditional Japanese green tea. The wine list offers a small but interesting selection of California wines. Specialty drinks offered from the full bar in the adjacent Matsu No Ma Lounge include the *Matsu,* made from gin, melon liqueur, pineapple, and lemon juices.

**AVERAGE PRICE RANGE:** Lunch entrees $$, dinner entrees $$$.

**FEATURES:** Since no reservations are taken, Tempura Kiku is a good choice for visitors who do not have dining reservations, especially during off-peak hours. Guests waiting for seats can enjoy the view of the World Showcase Lagoon from the adjacent Matsu No Ma Lounge.

The counter service is fast and efficient, making Tempura Kiku an excellent choice for lunch.

**DRAWBACKS:** Groups of more than three will find it difficult to conduct conversations because of the counter seating.

**RESERVATIONS:** No reservations are taken at this restaurant. The counter seats twenty-five.

### REVIEWERS' RATINGS
**XXXX** – As good as it gets. **XXX** – Better than most. **XX** – Adequate. **X** – Of limited appeal.

**XX** FOOD *(Very typical, modern tempura-style cooking.)*
**XXXX** SERVICE *(Fast, pleasant, and professional.)*
**XXX** AMBIENCE *(Friendly Japanese-style counter dining with interesting goings-on.)*

# TEPPANYAKI DINING

**FOOD:** Teppanyaki Dining offers meat, seafood, poultry, and vegetable dishes deftly prepared at the table by a white-hatted stir-fry chef. All the entrees are fresh, crisp, and sizzling.

**LOCATION:** Teppanyaki Dining is located in the Japan pavilion in the World Showcase at Epcot Center. Guests enter this second-floor restaurant from the wide staircase at the side of the Mitsukoshi Department Store.

**DINING HOURS:** 11:30 AM for lunch, 4:30 PM for dinner.

**AMBIENCE:** Guests are seated in one of the five tatami-floored rooms, which are separated by movable hand-painted shoji screens. Each dining room has four black-lacquered tables under gleaming copper venting hoods. The tables accommodate eight guests around the teppan grill, where the stir-fry chef prepares the meals. Once the orders are placed, the entertainment begins. The chef dons a large white hat, pulls knives from a holster, and artfully slices, dices, seasons, and stir-fries each order. Those familiar with the Benihana of Tokyo restaurant chain will notice a striking, but more low-key similarity. In the background are the sounds of traditional Japanese *koto* music.

**SAMPLE DINNER ENTREES:** *Ebi* (grilled shrimp); *Beef Tenderloin* (grilled steak); *Fujiyama* (grilled sirloin and shrimp); *Nihon-kai* (grilled shrimp, scallops, and lobster). All entrees are served with salad, grilled fresh vegetables with udon noodles, and steamed rice.

**HEALTHY-CHOICE ENTREES:** *Tori* (grilled chicken); *Kaibashira* (grilled scallops). Chefs will prepare vegetarian meals on request.

**LUNCH:** Lunch and dinner menus are very similar, although lunch does not include a salad, and prices are much lower, almost by half, than they are at dinner.

**BEVERAGES:** A fair selection of American wines is offered, as is plum wine from Japan. Kirin beer and hot sake are also available, as are cocktails from the full bar. A popular specialty drink, *Tachibana,* is concocted from light rum, orange Curaçao, mandarin orange, and orange juice. Soft drinks, green tea, and coffee are also available.

**AVERAGE PRICE RANGE:** Lunch entrees $$$, dinner entrees $$$$.

**FEATURES:** With their speedy chopping and clever preparation and cooking techniques, the stir-fry chefs provide memorable mealtime entertainment.

The nearby Matsu No Ma Lounge, overlooking the World Showcase Lagoon, makes waiting for tables a painless and relaxing experience.

Individuals and parties of two can frequently get seating without reservations.

**DRAWBACKS:** The communal seating may disappoint those looking for a private, intimate meal together.

**RESERVATIONS:** All Walt Disney World visitors can make reservations up to sixty days in advance by calling Disney Dining Reservations (407 939-3463). Same-day reservations can be made through WorldKey Information Service at Epcot Center, at the restaurant itself, or by calling Same Day Reservations after 10 AM (939-3463).

### REVIEWERS' RATINGS

**XXXX** – As good as it gets.  **XXX** – Better than most.  **XX** – Adequate.  **X** – Of limited appeal.

**XXX**  FOOD  *(The cuisine is Americanized and may disappoint diners expecting the real thing.)*
**XXXX**  SERVICE  *(Entertaining service: fast, funny, polite, and efficient.)*
**XXX**  AMBIENCE  *(Plenty of camaraderie, if you're in the mood for communal dining.)*

# TONY'S TOWN SQUARE RESTAURANT

**FOOD:** Tony's Town Square Restaurant offers Italian-style hot entrees and lighter dishes such as pizza, calzone, pasta, frittatas, and Italian sandwiches.

**LOCATION:** Tony's Town Square Restaurant is located at the beginning of Main Street, across Town Square from City Hall and next to Disneyana Collectibles in the Magic Kingdom.

**DINING HOURS:** Open all day. Breakfast from park opening, lunch from noon, dinner from 4:30 PM.

**AMBIENCE:** The welcoming centerpiece at Tony's Town Square Restaurant is a large statue of the leading characters in *Lady and the Tramp.* Other reminders of the delightful Walt Disney film are placed throughout the comfortable waiting area and dining rooms. Guests may choose to dine in the main dining room, with its stained-glass windows, mahogany-beamed ceilings, and banquette seating, or in the sunny glassed-in patio, with its ceiling fans, terra cotta–tiled floors, and view of bustling Town Square.

**SAMPLE DINNER ENTREES:** *Strip Steak with Lobster and Pasta* (twelve-ounce strip steak seasoned with garlic and served with sautéed lobster tossed with linguine and a light garlic-cream sauce); *Chicken Florentine with Pasta* (grilled chicken breast with spinach sauce and a blend of five cheeses); *Tony's Shrimp Sauté* (shrimp sautéed with garlic and seasonal vegetables, then tossed with linguine and a light cream sauce); *Joe's Linguine* (sautéed prosciutto ham, plum tomatoes, artichoke hearts, garlic, and linguine, tossed with a blend of five cheeses and cream).

**HEALTHY-CHOICE ENTREES:** *Turkey Piccata with Pasta* (escalope of turkey breast sautéed with lemon juice, white wine, and wild mushrooms); *Joe's Catch* (fresh catch of the day).

**BREAKFAST AND LUNCH:** *Tony's Italian Toast* and *Lady and the Tramp Waffles* are the breakfast specialties at Tony's, along with a selection of egg dishes. The lunch menu has fewer hot entrees than the dinner menu, and features frittatas, salads, and hot sandwiches. Prices are considerably lower at lunch.

**BEVERAGES:** Coffee, tea, and soft drinks are served, along with espresso and cappuccino.

**AVERAGE PRICE RANGE:** Breakfast entrees $$; lunch entrees $$; dinner entrees $$$.

**FEATURES:** Among the Magic Kingdom restaurants, Tony's is a good choice for those who enjoy Italian food. Although the cuisine is quite Americanized, it's still tasty and satisfying.

The lunch menu has a large selection for light eaters, including a variety of healthful salads.

On hot afternoons, Tony's is a great place to relax and cool off. After 2:30 PM, there are many empty tables and guests may order beverages or appetizers only, if they wish. Tony's *Fried Calamari with Marinara Sauce* is popular among frequent diners here.

Tony's Town Square Restaurant has compiled a menu for guests with special dietary concerns.

**DRAWBACKS:** The restaurant is located in a very busy part of the Magic Kingdom and attracts many families; it is not the best choice for a quiet lunch or dinner.

**RESERVATIONS:** All Walt Disney World visitors can make reservations up to sixty days in advance by calling Disney Dining Reservations (407 939-3463). Same-day reservations can be made at City Hall or at the restaurant itself, or by calling Same Day Reservations after 10 AM (939-3463).

## REVIEWERS' RATINGS

**XXXX** – As good as it gets. **XXX** – Better than most. **XX** – Adequate. **X** – Of limited appeal.

**XXX** FOOD *(Fair Italian food with a wide selection of entrees. A good bet for breakfast.)*

**XXX** SERVICE *(Polite, snappy, and informed.)*

**XX** AMBIENCE *(Pleasant, but often filled with children during mealtimes.)*

# TRAIL'S END BUFFETERIA

**FOOD:** Trail's End Buffeteria offers hearty all-you-can-eat country-style buffets for breakfast, lunch, and dinner. Lunch and dinner buffets include freshly made soup, sandwiches, and casseroles. An all-you-can-eat pizza buffet is also offered nightly after 9 PM.

**LOCATION:** Trail's End Buffeteria is located at Pioneer Hall in the Settlement Recreation Area at Fort Wilderness. Guests can reach Pioneer Hall by ferrying to the Fort Wilderness Marina or by taking a bus from the Fort Wilderness Guest Parking Lot or a shuttle from Disney's Wilderness Lodge.

**DINING HOURS:** Open all day. Breakfast from 7:30 AM, lunch from 11:30 AM, dinner from 4:00 PM, pizza buffet from 9:30 PM.

**AMBIENCE:** Trail's End Buffeteria is a very casual restaurant with an Old West, log-cabin ambience. Painted animal hides, antlers, horseshoes, and other frontier artifacts decorate the walls, and the small dining room has Formica-topped Early American tables and a rustic log-beamed ceiling. Music from a player piano entertains guests as they dine. Guests serve themselves from a variety of hot and cold entrees at the buffet and salad bar.

**SAMPLE DINNER ENTREES:** *Carved Steamship Round of Beef; Chicken and Dumplings; Sweet and Sour Pork Spareribs; Fried Chicken; Catfish Strips.* Soups, salads, and desserts are also included.

**HEALTHY-CHOICE ENTREES:** *Fresh Catch of the Day; Assorted Fresh Garden Vegetables; Salad Bar.*

**BREAKFAST AND LUNCH:** The breakfast buffet features egg dishes, pancakes, waffles, biscuits, fruit, pastries, and a seven-inch breakfast pizza. At lunch the buffet offers hamburgers, hot dogs, fried chicken, spaghetti, and personal pizzas.

**BEVERAGES:** Beer is available at lunch, as are coffee, tea, and soft drinks. At dinner, wine and spirits are also available. Nonalcoholic beverages are included in the price of the meal.

**AVERAGE PRICE RANGE:** Breakfast buffet **$**, lunch buffet **$**, dinner buffet **$$**.

**FEATURES:** Trail's End Buffeteria opens at 7:30 AM, giving early birds camping at Fort Wilderness a head start to the theme parks, and providing early arrivals for Fort Wilderness activities with a convenient breakfast spot.

   Trail's End will prepare foods to go, which makes it an ideal choice for visitors who would like to picnic at the beach or along the nature trails of Fort Wilderness.

   The restaurant offers a late-night pizza buffet from 9:30 until 11 PM every night of the week.

**DRAWBACKS:** This restaurant is small, so there can be a wait for a table during peak dining hours, except at lunch, when most Fort Wilderness guests are at the theme parks.

   Due to the isolation of Pioneer Hall within Fort Wilderness, Trail's End Buffeteria can be difficult to reach from other locations in Walt Disney World. Since the food here is not exceptional, it is only a worthwhile meal destination for visitors who are participating in Fort Wilderness activities.

   Trail's End Buffeteria is popular with families and can get very noisy and crowded.

**RESERVATIONS:** Buffet-style service. No reservations.

### REVIEWERS' RATINGS

**XXXX** – As good as it gets.   **XXX** – Better than most.   **XX** – Adequate.   **X** – Of limited appeal.

   **XX**   FOOD   *(Ordinary, but plenty of it. A good value, everything considered.)*
   **XX**   SERVICE   *(Guests serve themselves from the buffet; servers bring beverages and clear tables.)*
   **X**   AMBIENCE   *(Rustic and plain. Don't go out of your way.)*

WDW FOR ADULTS **ONE FREE** DINNER AT THE **OUTBACK** ★ SEE PAGE 272

# RESORT DINING

The resort restaurants offer some of the best dining experiences at Walt Disney World. Very often, the resort coffee shops are also surprisingly good, especially in the premier resorts, and the prices are reasonable. Any WDW visitor can make reservations at WDW resort restaurants up to sixty days in advance by calling the restaurant directly, or through Disney Dining Reservations (407 939-3463), which is open from 7 AM until 10 PM (EST) Monday through Friday and from 7 AM until 8 PM (EST) on Saturday and Sunday. Restaurants at non-Disney owned hotels take their own reservations and their phone numbers are noted in the review. Reservations at all the restaurants should be made well in advance for holidays such as Thanksgiving and Easter. Kosher, vegan, and other special meals can be requested when reservations are made, or can be requested twenty-four hours in advance. Wine, beer, and spirits are served in all resort restaurants and they are open every day. Some resort restaurants have smoking sections, which are noted in the reviews; however, smoking is not permitted in any of the Disney-owned restaurants. Listed below are some of the favorite resort eating spots among readers, including The Outback restaurant, which has been one of the most frequently mentioned. Readers' ratings were incorporated with those of the reviewers for overall quality and dining enjoyment as shown below: *(See page 163 for pricing codes.)*

**XXXX** – EXCELLENT OVERALL.   **XXX** – AMONG THE BEST.   **XX** – PLEASANT AND SATISFYING.

## The Outback
*Buena Vista Palace Resort and Spa*

Aboriginal designs, weathered woodwork, and an indoor waterfall that cascades down three stories of rough-hewn rock into a pond sparkling with swimming koi surround guests with the rustic ambience of Australia's outback. Servers dressed in "bush" outfits dish up surf-and-turf specialties that are grilled on open pits in the center of the restaurant. As they dine, guests are entertained with traditional folk tales and other interesting lore by an Australian storyteller who visits their tables.

**FOOD:**  The Outback features the flame-grilled cooking style of Australia's bush country. Entrees include meats, poultry, seafood, and fresh fish from Florida waters, served with a variety of tangy sauces.

**DINING HOURS:**  The Outback is open for dinner from 5:30 until 11 PM.

**SAMPLE DINNER ENTREES:**  *The Porterhouse 22 oz.* (the best of both steaks, served with creamed spinach in a puff pastry); *Barbecue Baby Back Ribs* (served with spicy Aussie barbecue sauce and seasonal vegetable); *Florida Catch* (Florida's freshest fish, prepared grilled, poached, or baked, served with seasonal vegetable). All entrees are served with baked potato, rice, or pasta.

**BEVERAGES:**  Soft drinks, mineral water, tea, and coffee, including espresso and cappuccino, are served. The restaurant's full bar features selected beers and wines from Australia, as well as specialty drinks such as *Outback Coffee* (Courvoisier, Kahlúa, Frangelico, and coffee, topped with whipped cream and chocolate sprinkles).

**AVERAGE PRICE RANGE:**  Dinner entrees $$$.

**RESERVATIONS:**  Reservations are suggested (407 827-3430). There is a smoking section.

**OVERALL RATING: XXXX**

**ARIEL'S:** *Disney's Beach Club Resort* — Named after the feisty princess in *The Little Mermaid,* Ariel's is a first-rate choice for seafood. Entrees also include pasta, beef, and chicken, and there is a separate menu section for the specialty of the house, lobster. The dining room decor has an undersea theme, featuring a twenty-five-hundred gallon aquarium. The wine list offers vintage California wines.

**DINING HOURS:** Ariel's is open for dinner from 6 until 10 PM.

**AVERAGE PRICE RANGE:** Dinner entrees $$$$.

**RESERVATIONS:** Reservations are required.

**OVERALL RATING: ✗✗✗✗**

**ARTHUR'S 27:** *Buena Vista Palace Resort and Spa* — Arthur's 27 serves elegant international cuisine in a traditionally decorated dining room with a panoramic view. Specialty entrees include Dover sole, venison, and duck. A seven-course prix-fixe banquet is also available. The wine list is extensive and well developed, and special dietary requests are accommodated with style. The service at Arthur's 27 is impeccable, and the restaurant holds a four-diamond rating from the American Automobile Association.

**DINING HOURS:** Arthur's 27 is open for dinner from 6 until 10:30 PM.

**AVERAGE PRICE RANGE:** Dinner entrees $$$$, prix-fixe dinners $$$$$$.

**RESERVATIONS:** Reservations are highly recommended (407 827-3450). Jackets are required for men; women tend to dress up. There is a smoking section.

**OVERALL RATING: ✗✗✗✗**

**ARTIST POINT:** *Disney's Wilderness Resort* — Artist Point serves a changing menu of seasonal Pacific Northwest specialties in a spacious dining area overlooking Bay Lake and the resort's gardens. Entrees include fresh seafood, poultry, steaks, game, and other delicacies, many of them smoked on the premises. A prix-fixe menu is also offered. The wines of Oregon and Washington are featured, along with a specially microbrewed house beer. The daily Character Breakfasts are lively and popular with families.

**DINING HOURS:** Artist Point is open for breakfast from 7:30 until 11:30 AM and dinner from 5:30 until 10 PM (until 10:30 PM on Friday and Saturday).

**AVERAGE PRICE RANGE:** Breakfast entrees $$, dinner entrees $$$, prix-fixe dinner $$$$$.

**RESERVATIONS:** Reservations are recommended.

**OVERALL RATING: ✗✗✗✗**

**BASKERVILLES:** *Grosvenor Resort* — Complete with a replica of Sherlock Holmes' Baker Street study, Baskervilles challenges diners to keep an observant eye out for Holmes memorabilia throughout the dining room. Dinner buffets feature different food themes nightly, including Italian, seafood, and Caribbean, all with carved prime rib. Breakfast is also served buffet-style, and lunch is a la carte, featuring salads, sandwiches, and light entrees.

**DINING HOURS:** Baskervilles is open for breakfast from 7 until 11:30 AM, lunch seasonally from 11:30 AM until 1:30 PM, and dinner from 6 until 10 PM. ★ The MurderWatch Mystery Dinner Theatre is held here on Saturday nights and selected nights (see "Dining Events," page 209).

**AVERAGE PRICE RANGE:** Breakfast entrees $$, lunch entrees $$, dinner entrees $$$.

**RESERVATIONS:** Dinner reservations are recommended (407 828-4444). The restaurant has a smoking section.

**OVERALL RATING: ✗✗✗**

WDW
FOR ADULTS
$ 5 OFF PER PERSON
MurderWatch
MYSTERY DINNER
THEATER
SEE PAGE 272

**BOATWRIGHT'S DINING HALL:** *Disney's Dixie Landings Resort* — The hospitality and cooking of the Old South dominate the entrees at Boatwright's Dining Hall, including tin-pan breakfasts, seafood jambalaya, steaks, prime rib, and Cajun specialties. Also featured are family-style dinners of chicken, ribs, or catfish, and fresh-baked breads and pastries.

> **DINING HOURS:** Boatwright's Dining Hall is open for breakfast from 7 until 11:30 AM and dinner from 5 until 10 PM.
>
> **AVERAGE PRICE RANGE:** Breakfast entrees $, dinner entrees $$.
>
> **RESERVATIONS:** Dinner reservations are recommended.
>
> **OVERALL RATING:** ✗✗✗

**BONFAMILLE'S CAFE:** *Disney's Port Orleans Resort* — First conceived in the classic Disney movie *The Aristocats,* Bonfamille's Cafe is a casual restaurant that evokes the Old French Quarter of New Orleans in its decor. Dinner entrees include steaks, seafood, and Creole specialties such as seafood jambalaya and spicy shrimp, crawfish, and oyster dishes. Breakfasts are lively and tend to be crowded.

> **DINING HOURS:** Bonfamille's Cafe is open for breakfast from 7 until 11:30 AM and dinner from 5 until 10 PM.
>
> **AVERAGE PRICE RANGE:** Breakfast entrees $$, dinner entrees $$.
>
> **RESERVATIONS:** Dinner reservations are recommended.
>
> **OVERALL RATING:** ✗✗✗

**CALIFORNIA GRILL:** *Disney's Contemporary Resort* — Located on the resort's fifteenth floor, California Grill offers a spectacular view and theatrical food preparation. Guests seated in the moderately sized dining area can watch as the restaurant's chefs prepare seafood, poultry, and meat dishes, along with gourmet pizzas, in the open kitchen. The focus is on using the freshest ingredients available seasonally, and portions are small. The wine list is extensive and features fine wines from California vineyards.

> **DINING HOURS:** California Grill is open for dinner from 5:30 until 10 PM.
>
> **AVERAGE PRICE RANGE:** Dinner entrees $$$$.
>
> **RESERVATIONS:** Reservations are highly recommended.
>
> **OVERALL RATING:** ✗✗✗✗

**CAPE MAY CAFE:** *Disney's Beach Club Resort* — Beach scenes and striped umbrellas create a casual seashore atmosphere at the Cape May Cafe. The buffet-style meals feature a daily New England–style clambake including fish, mussels, oysters, and shrimp, along with a variety of chowders. Whole steamed lobster can be ordered as a separate entree. The popular Character Breakfast buffet is served daily.

> **DINING HOURS:** Cape May Cafe is open for breakfast from 7:30 until 11 AM and dinner from 5:30 until 9:30 PM.
>
> **AVERAGE PRICE RANGE:** Character Breakfast buffet $$, dinner buffet $$$.
>
> **RESERVATIONS:** Reservations are recommended.
>
> **OVERALL RATING:** ✗✗✗

**CONCOURSE STEAKHOUSE:** *Disney's Contemporary Resort* — Located in a large atrium with the monorail passing overhead, the Concourse Steakhouse has a high-tech, yet comfortable ambience. Grilled steaks and prime rib are featured, along with poultry, seafood, and pasta dishes. For the pleasure of diners who enjoy wine with their meals, the restaurant's menu lists selected wines from California, Oregon, and

Washington alongside the appetizers and entrees they complement. Breakfast and lunch can be very noisy, but dinners are usually pleasant, intimate, and sophisticated.

**DINING HOURS:** Concourse Steakhouse is open for breakfast from 7 until 11 AM, lunch from noon until 3 PM, and dinner from 5 until 10 PM.

**AVERAGE PRICE RANGE:** Breakfast entrees $$, lunch entrees $$, dinner entrees $$$.

**RESERVATIONS:** Reservations are recommended.

**OVERALL RATING: ✗✗✗**

**FINN'S GRILL:** *The Hilton Resort* — Finn's Grill serves up seafood and steaks in an informal Key West style. Individual wood tables have comfortable wood chairs, and fanciful interpretations of fish fins adorn the walls and booths. Entrees can be grilled, fried, blackened, steamed, sautéed, or broiled, and most reflect a mix of Floridian and Caribbean styles. Pasta and pizza are also served. Finn's Grill has a limited wine list, and draft beer seems to be the popular pick here.

**DINING HOURS:** Finn's Grill is open dinner from 5:30 until 11 PM.

**AVERAGE PRICE RANGE:** Dinner entrees $$$.

**RESERVATIONS:** Reservations are accepted (407 827-4000). There is a smoking section.

**OVERALL RATING: ✗✗**

**FLAGLER'S:** *Disney's Grand Floridian Beach Resort* — A charming, elegant Old World atmosphere is re-created in this upscale restaurant. Entrees are prepared Italian style and include pasta, seafood, chicken, beef, and veal dishes. The wine list offers selections that complement the menu.

**DINING HOURS:** Flagler's is open for dinner from 5:30 until 10 PM.

**AVERAGE PRICE RANGE:** Dinner entrees $$$$.

**RESERVATIONS:** Reservations are recommended.

**OVERALL RATING: ✗✗✗**

**GRAND FLORIDIAN CAFE:** *Disney's Grand Floridian Beach Resort* — The Grand Floridian Cafe, located on the resort's ground floor, is a spacious light-filled room with tables, cozy booths, and tall arched windows that overlook the pool and courtyard. The menu features seafood, meats, and poultry prepared southern style, and a selection of specialty sandwiches.

**DINING HOURS:** Grand Floridian Cafe is open for breakfast from 7 until 11 AM and all-day dining from noon until 11 PM.

**AVERAGE PRICE RANGE:** Breakfast entrees $$, lunch entrees $$, dinner entrees $$$.

**RESERVATIONS:** Reservations are recommended.

**OVERALL RATING: ✗✗**

★ **HARRY'S SAFARI BAR & GRILLE:** *Walt Disney World Dolphin* — Tropical murals, tiger-stripe carpets, and a menu with prices listed in British pounds as well as U.S. dollars impart an international jungle-explorer flavor to the civilized dining experience here. Entrees feature beef, chicken, and seafood grilled to order. A "yard of beer" is also available for the intrepid bon vivant. The restaurant has a Sunday Character Brunch.

**DINING HOURS:** Harry's Safari Bar & Grille is open for dinner from 6 until 11 PM. The Sunday Character Brunch is offered from 8:30 AM until noon.

**AVERAGE PRICE RANGE:** Character Brunch $$$, dinner entrees $$$$.

**RESERVATIONS:** Reservations are recommended (407 934-4000). There is a smoking section.

**OVERALL RATING:** ✗✗✗

★ **JUAN & ONLY'S:** *Walt Disney World Dolphin* — A casual, yet sophisticated restaurant, Juan & Only's is decorated with festive piñatas, bright floral arrangements, carved wooden furnishings, and a bar with a timbered turn-of-the-century jail motif. The menu features traditional Mexican entrees such as enchiladas, burritos, and chimichangas, as well as seafood, poultry, and meat dishes prepared in a variety of regional Mexican cooking styles.

**DINING HOURS:** Juan & Only's is open for dinner from 5 until 11 PM.

**AVERAGE PRICE RANGE:** Dinner entrees $$.

**RESERVATIONS:** Reservations are recommended (407 934-4000). There is a smoking section.

**OVERALL RATING:** ✗✗✗

**NARCOOSSEE'S:** *Disney's Grand Floridian Beach Resort* — The octagonal shape, open central kitchen, outdoor deck, and sensational waterside view of the Seven Seas Lagoon and the Magic Kingdom create an upbeat mood for diners at Narcoossee's. The restaurant features blackened alligator steak along with entrees that include chicken, veal, lamb, beef, and seafood (lobster is a specialty).

**DINING HOURS:** Narcoossee's is open for lunch from 11:30 AM until 3 PM and dinner from 5 until 10 PM. Snacks and appetizers are served from 3 until 5 PM.

**AVERAGE PRICE RANGE:** Lunch entrees $$, dinner entrees $$$.

**RESERVATIONS:** Reservations are recommended.

**OVERALL RATING:** ✗✗✗✗

**OLIVIA'S:** *Disney Vacation Club Resort* — Evoking the ambience of Old Key West, Olivia's has a light and airy dining room and tables outdoors on the veranda. At dinner, prime rib is featured, along with entrees of seafood, poultry, and meat dishes prepared in the culinary style of the Florida Keys.

**DINING HOURS:** Olivia's is open for breakfast from 7:30 until 10:30 AM, lunch from 11 AM until 2 PM, and dinner from 5 until 10 PM.

**AVERAGE PRICE RANGE:** Breakfast entrees $, lunch entrees $$, dinner entrees $$.

**RESERVATIONS:** Reservations are recommended.

**OVERALL RATING:** ✗✗

**PALIO:** *Walt Disney World Swan* — Palio serves fine Italian cuisine in an elegant and festive dining room with an open kitchen. Entrees include specialty pizzas baked in a wood-burning oven, as well as veal, pasta, and seafood dishes. Strolling musicians provide tableside entertainment.

**DINING HOURS:** Palio is open for dinner from 6 until 11 PM.

**AVERAGE PRICE RANGE:** Dinner entrees $$$$.

**RESERVATIONS:** Reservations are recommended (407 934-3000). There is a smoking section.

**OVERALL RATING:** ✗✗✗

**SEASONS:** *Disney Institute* — Comfortably ensconced at the Village Green, Seasons is a great place to relax with a beautiful view of the Disney Village Waterways. The large dining area is divided into four sections, each decorated as a season: winter, spring, summer, and fall. The ever-changing menu features a breakfast buffet and New American and international cuisines, sometimes prepared by visiting chefs who are teaching at the Disney Institute. A Sunday brunch is also served.

**DINING HOURS:** Seasons is open for breakfast from 7 until 11 AM, lunch from 11:30 AM until 3 PM, dinner from 5:30 until 10 PM, and Sunday brunch from 9 AM until 2 PM.

**AVERAGE PRICE RANGE:** Breakfast buffet $$, lunch entrees $$, dinner entrees $$$, Sunday brunch buffet $$$.

**RESERVATIONS:** Dinner reservations are recommended.

**OVERALL RATING:** ✗✗✗✗

★ **SUM CHOWS:** *Walt Disney World Dolphin* — Sum Chows serves a sophisticated selection of regional Asian dishes in an elegant environment with white paper lanterns, black lacquer chairs, and deep red tablecloths. The varied prix-fixe menus incorporate seafood, beef, pork, lamb, chicken, and duck. Meals are prepared with great attention to presentation.

**DINING HOURS:** Sum Chows is open for dinner from 6 until 10 PM.

**AVERAGE PRICE RANGE:** Prix-fixe dinners $$$$$.

**RESERVATIONS:** Reservations are recommended (407 934-4000). There is a smoking section.

**OVERALL RATING:** ✗✗✗

**VICTORIA & ALBERT'S:** *Disney's Grand Floridian Beach Resort* — Award-winning Victoria & Albert's preserves the grand dining tradition in a formal, elegant dining room set with Royal Doulton china. The seven-course prix-fixe menu (with optional wine pairings) changes nightly and reflects the foods of the season. Entrees include seafood, poultry, beef, veal, lamb, and game. Soup, salad, appetizers, and dessert round out the menu. An excellent selection of wines, aperitifs, and cordials is also featured. Special seating at the Chef's Table in the kitchen area allows culinary fans to watch the chef in action.

**DINING HOURS:** Victoria & Albert's has two dinner seatings, 6 PM and 9 PM.

**AVERAGE PRICE RANGE:** Prix-fixe dinner $$$$$$ (about $25 additional with wine pairings).

**RESERVATIONS:** Advance reservations are required. Jackets and ties are required for men.

**OVERALL RATING:** ✗✗✗✗

**WHISPERING CANYON CAFE:** *Disney's Wilderness Lodge* — A boisterous atmosphere, rustic wooden tables, and comfortable chairs make guests feel welcome at this casual, friendly restaurant. Skillet breakfasts, hot or cold family-style lunches, and a cook-out themed dinner are featured. Entrees are prepared using a variety of techniques such as roasting, smoking, grilling, and barbecuing.

**DINING HOURS:** Whispering Canyon Cafe is open for breakfast from 7 until 11 AM, lunch from 11:30 AM until 3 PM, and dinner from 4:30 until 10 PM.

**AVERAGE PRICE RANGE:** Breakfast skillets $$, lunch entrees $$, dinner entrees $$$.

**RESERVATIONS:** Reservations are not accepted; guests are seated on a first-come, first-served basis.

**OVERALL RATING:** ✗✗✗

**YACHTSMAN STEAKHOUSE:** *Disney's Yacht Club Resort* — Wood-plank flooring, private booths, and intimate dining areas provide a clubby atmosphere for meat-lovers. The entrees prepared in the glassed-in kitchen include prime cuts of beef, lamb, and pork. A limited selection of chicken and seafood dishes is also available. The list of wines and domestic and international beers is impressive.

**DINING HOURS:** Yachtsman Steakhouse is open for dinner from 6 until 10 PM.

**AVERAGE PRICE RANGE:** Dinner entrees $$$$.

**RESERVATIONS:** Reservations are required.

**OVERALL RATING:** ✗✗✗

WDW FOR ADULTS
**$50 OFF**
ANY RESTAURANT AT THE
**DOLPHIN**
★
SEE PAGE 272

# DINING EVENTS

Dinner shows and entertainment dining are very popular at Walt Disney World, and reservations should be secured well in advance of your visit. Walt Disney World continues to add more evening entertainment to the lineup of events for adult visitors, including the new Disney's BoardWalk, an attraction and resort complex complete with restaurants, dance and music clubs, and ESPN Sports World entertainment center (see "Disney's BoardWalk," page 96). The premier late-night entertainment and club scene can be found on Pleasure Island (see "Pleasure Island," page 61). Also popular with insiders, but less well known among visitors, are the clubs at Hotel Plaza, which are frequented by locals and Disney Cast Members. A big hit with both families and hardcore Disney fans are Disney Character Meals, usually for breakfast or dinner.

**LAUGHING KOOKABURRA:** *Buena Vista Palace Resort and Spa* — This energetic dance club, the largest at Hotel Plaza, is located in the lower level of the hotel. Starting at 4 PM, deejays play a mix of soft rock and Top 40 tunes, throw trivia and "name-that-tune" questions to the crowd, and award prizes for the right answers. At 9 PM, the featured band comes onstage and the dancing heats up. The crowds are made up of locals, convention attendees, and guests staying in the Hotel Plaza area.

    **HOURS:** Nightly from 4 PM until 2 AM.

    **FEATURES:** Happy hour from 4 until 8 PM, including a complimentary buffet. On Ladies' Night Tuesdays, women receive free drinks. Free valet parking at the Laughing Kookaburra entrance.

**TOP OF THE PALACE LOUNGE:** *Buena Vista Palace Resort and Spa* — Located on the hotel's twenty-seventh floor, this elegant lounge provides a perfect setting for guests seeking an intimate spot for cocktails or after-dinner drinks. At 8:30 PM Wednesday through Sunday, a singer accompanied by piano appears. The lounge attracts a sophisticated crowd, which spills over from the elegant Arthur's 27.

    **HOURS:** Nightly from 5 PM until 1 AM.

    **FEATURES:** Nightly Champagne Sunsets feature a complimentary champagne toast every evening, followed by an excellent view of WDW's fireworks shows. Appetizers and desserts from Arthur's 27 are served. Free valet parking at the Laughing Kookaburra entrance, downstairs.

**TOPPERS:** *Travelodge Hotel* — This club, on the hotel's top floor, is frequented by locals and Cast Members who drop by after work to catch sporting events on the club's twelve monitors, watch WDW's fireworks shows, and enjoy Margaritas by the pitcher. From 8 PM until midnight Wednesday through Saturday, music videos fill the monitors, turning the club into a lively social scene.

    **HOURS:** Nightly from 5 PM until 2 AM.

    **FEATURES:** Happy hour from 4 until 8 PM. Snack foods are available from 8 PM until 1 AM, and the club has an excellent view of all theme park fireworks. On selected nights, Toppers offers two-for-one drink specials; Cast Members have discounts every night.

**CHARACTER MEALS:** Several types of Character Meals are scheduled daily at the theme-parks restaurants and at the resorts, including Hotel Plaza resorts. Popular Disney characters act as hosts and drop by tables to greet diners, sign autographs, and have their pictures taken with guests. While popular with the kids, Character Dinners can also be quite charming for adult visitors. The later the meal, the better. For information about Character Meals and times, or to make reservations, call Disney Dining Reservations (407 939-3463) or consult Guest Services at your resort. ◆

# HOOP-DEE-DOO MUSICAL REVUE

**LOCATION:** The Hoop-Dee-Doo Musical Revue is held nightly at Pioneer Hall, in the heart of 740-acre Fort Wilderness. Visitors can catch shuttle buses to Pioneer Hall from the Fort Wilderness Guest Parking Lot, or ferry across Bay Lake from the Contemporary Marina or the Magic Kingdom Dock.

**ENTERTAINMENT:** The dinner show, performed by the enthusiastic Pioneer Hall Players, starts with a banjo and piano serenade followed by a song-and-dance vaudeville performance that relies heavily on broad humor, sight gags, pratfalls, puns, and audience participation. The colorfully costumed performers mingle with the audience, asking them where they're from, then sing little ditties based on the replies. Guests with birthdays or anniversaries are singled out for special attention, as are newlyweds. For the finale, washboards are handed out to the audience, who are encouraged to play them with their spoons.

**DINING ROOM:** The large pine-log lodge has two levels: a ground floor with a stage at one end, and a balcony supported by large rock pillars. The room is lit with hanging wagon-wheel fixtures and decorated in a wilderness motif with stuffed animal heads, snowshoes, and antlers.

**SAMPLE MENU:** The family-style all-you-can-eat dinner includes *Appetizer* (chips and salsa, and fresh-baked bread); *Salad* (lettuce, slices of cucumber, carrot, and cabbage) with *Vinaigrette Dressing*; *Pieces of Golden, Brown, Country Fried Chicken; Barbecued Ribs* (tasty short ribs cooked in barbecue sauce); *Corn-Right-on-the-Cob; Beans;* and *Mom's Homemade Strawberry Shortcake.* The menu may vary.

Kosher, vegetarian, or low-sodium meals may be ordered twenty-four hours in advance through the Hoop-Dee-Doo Musical Revue Office (407 824-2803).

**BEVERAGES:** Soft drinks, coffee, and iced tea are included with the meal. Beer, wine, and sangría (recently strengthened with the addition of rum) are also offered.

**PRICE:** The ticket price is about $40 ($27 for juniors, $20 for children). Taxes and gratuities are not included in the ticket price, and servers expect a 15 to 20 percent tip.

**SHOW TIMES:** Shows are scheduled at 5 PM, 7:15 PM, and 9:30 PM. Families frequent the early show.

**MAKING RESERVATIONS:** Reservations for the popular Hoop-Dee-Doo Musical Revue should be made as far in advance as possible. All Walt Disney World visitors may book dinner shows up to one year in advance by calling Disney Dining Reservations (407 939-3463). Same-day reservations may be made by calling 824-2858 between 8 AM and 6 PM.

Reserved dinner-show tickets, which must be obtained before show time, may be purchased up to five days in advance at Guest Services in any WDW resort, or at the Guest Services Window at Pioneer Hall.

**TIPS:** Pioneer Hall is not easy to find at night, and it takes longer than you think to get there. (See "Fort Wilderness & River Country," page 69.) Busing from another resort is difficult; you must change buses. (Some WDW resorts now run direct buses at times.) If you are driving (or busing directly from a theme park), it's a smart idea to go to Disney's Wilderness Lodge Resort and catch their shuttle to Pioneer Hall.

**NOTE:** There is no smoking permitted at the Hoop-Dee-Doo Musical Revue. Dress is very casual. Arrive one half hour before the scheduled show time, or your reservation may be cancelled.

### REVIEWERS' RATINGS

**XXXX** – Top-notch. **XXX** – Makes the evening worthwhile. **XX** – Pleasantly adequate. **X** – Of limited merit.

**XXX** ENTERTAINMENT *(Very hokey material executed by very talented performers.)*

**XX** FOOD *(Ample portions, but the quality frequently varies from good to disappointing.)*

**XXX** SERVICE *(Polite, fast, friendly, and professional.)*

**XXX** AMBIENCE *(Boisterous. Kids have a great time here, and many adults are great fans.)*

# HOUSE OF BLUES

**LOCATION:** Slated to open in 1996, the House of Blues is located adjacent to Pleasure Island, beyond the AMC Pleasure Island Theatres at the edge of Buena Vista Lagoon.

**ENTERTAINMENT:** This combination restaurant and concert hall features live performances by top-rated musicians. Concert-goers can attend the House of Blues concert performances only, or they can make an evening of it with dinner, as well. House of Blues also serves an all-you-can-eat Gospel brunch every Sunday, complete with gospel music entertainment. The creators of House of Blues (who include Dan Ackroyd, Jim Belushi, and the rock band Aerosmith) consider blues the taproot of many American musical forms, so the performances range across all styles, including rhythm and blues, reggae, country, gospel, pop, jazz, and of course, the blues.

**DINING ROOM:** As much a noted restaurant as a concert hall, the House of Blues features an inspired menu from the Mississippi Delta, served in a large comfortable dining room that captures the welcoming ambience of a Delta home of the Old South. Throughout the room, numerous works of African-American folk art are exhibited (which the club owners call the "visual blues") and the ceilings are adorned with original bas-reliefs of legendary "bluesmen." Typically, House of Blues is designed with a spacious ground floor concert-hall that has a stage filling one end, a dance area in front of the stage, and several bars. The dining area is situated on a large second-level loft overlooking the stage.

**SAMPLE MENU:** The chefs at House of Blues have creatively adapted the cuisine of the Mississippi Delta region to incorporate seasonal ingredients in the traditional dishes, which include their signature *Jambalaya* (shrimp, scallops, tender chicken, and Andouille sausage tossed in a Creole sauce with Cajun rice). The menu also features a number of standard American favorites, including pastas, salads, barbecued meats, hamburgers, and pizzas fired in a wood-burning oven. The tempting array of desserts includes the house favorite, *Warm Bread Pudding with Whiskey Sauce.*

**BEVERAGES:** Soft drinks, juices, coffee, cappuccino, and espresso are available. There are full bars throughout the club that feature domestic and imported beers, vintage wines, and a number of specialty drinks, including their infamous *Blues Mobile,* made with vodka, rum, triple sec, gin, tequila, Roses Lime Juice, and Blue Curaçao for color.

**PRICE:** Depending on the featured performer, ticket prices for the performances range from about $8 to $15. Lunch and dinner entrees range from $10 to $20. The Sunday Gospel Brunch is about $20. (Prices do not include beverages, taxes, and gratuities.)

**SHOW TIMES:** The House of Blues is open from 11:30 AM for lunch and from 6 PM for dinner. Performances generally start between 8 and 9 PM. (There is no live music at lunch.) There are three Gospel Brunch seating on Sundays: 10 AM, 12:15 PM, and 2:30 PM.

**MAKING RESERVATIONS:** Reservations for the House of Blues performances and dinner can be made about thirty days in advance. Brunch reservations can be made up to sixty days in advance. No reservations are taken for lunch. For information, call Disney Dining Reservations (407 939-3463). House of Blues also has a walk-up box-office where tickets can be picked-up and purchased for both future and same-day events.

**TIPS:** The rest room attendants keep a supply of lotions, colognes, and other grooming accessories on hand for guest use. If you will be using them, take tipping change with you.

**NOTE:** Generally, guests must be twenty-one for evening performances, although there are frequently early-evening performances for visitors of all ages.

    Both the club and restaurant have smoking sections. Dress is casual. ◆

# JOLLY HOLIDAYS

**LOCATION:** The Jolly Holidays dinner show and Christmas celebration is staged in the Fantasia Ballroom at Disney's Contemporary Resort, which is located on the monorail line in the Magic Kingdom Resorts Area.

**ENTERTAINMENT:** Guests are entertained periodically during dinner by carolers, but it is after dinner that the action really begins. The lights go down and all four stages in the ballroom are used, which keeps guests swiveling in their seats. The show is modified and new elements are added yearly, but the theme is generally centered around Toyland on Christmas Eve, performed by a cast of more than one hundred elaborately costumed singers and dancers. Popular Disney characters and a parade of toy soldiers star in this well-crafted extravaganza, and the action takes place on the stages and throughout the huge ballroom. The show runs heavy on the sentimental, but what could be more appropriate for Christmas?

**DINING ROOM:** The Fantasia Ballroom is on the ground floor of the Contemporary's large convention center. The four walls of this vast ballroom are turned into elaborate stages, and the room is filled with round tables that seat twelve and are festively decorated with green tablecloths, red napkins, and a center-piece of brightly wrapped gifts. Most tables are near at least one stage, and the aisles between tables are also used by the performers, so everyone has a unique view. The ballroom's prismatic mirrored ceiling is used to created special lighting effects with spotlights, lasers, and strobes.

**SAMPLE MENU:** The all-you-can-eat turkey dinner, with all the trimmings, is served family style at each table. The menu includes *Platters of Sliced Roast Turkey and Ham, Gravy, Mashed Potatoes, Sweet Potatoes, Green Beans, Cranberry Sauce,* and *Hot Apple Cobbler with Fresh Whipped Cream.* Food and beverages are frequently replenished by servers. The menu may vary.

**BEVERAGES:** Unlimited soft drinks, coffee, tea, and red and white wine are included with the meal.

**PRICE:** The ticket price is about $60 ($55 for juniors, $35 for children). Taxes and gratuities are included in the ticket price.

**SHOW TIMES:** Jolly Holidays plays nightly from just after Thanksgiving until just before Christmas. Shows are generally scheduled at either 5 or 8:30 PM. Families with young children frequent the early shows.

**MAKING RESERVATIONS:** This dinner show is produced in conjunction with Disney's Jolly Holidays Vacation Package, which may be booked up to one year in advance and includes accommodations, the Jolly Holidays dinner show, holiday receptions at resorts throughout the property, and theme park admissions. Usually beginning in October, any visitor can make dinner-show-only reservations by calling Disney Dining Reservations (407 827-7200). The show is paid for at the time it is booked, with a credit card or by check. There is a forty-eight-hour cancellation policy. For information on same-day reservations, call Disney's Contemporary Resort's Guest Services desk (824-1000).

**TIPS:** Seating begins about twenty minutes before show time. Several bars, usually set up in the large lobby outside the ballroom, dispense Christmas spirits.

Guests are seated communally at tables for twelve on a first-come, first-served basis.

**NOTE:** There is no smoking permitted at Jolly Holidays. Dress tends to be festive.

## REVIEWERS' RATINGS

**XXXX** – Top-notch. **XXX** – Makes the evening worthwhile. **XX** – Pleasantly adequate. **X** – Of limited merit.

**XXXX** ENTERTAINMENT *(Great sound, lighting, and performances. A pleaser for all ages.)*
**XXXX** FOOD *(This is among the best food served at any Disney dinner show.)*
**XXX** SERVICE *(The servers are unobtrusive and skilled professional convention workers.)*
**XXX** AMBIENCE *(It's remarkable that a ballroom can be made to feel so cozy and homey.)*

# MURDERWATCH MYSTERY DINNER THEATRE

**LOCATION:** MurderWatch Mystery Dinner Theatre is staged at the Grosvenor Resort, located on Hotel Plaza in the Disney Village Resorts Area. The show is held in Baskervilles restaurant.

**ENTERTAINMENT:** Guests are asked to help solve a murder with a zany and animated group of players, some of whom are clandestinely planted in the audience before the show. Most of the action takes place after guests have served themselves at the buffet. Some subtle altercations occur while guests are dining, to attract attention to the large cast and to create suspicion. After witnessing a murder, compiling clues, guessing at motives, and listening to a number of hilarious, heartrending confessions, guests are asked to choose the most likely suspect. The winners receive their awards on stage.

**DINING ROOM:** Guests are seated at tables for two, four, or six in a spacious but intimately proportioned Edwardian-style dining room. The walls of the restaurant are decorated with framed plates from Sherlock Holmes editions, drawn for London's *Strand Magazine* in the 1890s.

**MENU:** The all-you-can-eat buffet includes *Roast Prime Rib of Beef, Fresh Red Snapper, Coq au Vin, Baked Stuffed Shells, Fresh Mixed Vegetables,* and a complete *Salad Bar.* Side dishes include *Wild-Blend Rice with Raisins and Almonds* and *Duchèse Potatoes.* Guests select from an array of desserts at the *Dessert Buffet.* The menu may vary.

**BEVERAGES:** Coffee and tea are available at the buffet. Soft drinks, wine, and beer are brought to the table by servers. Guests can order cocktails from Moriarty's Pub, next door.

**PRICE:** The ticket price is about $35 (about $15 for children). The admission price includes taxes and gratuities. Guests pay as they enter the restaurant.

**SHOW TIMES:** There is always one show at 6 PM on Saturday nights; during busy seasons, show times are at 6 and 9 PM. Shows may be scheduled on other selected nights.

**MAKING RESERVATIONS:** Reservations for the MurderWatch Mystery Dinner Theatre should be made well ahead of time. Reservations may be made up to two months in advance and are taken on a first-come, first-served basis. There is no preference for guests staying at the Grosvenor Resort. Reservations made during low-attendance times require a two-day advance notice. Reservations can be made by calling the Grosvenor Resort (800 624-4109 or 407 827-6500).

**TIPS:** The dining room has several large square pillars in the center, which can obscure the action taking place throughout the show. Ask for a table "in the middle of the action" when booking reservations.

Don't miss the Grosvenor's Sherlock Holmes Museum, a replica of the famous detective's 221B Baker Street digs, tucked in the back of the restaurant. It includes such props as the famous Stradivarius, Holmes' purple dressing gown and Meerschaum pipe, and the remains of a meal interrupted by a client in distress. Give yourself a little extra time before or after the show to view it.

There are very few little children at these shows; the atmosphere is more like a supper club. The children who do attend are usually older and are drawn into the action as clue hunters by the hosts.

**NOTE:** Guests may wish to dress up a bit for this buffet dinner. Smoking is not permitted during the show.

### REVIEWERS' RATINGS

**XXXX** – Top notch.  **XXX** – Makes the evening worthwhile.  **XX** – Pleasantly adequate.  **X** – Of limited merit.

**XXXX**  ENTERTAINMENT  *(An outstanding professional cast. One of the best shows at WDW.)*

**XXX**  FOOD  *(Above-average buffet-style food, good prime rib, and a very good value.)*

**XXX**  SERVICE  *(Self-service. Very attentive, helpful servers bring beverages and clear plates.)*

**XX**  AMBIENCE  *(A functional, pleasant dining room; intimate and charming at night.)*

WDW FOR ADULTS
$5 OFF PER PERSON
MURDERWATCH MYSTERY DINNER THEATER
SEE PAGE 272

# 'OHANA

LOCATION: 'Ohana restaurant is located on the second floor of the Great Ceremonial House at Disney's Polynesian Resort. This restaurant is housed in what was formerly the Papeete Bay Verandah.

ENTERTAINMENT: 'Ohana means "family" in Hawaiian, and this is how guests are treated from the moment they enter. Servers sound the *Pu,* or ceremonial conch shell, to signal the arrival of "the King's Storyteller," who sings an Hawaiian welcoming song. The show is a performance of Hawaiian culture told in stories and song. During dessert, guests are given Hawaiian instruments to play along with the traditional songs. From 'Ohana's windows, guests are treated to a view of the Magic Kingdom fireworks and the Electrical Water Pageant.

DINING ROOM: Giant tikis, slate and wooden floors, and Polynesian artifacts enhance 'Ohana's Southern Pacific Islands motif. In the center of the restaurant, the ceiling is reminiscent of a thatched roof with small spots of sun (high-intensity halogen lights) beaming through. Tables for individual dining are scattered throughout the restaurant. The open kitchen features a sixteen-foot grill that flames dramatically while the meats are being cooked.

SAMPLE MENU: Much of the all-you-care-to-eat dinner is served family style with large lazy Susans filled with *Polynesian Dim Sum; Napa Cabbage Slaw, Green Salad; Roasted Sesame Dressing,* and tangy *'Ohana Salsa,* served with *Toasted Bread with Rosemary Seasoning.* Main courses include *Vegetable Stir-fried Lo Mein* and three-foot long skewers of flame-seared meats such as *Hawaiian Sausage Flavored with Parsley and Garlic; Grilled Chicken; Spicy Grilled Jumbo Shrimp; Turkey Marinated in Malt Vinegar, Brown Sugar, Cracked Black Pepper, Lemon Juice, and Tabasco; Pork Ribs in a Mild Teriyaki Seasoning; Beef Tenderloin Rubbed with Mesquite Seasoning;* and a palate cleanser of *Sliced Pineapple with Caramel Dipping Sauce.* Dessert choices include *Passion Fruit Crème Brûlée, Coconut Snowball, Apple Torte with Mango Slice,* and *Chocolate Diablo Fudge Cake.* The menu may vary.

BEVERAGES: Soft drinks, coffee, and iced tea are included with the meal. The wine list is very limited but includes 'Ohana's own Johannesburg Riesling, which is an excellent accompaniment to the dishes served. The adjacent Tambu Lounge has a full bar and features frozen tropical drinks.

PRICE: The prix-fixe dinner is about is about $25 (about $15 for juniors and $10 for children). Desserts are not included in the dinner price. Taxes and gratuities are not included in the dinner price, and servers expect a 15 to 20 percent tip.

SHOW TIMES: Open from 5 until 10 PM; continuous entertainment throughout the evening.

MAKING RESERVATIONS: Reservations can be made by all guests up to sixty days in advance by calling Disney Dining Reservations at 407 939-3463. Kosher, vegetarian, or low-fat meals may be requested at that time, or ordered no later than twenty-four hours in advance. For same-day reservations, call 939-3463 after 10 AM.

TIPS: If you do not want to be actively involved in the show, let the host know before you are seated.

NOTE: No smoking is permitted at 'Ohana. Dress is casual.

### REVIEWERS' RATINGS

✘✘✘✘ – Top-notch. ✘✘✘ – Makes the evening worthwhile. ✘✘ – Pleasantly adequate. ✘ – Of limited merit.

✘✘✘ ENTERTAINMENT *(An audience-engaging show of traditional Hawaiian hospitality.)*

✘✘✘✘ FOOD *(An enjoyable mix of tasty dishes with unique presentations; meat oriented.)*

✘✘✘✘ SERVICE *(A friendly, informative, and personable staff, well versed in Hawaiian culture.)*

✘✘✘ AMBIENCE *(You feel like an honored guest at an authentic Hawaiian fete.)*

# POLYNESIAN LUAU

**LOCATION:** The Polynesian Luau dinner show is staged nightly in Luau Cove, an open-air dinner theater near the beach at Seven Seas Lagoon, behind Disney's Polynesian Resort.

**ENTERTAINMENT:** The show begins after dinner, with a South Seas island fashion show and the music of a five-piece Hawaiian band. After a brief intermission, the talented dancers appear on stage and the action gets going: graceful hulas interpreted by women in ti-leaf skirts, ritual dances from the Kingdom of Tonga performed by men in traditional face paint, fast-moving Tahitian dances driven by staccato drumbeats, and a dramatic Samoan fire-dance finale with burning torches and a great deal of good humor.

**DINING ROOM:** A partial roof covers the large fan-shaped dining room, protecting guests from the occasional rains but leaving the stage open to the sky. Guests are seated at long, candlelit quasi-communal tables that radiate out from the stage.

**SAMPLE MENU:** The family-style all-you-can-eat dinner includes *Zucchini-Carrot Salad with Vinaigrette Dressing; Roasted Boneless Chicken with Hawiian Brown Sauce; Seafood Stir-Fry; Spareribs in Barbecue Sauce; Steamed Rice; Banana Bread with Honey-Cinnamon Butter; Polynesian-Themed Dessert.* The menu may vary.

Kosher, vegetarian, or low-fat meals may be ordered twenty-four hours in advance through the Polynesian Luau Office (824-1593).

**BEVERAGES:** Soft drinks, coffee, and iced tea are included with the meal. You may also select a *Mai Tai* (rum and fruit juices) or *Melon Colada* (melon liqueur, rum, and fruit juices). They may sound potent but they're very mild. Beer and wine are also offered.

**PRICE:** The ticket price is about $36 (about $27 for juniors and $20 for children). Taxes and gratuities are not included in the ticket price, and servers expect a 15 to 20 percent tip.

**SHOW TIMES:** The early show seating is at 6:45 PM; the late show seating is at 9:30 PM.

**MAKING RESERVATIONS:** Reservations for the Polynesian Luau should be made well in advance. All Walt Disney World visitors may book dinner shows up to one year in advance by calling Disney Dining Reservations (407 939-3463). Same-day reservations may be made by calling 824-1593.

Reserved dinner-show tickets, which must be obtained before show time, may be purchased up to seven days in advance at Guest Services at the Polynesian or any other WDW resort. You are assigned a table number at that time.

**TIPS:** The performance is most dramatic when it is dark, so try to book the late show during the summer. If your timing is right, you can see the Magic Kingdom fireworks show during dinner.

Visitors who would like a sneak preview of the Polynesian Luau should venture out to Luau Cove at about 8 or 10:45 PM. The stage can be seen from the courtyard at the entrance.

**NOTE:** There is no smoking permitted at the Polynesian Luau. Dress casually for an outdoor setting. Arrive about one half hour before the scheduled show time. Shows are rarely cancelled, even in the rain, but if the weather is very cold, call 824-2189 to confirm.

### REVIEWERS' RATINGS

**XXXX** – Top-notch. **XXX** – Makes the evening worthwhile. **XX** – Pleasantly adequate. **X** – Of limited merit.

**XXX** ENTERTAINMENT *(An enjoyable, well-crafted show with highly skilled performers.)*

**XX** FOOD *(Not exactly a gourmet feast, but enjoyable and filling.)*

**XX** SERVICE *(Family-style service by polite but rushed and impersonal staff.)*

**XXXX** AMBIENCE *(The tropical atmosphere is especially compelling after dark.)*

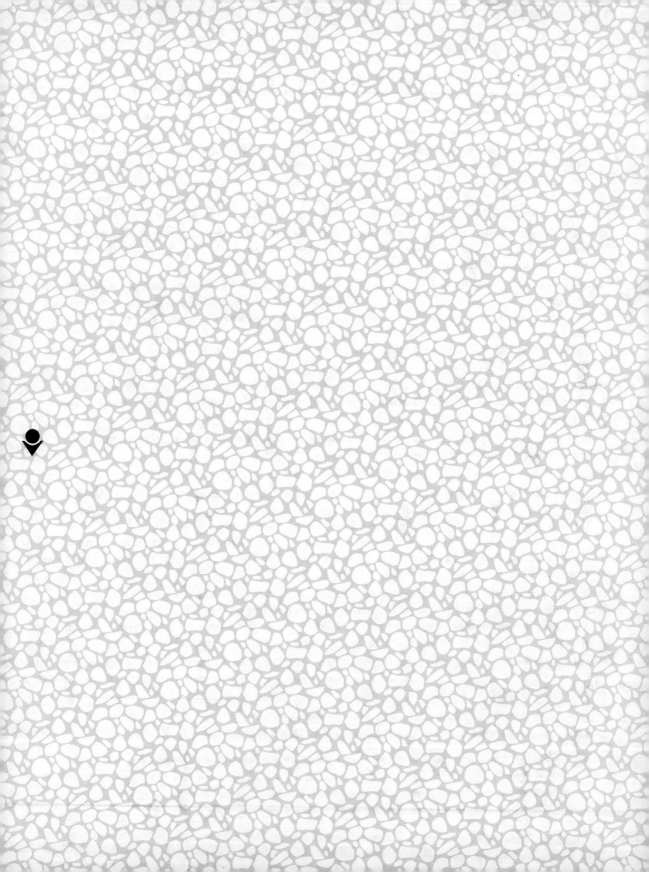

# SPORTS

Visitors who like to combine sports activities with their vacations will find plenty of options at Walt Disney World, which prides itself on the quality and diversity of its recreational facilities. Over the past two years, WDW has positioned itself as a premier sports vacation destination by focusing on the needs of guests who wish to watch or participate in sports. The Walt Disney Company recently acquired ESPN, and will open ESPN Sports World entertainment center at Disney's BoardWalk; and in 1997, Disney's International Sports Complex will open with facilities for professional and amateur competitions in more than twenty five different sports. Walt Disney World also hosts a number of sports events that attract participants and spectators from around the world (call 407 939-7810 for information about these events), which include:

**WALT DISNEY WORLD MARATHON:** In early January, thousands of runners gather to compete on a 26.2-mile course that begins near Epcot Center and passes through the three major theme parks and a number of WDW resorts. On the two days preceding the race, a Sports and Fitness Expo is open to all visitors. Participation in the marathon is open to the first 12,000 people who register, and the slots fill quickly. For information and registration forms, call 407 939-7810.

**THE INDY 200 AT WALT DISNEY WORLD:** The Indy 200 at Walt Disney World, premiering in 1996, brings members of the Indy Racing League together each January for a high-speed auto race on the 1.1-mile tri-oval track located near the Magic Kingdom. Three Day Tickets, good for race day and all practice and qualification trials, range in price from about $40 to $100. Race Day Tickets range in price from about $35 up to $90. Call 800 822-4639 to request a brochure or purchase tickets.

**BRYANT GUMBEL/WALT DISNEY WORLD CELEBRITY–AM GOLF TOURNAMENT:** NBC "Today" show anchor Bryant Gumbel hosts this tournament every March to raise funds for the United Negro College Fund. The benefit attracts top celebrities in the entertainment, sports, and other fields for some good-natured competition on WDW's PGA golf courses. For information, call 407 824-2250.

**DISNEY'S TOUR "D" FUN BIKE TRIP:** For three days in September, bicyclists compete seriously or simply coast along and enjoy the view on this scenic ride from Tampa Bay to Walt Disney World, cheered on by fans and Disney characters. For information and registration forms, call 407 939-7810.

**OLDSMOBILE SCRAMBLE CHAMPIONSHIP:** This golf competition is held a few days before the Walt Disney World/Oldsmobile Golf Classic in October. The tournament pits teams made up of one professional and four amateur golfers against each other, with a prize of over $15,000 going to the winning pro. Call 800 582-1908 for information.

**WALT DISNEY WORLD/OLDSMOBILE GOLF CLASSIC:** Since 1971, Walt Disney World has been the site for this major and most famous PGA Tour event, held in October. The tournament attracts about 200,000 spectators to watch the top names in golf compete on Disney's Palm, Magnolia, and Lake Buena Vista golf courses. For information, call 407 824-2270.

**CLASSIC CLUB PRO-AM:** A concurrent event with the Walt Disney World/Oldsmobile Golf Classic, the Classic Club Pro-Am gives golf enthusiasts willing to pay annual Golf Classic Club membership fees of about $5,000 the chance to play alongside the pros. For information, call 407 824-2255. ◆

# BICYCLING

Bicycling is one of the more pleasant exercise diversions at Walt Disney World, offering an array of scenic views and landscapes. Many Walt Disney World resorts have bicycling areas ranging from beach promenades and wilderness areas to manicured fairways and flower-lined streets. Rental fees range from about $3 to $5 per hour and $6 to $10 per day, depending on the resort and type of bike. Florida weather permits bicycling at any time of the year, but in the summer, visitors will find early-morning rides the most pleasant, since afternoons tend to be hot, humid, and often rainy. Bicycle rentals end at sundown.

## WILDERNESS RIDE

*Disney's Wilderness Lodge and Fort Wilderness Resort and Campground*

Nine miles of roads and trails throughout Fort Wilderness are available to visitors riding either single or tandem bicycles. The lightly traveled paved roads have occasional cars and buses, but the off-road trail system is a biker's dream. It meanders along waterways, past beaches, through shady forests, and across bridges and boardwalks. This is considered one of the best bicycle paths in Walt Disney World.

**WHERE TO RENT:** Bicycles, including tandem bikes, can be rented at the Bike Barn, in the Meadow Recreation Area at Fort Wilderness, and at the Teton Boat and Bike Rental at Wilderness Lodge.

**WHO MAY RENT:** Bicycles are available to both WDW resort guests and day visitors.

**BIKING AREAS:** Bikers may use all roads, paths, and trails throughout Fort Wilderness. The overall path length is about nine miles.

**MAPS:** Maps showing the roads and trails of Fort Wilderness are available at the Bike Barn, where bicycles are rented. (See also "Fort Wilderness & River Country," page 68.)

**NOTE:** Bike paths are shared with pedestrians and electric carts, and sometimes buses and cars, so bikers should use caution.

## OLD KEY WEST AND COUNTRY CLUB RIDE

*Disney Vacation Club and Disney Institute*

Combining the features of two adjoining resorts, the path meanders through the winding streets at the Disney Vacation Club, lined with Key West–styled vacation cottages. It runs past the green fairways of the Buena Vista Golf Course and crosses footbridges over the waterways. It continues along shady forest lanes past the Treehouses at the Disney Institute, and continues all the way to the Disney Village Marketplace.

**WHERE TO RENT:** Bicycles, including tandem bikes, may be rented at either Hank's Rent 'N Return at the Disney Vacation Club or at the marina at Disney Institute.

**WHO MAY RENT:** Only guests staying at a WDW resort may rent bicycles at these two resorts.

**BIKING AREAS:** At both resorts, bikes may use resort roadways and all paths designated for joggers, but may not leave the paved areas or travel on the golf paths. The overall path length is about three miles.

**MAPS:** Maps showing bike paths are available at Guest Services at either the Disney Vacation Club or at Disney Institute.

**NOTE:** Bike paths are shared with pedestrians and electric carts, so bikers should use caution.

## TROPICAL ISLAND BICYCLE CRUISE
### Disney's Caribbean Beach Resort

The paved promenade encircling forty-acre Barefoot Bay lake lets bikers spin casually past white sand beaches and sample a range of exotic tropical landscaping and colorful Caribbean-style lodges. Bicycles may cross the wooden bridges leading to Parrot Cay island, where the path meanders along the shore, by clusters of water-lilies and reeds that ring the island. The island has the themed architecture of an old Caribbean fortress, complete with cannons pointing out over the lake. The path travels past aviaries filled with colorful birds before continuing across Barefoot Bay to the main promenade.

**WHERE TO RENT:** Bicycles may be rented at the Barefoot Bay Boat Yard, located in the center of the Caribbean Beach Resort at Old Port Royale.

**WHO MAY RENT:** Bicycles are available to both WDW resort guests and day visitors. Day visitors must stop at the Caribbean Beach resort entrance check-in to get a nonregistered-guest pass that will allow them to enter the resort.

**BIKING AREAS:** Bicycles may use the promenade that encircles Barefoot Bay and the sidewalks of the individual island villages. Bicycles are not permitted on the perimeter roads of the resort. The overall path length is about 1.5 miles.

**MAPS:** Maps of the promenade at Disney's Caribbean Beach Resort are available at the Barefoot Boat Yard, where bicycles are rented.

**NOTE:** Joggers and pedestrians share the promenade with bikers. The best time for a bicycle ride is mid-morning, after resort guests have departed for the theme parks.

## EASY RIDER
### Disney's Port Orleans and Dixie Landings Resorts

Bikers riding single or tandem bicycles can follow the paved areas and rustic paths of these two resorts on a town-and-country tour through the Old South. The path follows the Carriage Path encircling Port Orleans, a fanciful replica of the French Quarter in New Orleans. It continues along the riverfront to Dixie Landings, on a winding path past graceful plantation mansions and continuing past deep-country bayou lodges sheltered by tall pines draped with Spanish moss.

**WHERE TO RENT:** Single and tandem bikes are available at both resorts. At Port Orleans, bicycles can be rented at Port Orleans Landing, near the marina. At Dixie Landings, bicycles can be rented at Dixie Levee, near the marina.

**WHO MAY RENT:** Bicycles may be rented by registered guests only.

**BIKING AREAS:** Bikers may ride on any of the sidewalks and inner roadways of both resorts, as well as all along the Carriage Path. Bicycles are not permitted on the perimeter roads of the resorts. The overall path length is about 2.5 miles.

**MAPS:** Resort maps are available at Guest Services in both resorts.

**NOTE:** Pedestrians, joggers, and luggage-conveyance vehicles share this path with bikers. ◆

# BOATING

Walt Disney World is home to the largest privately owned fleet of watercraft in the world — and much of it is available to visitors who would like to explore the extensive waterways and interconnected lakes that span the forty-three square miles of Walt Disney World. A variety of rental boats is available at all of the Walt Disney World lakes: Bay Lake, Seven Seas Lagoon, Buena Vista Lagoon, Lake Buena Vista, Crescent Lake, Stormalong Bay, and Barefoot Bay. Boats may also be rented to explore Walt Disney World's canal and inland waterway systems. Disney's Fort Wilderness Resort and Campground and the marinas in the Disney Village Resorts Area provide access to these waterways.

## LAKES, WATERWAYS, AND MARINAS

*The Walt Disney World marinas are open every day from about 10 AM until sundown, and by reservation afterward at select resorts. Visitors may dock their boats at other marinas in the area to tour various theme resorts or explore recreation facilities. Each lake and waterway has unique characteristics and touring opportunities. The watercraft are available on a first-come, first-served basis.*

**SEVEN SEAS LAGOON AND BAY LAKE:** Together, these lakes make up the largest body of water at Walt Disney World, covering 650 acres. The lakes are connected by a unique water bridge and are also used by ferries, waterskiers, and fishing excursions. Forests and wetlands surround the lakes, which are accented by miles of white sand beaches. The wetlands are home to a large population of native waterfowl, including great white egrets, herons, and pelicans. Discovery Island zoological park lies in the middle of Bay Lake, and although boaters cannot dock at Discovery Island, they can dock their craft at the following marinas during their excursion (boats must be returned to the marina where rented):

- Marina Pavilion at Disney's Contemporary Resort
- The Marina at Disney's Fort Wilderness Resort and Campground
- The Marina at Disney's Polynesian Resort
- Captain's Shipyard at Disney's Grand Floridian Beach Resort.

**BUENA VISTA LAGOON AND THE DISNEY VILLAGE WATERWAYS:** Buena Vista Lagoon, thirty-five acres of man-made lake, is the showcase lake of the Disney Village Resorts Area. Along its shores are the Disney Village Marketplace and Pleasure Island. A Mississippi riverboat replica, the *Empress Lilly,* is docked at Buena Vista Lagoon, and the lagoon's waters are used by ferries and fishing excursions. The narrow Disney Village Waterways lead off from the lagoon and wind through pine forests and bayous where the trees are overhung by vines. The waterways pass under footbridges and flow by fairways populated with golfers, while snowy white long-necked egrets pose among the water reeds, hoping the boat wake will wash something edible their way. The waterways lead to the Trumbo Canal and the Sassagoula River, and boaters can dock at the following marinas during their excursion:

- Cap'n Jack's Marina at Disney Village Marketplace
- Hank's Rent 'N Return at Disney Vacation Club
- The Landing at Disney's Port Orleans Resort
- Dixie Levee at Disney's Dixie Landings Resort
- The Marina at the Disney Institute.

**Crescent Lake and Stormalong Bay:** These two small interconnected lakes are surrounded by some of the most intriguing architecture at Walt Disney World, including the fanciful Dolphin and Swan resorts, the faithfully replicated New England seaside architecture of the Yacht Club and Beach Club resorts, and the lively Atlantic City–style waterfront at Disney's BoardWalk. On the other side of the lakes, in the World Showcase, the tops of the replicas of the Eiffel Tower and the Campanile of St. Mark's Square in Venice can be seen. Along the shores are white sand beaches, arched bridges, and boardwalks filled with strolling pedestrians and colorful trams on their way to the International Gateway. The lakes are also used by ferries. Boaters can rent their craft at the following marinas:

- The Hot Spot at Walt Disney World's Dolphin and Swan
- Bayside Marina at Disney's Yacht Club and Beach Club Resorts.

**Barefoot Bay:** This forty-acre lake is actually three interconnected lakes, one of which has Parrot Cay island in its center, spanned on both sides by wooden footbridges. A white sand beach follows the shoreline, which is encircled by a promenade used by pedestrians and bicyclists. Clusters of brightly colored Caribbean cottages are nestled in the lush tropical landscaping. Boaters can rent their craft at the following marina:

- Barefoot Bay Boat Yard at Disney's Caribbean Beach Resort.

**Fort Wilderness Waterways:** Friendly ducks and not-so-friendly swans share these narrow waterways with native waterfowl and canoers. At times, the waterways give way to open grassy banks where hopeful anglers patiently hold their poles. More often, the canals become bayoulike, closed in by pine forests hung with gray-green Spanish moss. Here and there, canoers will find picnic-perfect shady inlets filled with water reeds and an occasional blue heron standing guard. Canoers may rent their craft at the following marina:

- The Bike Barn at Disney's Fort Wilderness Resort and Campground.

**Lake Buena Vista:** This is both a natural lake and an extension of the man-made Buena Vista Lagoon, nearby. Lake Buena Vista is on the grounds of the Buena Vista Palace Resort and Spa at Hotel Plaza. The shores are surrounded by dark green water reeds with a dense stand of pine forest beyond. The glassy surface of the lake's dark waters is ideal for the Sunkats that use it exclusively, and, of course, ideal for the swans and ducks that populate it prettily. Boaters can rent their craft at the following marina:

- Recreation Island Marina at Buena Vista Palace Resort and Spa.

## SELF-OPERATED WATERCRAFT

*Visitors can select from a wide variety of watercraft at the Walt Disney World marinas including speedboats, sailboats, canopy boats, pontoon boats, pedal boats, canoes, and rowboats. Boats can be rented by the hour or half hour and are available to both Walt Disney World resort guests and day visitors with a valid driver's license (a few exceptions are noted below). The fees for rentals and the types of boats available vary from marina to marina. Generally, the least-expensive rentals are at the lower-priced resorts. Self-operated boats are rented on a first-come, first-served basis and cannot be reserved.*

**Water Sprites:** These tiny, one- to two-passenger mini speedboats sit low in the water and zip along at about ten miles per hour. Water Sprites are used exclusively on the lakes and are not allowed in the canals or narrow waterways.

**CAPACITY:** Water Sprites hold two passengers weighing up to three hundred pounds total.

**RENTAL FEE:** Depending on the marina, Water Sprite rentals start at about $32 per hour.

**WHO MAY RENT:** Water Sprites are available to both WDW resort guests and day visitors.

**MARINAS:** Water Sprites are available at the following marinas and resorts: Contemporary, Grand Floridian, Wilderness Lodge, Polynesian, Yacht Club, Beach Club, Fort Wilderness Marina, and Cap'n Jack's Marina at the Disney Village Marketplace.

**SAILBOATS:** Sailboats and catamarans are available in a variety of sizes and styles. Visitors who wish to rent catamarans must be experienced sailors.

**CAPACITY:** The Sunfish holds two passengers; the Cray Cat holds two passengers; the Com-Pac holds four passengers; the Capri holds up to six passengers; the Hobie Cat 14 holds two passengers; the Hobie Cat 16 holds three passengers.

**RENTAL FEE:** Depending on the marina, sailboat rentals start at about $12 per hour.

**WHO MAY RENT:** Sailboats are available to both WDW resort guests and day visitors. The sailboats at the Dolphin and Swan are available to WDW resort guests only.

**MARINAS:** Sailboats are available at the following marinas and resorts: Contemporary, Wilderness Lodge, Grand Floridian, Polynesian, Yacht Club, Beach Club, Caribbean Beach, Swan, Dolphin, and Fort Wilderness Marina.

**PONTOON BOATS:** These motor-powered watercraft, also known as float boats, are canopied and sit high in the water atop gleaming stainless-steel pontoons. The twenty-foot self-operated Pontoon Boats are ideal for groups of up to ten passengers, and may cruise either the lakes or the waterways. For larger pontoon boats, which require a driver along, see "Excursion Cruises," page 220.

**CAPACITY:** Twenty-foot pontoon boats hold eight to ten passengers.

**RENTAL FEE:** Depending on the marina, pontoon boat rentals start at about $45 per hour for twenty-foot boats.

**WHO MAY RENT:** Pontoon boats are available to both WDW resort guests and day visitors.

**MARINAS:** Pontoon boats are available at the following marinas and resorts: Contemporary, Grand Floridian, Polynesian, Yacht Club, Beach Club, Vacation Club, Port Orleans, Dixie Landings, Caribbean Beach, Fort Wilderness Marina, Wilderness Lodge, and Cap'n Jack's Marina at Disney Village Marketplace.

**CANOPY BOATS:** Motorized canopy boats may be used on both the lakes and waterways. Their striped canvas canopies provide shade and they are ideal sightseeing craft for small groups. At some marinas, larger canopy boats are available.

**CAPACITY:** Small canopy boats hold four passengers; large canopy boats hold six passengers.

**RENTAL FEE:** Depending on the marina, rental fees for canopy boats range from about $25 to $36 per hour. Large canopy boats rent for about $40 per hour.

**WHO MAY RENT:** Canopy boats are available to both WDW resort guests and day visitors.

**MARINAS:** Canopy boats are available at the following marinas and resorts: Contemporary, Grand Floridian, Polynesian, Yacht Club, Beach Club, Vacation Club, Port Orleans, Dixie Landings, Caribbean Beach, Fort Wilderness Marina, Wilderness Lodge, and Cap'n Jack's Marina at Disney Village Marketplace.

**PEDAL BOATS:** These small, colorful, human-powered watercraft, also called paddle boats, will cruise along as fast as you can pedal. They're very light and are ideal for lazy explorations of the shoreline and for sneaking up on waterfowl for a closer look. Only the front seats have pedals, so passengers in the back get a free ride.

    **CAPACITY:** Pedal boats hold up to four passengers.

    **RENTAL FEE:** Depending on the marina, pedal boat rentals start at about $10 per hour.

    **WHO MAY RENT:** Pedal boats are available to both WDW resort guests and day visitors. Pedal boats at the Dolphin and Swan are available to WDW resort guests only.

    **MARINAS:** Pedal boats are available at the following marinas and resorts: Polynesian, Yacht Club, Beach Club, Port Orleans, Dixie Landings, Vacation Club, Caribbean Beach, Swan, Dolphin, and the Bike Barn at Fort Wilderness.

**ROWBOATS:** Two resorts maintain a small fleet of rowboats for visitors who want to see if that rowing machine at the gym actually pays off. These nifty boats are great for getting in close to the shore or exploring small inlets that other boats cannot reach.

    **CAPACITY:** Rowboats hold up to two passengers.

    **RENTAL FEE:** Rowboats rentals start at about $5 per half hour and $7 per full hour.

    **WHO MAY RENT:** Rowboats are available to both WDW resort guests and day visitors.

    **MARINAS:** Rowboats are available at Port Orleans and Dixie Landings.

**CANOES:** Canoes are the official watercraft of the Fort Wilderness Waterways, which wind through hundreds of acres of forest and wetlands, and are home to numerous waterfowl. These canals are a favorite spot for fishing, and canoers can buy bait and rent fishing poles, as well.

    **CAPACITY:** Canoes hold up to three passengers.

    **RENTAL FEE:** Canoe rentals start at about $4 per hour or $10 per day.

    **WHO MAY RENT:** Canoes are available to both WDW resort guests and day visitors.

    **MARINAS:** Canoes are available at the Bike Barn at Fort Wilderness and the Disney Institute marina.

**OUTRIGGER CANOES:** These are the canoes that were fashioned by the Polynesians for steady travel through the pounding surf. Outrigger canoes are restricted to Seven Seas Lagoon, and they require a minimum of six persons to row.

    **CAPACITY:** Outrigger canoes hold up to eight passengers.

    **RENTAL FEE:** Rental fees for outrigger canoes start at about $2 per person per hour.

    **WHO MAY RENT:** Outrigger canoes are available to both WDW resort guests and day visitors.

    **MARINAS:** Outrigger canoes are available at the Polynesian resort.

**SUNKATS:** These motorized lounge chairs for two are ideal for drifting along and soaking up the sun on a lazy afternoon. They float high above the water on rubber pontoons.

    **CAPACITY:** Sunkats hold up to two passengers.

    **RENTAL FEE:** Depending on the marina, Sunkat rentals start at about $30 per hour.

    **WHO MAY RENT:** Sunkats are available only to WDW resort guests.

    **MARINAS:** Sunkats are available at the following resorts: Buena Vista Palace Resort and Spa, Swan, and Dolphin.

B O A T I N G

## EXCURSION CRUISES

Excursion cruises take visitors onto Bay Lake, Seven Seas Lagoon, or Crescent Lake, or through the bayoulike Disney Village Waterways. In the evenings, the excursion cruises provide views of the dramatic lighting at the resorts and theme parks, including the fireworks shows. Any WDW visitor may book a private or public excursion cruise. There is even a private dining cruise, ideal for special occasions.

**THE BREATHLESS:** The Bayside Marina at the Yacht Club is home to this mahogany ChrisCraft boat. It takes visitors for private cruises over Crescent Lake and Stormalong Bay. The evening excursions offer a unique view of the fireworks at Epcot Center and Disney-MGM Studios.

**CAPACITY:** The *Breathless* carries up to seven passengers plus a driver.

**TIMES:** Available all year; times vary according to the fireworks show schedules.

**FEES:** About $50 per half hour in the daytime; about $75 per half hour at night, including driver.

**RESERVATIONS:** Reservations are required and can be made up to two weeks in advance at the Bayside Marina at the Yacht Club (407 934-8000).

**FIREWORKS CRUISES:** These pontoon boats carry passengers across Bay Lake and Seven Seas Lagoon for views of the Magic Kingdom fireworks show and the Electrical Water Pageant.

**CAPACITY:** The boats carry up to fourteen passengers.

**TIMES:** Times vary according to the fireworks show schedules. Cruises operate seasonally.

**FEES:** About $28 for a one-hour cruise. Snacks and beverages are served.

**RESERVATIONS:** Reservations are required and can be made up seven days ahead. For departures from the Contemporary, call 407 824-1000; for departures from the Polynesian, call 407 824-2000.

**STARLIGHT CRUISE:** This pontoon boat departs in the evening from the Grand Floridian resort for a romantic private cruise on Seven Seas Lagoon and Bay Lake. Visitors can watch the Electrical Water Pageant and Magic Kingdom fireworks while dining, if they wish, on a catered meal from either Flagler's or Narcoossee's restaurant.

**CAPACITY:** The Starlight Cruise carries up to four passengers plus a driver and optional server.

**TIMES:** Available all year; times start after 5 PM and vary according to each reservation.

**FEES:** About $75 per hour; one-hour minimum (does not include dinner). Dinner prices will vary according to the meal. An additional $50 is charged if a waiter is requested to serve dinner on board.

**RESERVATIONS:** Reservations are required at least twenty-four hours in advance and can be made up to two weeks ahead by calling Captain's Shipyard at the Grand Floridian (407 824-2439). Dinner can be ordered at the same time from Private Dining (407 824-2474).

**PONTOON BOAT CRUISES:** These twenty-four-foot pontoon boats can be booked by private groups and include a driver. They can cruise either the lakes or the waterways.

**CAPACITY:** Twenty-four-foot pontoon boats hold up to twenty passengers plus a driver.

**TIMES:** Daytime cruises only. Times vary according to reservation requests.

**FEES:** Twenty-four-foot-pontoon boats rent for about $70 per hour, including driver.

**RESERVATIONS:** Pontoon boats with drivers must be reserved and are available at most marinas. Reservations can be made up to two weeks in advance by calling a resort that has a marina located on the lake or waterway you wish to tour. ◆

# FISHING

In recent years, fishing at Walt Disney World has become increasingly popular. In fact, during the summer months, excursions fill quickly. The fishing guides who lead the excursions are professional anglers, and they know well the best fishing spots in the waterways they tour. There are two main fishing areas at Walt Disney World: Bay Lake and Buena Vista Lagoon. A large number of native fish were found in Bay Lake at the time that Disney began development, including largemouth bass, bluegill, Seminole killfish, lake chubsuckers, and spotted gar. As new lakes, lagoons, and waterways were created in order to drain parts of the swampland, the waters were further stocked with brown bullhead catfish and at least eight species of sunfish. The lakes, lagoons, and waterways are no longer stocked, since the fish now propagate well and provide a naturally balanced ecology that supports a large waterfowl population and other local denizens.

Visitors who would like to join a fishing excursion should make reservations well in advance. They can use their own equipment, if they wish, although tackle is provided and bait is readily available. No fishing license is required at Walt Disney World. A catch-and-release policy is strongly encouraged, although resort guests with kitchen facilities may keep fish caught from some areas (ask the excursion guide).

## FORT WILDERNESS FISHING EXCURSION

Bay Lake, the largest natural lake at Walt Disney World, is the fishing ground for this excursion. Forests and wetlands surround the lake and are home to a large population of native waterfowl, including great white egrets, herons, and pelicans. Bay Lake is large and well aerated, so the fish caught here are relatively free of pesticides and bacteria. Visitors with kitchen facilities may keep their catch if they plan to dine on it. Some of the largemouth bass that have been caught here weigh as much as thirteen pounds. Pontoon boats are used for the fishing excursions, which leave three times daily from the Fort Wilderness Marina.

**EXCURSION FEES:** About $125 for two hours, which includes boat, guide, all tackle, bait, and refreshments. Maximum of five persons. Participants may bring their own fishing equipment.

**TIMES:** 8 AM, 12 PM, and 3 PM. Times vary throughout the year.

**RESERVATIONS:** Space can be reserved up to two weeks in advance (407 824-2621). Reservations are recommended, and visitors will find them to be essential during the busy summer months. The excursion is available to both Walt Disney World resort guests and day visitors.

**NOTE:** Excursion boats will also pick up guests at the following resorts: Polynesian, Wilderness Lodge, Grand Floridian, and Contemporary.

## BUENA VISTA LAGOON FISHING EXCURSION

The waters of both Buena Vista Lagoon and the Disney Village Waterways are the fishing grounds for this excursion. Because Buena Vista Lagoon and the picturesque bayoulike waterways that feed it were excavated from swampland, this system is smaller and less aerated than Bay Lake, and the fish caught may not be kept to eat. However, a mounting service is available for visitors who catch fish weighing in at over eight pounds. Pontoon boats are used for the excursion. Visitors holding a current Florida fishing license enjoy a 10 percent discount. The excursions leave twice daily from Cap'n Jack's Marina at Disney Village Marketplace.

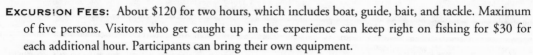

**EXCURSION FEES:** About $120 for two hours, which includes boat, guide, bait, and tackle. Maximum of five persons. Visitors who get caught up in the experience can keep right on fishing for $30 for each additional hour. Participants can bring their own equipment.

**TIMES:** 6:30 AM, 8:30 AM, 10:30 AM, and 12:30 PM. Times vary throughout the year.

**RESERVATIONS:** Reservations are required at least twenty-four hours in advance and can be made up to three months ahead (407 828-2461). This fishing excursion is one of the most popular at WDW and fills quickly in summer months, so visitors planning a summer trip should book this excursion well in advance. The excursion is available to both Walt Disney World resort guests and day visitors.

**NOTE:** Excursion boats will also pick up guests at the following resorts: Vacation Club, Port Orleans, Dixie Landings, and Disney Institute.

## CRESCENT LAKE FISHING EXCURSION

This excursion on the waters of Crescent Lake gives visitors the feel of fishing from a New England coastal resort. The two-hour fishing excursion is limited to a maximum of five participants on each trip and leaves three times daily from the Bayside Marina at Disney's Yacht Club Resort. A policy of catch and release is strongly encouraged.

**EXCURSION FEES:** About $120 for two hours, which includes boat, guide, all tackle, bait, and snacks.

**TIMES:** 7 AM, 9 AM, and 1 PM. Times vary throughout the year.

**RESERVATIONS:** Reservations are required at least twenty-four hours in advance and can be made up to seven days ahead (407 934-3256: Ship Shape Health Club). The excursion is available to both Walt Disney World resort guests and day visitors.

**NOTE:** The first fishing excursion of the day, departing at 7 AM, can be the most enjoyable for both atmosphere and catch ratio.

## SASSAGOULA RIVER FISHING EXCURSION

This two-hour fishing excursion begins along the tree-lined Sassagoula River, which feeds into Buena Vista Lagoon. The Buena Vista Lagoon is also a primary fishing site on this excursion. The early-morning fishing trip departs once daily from the Dixie Levee at Disney's Dixie Landings Resort. The fish caught on this excursion must be released, and may not be kept to eat.

**EXCURSION FEES:** About $35 per person, which includes boat, guide, tackle, bait, and beverage. The excursion is booked on a party-boat basis, with a minimum of one person and a maximum of five people at a time.

**TIMES:** One excursion daily at 6:30 AM.

**RESERVATIONS:** Reservations are required at least twenty-four hours in advance and can be made up to two weeks ahead at the Fishing Hole (407 934-5409). The excursion is available to both Walt Disney World resort guests and day visitors.

**NOTE:** One of the best features of this fishing excursion is that it will sail even if only one participant is aboard, making this a real treat during the occasional times when bookings are slow.

FISHING

## FISHING THE FORT WILDERNESS WATERWAYS

Fishing is permitted in the miles of picturesque waterways that traverse Fort Wilderness. Fish may be caught from the grassy banks of the canals, or visitors can rent pedal boats or canoes and seek out likely looking fishing holes in the heavily forested areas. Guests with kitchen facilities may keep and eat fish caught in these waterways, although a policy of catch and release is strongly encouraged.

**EQUIPMENT:** Fishers can use their own equipment, if they wish. Canoes, pedal boats, and cane poles can be rented at the Bike Barn in the Meadow Recreation Area at Fort Wilderness. Bait is sold at the Meadow Trading Post, nearby.

**RENTAL FEES:** Canoes rent for about $4 per hour or $10 per day. Pedal boats rent for about $10 per hour. Cane poles rent for about $2 per hour or $8 per day; rod-and-reel combinations rent for about $4 per hour or $8 per day.

**TIMES:** The Bike Barn is open from 8 AM until sundown.

**RESERVATIONS:** No reservations are taken for canoes or pedal boats. Fishing at Fort Wilderness is available to both Walt Disney World resort guests and day visitors.

**NOTE:** Canoes hold up to three persons; pedal boats hold up to four people.

## DOCK FISHING AT CAP'N JACK'S MARINA

All visitors at Walt Disney World can rent old-fashioned cane poles to fish for bluegill in the Buena Vista Lagoon from the dock at Disney Village Marketplace. All fish caught here, however, must be released.

**EQUIPMENT:** Cane poles can be rented at Cap'n Jack's Marina.

**RENTAL FEES:** Cane poles rent for about $3 per half hour or $5 per hour, including bait.

**TIMES:** Cap'n Jack's Marina is open from 10 AM until sundown.

**RESERVATIONS:** No reservations are taken. Fishing at Cap'n Jack's Marina is available to both Walt Disney World resort guests and day visitors.

## THE FISHING HOLE AT DIXIE LANDINGS

Disney's Dixie Landings Resort has its very own fishing hole on the Sassagoula River, which is part of the Disney Village Waterways. The fishing hole is stocked with bass, bluegill, and catfish, and visitors fish from an old-fashioned roped-off dock. A catch-and-release policy is encouraged. So far, the biggest catfish pulled from this fishing hole weighed in at seven pounds.

**EQUIPMENT:** Cane poles can be rented at the Fishing Hole on Ol' Man Island. Bait is provided and worm-hooking instructions are offered, a rare treat for the squeamish.

**RENTAL FEES:** Cane poles rent for about $3 per hour, including bait.

**TIMES:** The Fishing Hole is open from 7 AM until 3 PM.

**RESERVATIONS:** No reservations are taken. Fishing at Dixie Landings is available to both Walt Disney World resort guests and day visitors.

**NOTE:** For about $2, visitors can get a souvenir Polaroid of themselves and their catch. ◆

FISHING

# FITNESS CENTERS & SPAS

Many of the Walt Disney World resorts have well-appointed fitness centers offering a range of equipment and services. The most handsomely appointed fitness centers are the St. John's Health Club at the Grand Floridian, Body By Jake Health Studio at the Dolphin, and Ship Shape Health Club at the Yacht and Beach Club. Most resort fitness centers can be used only by registered guests, however, the Contemporary, Dolphin, and Buena Vista Palace have facilities that are available to both resort guests and day guests. In 1996, two full-service spas will open at Walt Disney World: The Spa at Buena Vista Palace, and the Sports and Fitness Center at the Disney Institute — both ideal resort destinations for visitors who would like to include a spa getaway in their Walt Disney World vacation.

## FULL-SERVICE SPAS

**BUENA VISTA PALACE:** *The Spa at Buena Vista Palace & The Fitness Center* — Opening in 1996 as the only European-style spa in the area, this fully staffed nine-thousand-square-foot facility pampers guests with a wide range of health and beauty services. Its sleek interior is spacious, light filled, and ultra-modern in design, and includes its own lap pool, fully appointed personal-care salon, and fourteen treatment rooms that offer guests complete privacy for therapeutic services such as herbal wraps, massages, and body scrubs. Spa vacation packages are available. The new Fitness Center, upstairs, offers personal training services and high-quality workout equipment.

    **EQUIPMENT AND FACILITIES:** State-of-the-art CYBEX weight-resistance and cardiovascular equipment, steam room, sauna, lap pool, and whirlpools.

    **SERVICES:** Water aerobics, individualized personal training, massage, reflexology, herbal wraps, body scrubs, body polish, hair salon, facials, manicures, pedicures, and waxing. Advance reservations are recommended; for appointments call 407 827-2727.

    **FEES:** Guests are charged a moderate daily fee for use of The Spa facilities. Spa services are a la carte, and spa facilities are included in full- or half-day spa packages. Buena Vista Palace guests are charged a nominal daily fee for use of The Fitness Center. Day visitors are also charged a modest per-visit fee.

    **HOURS:** The Spa is open from 9 AM until 7 PM. The Fitness Center is open from 7 AM until 10 PM.

    **WHO MAY ATTEND:** Both The Spa and The Fitness Center are available to any WDW visitor.

**THE VILLAS AT THE DISNEY INSTITUTE:** *Sports and Fitness Center* — As part of Disney's expanding focus on wellness, this brand-new facility offers the latest exercise equipment along with a large full-service spa. Individualized weight circuit training, classes in relaxation techniques and self-defense, and even rock climbing are some of the unique services available here.

    **EQUIPMENT AND FACILITIES:** Jogging track, up-to-the-minute CYBEX cardiovascular and strength training machines, rock climbing, aerobic room, indoor current pool, professional NBA basketball court, sauna, steam room, and whirlpool.

    **SERVICES:** Fitness and relaxation classes, personal training, massage, body wraps, facials, manicures, and pedicures. For information and appointments call 407 827-1100.

    **FEES:** The Sports and Fitness Center is complimentary. Spa services and treatments are a la carte.

    **HOURS:** 7 AM until 8 PM.

    **WHO MAY ATTEND:** The Spa and Fitness Center is available only to guests at the Disney Institute.

# FITNESS CENTERS

**DISNEY VACATION CLUB:** *R.E.S.T. Fitness Center* — The fitness center at the Vacation Club is located in the resort's recreation complex, facing the pool area and lagoon. A mirrored wall and French doors create an impression of spaciousness in this otherwise modest-sized, equipment-filled room. The fitness center is unstaffed, and there is one television and a separate massage room off to the side. The sauna-steam room is outside the club, in the cute red lighthouse at the edge of the lagoon.

  **EQUIPMENT AND FACILITIES:** Nautilus, Liferower, Lifestep, Lifecycle, free weights, combination sauna and steam room (coed), and whirlpool (outside).

  **SERVICES:** Massage and personal training by appointment (407 827-7700: hotel).

  **FEES:** Complimentary.

  **HOURS:** 7 AM until midnight.

  **WHO MAY ATTEND:** The fitness center is available only to registered guests.

**DISNEY'S YACHT CLUB AND BEACH CLUB RESORTS:** *Ship Shape Health Club* — The main room of this elegant, fully staffed health club has French doors and large windows looking out over Stormalong Bay. The whirlpool is in its own room, with a domed portico overhead. All the rooms are furnished in blue and white, and the sauna and steam rooms are off to the side. Televisions are interspersed throughout the main exercise room, which is furnished with the latest top-of-the-line equipment.

  **EQUIPMENT AND FACILITIES:** Lifecircuit, Nautilus, Lifestep, Lifecycle, Liferower, Gravitron, NordicTrack, StairMaster, treadmill, free weights, steam room (coed), sauna, and whirlpool.

  **SERVICES:** Massage and personal training by appointment (407 934-3256).

  **FEES:** About $7 per visit; $10 for an entire stay; $20 per family stay.

  **HOURS:** 6:30 AM until 10 PM.

  **WHO MAY ATTEND:** The health club is available only to registered guests.

**DISNEY'S CONTEMPORARY RESORT:** *Olympiad Health Club* — The Olympiad Health Club is located on the third floor of the Contemporary resort, near the hotel's executive offices. The modestly sized carpeted room has mirrored walls, low ceilings, and no television. The club is staffed and has a good selection of modern equipment and adjacent tanning and massage rooms.

  **EQUIPMENT AND FACILITIES:** Nautilus, StairMaster, Lifecycle, Aerobicycle, NordicTrack, rowing machine, treadmill, free weights, sauna (coed), whirlpool (outside), and tanning booth.

  **SERVICES:** Personal training and massage by appointment (407 824-3410).

  **FEES:** About $7 per visit; $10 for an entire stay; $20 per family stay. Tanning booth $5 for ten minutes.

  **HOURS:** 6:30 AM until 8 PM.

  **WHO MAY ATTEND:** The health club is available to guests staying at any WDW resort.

**DISNEY'S GRAND FLORIDIAN BEACH RESORT:** *St. John's Health Club* — This fully staffed health club is located in a freestanding white Victorian cottage overlooking the pool. Although modest in size, the room has mirrored walls and paned windows, which create a spacious, airy atmosphere. There are two televisions and pink-upholstered Nautilus equipment to match the pink-and-black multicolored floor. A large basket of fresh fruit is provided for exercising guests.

**EQUIPMENT AND FACILITIES:** Nautilus, StairMaster, Liferower, Lifestep, Aerobicycle, treadmill, free weights, sauna, and whirlpool (outside).

**SERVICES:** Fitness classes, personal training, nutrition and exercise counseling, and massage by appointment (407 824-2433).

**FEES:** About $7 per visit; $10 for an entire stay; $20 per family stay.

**HOURS:** 6 AM until 10 PM.

**WHO MAY ATTEND:** The health club is available only to registered guests.

**THE HILTON RESORT:** *Hilton Health Club* — This modestly sized green-carpeted exercise room is located behind the hotel, near the pools and tennis courts. Mirrors and tiles cover the walls and, on one side, large windows overlook the pool area. The health club has one television, but no staff.

**EQUIPMENT AND FACILITIES:** Nautilus, Lifestep, exercise bikes, treadmill, free weights, sauna (coed), and whirlpool (outside).

**SERVICES:** Massage by appointment (407 827-4000: hotel).

**FEES:** Complimentary.

**HOURS:** 6:30 AM until 10 PM.

**WHO MAY ATTEND:** The health club is available only to registered guests.

**WALT DISNEY WORLD DOLPHIN:** *Body By Jake Health Studio* — This handsome, fully staffed fitness center is operated by television workout professional Jake Steinfeld, who is occasionally on the premises and available for personal training. The carpeted weight room has windows overlooking Crescent Lake. The coed whirlpool is in a spacious tiled room furnished with blue rattan seating, and the club features its own workout studio with classes held throughout the day. There are no televisions in the weight room, although there is a wide screen TV-video setup in the exercise studio.

**EQUIPMENT AND FACILITIES:** Polaris, Lifestep, Lifecycle, Liferower, treadmill, free weights, sauna, and whirlpool (coed).

**SERVICES:** Fitness classes, personal training, massage, and body wraps by appointment (407 934-4264).

**FEES:** About $8 per visit; $16 for an entire stay; $26 per family stay. From noon until 1 PM, visits are free to any WDW resort guests.

**HOURS:** 6 AM until 8 PM.

**WHO MAY ATTEND:** The health club is available to guests staying at any WDW resort.

**WALT DISNEY WORLD SWAN:** *Swan Health Club* — This modest, but fully staffed health club is entered from outside the hotel through large glass doors that overlook the lap pool. Potted plants and peach and blue trim create a sense of openness in the rectangular exercise room, which houses a selection of Sprint Circuit machines and one television. A massage room is attached, and saunas are located in the adjoining locker rooms.

**EQUIPMENT AND FACILITIES:** Sprint Circuit machines, treadmill, free weights, sauna, and whirlpool (outside).

**SERVICES:** Massage by appointment (407 934-1360).

**FEES:** Complimentary.

**HOURS:** 7 AM until 11 PM.

**WHO MAY ATTEND:** The health club is available only to registered guests. ◆

# GOLF

Walt Disney World sometimes calls itself *The Magic Linkdom,* and with good reason: It boasts five outstanding PGA golf courses, as well as a par-36 practice course. With ninety-nine holes of golf and nearly twenty-five thousand guest rooms, Walt Disney World is the largest golf resort in the world. The golf courses here host more than four hundred golf tournaments each year, including the world's biggest: the PGA Tour's Walt Disney World/Oldsmobile Golf Classic (see page 213).

All visitors at Walt Disney World may use the golf courses. Advance reservations are necessary for all the courses, especially during peak seasons and holidays. Vacationers who would like to golf frequently during their stay should inquire about WDW's all-inclusive Golf Package Vacations (407 934-7639) and, if available, the Walt Disney World Golf Season Badge (407 824-2729).

## MAGNOLIA GOLF COURSE

Designed by Joe Lee, the Magnolia Golf Course is long and tight and requires a great deal of accuracy. It is planted with more than fifteen hundred magnolia trees and features the unique "mousetrap" on the sixth hole, a sand trap shaped like Mickey. In fact, the course has a preponderance of sand and water, with large greens on a rolling terrain. The layout covers 6,642 yards from the middle tees. The final round of the PGA Tour's Walt Disney World/Oldsmobile Golf Classic is played on this course, and the Disney pros rate the Magnolia the third toughest of the five courses at WDW.

**GREENS FEES:** About $85 for WDW resort guests; about $95 for day visitors; twilight games (after 2 or 3 PM) range from $35 to $50. Includes electric cart.

**EQUIPMENT RENTAL:** Clubs, shoes, and range balls are available at the Palm and Magnolia Pro Shop.

**FACILITIES:** The golf course has two driving ranges, putting green, locker rooms, and a beverage cart on the course. The Pro Shop carries golf apparel, equipment, and accessories. The Garden Gallery restaurant, nearby, is open for breakfast, lunch, and dinner, and the adjoining Back Porch Lounge is open all day. The Golf Studio offers personalized swing analysis using videotape, as well as both private and group lessons with PGA and LPGA instructors. Call 407 824-2270 for Golf Studio reservations.

**RESERVATIONS:** To reserve tee times, call the Walt Disney World Master Starter (407 824-2270) between 8 AM and 5 PM (EST). Guests staying at WDW resorts may reserve tee times up to thirty days in advance. Day visitors may reserve up to four days ahead. Same-day reservations may be made by calling the Pro Shop directly (824-2288).

**HOW TO GET THERE:** The Magnolia Golf Course is located at Shades of Green, in the Magic Kingdom Resorts Area. There is free parking near the Pro Shop (day guests are charged $7 to enter this area). Complimentary taxi service to and from the golf course is available to guests staying at Disney-owned resorts. Guests at other WDW resorts should check with Guest Services for transportation options.

**NEAREST RESORTS:** Shades of Green, Grand Floridian, Polynesian, and Contemporary.

## PALM GOLF COURSE

Like the nearby Magnolia Golf Course, the graceful Palm Golf Course is lined with beautiful trees, and the greens are mature. It is a picturesque course on which it is not unusual to see deer and other wildlife in the early mornings, and a certain alligator has been known to take a stroll along the outlying fairways. This Joe Lee–designed course is a challenging one, with narrow greens, plenty of water hazards and sand traps, and some difficult doglegs. The layout covers 6,461 yards from the middle tees. The eighteenth hole has been rated the fourth toughest on the PGA Tour, and the Disney pros rate the Palm the second toughest of the five courses at WDW.

**GREENS FEES:** About $85 for WDW resort guests; about $95 for day visitors; twilight games (after 2 or 3 PM) range from $35 to $50. Includes electric cart.

**EQUIPMENT RENTAL:** Clubs, shoes, and range balls are available at the Palm and Magnolia Pro Shop.

**FACILITIES:** The golf course has two driving ranges, putting green, and locker rooms. The Pro Shop carries golf apparel, equipment, and accessories. The Garden Gallery restaurant, nearby, is open for breakfast, lunch, and dinner, and the adjoining Back Porch Lounge is open all day. The Golf Studio offers personalized swing analysis using videotape, as well as both private and group lessons with PGA and LPGA instructors. Call 407 824-2270 for Golf Studio reservations.

**RESERVATIONS:** To reserve tee times, call the Walt Disney World Master Starter (407 824-2270) between 8 AM and 5 PM (EST). Guests staying at WDW resorts may reserve tee times up to thirty days in advance. Day visitors may reserve up to four days ahead. Same-day reservations may be made by calling the Pro Shop directly (824-2288).

**HOW TO GET THERE:** The Palm Golf Course is located at Shades of Green, in the Magic Kingdom Resorts Area. There is free parking near the Pro Shop (day guests are charged $7 to enter this area). Complimentary taxi service to and from the golf course is available to guests staying at Disney-owned resorts. Guests at other WDW resorts should check with Guest Services for transportation options.

**NEAREST RESORTS:** Shades of Green, Grand Floridian, Polynesian, and Contemporary.

## LAKE BUENA VISTA GOLF COURSE

The play on the Lake Buena Vista Golf Course is short and tight, but the views and fairways are wide and open. The greens are fully mature on this course, although they can be bumpy at times because many beginning golfers play here. The island green at the sixteenth hole is considered particularly challenging. The beautiful country club–like course, designed by Joe Lee, is lined with pine forests, oaks, and magnolias. The layout covers 6,655 yards from the middle tees, and the Disney pros rate Lake Buena Vista the fifth toughest of the five courses at WDW.

**GREENS FEES:** About $85 for WDW resort guests; about $95 for day visitors; twilight games (after 2 or 3 PM) range from $35 to $50. Includes electric cart.

**EQUIPMENT RENTAL:** Clubs, shoes, and range balls are available at the Lake Buena Vista Pro Shop.

**FACILITIES:** The golf course has a driving range, putting green, locker rooms, and a beverage cart on the course. The Lake Buena Vista Pro Shop carries golf apparel, equipment, and accessories. Both private and group lessons with PGA and LPGA instructors are available. Call 407 824-2270 to arrange lessons.

**RESERVATIONS:** To reserve tee times, call the Walt Disney World Master Starter (407 824-2270) between 8 AM and 5 PM (EST). Guests staying at WDW resorts may reserve tee times up to thirty days in advance. Day visitors may reserve up to four days ahead. Same-day reservations may be made by calling the Pro Shop directly (828-3741).

GOLF

**HOW TO GET THERE:** The Lake Buena Vista Golf Course is located at the Disney Institute, in the Disney Village Resorts Area. There is free parking near the Pro Shop. The golf course is within walking distance of most of the Hotel Plaza resorts. Complimentary taxi service to and from the golf course is available to guests staying at Disney-owned resorts. Guests at other WDW resorts should check with Guest Services for transportation options.

**NEAREST RESORTS:** The Disney Institute, Buena Vista Palace, Hilton, Grosvenor, Hotel Royal Plaza, Courtyard by Marriott, Vacation Club, Port Orleans, Dixie Landings, Travelodge, and DoubleTree Guest Suites.

## OSPREY RIDGE GOLF COURSE

This extra-long course was designed by Tom Fazio, with plenty of berms and mounds, and some excellent par-3s. The lakes and creeks were excavated to create the elevated ridge that is the central feature of this course. Nesting platforms have attracted ospreys to the course, and red-tailed hawks can be seen perched in the tall pine trees or flying overhead as they patrol the area. The course features large greens interspersed with wilderness areas, and has become a favorite with experienced golfers. The layout covers 6,705 yards from the middle tees, and the Disney pros rate Osprey Ridge the toughest of the five courses at WDW.

**GREENS FEES:** About $100 for WDW resort guests; about $115 for day visitors; twilight games (after 2 or 3 PM) range from $35 to $50. Includes electric cart.

**EQUIPMENT RENTAL:** Clubs, shoes, and range balls are available at Bonnet Creek Golf Club Pro Shop.

**FACILITIES:** The golf course has a driving range, putting green, locker rooms, and a beverage cart on the course. The Pro Shop carries golf apparel, equipment, and accessories. The Sand Trap Bar and Grill in the Bonnet Creek Golf Club serves breakfast and lunch, and the adjoining lounge is open all day. The Bonnet Creek Golf Studio offers personalized swing analysis using videotape, as well as both private and group lessons with PGA and LPGA instructors. Call 407 824-2270 for Golf Studio reservations.

**RESERVATIONS:** To reserve tee times, call the Walt Disney World Master Starter (407 824-2270) between 8 AM and 5 PM (EST). Guests staying at WDW resorts may reserve tee times up to thirty days in advance. Day visitors may reserve four days ahead. Same-day reservations may be made by calling the Pro Shop directly (824-2675).

**HOW TO GET THERE:** The Osprey Ridge Golf Course is located at the Bonnet Creek Golf Club, which lies between Fort Wilderness and the Disney Village Resorts Area. There is free parking in the large lot at the club. Complimentary taxi service to and from the golf course is available to guests staying at Disney-owned resorts. Guests at other WDW resorts should check with Guest Services for transportation options.

**NEAREST RESORTS:** Fort Wilderness, Wilderness Lodge, Dixie Landings, Port Orleans, Vacation Club, and the Disney Institute.

## EAGLE PINES GOLF COURSE

This challenging course, designed by Pete Dye, requires strategic play. Golfers must think their way from tee to green through the undulating, low-profile terrain. Water comes into play at sixteen holes, and instead of rough, the fairways are lined with pine needles and sand, giving the course a distinctive look and allowing for fast play. The layout covers 6,224 yards from the middle tees, and the Disney pros rate Eagle Pines the fourth toughest of the five courses at WDW.

**GREENS FEES:** About $100 for WDW resort guests; about $115 for day visitors; twilight games (after 2 or 3 PM) range from $35 to $50. Includes electric cart.

**EQUIPMENT RENTAL:** Clubs, shoes, and range balls are available at Bonnet Creek Golf Club Pro Shop.

**FACILITIES:** The golf course has a driving range, putting green, locker rooms, and a beverage cart on the course. The Pro Shop carries golf apparel, equipment, and accessories. The Sand Trap Bar and Grill in the Bonnet Creek Golf Club serves breakfast and lunch, and the adjoining lounge is open all day. The Bonnet Creek Golf Studio offers personalized swing analysis using videotape, as well as both private and group lessons with PGA and LPGA instructors. Call 407 824-2270 for Golf Studio reservations.

**RESERVATIONS:** To reserve tee times, call the Walt Disney World Master Starter (407 824-2270) between 8 AM and 5 PM (EST). Guests staying at WDW resorts may reserve tee times up to thirty days in advance. Day visitors may reserve four days ahead. Same-day reservations may be made by calling the Pro Shop directly (824-2675).

**HOW TO GET THERE:** The Eagle Pines Golf Course is located at the Bonnet Creek Golf Club, which is between Fort Wilderness and the Disney Village Resorts Area. There is free parking in the club's lot. Complimentary taxi service to and from the golf course is available to guests staying at Disney-owned resorts. Guests at other WDW resorts should check with Guest Services for transportation options.

**NEAREST RESORTS:** Fort Wilderness, Wilderness Lodge, Dixie Landings, Port Orleans, Vacation Club, and the Disney Institute.

## OAK TRAIL COURSE

The Oak Trail Course, also called the Executive or Family Course, has some of the most challenging holes at Walt Disney World. The nine-hole, par-36 course features two par-5s, two par-3s, and five par-4s, and the local pros play here to work on their game. The layout covers 2,913 yards from the men's tees.

**GREENS FEES:** About $25 for one round; about $33 for two rounds. Includes pull-cart. Walking only.

**EQUIPMENT RENTAL:** Clubs and shoes are available at the Palm and Magnolia Pro Shop.

**FACILITIES:** The Pro Shop carries golf apparel, equipment, and accessories. The Garden Gallery restaurant, nearby, is open for breakfast, lunch, and dinner, and the adjoining Back Porch Lounge is open all day.

**RESERVATIONS:** To reserve tee times, call the Walt Disney World Master Starter (407 824-2270) between 8 AM and 5 PM (EST). Guests staying at WDW resorts may reserve tee times up to thirty days in advance. Day visitors may reserve four days ahead. Same-day reservations may be made by calling the Pro Shop directly (824-2288).

**HOW TO GET THERE:** The Oak Trail Course is located at Shades of Green, in the Magic Kingdom Resorts Area. There is free parking near the Pro Shop (day guests are charged $7 to enter the area). Complimentary taxi service to and from the golf course is available to guests staying at Disney-owned resorts. Guests at other WDW resorts should check with Guest Services for transportation options.

**NEAREST RESORTS:** Shades of Green, Grand Floridian, Polynesian, and Contemporary. ◆

# HORSEBACK RIDING

Any Walt Disney World visitor can join a guided wilderness trail ride at either Fort Wilderness or at the nearby Hyatt Regency Grand Cypress Resort. Both facilities offer trail rides suited for inexperienced riders whose primary interest is sightseeing. The Grand Cypress Equestrian Center also offers riding adventures for intermediate and advanced riders. Shoes (not sandals or high heels) are required, and long pants are suggested. Spring and fall are the best seasons for trail rides. In the summer, morning rides are the most pleasant, the earlier the better. In winter, afternoon rides are the nicest. Check-in time for all rides is thirty minutes prior to the scheduled departure. Times vary with the season, and rides may be cancelled in poor weather.

## FORT WILDERNESS TRAIL RIDE

Visitors led by cowboy guides ride along a packed-sand trail wending through shady forests and sunny glades. Novices will feel comfortable on this walk-paced ride (no trotting or galloping) astride well-behaved horses that are sometimes used in the Magic Kingdom parades.

FEE: About $18 per person for a forty-five-minute ride. A maximum of twenty participants per ride.

RESERVATIONS: Reservations are required and may be made up to two weeks ahead (407 824-2832). Same-day reservations can be made by calling 824-2832.

SCHEDULE: Rides leave daily at 8:30 AM, 10 AM, 11:30 AM, 1 PM, 2:30 PM, and 4 PM from the Trail Blaze Corral at Tri-Circle-D Livery, behind the Fort Wilderness Guest Parking Lot. Parking in the lot is free to guests at all Disney-owned resorts (others are charged about $6).

## HYATT REGENCY GRAND CYPRESS TRAIL RIDES

Mounted on gentle horses, a maximum of four riders is led along the shady trails of the resort's extensive nature area. Three different types of rides are offered, and are available to all visitors. Reservations are required at least twenty-four hours in advance and may be made up to thirty days ahead (407 239-1938).

WESTERN TRAIL RIDE: This walking-pace ride is ideal for novices. The ride departs from the resort's Western Trail Barn. Visitors park free at the resort's main lot and travel by shuttle or trolley to the barn.

FEE: About $30 per person for a fifty-minute ride.

SCHEDULE: Seasonally at 8 AM, 9 AM, 10 AM, and 11 AM.

INTERMEDIATE WALK-TROT WESTERN TRAIL RIDE: The intermediate ride is geared to more practiced riders who can sit a trot. The ride departs from the resort's Western Trail Barn. Visitors park free at the resort's main lot and travel by shuttle or trolley to the barn.

FEE: About $30 per person for a fifty-minute ride.

SCHEDULE: The Intermediate Walk-Trot Western Trail Ride leaves daily at 11 AM.

GRAND CYPRESS EQUESTRIAN CENTER TRAIL RIDE: This advanced trail ride, for riders with English-saddle and cantering experience, follows the trails surrounding the Grand Cypress Golf Course. It is headquartered at the Grand Cypress' exclusive Equestrian Center, where visitors park free.

FEE: About $45 per person for a fifty-minute ride.

SCHEDULE: The Advanced Trail Ride is scheduled by appointment only. ◆

# JOGGING

Most of the resorts at Walt Disney World have jogging courses or designated paths located on their grounds or nearby. Some of the courses are serious and spectacular, such as the exercise courses at the Disney Institute and in Fort Wilderness, while others pass through specially themed environments such as the promenade at the Caribbean Beach resort and the carriage path at Port Orleans. Maps of designated jogging paths are available at Guest Services in most resorts. Any visitor to Walt Disney World can use the jogging paths.

## POLYNESIAN RUN
### *Disney's Polynesian Resort and Shades of Green*

The trail starts in the exotic tropical landscaping at the Polynesian resort's Luau Cove, and runs past the long South Pacific–style lodges. It emerges at the fairways of the Magnolia Golf Course, then travels alongside them before looping back at Shades of Green resort. Passing under the monorail tracks, the path again enters the Polynesian's jungle environment, goes by the huge cross-beamed Great Ceremonial House, and exits on the beach at Seven Seas Lagoon. The trail runs along the beach, past the marina, and returns to Luau Cove.

**LENGTH:** The path is about 1.5 miles long.

**MAPS:** Jogging maps are available at the Polynesian resort Guest Services.

## CRESCENT LAKE AND BOARDWALK RUN
### *Walt Disney World Swan and Dolphin*

The trail begins at the Beach Hut near the Grotto Pool between the Swan and Dolphin. The path loops through the plaza that connects the two hotels and then circles Crescent Lake, following the wood-slatted BoardWalk toward Epcot Center and returning along the Stormalong Bay beach in front of the Beach Club and Yacht Club resorts. It circles the parking area of the Swan, runs past the tennis courts, and continues along the perimeter of the Dolphin, Yacht Club, and Beach Club parking areas before returning.

**LENGTH:** The trail is designed in three lengths, depending on the turnaround: 3.1 miles (5K), 1.86 miles (3K), and 1.24 miles (2K).

**MAPS:** Jogging maps are available at the Swan and Dolphin resorts' Guest Services, at the Body By Jake Health Studio in the Dolphin, and at the Swan Health Club in the Swan.

## COUNTRY CLUB FITNESS COURSE AT LAKE BUENA VISTA
### *Disney Institute, Disney Vacation Club, and Hotel Plaza at Disney Village*

The trail begins at the Disney Institute's Village Green and winds its way through a country club–like scattering of vacation villas surrounding the fairways of the Buena Vista Golf Course. The path follows the resort lanes to the Vacation Club, where it loops back and plunges into the forest along Treehouse Lane. Emerging from the forest, it crosses a grassy-banked waterway and follows a path lined with exercise stations. A footbridge takes the path back across the water to the starting point. From the Vacation Club, the path begins behind Building No. 54.

**LENGTH:** This jogging course is designed in two lengths, depending on the turnaround: 3.4 miles and 2.4 miles. A section of the trail — 1.8 miles — has thirty-two exercise stations with instructions.

**MAPS:** Jogging maps are available at Guest Services at the Disney Institute, the Vacation Club, and the Hotel Plaza resorts.

## BAREFOOT BAY BEACH AND ISLAND RUN
### *Disney's Caribbean Beach Resort*

The path begins at any point along the promenade encircling forty-acre Barefoot Bay lake. The promenade parallels the beach in front of the resort's Caribbean-style lodges and tropical landscaping. For a sightseeing break from the promenade, joggers may run the path encircling Parrot Cay, a Caribbean-themed garden island in the center of the lake, complete with parrots and other colorful birds. Wooden footbridges connect Parrot Cay to the promenade from either side of the lake.

**LENGTH:** The promenade around the lake is approximately 1.4 miles long, and slightly longer if you loop through Parrot Cay island.

**MAPS:** Resort maps showing the jogging path are available at the Caribbean Beach resort Guest Services.

## TOWN AND COUNTRY RUN THROUGH THE OLD SOUTH
### *Disney's Port Orleans and Dixie Landings Resorts*

The trail starts at any point in either resort. It follows the Carriage Path that encircles Port Orleans resort and passes through the streets designed after New Orleans' French Quarter, with row house brick buildings and pleasant park squares. The run follows the banks of the Sassagoula River, and enters the Old South at Dixie Landings resort. The trail continues along the river past large plantation mansions with sweeping lawns, then winds through a shady, wooded area where rustic bayou lodges are tucked among the cypresses and pines. The path crosses the river to Ol' Man Island, runs along the opposite shore past the Dixie Landings marina, and returns to the Port Orleans Carriage Path.

**LENGTH:** The trail length varies according to the winding paths chosen through the Dixie Landings resort, but averages about 1.5 miles.

**MAPS:** Jogging maps are available at the Port Orleans and Dixie Landings resorts Guest Services.

## ATLANTIC CITY BOARDWALK RUN
### *Disney's BoardWalk*

The trail begins in front of Disney's BoardWalk Inn, on the stretch of the BoardWalk Promenade by the BoardWalk Green. It crosses the bridge over the waterway toward Epcot Center, then runs along the waterfront at Stormalong Bay past the Beach Club and Yacht Club resorts. It follows the winding walkways to the Dolphin hotel, then continues on past the Swan hotel and passes behind Disney's BoardWalk before it emerges onto the wood-slatted BoardWalk Promenade. The long Promenade curves around Crescent Lake, leading back to the BoardWalk Inn, where joggers can stop or repeat the circuit.

**LENGTH:** The circuit is approximately 2.5 miles.

**MAPS:** Jogging maps are available at Guest Services at Disney's BoardWalk Inn and at Disney Vacation Club Villas at the BoardWalk.

## LAGOON RUN THROUGH TURN-OF-THE-CENTURY FLORIDA
### Disney's Grand Floridian Beach Resort

The path starts at the Grand Floridian's wood-planked dock and shoreline restaurant, Narcoossee's, at Seven Seas Lagoon, and heads inland to wind past the resort's elegant lawns and flower gardens in the wide courtyard. Passing by the free-form Courtyard Pool, the path travels between the Summer House and the majestic Victorian lobby building, continuing along the white sand beach at the edge of the lagoon and past the tennis courts before looping back to the Grand Floridian dock.

**LENGTH:** The path is about 1.3 miles long.

**MAPS:** Jogging maps are available at the Grand Floridian resort Guest Services.

## WILDERNESS EXERCISE TRAIL
### Disney's Fort Wilderness Resort and Campground and Disney's Wilderness Resort

The trailheads to the Wilderness Exercise Trail can be found across the road from the Tri-Circle-D Ranch in Fort Wilderness and at the side of the Wilderness Lodge. The asphalt-surfaced course enters the cool shade of a dense pine forest, which conveys a sense of quiet isolation. Ferns and palmettos line the course, giving way ever so often to the exercise stations placed alongside the path. Birds, marsh rabbits, and small lizards populate the area and watch the goings-on from the sidelines.

**LENGTH:** The fitness course is a 1-mile round trip, with exercise stations about every quarter mile along the way.

**MAPS:** Maps showing the exercise trail are available at Guest Services in the Fort Wilderness Reception Outpost, located in the Fort Wilderness Guest Parking Lot; at the Pioneer Hall Ticket and Information Window, near the Fort Wilderness Marina; and at Wilderness Lodge Guest Services.

## THE SURF AND TURF RUN
### Disney's Yacht Club and Beach Club Resorts

The trail begins on the waterfront walkway at the shore of Stormalong Bay and curves along the beach past a long stretch of red and white cabanas. It continues across to the wood-slatted BoardWalk Promenade that curves around Crescent Lake. The trail exits behind Disney's BoardWalk and continues past the Swan resort, where it circles the parking area, runs past the tennis courts, and continues along the perimeter of the Dolphin, Yacht Club, and Beach Club parking areas, ending back at the front entrances of the Yacht Club and Beach Club resorts.

**LENGTH:** The trail has two lengths, 2 miles and 1 mile, depending on the turnaround.

**MAPS:** Jogging maps are available at Guest Services at the Yacht Club and Beach Club resorts. ◆

# NATURE WALKS

Visitors who would like a change of pace from the intense stimulation of the theme parks can enjoy leisurely strolls along some of Walt Disney World's nature walks. The trails explore a variety of environments including wooded wilderness areas, marshy wetlands, and lush tropical groves, which are populated with birds, rabbits, squirrels, deer, lizards, and numerous other creatures.

## WILDERNESS SWAMP TRAIL
### *Disney's Fort Wilderness Resort and Campground*

The Wilderness Swamp Trail is one of the most serene and varied of the nature trails at Walt Disney World, and one of the least traveled. The 2.2-mile-long trail starts in an old-growth forest of tall moss-draped trees. Ferns, vines, and low shrubs grow untamed along the trail, which emerges on the shore of an estuary. Here, a secluded sitting area provides the perfect spot for a picnic. The trail plunges back into the dense forest before leading onto a boardwalk that crosses the wetlands of a wilderness swamp. Water reeds and cattails grow among the partially submerged cypress forest, where wild waterfowl live. The trail once again enters the tree-canopied forest. Wildflowers, berries, woodpeckers, fluttering butterflies, chirping birds, humming insects, and tiny yellow-striped lizards add splashes of color, sound, and movement. The trail crosses the grassy banks of Chickasaw Creek and returns through the forest.

MAPS: A map of Fort Wilderness showing the trailhead is available at Guest Services in the Fort Wilderness Reception Outpost (located in the Fort Wilderness Guest Parking Lot) and at the Pioneer Hall Ticket and Information Window (near the Fort Wilderness Marina). See also "Fort Wilderness & River Country," page 68.

NOTE: Snacks, beverages, and picnic supplies are available at the Settlement Trading Post, located between Pioneer Hall and the beginning of the Wilderness Swamp Trail. The Trail's End Buffeteria at Pioneer Hall also will prepare meals to go for those who wish to picnic. The Wilderness Swamp Trail is a wonderful walk at any time of the day, but the early mornings and dusky evenings are the most dramatic, with deep shadows and much animal activity.

## PARROT CAY ISLAND AND AVIARY WALK
### *Disney's Caribbean Beach Resort*

The walk through Parrot Cay, a Caribbean-themed garden island in the center of forty-acre Barefoot Bay lake, is a short, leisurely stroll that covers about a quarter mile and is sure to delight bird-lovers. The walk starts at either of the wooden footbridges that connect the island to the promenade encircling the lake, and twists and turns through a lush tropical garden of palm and banana trees and bamboo. The walk continues past a rustic octagonal gazebo fashioned of lodgepole pines, and over to Parrot Cay's highlight, an aviary populated with a variety of exotic birds. Here, cherry-headed conures and gold-cap conures from South America preen and display their colorful feathers, while a blue-front Amazon parrot from Central America talks to visitors astute enough to greet him. Try opening the conversation with a simple "Hello!" Nearby is a pleasant shaded area with picnic tables.

**MAPS:** There is no map available that focuses on Parrot Cay; however, a map of the resort is available at Caribbean Beach resort Guest Services.

**NOTE:** Snacks, beverages, and other picnic supplies are available at the food court in Old Port Royale, located just across the footbridge to Parrot Cay. The Parrot Cay Island and Aviary Walk is pleasant at any time of the day, but the island's playground attracts large groups of children in the afternoons, so early mornings and evenings are best for quiet strolls. Parrot Cay is wheelchair accessible.

## ZOOLOGICAL GARDENS WALK
### *Discovery Island*

Discovery Island was designed to be the quintessential nature walk at Walt Disney World. Ferries carry visitors to the island from the Magic Kingdom Dock, the Marina Pavilion at the Contemporary Resort, and the Fort Wilderness Marina. The island's tree-canopied path wanders through a jungle lush with palm trees, flowering plants, curling vines, and exotic shrubs from around the world. Tweets, chirps, screams, honks, and caws can be heard as the path enters a vast walk-through aviary suspended high above a sheltered lagoon. It exits at an inlet that is the home to brown pelicans, once an endangered species due to the pesticide DDT. The boardwalk to the right follows the beach to a wrecked "pirate ship"; to the left it runs alongside a flamingo-filled lagoon and a section of beach favored by giant Galapagos tortoises. As the path returns to the dock, visitors can catch an up-close view of the island's resident alligators.

**MAPS:** A map of the trail is available at the Discovery Island dock where the ferries land. (See also "Discovery Island," page 76.)

**NOTE:** Admission is charged at Discovery Island, but is included in Length of Stay Passes and some Multiday Passes. Snacks, beverages, and other picnic supplies are available at the Thirsty Perch. Animal-lovers should try to see one of the bird or reptile shows scheduled throughout the day. Discovery Island is wheelchair accessible.

## CYPRESS POINT NATURE TRAIL
### *River Country at Fort Wilderness*

This trail is actually a narrow roped boardwalk leading visitors on a quarter-mile path that follows the shoreline of Bay Lake into the wetlands. Moss-hung bald cypresses grow up out of the water and shade the path. These trees are native to the wetlands and were here long before the land was developed. In the shallow water, among the roots of the trees, are colonies of freshwater mollusks, extremely important to the food chain in this ecosystem. Small fish dart through the water, and egrets and heron stand among the water reeds fishing. One aviary along the way holds a white-necked raven and another is the home of a red-tailed hawk. The birds at Cypress Point have been injured in the wild and rehabilitated, but cannot survive unaided.

**MAPS:** There are no official maps of the trail or of River Country. See "Fort Wilderness & River County," page 68, for a map of the area.

**NOTE:** Admission is charged at River Country, but is included in Length of Stay Passes and some Multiday Passes. Snacks, beverages, and other picnic supplies are available at Pop's Place or the Waterin' Hole. There is a shaded picnic area at the end of the trail on the white sand beach. ◆

# SWIMMING

All Walt Disney World resorts have swimming pools, usually more than one. The resort pools are generally restricted to guests registered at a particular resort (except for Vacation Club Members). Visitors who want to engage in serious water play should visit the water parks at River Country (see "Fort Wilderness & River Country," page 68); Typhoon Lagoon (see "Typhoon Lagoon," page 84); or Disney's newest water park, Blizzard Beach (see "Blizzard Beach," page 90). There is also an extensive beach scene at the Walt Disney World resorts, and anyone bringing along a towel can venture out and stake a place in the sand. All beaches have snack bars, rest rooms, and lockers nearby. From time to time, usually in late spring and autumn, the lakes and waterways at Walt Disney World undergo a "seasonal turnover," with an increase in bacteria and algae levels. During those periods, swimming is prohibited in any area except resort pools. Signs are posted.

**LAP POOLS:** Swimmers who would like to exercise during their vacation should consider staying at a resort that offers a lap pool. Lap pools are usually one of several pools, and are set apart from the family pools. Lap pools tend to be deserted in the mornings. Lap pools or Olympic-sized pools can be found at:
- Disney's Contemporary Resort (a seventy-five-foot pool)
- Walt Disney World Swan (shared by guests at the Walt Disney World Dolphin)
- Buena Vista Palace Resort and Spa (at The Spa)
- Disney Institute Sports and Fitness Center.

**WALT DISNEY WORLD RESORTS WITH POOLS LARGE ENOUGH FOR LAP SWIMMING INCLUDE:**
- Lake Buena Vista Clubhouse at Disney's Village Resort (the loveliest at Walt Disney World)
- Fort Wilderness Resort and Campground (in the Meadow Recreation Area)
- Buena Vista Palace Resort and Spa (on Recreation Island)
- Disney's Yacht Club Resort (the "quiet pool")
- Disney's Beach Club Resort (the "quiet pool")
- Disney's Yacht and Beach Club Resorts — Stormalong Bay water park (the oval "current" pool).

**WHITE SAND BEACHES:** Most of the Walt Disney World resorts offer stretches of pure white sand beach for the enjoyment of guests. Many of the beaches are equipped with comfortable lounge chairs to relax in, or rows of jaunty striped cabanas for shelter from the sun. Besides the resort beaches listed below, there is also a charming deserted beach on Discovery Island, although swimming is not permitted there. During certain months, when bacteria counts rise, all beaches at Florida lakes are closed. Beaches can be found at the following resorts and parks:
- Fort Wilderness Marina and Beach (a large beach on Bay Lake)
- Disney's Contemporary Resort (a large beach on Bay Lake)
- Disney's Polynesian Resort (a large beach on Seven Seas Lagoon)
- Disney's Grand Floridian Beach Club Resort (a large beach on Seven Seas Lagoon)
- Disney's Beach Club Resort (a large beach on Stormalong Bay — swimming seasonally)
- Walt Disney World Swan and Dolphin (a small beach on Crescent Lake — swimming seasonally)
- Disney's Caribbean Beach Resort (a large beach on Barefoot Bay)
- Disney Vacation Club (a small beach on the Trumbo Canal — no swimming)
- Disney's Wilderness Lodge (a small beach on Bay Lake). ◆

# TENNIS & VOLLEYBALL

Visitors who enjoy tennis can choose from a variety of tennis environments at Walt Disney World. Most of the resorts have well-designed tennis courts in a number of interesting settings: tucked into the forest, or overlooking beaches, lakes, golf courses, and pools. For casual play, the tennis courts at the resorts are well kept and pleasant; however, serious tennis players may want to take advantage of the professional facilities at Walt Disney World's full-service tennis clubs.

## TENNIS CLUBS

*The full-service tennis clubs at Walt Disney World are staffed by tennis pros certified by the United States Professional Tennis Association, who offer private tennis lessons and challenging tennis clinics. Tennis equipment and ball machines can be rented at the pro shops, and the clubs will arrange tournaments for groups. Appropriate tennis attire is required. No track shoes, running shoes, or cross trainers.*

**DISNEY'S RACQUET CLUB AT THE CONTEMPORARY:** The tennis courts at Disney's Racquet Club are located next to the Contemporary resort's north garden wing, along the shore of Bay Lake. All six courts were recently resurfaced to state-of-the-art Hydro-Grid clay. Several of the courts are set up for competition play, complete with bleacher areas.

   **COURTS:** Six, lighted.

   **HOURS:** 8 AM until 9 PM.

   **FEES:** About $12 per hour (about $40 per family for an entire stay). Private lessons are about $40 per hour. The Tennis Clinic is available for about $35 per person, and features video analysis. To arrange for tennis instruction, call 407 824-3578.

   **RESERVATIONS:** Recommended. Courts can be reserved twenty-four hours in advance (824-3578).

   **NOTE:** Courts are available to both Walt Disney World resort guests and day visitors. Rental equipment is available at the Racquet Club pro shop, which also has two practice courts. The pro shop also offers a "Tennis Anyone" program that matches players with tennis partners. The Racquet Club pro shop is open from 9 AM until 9 PM and offers a restringing service.

**THE TENNIS CLUB AT WALT DISNEY WORLD DOLPHIN:** The Dolphin shares a deluxe full-service tennis club with the adjacent Swan resort. The Tennis Club is located on its own parcel of land across Epcot Resort Boulevard from the two resorts, which are connected to the tennis courts by a walkway. There is parking behind the tennis courts, although the lot is unmarked. The Tennis Club has a comfortable waiting area under a striped cabana.

   **COURTS:** Eight, lighted.

   **HOURS:** 9 AM until 6 PM.

   **FEES:** About $12 per hour, complimentary after 6 PM.

   **RESERVATIONS:** Recommended. Courts can be reserved twenty-four hours in advance (934-4396).

   **NOTE:** Courts are available to both Walt Disney World resort guests and day visitors. The Tennis Club offers a match-up service for players looking for partners. Instruction for both individuals and groups is available, and themed round-robin tournaments are scheduled weekly. The pro shop, open from 8 AM until 6 PM, carries tennis apparel and equipment and offers a restringing service.

## TENNIS COURTS

*The tennis courts at most of the resorts are available to players on a first-come, first-served basis, although some do accept reservations, and many may be used only by registered guests. Day visitors as well as guests at any Walt Disney World resort can play the courts at Fort Wilderness. Hotel tennis courts are complimentary except at the following resorts: Contemporary, Grand Floridian, Swan, and Dolphin. Appropriate tennis attire is required at all courts, and most resorts offer equipment rentals or loaners.*

**BUENA VISTA PALACE RESORT AND SPA:** Located on the resort's large Recreation Island, these tennis courts overlook Lake Buena Vista. A wide lawn leads from the pool area to the courts.
> **COURTS:** Three, lighted.
> **HOURS:** 6 AM until 10 PM.
> **FEES:** Complimentary.
> **RESERVATIONS:** None; courts are available on a first-come, first-served basis. There is no time limit.
> **NOTE:** Courts are available to registered guests only. Complimentary tennis equipment is available at the concierge desk in the Palace Suites, adjacent to the pool. Tennis lessons and tournaments can be arranged by the concierge.

**DISNEY INSTITUTE:** The Disney Institute offers a tennis studio complete with video playback, private and group lessons, a pro shop, and clay-surfaced courts, all with a panoramic view of the Disney Village Waterways. This all-new facility will occasionally feature a class taught by notable tennis pros. Private lessons and competition matches can be arranged through Disney Institute Guest Services.
> **COURTS:** Eight, lighted.
> **HOURS:** 6 AM until 10 PM.
> **FEES:** Complimentary.
> **RESERVATIONS:** Recommended, twenty-four hours in advance (827-1100).
> **NOTES:** Courts are available only to guests staying at the Disney Institute. Rental equipment is available at the Sports and Fitness Center. Tennis lessons can be arranged by appointment.

**DISNEY VACATION CLUB:** The tennis courts at the Vacation Club are located on the edge of the Trumbo Canal, in the resort's recreation complex. The courts are surrounded by a palmetto and pine tree grove and lie within viewing distance of the pool. Although the courts themselves have no viewing area, there are benches nearby for those waiting to play.
> **COURTS:** Two, lighted.
> **HOURS:** 7 AM until 11 PM.
> **FEES:** Complimentary.
> **RESERVATIONS:** None; courts are available on a first-come, first-served basis.
> **NOTE:** Courts are available to registered guests only. Rental equipment is at Hank's Rent 'N Return.

**DISNEY'S GRAND FLORIDIAN BEACH RESORT:** Located on the south side of the resort, these clay-surfaced courts are secluded in a charming tree-banked setting. The monorail track is located between the courts and Seven Seas Lagoon, and players can see and hear the trains gliding by as they play.
> **COURTS:** Two, lighted.
> **HOURS:** 8 AM until 8 PM.
> **FEES:** About $12 per hour. Private lessons are about $40 per hour.

RESERVATIONS: Recommended, twenty-four hours in advance (824-2433).

NOTE: Courts are available to Walt Disney World resort guests only. Rental equipment is available at the St. John's Health Club. Tennis lessons can be arranged by appointment.

DISNEY'S YACHT CLUB AND BEACH CLUB RESORTS: These two resorts share a set of tennis courts, located on the far side of the Beach Club. The courts are surrounded on three sides by a forest of pine trees and low-growing mulberry and jasmine bushes. In the nearby waiting area, players can view ongoing games in the shade of a large canvas awning.

COURTS: Two, lighted.

HOURS: 7 AM until 10 PM.

FEES: Complimentary.

RESERVATIONS: None; courts are available on a first-come, first-served basis.

NOTE: Courts are available to registered guests only. Complimentary equipment is available at the Ship Shape Health Club.

DOUBLETREE GUEST SUITES RESORT: The resort's tennis courts are located behind the hotel, near the pool. A lawn stretches out in front of the courts, which are surrounded by tall palms and pines. Although the belt of trees acts as a buffer, players can hear the sounds of the freeway behind the courts. A wood-shingled gazebo provides players with a shaded waiting and viewing area.

COURTS: Two, lighted.

HOURS: 7 AM until 11 PM.

FEES: Complimentary.

RESERVATIONS: None; courts are available on a first-come, first-served basis.

NOTE: Courts are available to Walt Disney World resort guests only. Complimentary racquets are available at the hotel bell desk.

FORT WILDERNESS: At Fort Wilderness, players can enjoy a quiet country setting for their tennis game. To reach the courts, guests must take a Fort Wilderness shuttle bus to the Meadow Recreation Area. The tennis courts are located adjacent to the Meadow swimming pool. Pine forest banks the courts on three sides, and there is a small waiting area near the pool.

COURTS: Two, lighted.

HOURS: 8 AM until 10 PM.

FEES: Complimentary.

RESERVATIONS: None; courts are available on a first-come, first-served basis. There is a one-hour playing-time limit if others are waiting to play.

NOTE: Courts are available to both Walt Disney World resort guests and day visitors. Equipment is available for rent at the Bike Barn, nearby.

GROSVENOR RESORT: The tennis courts at the Grosvenor Resort are located behind the pool area, and adjacent to the resort's handball and volleyball courts. Behind the courts, patches of pine forest lead down to the shores of Lake Buena Vista. There is a small waiting area with shaded tables, nearby.

COURTS: Two, lighted.

HOURS: 9 AM until 10 PM.

FEES: Complimentary.

**RESERVATIONS:** None; courts are available on a first-come, first-served basis.

**NOTE:** Courts are available to Walt Disney World resort guests only. Complimentary loaner equipment is available at the Recreation Office near the pool.

**HOTEL ROYAL PLAZA:** The courts at this hotel are located at the far end of the property, across from the parking lot. They are backed up against the freeway, with little landscaping to offer a buffer from the noise. There is a small waiting area on the lawn in front of the courts.

**COURTS:** Four, lighted.

**HOURS:** 7 AM until 11 PM.

**FEES:** Complimentary.

**RESERVATIONS:** None; courts are available on a first-come, first-served basis.

**NOTE:** Courts are available to Walt Disney World resort guests only. No equipment is available for rent. The hotel can arrange tennis lessons for registered guests.

**SHADES OF GREEN:** The tennis courts are located at the edge of the Palm Golf Course near the south wing of the resort. A small landscaped area, shaded by a smattering of palm trees, provides guests with a pleasant place to wait for a game. The courts are banked by forest with a view of the fairways.

**COURTS:** Two, lighted.

**HOURS:** Dawn until 10 PM.

**FEES:** Complimentary.

**RESERVATIONS:** None; courts are available on a first-come, first-served basis.

**NOTE:** Courts are available to registered guests only. Complimentary equipment is available at the Front Desk.

## VOLLEYBALL

There are more than a dozen sand volleyball courts scattered throughout Walt Disney World. Volleyball is a "pickup" sport, so visitors who begin a game may find they pick up more players as they go along; or if there is a game in progress, they can wait on the sidelines to be picked. The volleyball courts at Fort Wilderness are available to all WDW visitors. The courts at Typhoon Lagoon and River Country, where admission is charged, may also be used by any visitor. Hotel courts are for registered guests only. Locations include:

- **FORT WILDERNESS** — Meadow Recreation Area and on the Fort Wilderness beach.
- **TYPHOON LAGOON** — In the Getaway Glen Picnic Area, with a grassy berm for spectators.
- **RIVER COUNTRY** — On the beach near Pop's Picnic Area, overlooking Bay Lake.
- **DISNEY VACATION CLUB** — At the resort's recreation complex, near the tennis courts.
- **DISNEY'S BEACH CLUB RESORT** — In a secluded courtyard facing the beach at Stormalong Bay; shared by guests at the Yacht Club resort.
- **DISNEY'S CARIBBEAN BEACH RESORT** — On the beach at Barefoot Bay, near Old Port Royale.
- **DISNEY'S CONTEMPORARY RESORT** — On the beach at Bay Lake, adjacent to the Marina Pavilion.
- **DISNEY'S GRAND FLORIDIAN BEACH RESORT** — On the white sand beach at Seven Seas Lagoon.
- **DISNEY'S POLYNESIAN RESORT** — On the white sand beach at Seven Seas Lagoon.
- **GROSVENOR RESORT** — Behind the pool area, surrounded by lawn and pine forest. ◆

# WATERSKIING & PARASAILING

Waterskiers fly across the surface of Bay Lake all year long, and if you look up, you may see someone parasailing through the sky over Bay Lake, tethered by a rope to a speedboat below, with a brightly colored parachute soaring above. Everyone from novices to experts can make use of Walt Disney World's fleet of speedboats and waterskiing and parasailing equipment. The drivers are professional instructors and certified by the American Waterski Association. They offer instruction and helpful tips to both beginning and advanced skiers — from helping novices get up on skis for the first time to guiding more experienced skiers in how to perform complex turns and daredevil stunts. Waterskiing and parasailing excursions are available to all visitors at Walt Disney World.

**WATERSKIING:** Ski boats cruise along at about fifty miles per hour, and waterskiing excursions last one hour. Groups of up to five people can waterski together, with a two-person minimum. Since the fee for waterskiing excursions is per hour rather than per person, it can be economical to team up with other waterskiers. Along with standard waterskis, the excursion boats carry Scurfers (mini surfboards), Hydra-slides (knee boards), and slalom skis.

    **FEE:** About $80 per hour, which includes ski boat, driver-instructor, and all waterskiing equipment. Participants may bring their own waterskis, if they wish. There is a maximum of five persons per boat, with a two-person minimum. Excursion groups are not mixed, except by request.

    **RESERVATIONS:** Reservations are required at least one day in advance and can be made up to two weeks ahead (407 824-2621). Excursion boats pick up waterskiers at the Fort Wilderness, Wilderness Lodge, Contemporary, Polynesian, and Grand Floridian resort marinas — be sure to specify where you wish to board. Waterskiing excursions are extremely popular during peak-attendance seasons, on warm weekends, and during holidays, so make reservations as far in advance as possible if you will be traveling to WDW at any of these times.

    **EXCURSION SCHEDULE:** At least two waterskiing boats are in operation at all times on Bay Lake, where all waterskiing is done at Walt Disney World. Waterskiing excursions depart daily at 8:45 AM, 10 AM, 11:15 AM, 1:30 PM, 2:45 PM, and 4 PM. Excursion times may vary with the season, and excursions can sometimes be delayed or cancelled due to poor weather conditions.

**PARASAILING:** Parasailing may look very daring, but it requires no prior experience. Parasailers only need to settle into the parasail seat, put on the harness, and up and away they go, towed around Bay Lake by a speedboat as they soar to music from their speaker-mounted seat.

    **FEE:** About $45 per person for about 10 to 12 minutes of flight time; about $16 per person for visitors wishing to ride along on the boat without going aloft.

    **RESERVATIONS:** Reservations are required at least one day in advance and can be made up to two weeks ahead at the Contemporary's Marina Pavilion (407 824-1000: hotel).

    **SCHEDULE:** Parasailing excursions depart from the Contemporary's Marina Pavilion every morning at 6:45 AM, 7:30 AM, 8:15 AM, 9 AM, and 9:45 AM; and, during the summer, on Wednesday and Saturday evenings at 6:15 PM, 7 PM, and 7:45 PM. Times may vary with the season, and excursions can sometimes be delayed or cancelled due to poor weather conditions. ◆

# TOURING TIPS

## PACKING

Casual clothes are the norm throughout Walt Disney World. The only exceptions are in some of the more elegant restaurants or, if you want to make an impression, the night clubs at Pleasure Island. The budget resorts provide shampoo; the better resorts also supply conditioner, body lotion, and sometimes toothpaste, toothbrushes, sunblock, and hair dryers. In fall and winter, Orlando can get surprisingly cold, so before packing, check with Disney Weather (407 824-4104). The items listed below are absolute musts for touring Walt Disney World in comfort.

**CLOTHING:** Pack comfortable, well-broken-in walking shoes — you will be spending much of your time on your feet. Forget sandals except for poolside use, as these can cause blisters and problems when boarding and disembarking rides. In warm months, water sports are big at Walt Disney World, so if you plan to swim, don't forget your bathing suit. Women should bring a one-piece bathing suit for the wild water slides at Typhoon Lagoon and Blizzard Beach. In the winter, bring a sweatshirt or sweater for layering, and pack a jacket that is lined for warmth. Don't forget gloves to keep off the chill when standing in line and touring outdoors.

**SUN & WEATHER PROTECTION:** Pack a lightweight hat that shades your eyes; visors are also a good choice and are easy to pack and carry around. Sunglasses are a must, the larger the better. Bring a pair that provides full protection from UV rays. Choose a sunblock rated SPF 15 or higher; the Florida sun will burn you even in the winter. (Sunburn is the most frequently treated problem at first-aid stations in Walt Disney World.) It rains daily on summer afternoons and periodically throughout the year, so pack a collapsible umbrella that fits in your tote bag (rain ponchos can be a nuisance when wet).

**TOURING ESSENTIALS:** Bring a roomy, lightweight tote bag with a shoulder strap — you will find it invaluable for carrying around brochures, entertainment schedules, sunblock, purses, small purchases, and bottled water. Self-closing plastic bags are good for stashing wet bathing suits or food in your tote bag while you're touring. Pack a lightweight flashlight such as a penlight, which is useful for reading maps and entertainment schedules after dark, consulting guidebooks while waiting in line at dark attractions, and reading menus in dimly lit restaurants. To pass the time while waiting in lines, you might want to bring a book to read or a cassette player with headphones for audio books or music tapes.

**UPON ARRIVAL:** On your drive to Walt Disney World, you may want to pick up a few amenities for your room. The largest and most convenient store is Gooding's Supermarket at Crossroads Shopping Center. (See "Walt Disney World Overview" map, page 10.) Purchase enough bottled water for your stay (WDW water isn't very tasty), and include some small bottles of water you can refill and carry with you as you tour. Most people don't realize how dehydrated they can get here and how tired it can make them feel. You may also want to pick up fresh fruit and snack items for your room, as well as juice, soft drinks, coffee (if your room has a coffeemaker) beer, or wine. Spirits are available at Pacino's Liquors next door to Gooding's Supermarket. Most resort rooms have mini bars where you can store your beverages, and what you've purchased will cost much less than the hotel-stocked treats. ◆

PACKING

# DISCOUNT TRAVEL

Many Walt Disney World visitors join travel clubs to help take the bite out of their vacation budgets. Travel clubs affiliated with WDW include the American Automobile Association and American Express, as well as Orlando-based organizations and Disney-sponsored clubs. Most travel clubs offer discounts on accommodations, restaurants, vacation packages, and car rentals. (See also "Vacation Discount Coupons," page 272.)

## MAGIC KINGDOM CLUB GOLD CARD

The Magic Kingdom Club, operated by the Disney Company, has been around for more than forty years. Club members receive an embossed card that entitles them to benefits and discounts at Walt Disney World in Orlando, Disneyland in California, Disneyland Paris in France, and Tokyo Disneyland in Japan.

**WDW HOTEL DISCOUNTS:** A 10 to 30 percent discount at selected Disney-owned hotels year round; a 10 percent discount at independently owned hotels on Disney property (Swan, Dolphin, and Hotel Plaza resorts); and a wide selection of all-inclusive WDW vacation packages at discount rates.

**ADMISSION DISCOUNTS:** A slight (about 5 percent) discount on park admissions; a 10 percent discount on golf greens fees during selected seasons; and a 10 percent discount on some dinner shows.

**ADDITIONAL BENEFITS:** A 10 percent discount on selected meals at the Magic Kingdom, Epcot Center, and Disney-MGM Studios restaurants; a 10 percent discount on merchandise purchased at selected stores at Disney Village Marketplace, Pleasure Island, Crossroads Shopping Center, and at The Disney Stores anywhere in the world. Magic Kingdom Club members are given a toll-free telephone number for WDW reservations and information; a 10 percent discount on AAA memberships; restricted discounts with Delta Airlines and National Car Rental; a two-year subscription to *Disney News*, a members-only magazine; and a trial membership in Travel America at HalfPrice, a hotel discount club.

**MEMBERSHIP FEE:** The fee for a two-year family membership is about $65.

**REVIEWERS' COMMENTS:** An excellent value for those who want to stay on property at WDW. The admission ticket discounts are small, but frequent visitors who like to plan ahead will save quite a bit on telephone calls to WDW. The 10 percent Delta Airlines discount applies only to the higher fares, so it is of questionable value, as is the unimpressive National Car Rental discount.

**CONTACT:** Magic Kingdom Club, P.O. Box 3850, Anaheim, CA 92803-9831 (800 413-4763).

## DISNEY'S MAGIC YEARS CLUB

The Magic Years Club is designed for people aged fifty-five and over. It includes the same benefits and discounts at Walt Disney World and Disney properties throughout the world as the Magic Kingdom Club, above, but at a specially discounted membership price.

**ADDITIONAL BENEFITS:** Beyond the standard Magic Kingdom Club benefits, some additional benefits offered to Magic Years Club members include discount parking tickets, discount dining coupons for use at Walt Disney World and Disneyland, and a toll-free telephone number for WDW reservations and information for Disney's Magic Years Club members.

**MEMBERSHIP FEE:** The fee for a five-year individual membership (including one guest) is about $35.

**REVIEWERS' COMMENTS:** Because the length of membership is five years, this is a good value for seniors who travel to Walt Disney World frequently. The 10 percent Delta Airlines discount applies only to the higher fares, so it is of questionable value, but the toll-free telephone number can be a real plus.

**CONTACT:** Disney's Magic Years Club, P.O. Box 4709, Anaheim, CA 92803-4709 (714 520-2500).

## DISNEY'S FOOD 'N FUN CARD

The Disney Food 'N Fun Card is a dining voucher that can be added to any Walt Disney World vacation package. It entitles guests to two meals per day (breakfast, lunch, and/or dinner) at any of about sixty-five full-service restaurants in both the resorts and theme parks. As for the "Fun" portion, card holders have unlimited access to most of the recreational facilities throughout WDW (see "Sports," page 213).

**MEALS:** For breakfast, the plan includes one a la carte breakfast and beverage or a Character Breakfast; lunch and dinner include an appetizer or salad, entree, nonalcoholic beverage, and dessert. Taxes and gratuities are included. Not included in the plan are alcoholic beverages, snacks or refreshments, room service, fast food, lobster entrees, and restaurants at non-Disney-owned hotels. A few restaurants are not included in the plan, and some participate only at lunch. This list varies. Restaurants that have served only lunch include The Hollywood Brown Derby, King Stefan's Banquet Hall, Chefs de France, L'Originale Alfredo di Roma, Restaurant Marrakesh, and San Angel Inn. Restaurants not participating at all have included Au Petit Café, Bistro de Paris, Coral Reef, and Victoria and Albert's. Also generally not included are the Disney dinner shows. Check ahead to determine which restaurants are participating.

**RECREATION:** Card holders have unlimited access to WDW recreational facilities including tennis, waterskiing, watercraft and bicycle rentals, horseback riding, and most health clubs. Not included in the plan are golf green fees, golf cart rentals, golf and tennis lessons, fishing, massage, and arcade games.

**REVIEWER'S COMMENTS:** Many visitors find it more economical to buy fewer Food 'N Fun days than the number of days in their vacation package. Restaurant reservations are essential and can be made up to sixty days in advance through Disney Dining Reservations (407 939-3463). The card is an especially good value for those who plan to take advantage of WDW's recreational facilities.

**PROGRAM FEES:** As an add-on to Disney Vacation packages, the Food 'N Fun Card runs about $50 to $60 per day per person (about $35 for children).

**CONTACT:** The Food 'N Fun Card can be ordered at the time vacation packages are booked through Disney's Central Reservations Office (407 934-7639).

## ORLANDO MAGICARD

The Orlando Magicard is sponsored by the Orlando/Orange County Convention & Visitors Bureau, Inc., and offers visitors discounts on attractions, dinner shows, car rentals, factory outlet merchandise, and hotels throughout the Orlando attractions area, including hotels on Walt Disney World property.

**WDW HOTEL DISCOUNTS:** Special discount rates (ranging from 10 to 20 percent) on accommodations and vacation packages at Hotel Royal Plaza, Grosvenor Resort, Buena Vista Palace Resort and Spa, Courtyard by Marriott; and DoubleTree Guest Suites Resort.

DISCOUNT TRAVEL

**ADMISSION DISCOUNTS:** A 20 percent discount on admission to Pleasure Island; discounts on the Polynesian Luau dinner show; and limited discounts on some Multiday Passes.

**ADDITIONAL BENEFITS:** A 10 percent discount on Alamo, Avis, and Hertz rental cars, and a toll-free number for discount hotel reservations.

**MEMBERSHIP FEE:** The Orlando Magicard is free and can be used for groups of up to six persons.

**REVIEWERS' COMMENTS:** A true savings for active visitors. Be sure to call and request your discount card well ahead of your visit. It takes about three to four weeks to receive your card.

**CONTACT:** Orlando Magicard (800 643-9492).

## NATIONAL TRAVEL CLUBS

Several national travel clubs and other organizations, such as the American Association of Retired Persons, offer members travel discounts on selected Walt Disney World accommodations, vacation packages, and car rentals. Those listed here are among the most frequently used at Walt Disney World, although most of the Hotel Plaza resorts also offer discounts to a number of other travel clubs (see "Hotels," page 133).

**AMERICAN AUTOMOBILE ASSOCIATION:** Discounts ranging from 10 to 20 percent at Hotel Royal Plaza, Courtyard by Marriott, Grosvenor Resort, DoubleTree Guest Suites Resort, Travelodge Hotel, and the Hilton Resort; discounts on Walt Disney World vacation packages; and discounts at most car rental agencies. Parking at theme parks is free when admission tickets are purchased through AAA. Periodically, AAA members are also offered discounts at Disney-owned resorts.

> **MEMBERSHIP FEE:** Membership costs about $55 for the first year and about $40 thereafter.
>
> **CONTACT:** Call your local chapter of the American Automobile Association for an application.

**ENCORE:** Encore offers members a 50 percent discount at Hotel Royal Plaza, Travelodge Hotel, and many off-site hotels in the area; discount vacation packages to Walt Disney World; and discounts at most car rental agencies.

Membership Fee: A one-year membership for an individual or family is about $50.

> **CONTACT:** ENCORE Preferred Traveller Program, ENCORE Travel, 4501 Forbes Boulevard, Lanham, MD 20706 ( 800 638-8976).

**ENTERTAINMENT PUBLICATIONS:** This discount coupon book offers a 50 percent discount at Hotel Royal Plaza, Grosvenor Resort, Travelodge Hotel, and many off-site hotels in the area; discounts on Pleasure Island admissions; and discounts at most car rental agencies.

> **MEMBERSHIP FEE:** An Entertainment Publications discount book for Orlando or any other city in the United States, good for one year, is about $40.
>
> **CONTACT:** Entertainment Publications, P.O. Box 1068, Trumbell, CT 06611 (800 374-4464).

**AMERICAN EXPRESS:** American Express, the official charge card at Walt Disney World, offers credit card holders Disney Dollars Vacation Packages that include accommodations at a WDW resort, a rental car, park admissions, a 10 percent discount on some dinner shows, 250 Disney Dollars to spend, and a number of other amenities. The company also offers a 20 percent discount on Disney Backstage Tours.

> **MEMBERSHIP FEE:** The annual credit card fee is about $55.
>
> **CONTACT:** American Express Customer Service (800 528-4800). ◆

# ORLANDO INTERNATIONAL AIRPORT

This large futuristic airport is growing faster than any other in the United States. The main terminal has a variety of restaurants and retail shops, including gift shops for Universal Studios, Warner Brothers, Sea World, and Walt Disney World. The first-class Hyatt Regency hotel is inside the main terminal, and is particularly convenient for visitors who are arriving late or leaving early. Automated trams transport passengers from the outlying gates to the main terminal, where ticketing areas, baggage claim, and ground transportation are located. (See also "Local Transportation & Parking," page 249.)

**AIRPORT LAYOUT:** The airport layout can be confusing for travelers who have several things to accomplish there after they arrive, such as confirming tickets at different airlines, renting cars, storing baggage, or meeting others. Three distant airline gateways are serviced by automated transit systems that leave from either end of the very long main terminal: the East Hall or West Hall. The main terminal is further divided north and south into two long mirror-image service areas: Landside A (north) and Landside B (south). Each Landside is used by specific airlines, and each has its own ticket counters and baggage claim areas, duplicate car rental counters and ground transportation services, and parking lots. For example, every rental car company has at least two, often three counters; however, reservations are held only at the counter nearest the passenger's arrival gate.

Passengers arrive on Level Three, where the ticket counters, shops, restaurants, and hotel are located. Baggage claim and ground transportation services are on both Landsides of Level Two. Car rental counters are on both Landsides of Level One. Airlines serviced at Landside A (West Hall) include American, Continental, and TWA. Airlines serviced at Landside B (East Hall) include Delta and America West. Airlines serviced at Landside B (West Hall) include Northwest, USAir, and United. (Landside A East Hall gates have not yet been constructed.) Airport telephone numbers include:

- 407 825-2001 — Information about airline gate locations; open 8 AM until 5 PM.
- 407 825-2000 — Paging number for callers outside the airport.
- 407 825-2352 — General airport information and help with departure and arrival times.

**MEETING COMPANIONS AT THE AIRPORT:** Travelers arriving on different airlines who want to rendezvous at the airport should plan carefully, since mixups can easily occur. For example, there are three Dollar Rental Car counters, so if you decide to meet at Dollar on Level One, you must specify the Dollar location nearest the airline of the passenger holding the car rental reservation. There is no direct route between Landsides A and B at the lower levels, so you must return to Level Three to cross over.

If there is considerable time between arrivals, you may want to meet on Level Three after retrieving your luggage. (Note: The airport does not have rental luggage carts, but there are numerous storage lockers scattered throughout.) The most pleasant and reliable meeting spots on Level Three include:

- *Beauregard's Restaurant* — (West Hall, mezzanine level) — Closes between 8 and 9 PM.
- *Orlando Marketplace* — (West Hall) — The food court counters close between 8 and 9 PM. Nathan's Hot Dogs is open twenty-four hours. The tables can be used at anytime.
- *Glades Grill and Lounge* — (East Hall) — Closes between 7 and 8 PM.
- *The Atrium Rotunda* — (East Hall) — A large comfortable hall with fountain and seating areas.
- *Hyatt Regency* — (East Hall, mezzanine level) — Meeting spots include the comfortable lobby area and McCoy's bistro-style restaurant, which is open until 11 PM. ◆

AIRPORT

# HYATT REGENCY

**LOCATION:** The Hyatt Regency is located above the main terminal of the Orlando International Airport. It is accessible from within the airport and has its own entrance court outside.

**AMBIENCE:** Surrounding the upper floors of the East Hall of the main terminal, the Hyatt Regency overlooks the airport's spacious indoor atrium and fountain. The mezzanine-level lobby has a quiet, elegant atmosphere with luxurious Oriental decor and large, comfortable seating areas. The moderately sized guest rooms are pleasantly decorated in cool shades of aqua with a tropical motif and overhead fans. The hotel frequently hosts business travelers and seminar attendees.

**AVERAGE RATES:** Standard rooms about $175 Sunday through Thursday; about $110 on weekends.

**AMENITIES:** Twenty-four-hour room service, coffeemaker, in-room safe, newspaper delivery, turndown service, voice mail, and valet parking.

**RESTAURANTS:** *McCoy's Bar and Grill* — Lunch and dinner, featuring seafood and steaks. McCoy's Bar and Grill closes at midnight.

*Hemispheres Restaurant* — Breakfast is served daily, lunch is available Monday through Friday, and dinner is served Monday through Saturday. Hemispheres features Italian cuisine and closes at 10 PM.

**RECREATION:** Pool, fitness center, whirlpool.

**FEATURES:** While guests check in, bellhops will retrieve luggage from the baggage claim area and deliver it to guest rooms. Bags are also transported from rooms to the ticket counter for departing guests. The tenth floor provides rooms that are specially equipped for business travelers.

**DRAWBACKS:** There are no mini bars in the room, which can be inconvenient for travelers arriving late who would like a beverage or snack.

**TIPS:** Rooms facing the atrium (even-numbered rooms) open onto the interior of the airport. The odd-numbered rooms face the runways and have large furnished balconies with soundproof glass doors.

For guests flying into Orlando in the evening, it may be more convenient to spend the night at the Hyatt Regency than renting a car and trying to find Walt Disney World in the dark.

Guests with early departures may want to spend their last night at the Hyatt Regency, which allows for a relaxed departure in the morning. The hotel television broadcasts a listing of all flights, so guests can monitor departure times.

**MAKING RESERVATIONS:** First call Hyatt Central Reservations (800 233-1234), then call the hotel directly (407 825-1234) to compare rates. Inquire about weekend or promotional rates and corporate rates.

**XXX** ATMOSPHERE. **XXX** ATTITUDE. **XXX** QUALITY. **XXX** TRUE VALUE.

HYATT REGENCY ORLANDO INTERNATIONAL AIRPORT
A HYATT HOTEL
9300 AIRPORT BOULEVARD, ORLANDO, FLORIDA 32827
TELEPHONE (407) 825-1234 • FAX (407) 856-1672

AIRPORT

# LOCAL TRANSPORTATION & PARKING

Most visitors to Walt Disney World arrive in their own cars. About one third of all visitors will fly into the Orlando International Airport, from which they have a number of transportation options, including rental cars. It is not absolutely necessary to have a car at Walt Disney World, since its internal transportation system is an efficient network of buses, ferries, trams, and monorails; it all depends how much you want to see each day and where you are staying. The resorts with the most convenient WDW transportation are the Beach Club, Yacht Club, Swan, Dolphin, BoardWalk, Grand Floridian, Contemporary, and Polynesian.

## AIRPORT TRANSPORTATION SERVICES

Walt Disney World is a thirty-minute drive from the Orlando International Airport and lies south of Orlando. Several independent services provide transportation from the airport to Walt Disney World.

**SHUTTLE SERVICE:** Mears Transportation (407 423-5566) provides twenty-four-hour mini-van transportation from the airport to all WDW resorts. Vans leave every fifteen to twenty minutes from the baggage claim areas. No reservations; about $16 per person one way, $25 round trip. Passengers are responsible for lifting and stowing their own luggage, and the van may make several stops along the way.

**TAXIS:** Private taxis from the airport to WDW cost about $40 each way, plus gratuity. If you have a party of three, it is less expensive and faster to take a taxi than a shuttle. Taxi service is also available at all resorts, and is a useful adjunct to WDW transportation, especially for travel between resorts.

**LIMOUSINES:** For larger groups, limousines are the most convenient and comfortable way to travel, and often the most economical. Limousine drivers are customarily tipped about 15 to 20 percent. Mears Transportation (407 423-5566) provides limousine service from the airport to WDW, starting at about $45 each way or $80 round trip. Mears' larger stretch limousines seat six and cost about $90 each way. Florida TownCar (800 525-7246) provides clean, courteous, and prompt service for parties up to five for about $70 round trip. They will even stop on the way to your hotel so you can pick up snacks or items you have forgotten. For larger groups, Town Car Limousine (407 299-8696) has a fleet of fully equipped six- to ten-passenger late-model stretch limousines starting at $80 each way.

## RENTAL CARS

Although WDW provides internal transportation for as many as one-hundred thousand guests each day, it is often more convenient to drive a car, especially if you would like to do a great deal in just a few days. WDW buses do not travel between resorts, so transfers are necessary. If you plan to visit or dine at a distant resort without using a car or taxi, you will waste an hour or more of your vacation time each way.

**WHERE TO RENT:** Car rental companies that are not in the airport may offer better prices than those at the airport, but an additional 6 to 9 percent airport shuttle surcharge is added to off-site car rental charges — and the convenience of the airport rental location is considerable, especially on return. Car rental companies currently located at the airport include Avis, Budget, National, and ★ Dollar (Hertz is relocating off property). Visitors can also rent cars whenever they wish at Walt Disney World and drop them off at the airport at no extra charge. Car rental companies located at Walt Disney World include

National (at the Exxon station near the Magic Kingdom, and at the Dolphin and Swan), Avis (Hilton), Budget (DoubleTree), ★ Dollar (Royal Plaza), Alamo (Buena Vista Palace), and Thrifty (Grosvenor).

**DIRECTIONS TO WDW FOR RENTAL CAR DRIVERS:** WDW is located about twenty miles from the airport. As you leave, look for exit signs that read "Disney World/Tampa" (which is 417 South, the Central Florida Greeneway). There are two $1 tollbooths along the way. The toll road exits at the intersection of State Road 536 (west), which takes you to WDW's Epcot Resorts Area, and State Road 535 (north), which takes you into the WDW Village Resorts Area, via Hotel Plaza Boulevard. If you are approaching WDW from Interstate Highway 4, follow the signs that say "Tampa" and "Disney World" and take any of the numbered exits listed below (see "Walt Disney World Overview" map, page 10):

- **EXIT 27:** Hotel Plaza at Disney Village and The Villas at the Disney Institute (via 535).
- **EXIT 26B:** All Epcot Resorts and Dixie Landings, Port Orleans, and Vacation Club (via 536).
- **EXIT 25B:** Magic Kingdom Resorts, All-Star Resorts, and Disney-MGM Resorts Area (via 192).

**AUTO SERVICING AND CAR TROUBLE:** There are two service stations at WDW, one near the Magic Kingdom, and one on Buena Vista Drive, across from Pleasure Island. Neither offers repair service. If you have problems with your own car and are a member of the American Automobile Association, call 800 222-4357 for towing, roadside service, or repair shop referrals. Otherwise, contact Guest Services in your hotel for assistance. For rental car problems, call the company for assistance. If you have rented from a company with a rental office at WDW, you can exchange your car on property.

## PARKING AT WALT DISNEY WORLD

Overall, the parking system at Walt Disney World is well run and convenient. If you plan to travel from place to place in a single day, however, a little parking strategy goes a long way.

**THEME PARK PARKING:** To survive the parking experience at the theme parks, there are two things you must remember: your car's row number and its license plate number, especially if you've rented a car. The rental cars that fill the lots all look the same. The parking lots at the major theme parks are free to guests staying at WDW resorts. Other visitors are charged about $7 per day, which entitles them to park in any of the WDW parking lots. The major theme park lots are serviced by trams that carry visitors from their parking area to the main entrance.

**RESORT PARKING:** All resorts have free self-parking lots and many have valet parking services. At the WDW-owned resorts, valet parking is free, and guests merely tip the valet a dollar or two when they pick up their car. Valet parking fees (ranging from $5 to $10) are charged at the independently run resorts. Sometimes it can be more convenient to park at a resort near the theme park you are visiting than in the theme park lot, especially if you are planning a short visit or plan to move on to other recreation or dining destinations in the vicinity. Resorts with the most convenient WDW transportation to Epcot Center (trams or water launches) and Disney-MGM Studios (water launches) include the Swan, Dolphin, Board-Walk, Yacht Club, and Beach Club (which is within walking distance). Resorts with the most convenient WDW transportation to the Magic Kingdom include the Contemporary (monorail), Polynesian (monorail and ferry), Wilderness Lodge (ferry), and Grand Floridian (monorail and ferry). The Contemporary resort has convenient ferry service to Discovery Island and Fort Wilderness. Wilderness Lodge has shuttle buses that run from the resort to Pioneer Hall and River County at Fort Wilderness. ◆

WDW FOR ADULTS FREE NIGHT! DOUBLETREE GUEST SUITES RESORT AT DISNEY WORLD! SEE PAGE 272

# GROUP & FAMILY TRAVEL

The variety of activities, attractions, entertainment, and sporting events at Walt Disney World make it an ideal vacation destination for family, friends, and groups who are gathering for reunions, weddings, holidays, meetings, or other events. WDW features many programs designed for groups, including special tours, private parties, and educational vacations at the new Disney Institute (see "Disney Institute," page 254); the Disney resorts also offer conveniences that can be very useful to groups, such as resort-wide transportation, voice mail, and child care services.

## GROUP ACCOMMODATIONS

Because of the hundreds of conventions held at Walt Disney World each year, the WDW resorts are equipped with amenities that also make them ideal destinations for smaller, private groups. In addition to standard hotel room accommodations, WDW offers several unique lodging options for groups, ranging from campsites to spacious vacation homes with full kitchens, which give groups the option to prepare their own meals and dine together. Groups requiring ten or more adjacent rooms may book in advance through Disney Leisure Group Department (800 327-2989). For descriptions and reviews of the accommodations listed below, see "Hotels," page 133 and "Off-Site Hotels," page 159.

**VACATION HOMES:** One-, two-, and three-bedroom condominium-style accommodations and detached vacation homes with fully equipped kitchens are available at Disney Vacation Club and at The Villas at the Disney Institute. Groups seeking a rustic outdoors setting will enjoy the less-expensive Wilderness Homes at Disney's Fort Wilderness Resort and Campground. These one-bedroom trailer homes include full kitchens and outdoor grills. Nearby, the Embassy Grand Beach Vacation Resort features three-bedroom, three-bathroom suites with full kitchens for less than the cost of a single room at some of the premier hotels.

**EFFICIENCY SUITES:** Suites with separate bedrooms and mini kitchens equipped with refrigerators, coffeemakers, and microwaves are available at ★ DoubleTree Guest Suites Resort, Buena Vista Resort Palace Suites, and The Villas at the Disney Institute. There is also a wide selection of affordable suite-style hotels adjacent to Walt Disney World (see "Off-Site Hotels," page 159).

**BUDGET RESORTS:** WDW's limited-amenity resorts provide exceptional value for groups lodging together on a budget. Blocks of rooms may be booked at the following WDW resorts: Dixie Landings (refrigerator on request, for a fee), Port Orleans (refrigerator on request, for a fee), Caribbean Beach (mini bar and coffeemaker), All-Star Resorts (refrigerator on request, for a fee), Courtyard by Marriott (coffeemaker), Travelodge (mini bar and coffeemaker), and Grosvenor (refrigerator and coffeemaker).

**CAMPSITES:** The Fort Wilderness campsites offer the most economical stay at a WDW resort. Groups may reserve campsites for tents and RVs, equipped with electrical outlets, charcoal grills, picnic tables, water, and cable TV hookup. A private area, Creekside Meadow, provides groups of twenty or more with a back-to-nature setting (no hookups), and can be reserved through Group Camping Reservations (407 354-1856). Showers, rest rooms, and laundry facilities are adjacent to all campsites; tents and cots can be rented through Fort Wilderness Guest Services (407 824-2900).

GROUPS & FAMILIES

## TOURING IN GROUPS

The guided tours at the WDW theme parks allow groups to enjoy the sights and attractions together, and are especially useful for orienting first-time visitors. WDW also offers groups a selection of private, special-interest, and behind-the-scenes tours.

**THEME PARK TOURS:** The four-hour Keys to the Kingdom tour is offered daily at the Magic Kingdom. It presents an overview of the history and attractions of the Magic Kingdom, and gives visitors a glimpse of some of the backstage areas and the lower-level "utilidors." The tour should be booked in advance; for details, see "Magic Kingdom," page 46. At Epcot Center, two special-interest tours focusing on the World Showcase are staged on alternate days: "Hidden Treasures of the World Showcase" looks at the design and construction of the international pavilions, and "Gardens of the World" explores the horticultural efforts to create and maintain the pavilion gardens and plants that are native to the various nations represented. The three-hour tours must be reserved in advance; for details, see "World Showcase," page 25. Many of the attractions at Disney-MGM Studios are tours in and of themselves that explore the diverse aspects of movie and television production (see "Disney-MGM Studios," page 36).

**VIP TOURS:** VIP Tours are limited to the groups that book them and have itineraries designed to meet a group's special interests. VIP Tours may be reserved by individuals or groups of up to ten people per guide, and cost about $45 per hour per guide for a four- to eight-hour tour of one or more theme parks. (Groups touring for more than four hours must have a meal at a full-service restaurant; theme park admission is not included in the price of the tour.) VIP Tours may be booked from forty-eight hours to six months in advance through Disney Special Activities (407 560-6233).

**BACKSTAGE MAGIC:** Backstage Magic takes groups on a tour of the behind-the-scenes areas in the Magic Kingdom, Disney-MGM Studios, and Epcot Center, as well as some of the out-of-park sites, to explore how the Walt Disney World experience is created and maintained. The seven-hour tour is held on Mondays and Wednesdays, costs about $150 per person, and generally includes special meal breaks, such as a private Continental breakfast in the Magic Kingdom and a picnic on the lawn of the Residential Street set in Disney-MGM Studios. Backstage Magic tours must be booked in advance (407 939-8687).

**TOURING SEPARATELY:** Individuals traveling in groups often have divergent interests and energy levels, so touring the theme parks and recreation areas separately is a simple solution that can satisfy everyone. Walt Disney World provides several innovative ways for group members touring separately to coordinate meals and shared activities, and to stay in touch in case of a change in plans.

**STAYING IN TOUCH:** Message centers are located at Guest Relations in the Magic Kingdom, Epcot Center, and Disney-MGM Studios. Here, visitors can leave and retrieve messages on a computer network that connects the three parks. Guests also can call WDW General Information (824-4321) to leave or retrieve messages from other visitors. Voice-mail systems are available in all WDW resort rooms (with the exception of some resorts at Hotel Plaza).

Using voice mail, guests can leave personal outgoing messages and retrieve incoming messages from any phone. For example, a group organizer may leave rendezvous instructions for the group on the outgoing message; individuals may leave messages for the group organizer about delays or changes in plans.

Cellular phones and pocket pagers can be reserved in advance through Guest Services at any Walt Disney World resort. Cellular phones rent for about $9 per day plus call charges of about $1.50 per minute; pocket pagers rent for about $10 a day, or about $30 for the length of stay.

GROUP & FAMILY TRAVEL

## PRIVATE PARTIES

There are many options for group celebrations at Walt Disney World, including large or small parties in the resort banquet halls. Private parties, however, have even been held at such unlikely places as on the stage of Indiana Jones Epic Stunt Spectacular, and on the beach of Discovery Island at sunrise. For information and reservations, call Resort Sales and Service (407 828-3074). Groups staying in WDW vacation homes can arrange for catered meals or private cookouts through WDW's Black Tie to Barbecue (407 827-3549).

**DINING AT FULL-SERVICE RESTAURANTS:** All resort restaurants take reservations for groups. To reserve a large seating or make special requests (a birthday cake, for example), call the resort restaurant directly or book through Disney Dining Reservations (407 939-3463). The theme park restaurants can also accommodate large and small groups, and are also booked through Disney Dining Reservations.

**VIP BIRTHDAY CELEBRATION IN THE MAGIC KINGDOM:** Here, adult birthday celebrants and their guests can enjoy a party package that includes admission to the Magic Kingdom, a birthday cake, beverages, party favors, a VIP viewing of one attraction or show, a private character greeting with Mickey and Friends, and a special motorcade down Main Street. The price for this special event is about $60 per adult. For information and reservations, call VIP Reservations (407 354-1851).

**PRIVATE PARTIES AT PLEASURE ISLAND:** Private parties can be arranged in any of Pleasure Island's seven nightclubs, which offer a range of interesting atmospheres. Pleasure Island caters parties in the clubs from 5 PM until 8:30 PM (the average cost is about $1,000). For information, call WDW Park and Event Sales (407 828-2048). At Planet Hollywood, private parties for thirty to five hundred guests can be arranged by calling Planet Hollywood Catering Sales (407 827-7836).

## ORGANIZING TIPS FOR GROUPS

Groups who are meeting at the Orlando International Airport should plan their strategy carefully to avoid confusion. Groups scheduled to arrive in the evening might consider spending the first night at the Hyatt Regency, located inside the airport (see "Orlando International Airport," pages 247 and 248).

**HOLIDAYS:** Group trips are frequently arranged during holidays, when WDW is very festive but very crowded. The best time for group vacations is during the three weeks following Thanksgiving, which has the lowest attendance of the year, while offering a variety of holiday entertainment events. The best holidays for groups, considering crowds and weather, are Thanksgiving, Presidents' Day, and Easter. The most difficult holidays for group vacations are Memorial Day, Labor Day, the week between Christmas and New Year's, the Fourth of July, and during spring break (see "Holidays," page 132).

**GROUP DISCOUNTS:** There are a number of travel clubs that offer discounts on WDW accommodations, admissions, car rentals, and airfares (see "Travel Discounts," page 244). Many of these discounts require only one person in a group to be a member of the club. WDW also offers its own seasonal vacation packages at a discount (407 827-7200). Disney Leisure Group Department (800 327-2989) will discount blocks of ten or more rooms; discounts at WDW's budget resorts, however, may not apply.

**BABYSITTING:** The many child care services at Walt Disney World allow groups to enjoy adult-oriented activities and evening entertainment while their children are entertained by child care professionals in theme parks, hotel rooms, or day-care centers (see "Babysitting & Day Camps," page 256). ◆

GROUPS & FAMILIES

# DISNEY INSTITUTE

The Disney Institute, opening in 1996, will give visitors the opportunity to experience a unique "discovery vacation." Along with all the amenities of a luxury resort, the Disney Institute will offer more than eighty courses, ranging from art history to rock climbing. Set at the Village Green, which combines the laid-back bustle of a college campus with the civic ambience of a small town, guests can explore their personal interests, acquire hands-on experience, and expand their creative talents. The Disney Institute program is ideal for families and groups that would enjoy a shared experience. During the day, guests attend the learning program of their choice; in the evenings, everyone comes together for social activities and entertainment events. There are a variety of accommodations at the Disney Institute, which was formerly Disney's Village Resort.

**LOCATION:** Disney Institute is located in the Disney Village Resorts Area. The Village Green fronts Buena Vista Lagoon, along with the adjacent Disney Village Marketplace and Pleasure Island. Accommodations are scattered across 250 acres of woodlands, waterways, and golf greens.

**PROGRAMS:** Instructors, including the artists in residence at the Institute, are top professionals in their field, and the guest-to-instructor ratio is about fifteen to one. Two course sessions are scheduled each morning and afternoon, which guests can mix and match to fit their interests. The Disney Institute offers programs for adults, as well as for guests age ten to seventeen, in the following areas:

- **ENTERTAINMENT ARTS:** Film and video production, history, and criticism; animation and audio (including radio) production; and photography.
- **CULINARY ARTS:** Gourmet culinary techniques, international cuisines, and foods and technology.
- **SPORTS AND FITNESS:** Exercise and fitness programs, personal training, stress relief and relaxation classes, sports clinics, and skills assessment and development in a variety of sports activities.
- **LIFESTYLES:** Personal development and exploration, family history and dynamics, and successful adaptation techniques for living in a changing world.
- **STORY ARTS:** Storytelling, oral traditions, and the art and history of personal communication.
- **DESIGN ARTS:** The history and development of style, interior design, architecture, and the art of creating an enjoyable and functional personal environment.
- **ENVIRONMENT:** The wonders of nature, gardening and landscaping styles and techniques, and horticultural strategies for different ecologies.
- **PERFORMING ARTS:** The history of the performing arts, and the development and expansion of skills in music, dance, film, stage, and nightclub performance.

**FACILITIES:** The Village Green at the Disney Institute includes a large performance center, an outdoor amphitheater, radio and motion picture production studios, a sports and fitness center with full-service spa, swimming pool, clay tennis courts, a marina, a PGA golf course, and a full-service restaurant.

**ACCOMMODATIONS:** Disney Institute guests may choose to stay in either a Club Suite or a one- or two-bedroom Townhouse, both with kitchenettes (see "The Villas at the Disney Institute," page 155).

**RESERVATIONS:** For program information, call 800 496-6337. A three-day minimum stay is required. A typical three-day package, which includes programs, accommodations, three meals per day, and a special one-day theme parks admission is about $700 per person (about $575 without meals).

**TIPS:** The programs are designed for guest arrivals on Mondays and Fridays. Although optional, a stay of seven days is considered the ideal to take full advantage of the Disney Institute programs. ◆

# WEDDINGS & HONEYMOONS

With over a thousand weddings each year at its resorts, and already the world's top honeymoon destination, Walt Disney World opened Disney's Wedding Pavilion in July 1995 to capitalize on the growing trend in destination weddings, which are held at unique and sometimes distant locations. The Wedding Pavilion's picturesque Seven Seas Lagoon setting and Disney's Fairy Tale Weddings event-planning services combine to position Walt Disney World as a premier wedding site.

**WEDDINGS:** Imagine arriving at your wedding in Cinderella's glass coach, drawn by six white horses, or perhaps in a vintage limousine, Great Gatsby style. These and other wedding fantasies can be satisfied at Disney's Wedding Pavilion, at the WDW resorts, and even inside the theme parks.

**DISNEY'S FAIRY TALE WEDDINGS:** These wedding packages are tailored to fit each couple's budget and taste by the wedding consultants at Franck's, a bridal salon patterned after the one in the film *Father of the Bride*. Located at Disney's Wedding Pavilion, the Fairy Tale Weddings consultants offer "one-stop-shopping" for invitations, welcome parties, customized ceremonies, music, flowers, wedding cakes, photographs, receptions, and even marriage licenses. Specially priced resort accommodations, entertainment, and outings for couples and their guests can also be arranged. Fairy Tale Wedding packages start at about $3,000 and can range up to $100,000 (some wedding parties have spent as much as $250,000). For information about Disney's Fairy Tale Weddings, call 407 828-3400.

**DISNEY'S WEDDING PAVILION:** This Victorian-style lakeside summerhouse, with large light-filled rooms, sits on a richly landscaped island in Seven Seas Lagoon, between Disney's Grand Floridian Beach Resort and Disney's Polynesian Resort. Disney's Wedding Pavilion is designed to accommodate weddings ranging from the most intimate ceremony to a gala gathering for 250. The Pavilion has an on-site floral work room, dressing rooms, sophisticated sound and lighting systems, and Franck's, the full-service salon where Disney's Fairy Tale Weddings are planned.

**HONEYMOONS:** At Walt Disney World, honeymooning couples can enjoy a different romantic adventure every day. A day of frolicking on white sand beaches, a tour of the world at Epcot Center's international pavilions, or a romantic candlelight dinner followed by a night of dancing — these are just some of the activities that make true honeymoon memories, and make Walt Disney World the number-one honeymoon destination in the world.

**DISNEY'S FAIRY TALE HONEYMOONS:** The Fairy Tale Honeymoon vacation packages are designed to help couples make the most of their honeymoon. The packages include accommodations at a Disney-owned resort, theme park admissions, and romance-oriented amenities such as a floral greeting or a chilled bottle of champagne in the room. Honeymoon packages range in price from about $800 to $3,600 per couple. For information about Disney's Fairy Tale Honeymoons, call Disney Resort Reservations (407 827-7200). Honeymoon packages that include a Fairy Tale Wedding are also available. Call Disney's Fairy Tale Weddings for information (407 828-3400).

**ADDITIONAL HONEYMOON PACKAGES AT WDW:** Honeymoon vacation packages are also available at the following privately owned resorts located on WDW property: Buena Vista Palace, Grosvenor, Hilton, Courtyard by Marriott, ★ DoubleTree Guest Suites Resort, Hotel Royal Plaza, Travelodge, Dolphin, and Swan. The honeymoon vacation packages offered by each hotel vary; call the hotel directly to request a brochure or additional information. (See "Hotels," page 133.) ◆

# BABYSITTING & DAY CAMPS

Visitors with children have a wealth of child care options at Walt Disney World so they can be free to enjoy the many adult-oriented events and activities offered during the day and evening. The child care centers and camps create unique environments where kids will feel entertained and not "sat." All drop-off programs require that children be completely toilet trained and able to dress themselves. No diapers, including pull-ups, are allowed. Some child care services are for hotel guests only, but many are open to all visitors.

**CAMP DOLPHIN:** *Walt Disney World Dolphin* — This child care and activity center is designed for children ages three through twelve (ages three to five attend Junior Dolphins). Activities include crafts, games, and sports activities by day, and a Dinner Club and movies in the evening. Priority is given to guests staying at the Dolphin and Swan hotels, but guests staying at other WDW resorts can reserve on a space-available basis. Occupancy is limited to twelve children.

   **RESERVATIONS:** Open 2 until 5 PM. About $7 per hour. Dinner Club from 6 until 10 PM. Dinner and entertainment is about $27. Reservations suggested (407 934-4241).

**CAMP SWAN:** *Walt Disney World Swan* — Designed for children ages three to twelve, this child care and entertainment center offers both individual and group activities, and features Disney movies in the evening. Meals are not included but may be brought by parents or pre-ordered from room service. While this program is offered to guests at the Swan and Dolphin resorts, guests staying at other WDW resorts are accepted subject to availability. Occupancy is limited to fifteen children.

   **RESERVATIONS:** Open 4 PM until midnight. About $5 per hour for the first child, and $3 for each additional child from the same family. Reservations should be made a day ahead (407 934-1620).

**CUB'S DEN:** *Disney's Wilderness Lodge Resort* — The Cub's Den is a fully supervised Western-themed dining and entertainment club for children ages four through twelve. Children are treated to a kid-friendly dinner buffet and enjoy a live-animal visit from Discovery Island, computer games, and art activities. As children get tired, they can cuddle up with a pillow and blanket in front of a wide-screen television to watch Disney movies. Available to guests staying at any Disney-owned resort. Occupancy is limited to twenty-eight children.

   **RESERVATIONS:** Open 5 PM until midnight. About $6 per hour for each child, which includes the buffet. One-hour minimum. Reservations suggested (407 824-1083).

**HILTON YOUTH HOTEL:** *The Hilton Resort* — In addition to the usual array of games, movies, and activities, this child care facility offers small beds set off in a quiet area for children who wish to take a nap or go to sleep before their parents return. Don't let the name fool you, though — this children's "hotel" is only open until midnight. Available to children ages four through twelve staying at any resort on WDW property.

   **RESERVATIONS:** Open 5 PM until midnight. About $5 per hour for one child, $7 per hour for two, and $8 per hour for three. If you arrive to pick up your children after midnight, there is an additional charge. Reserve a day in advance (827-4000: hotel).

**KINDERCARE IN-ROOM AND IN-PARK BABYSITTING:** KinderCare-trained sitters provide both in-room and in-park child care and touring. This service is available to guests at all resorts on WDW property, except the Dolphin and Swan. In-room sitting is the only option for children who are too young to tour the parks or who are not yet toilet trained. In-park child care is limited to no more than two children per sitter and guests are required to pay the price of the sitter's park admission plus the hourly fee. Guests are asked to provide the sitter with a meal if the sit time is six hours or more.

RESERVATIONS: Open twenty-four hours a day. Rates start at about $10 per hour; four-hour minimum with 30 minutes' travel time. Reserve at least a day in advance (407 827-5444).

KIDS' STUFF PROGRAM: *Buena Vista Palace Resort and Spa* — This educational and recreational camp is designed for children ages four to twelve. Enrollment is on a first-come, first-served basis, and is available to Buena Vista Palace Resort and Spa guests and those using the conference facilities.

RESERVATIONS: Daily from 10 AM until 1 PM and 2 until 5 PM daily. Evening camp on Monday, Wednesday, and Friday, from 6 until 9 PM. Day camps are complimentary; evening camps are $8 per child, which includes dinner. For additional information, call 800 327-2906.

MOUSEKETEER CLUB: *Disney's Grand Floridian Beach Resort* — This small, pleasantly decorated club accepts a maximum of twelve children at one time and provides an assortment of toys, board games, computer games, books, and Disney movies. Available to children ages four to nine who are staying at any Disney-owned resort. Cookies and a beverage are provided.

RESERVATIONS: Open 4:30 PM until midnight. About $5 per hour for each child. Reservations recommended. Call Guest Services at the Grand Floridian (407 824-2985).

MOUSEKETEER CLUBHOUSE: *Disney's Contemporary Resort* — The Mouseketeer Clubhouse is basically a short-term care center with limited facilities and amusements. Designed for children ages four through nine, it offers computer games and an assortment of toys. The Clubhouse accepts guests from any Disney-owned resort and is limited to ten children.

RESERVATIONS: Open 4:30 PM until midnight. Two-hour minimum, four-hour maximum; no meals. About $5 per hour. Reserve at least two days in advance (407 824-3038).

NEVERLAND CLUB: *Disney's Polynesian Resort* — Based on the story of Peter Pan, this themed club is very popular. Guests enter the building and find themselves in Wendy's bedroom, where they watch as their child is sprinkled with pixie dust and climbs through the window into the wonderful world of Never-Never Land. The fun includes a character visit, with a photo session and autograph; a visit from some of the feathered and scaly inhabitants of Discovery Island; unlimited arcade games; and a wealth of Disney toys. The children are supervised in both group and individual activities, and a kid-pleasing buffet dinner is included. Open to children ages four to twelve. Available to all WDW visitors.

RESERVATIONS: Open 5 PM until midnight, with hours extended to 2 AM on New Year's Eve. A buffet is served from 6 until 8 PM. Children arriving after the buffet get a peanut butter and jelly sandwich and dessert. About $8 per hour per child, with a three-hour minimum. Reservations suggested, especially during peak seasons. Call Disney Dining Reservations (407 939-3463).

SANDCASTLE CLUB: *Disney's Beach Club Resort* — This child care and activity center is open to children ages four to twelve and features computer games, arts and crafts projects, and a library of children's books and movies. Available to guests at the Yacht and Beach Club resorts; guests staying at other WDW resorts can use the facility on a drop-in basis after 4 PM, if space is available.

RESERVATIONS: Open 4:30 PM until midnight. About $5 per hour. Provision for a meal must be made for any child left more than four hours. Parents can provide the meal or pre-order from room service. Reserve at least one day ahead (934-6290). ◆

BABYSITTING

# VISITORS WITH DISABILITIES

In keeping with the cutting-edge technologies used throughout Walt Disney World, the facilities for visitors with disabilities, although mostly invisible to the general traveler, are unparalleled in the travel industry. Both current and experimental technologies are brought into play, from the closed-caption cable television in most resort rooms, to the wheelchairs and Electric Convenience Vehicles that make up the largest wheelchair fleet in the world. To accommodate visitors with hearing impairments, many attractions are designed with antennas built into the ceilings to beam sound down to tiny FM headsets. Guests with sight impairments are given Braille guidebooks or cassette players that help them tour the parks using sounds and smells. First-aid offices in all the parks will let guests take a break from their wheelchair to rest on a cot. (They will also refrigerate insulin for visitors who suffer from diabetes.) And, of course, all WDW hotels and public transportation are outfitted with devices for the convenience of visitors with disabilities. Overall, visitors with disabilities will find WDW to be one of the most accessible vacation experiences anywhere in the world.

## VISITORS WITH MOBILITY PROBLEMS

*Visitors should specify their needs when making hotel reservations and request that a complimentary copy of Walt Disney World's* Guidebook for Guests with Disabilities *be mailed to them or be waiting for them at check-in. Rental car companies or hotels can provide handicapped stickers for visitors who are driving.*

**HOTELS:** All WDW resorts have rooms for guests with mobility problems. The best facilities can be found at the following resorts: Vacation Club (lower beds, roll-in showers, handicapped parking near rooms), Caribbean Beach (handicapped parking near rooms), Polynesian (automatic entrance doors, elevator access to the monorail), Dixie Landings (handicapped parking near rooms), and Grand Floridian (door peepholes at wheelchair level, hand-held showers, elevator access to the monorail). The best off-site hotel for visitors with mobility problems is the Embassy Suites Resort Lake Buena Vista, which provides exceptional rooms that include bathrooms with roll-in showers, push-handle doorknobs, and low-height kitchen facilities and control switches (see "Off-Site Hotels," page 160).

Resorts presenting physical challenges to visitors with mobility problems include the Contemporary (no elevator access to the monorail), Port Orleans (many curbs and sidewalks throughout the resort), Beach Club (inconvenient wheelchair ramps), Fort Wilderness Campground (while some trailer homes are wheelchair accessible, campsite ground surfaces may be too soft for wheelchairs), and Wilderness Lodge (steep inclines and inconvenient wheelchair access).

**WHEELCHAIRS AND ELECTRIC CONVENIENCE VEHICLES:** Complimentary wheelchairs (with refundable deposit) are available at all WDW resorts for guests to use throughout their stay. The following theme parks and recreation areas have rental wheelchairs and Electric Convenience Vehicles: Magic Kingdom, Epcot Center, Disney-MGM Studios, and Disney Village Marketplace (wheelchairs only). The following parks have a limited number of complimentary wheelchairs (deposit required): Discovery Island, Typhoon Lagoon, Blizzard Beach, and Fort Wilderness (through Guest Services).

**PARKING AT THEME PARKS:** All theme parks provide handicapped parking areas. At the major theme parks, tell the tollgate attendant what your needs are, and you will be issued a pass and directed to the handicapped parking lot (if you cannot leave your wheelchair), or to handicapped-designated end spots in the main lot with easy access to the trams (if you can take a few steps and your chair folds). The smaller parks and recreation areas have handicapped parking near entrances. Pleasure Island offers valet parking after 5 PM.

**PARKING AT HOTELS:** The following WDW resorts offer complimentary valet parking: Polynesian, Grand Floridian, Contemporary, Yacht Club, Beach Club, Wilderness Lodge, and Hotel Royal Plaza. Valets expect a tip when you pick up your car. Valet parking fees (ranging from $5 to $10) are charged at the following resorts: Swan, Dolphin, Hilton, Grosvenor, and Buena Vista Palace.

**PUBLIC TRANSPORTATION:** Many, but not all, WDW buses are wheelchair accessible. You may have to wait for a specially equipped bus. All monorail stations, except at the Contemporary resort, are wheelchair accessible. All ferries are wheelchair accessible, except some that travel to Discovery Island and Fort Wilderness. Visitors may have to wait for a specially equipped ferry. WDW resort guests can arrange for a courtesy van to take them from one site to another within WDW by calling 824-6129.

**TELEPHONES:** All theme parks have wheelchair-accessible pay phones. Check with Guest Relations as you enter for a map showing telephone locations.

**TOURING:** The *Guidebook for Guests with Disabilities* explains which attractions are wheelchair accessible and which ones you must leave your chair in order to ride. WDW staff are not trained in transferring guests to and from wheelchairs, so if you need help, plan on visiting with a companion who can assist you. Guests using Electric Convenience Vehicles must transfer to standard wheelchairs before entering many attractions. Visitors who bring their own wheelchairs are sometimes given preferences in line over visitors in rented wheelchairs, and disability passes are sometimes issued to visitors with special problems. Call Disney Information (407 824-4321) and ask for Disney Special Activities.

## VISITORS WITH SIGHT IMPAIRMENTS

*Visitors who travel with guide dogs should inform the hotel when making reservations. They may keep their animals with them or they can arrange to board them at a WDW kennel. Visitors should request that a copy of Walt Disney World's* Guidebook for Guests with Disabilities *be mailed to them, listing attractions that accommodate guide dogs. All major theme parks have Braille guidebooks available at Guest Relations.*

**HOTELS:** Braille-marked elevators can be found at the following resorts: Polynesian, Contemporary, Grand Floridian, Port Orleans, Beach Club, Yacht Club, BoardWalk, Wilderness Lodge, All-Star Sports, All-Star Music, Dolphin, Swan, Grosvenor, and Buena Vista Palace. The highrise hotels are the easiest to get around in, with the exception of the Dolphin, where the floor plan is very confusing. The Polynesian, Port Orleans, Dixie Landings, All-Star Sports, All-Star Music, and Caribbean Beach resorts have sprawling layouts that may present a challenge to guests with sight impairments. The Grand Floridian resort also has rambling grounds, but offers trolley escort service from its outbuildings to the main lobby.

**TOURING:** All major theme parks have Braille maps at the entrance. Braille guidebooks and complimentary tape players with touring cassettes (deposit required) are available at Guest Relations in the Magic Kingdom, Epcot Center, and Disney-MGM Studios. Visitors with guide dogs may want to bring a companion to take charge of the dog while they enjoy attractions that restrict guide dogs. WDW staff are not permitted to take charge of guide animals.

DISABILITIES

**GUIDED TOURS:** Visitors with sight impairments may arrange for a complimentary guided overview of the major theme parks. The guide will provide a general sense of how to locate and enjoy the attractions. These tours, designed for visitors who wish to explore the parks on their own, must be booked in advance through Disney Special Activities (407 560-6233).

## VISITORS WITH HEARING IMPAIRMENTS

*Visitors with hearing impairments who would like their hotel room fitted with special equipment should specify their needs at the time they make reservations and request that a complimentary copy of Walt Disney World's* Guidebook for Guests with Disabilities *be mailed to them or be waiting at check-in.*

**HOTELS:** All WDW resorts can supply guest rooms with strobe lights and a telecommunications device for the deaf (TDD). Visitors can also use TDDs to make hotel reservations and special requests by calling 407 827-5141. Closed-caption television is available in guest rooms throughout WDW, except at some Hotel Plaza resorts.

**TELEPHONES:** All theme parks have amplified and hearing aid–compatible pay phones. Check with Guest Relations as you enter for a map showing telephone locations. TDDs for hearing-impaired visitors are available at Guest Relations in the Magic Kingdom and Disney-MGM Studios, and at The AT&T Global Neighborhood at Epcot Center.

**TOURING:** A complimentary written text of the narration for attractions is available at Guest Relations in the Magic Kingdom, Epcot Center, and Disney-MGM Studios. The major theme parks offer assistive listening devices at either Guest Relations or at the attractions where this technology is in use. A list of these attractions can be obtained through Guest Relations at the parks.

**SIGNING TOURS:** Visitors with hearing impairments can arrange for a brief complimentary tour of the theme parks in American Sign Language. These park overviews explain how to locate and enjoy the attractions. Four- to five-hour tours in American Sign Language that offer a more structured experience are also available for a minimal fee. Both the brief and extended tours must be booked in advance through Disney Special Activities (407 560-6233) or by TDD (407 827-5141).

## OTHER ASSISTANCE FOR VISITORS WITH DISABILITIES

*While Walt Disney World is committed to making its attractions accessible to everyone, WDW employees are not trained to help guests physically. Visitors who require assistance to ride attractions may want to bring a companion along. Orlando has a number of independent services that provide touring companions for visitors with disabilities, as well as companies that supply medical equipment and referrals.*

**HOLIDAY ASSISTANCE:** This service provides helpers who will push visitors in wheelchairs as needed at the parks, the airport, and at recreational activities. Companions are available for about $15 per hour (plus meals and park admissions), with a five-hour minimum (407 397-4845).

**CARE MED:** This medical supply and referral service helps visitors find a variety of medical resources, such as wheelchair and electrical wheelchair rentals, hospital beds, portable oxygen machines, insulin, dialysis assistance, and additional aids. They deliver to any area hotel (800 741-2282). ◆

DISABILITIES

# SHOPPING & SERVICES

Walt Disney World has it pretty well covered when it comes to supplying visitors' needs. The most sought after items and services are listed below. (See "Walt Disney World Overview" map, page 10, for locations.)

**BANKING & MONEY:** The WDW resorts offer check cashing for guests (up to $50). There is also an automatic teller machine (ATM) at the Contemporary resort.

*Theme Parks* — Guest Relations at all theme parks will cash checks for visitors (up to $25). The Magic Kingdom has a branch of the Sun Bank. There are ATMs at all major theme parks. Epcot Center also has an American Express Cash Machine and American Express Travel Services.

*Disney Village Marketplace* — There is an ATM located outside of Guest Services. A full-service branch of the Sun Bank is located across the street.

*Crossroads* — Gooding's Supermarket has an ATM and also provides foreign currency exchange.

**EYEGLASSES:** *Crossroads* — Gooding's Pharmacy carries both reading and sunglasses

**FLORIST:** Floral arrangements and fruit baskets can be ordered from WDW Florist (407 827-3505).

*Crossroads* — Gooding's Florist delivers to all area resorts (407 827-1206).

**GROCERIES:** Most WDW budget resorts offer a limited selection of groceries, beverages, and snacks.

*Disney Village Marketplace* — Gourmet Pantry has limited groceries, a bakery, and a deli.

*Crossroads* — Gooding's Supermarket, the largest in the area, is open twenty-four hours.

**LIQUOR:** Most WDW resorts sell wine and beer, and many carry spirits.

*Disney Village Marketplace* — Gourmet Pantry sells wine, beer, and spirits.

*Crossroads* — Gooding's Supermarket sells wine and beer; ★ Pacino's Liquors sells wine, beer, and spirits.

*Vista Center* — Johnny's Liquor sells wine, beer, and spirits.

**MEDICAL CARE & MEDICATIONS:** House+Med Service provides twenty-four-hour physician house calls to all WDW resorts (396-1195). Guest Services at all resorts will provide dental referrals.

*Buena Vista Walk-in Medical Center* — Located in the Disney Village Resorts Area, the Medical Center is open daily from 8 AM until 9 PM (828-3434). It provides free shuttle service for resort guests. Their pharmacy, Turner Drugs (828-8125), will deliver prescriptions to WDW resort guests.

*Medi+Clinic* — This walk-in clinic, open daily from 8 AM until 9 PM, is just east of Walt Disney World off Highway 192 at Parkway Boulevard (396-1195).

*Hospital* — Emergency services are provided by Sand Lake Hospital, just north of Walt Disney World on Interstate 4 at Exit 27A (351-8500).

*Crossroads* — Prescriptions can be filled at Gooding's Pharmacy (827-1207).

**SHIPPING:** Most shops at Walt Disney World will ship purchases for guests.

*Crossroads* — A U.S. Post Office is located here.

*Vista Center* — Mail and Parcels Plus provides shipping materials and uses all major carriers.

**SUNGLASSES:** Most WDW resorts carry sunglasses; the best selections are in the premium resorts.

*Crossroads* — ★ Ken Done features fashion sunglasses; Sunglass Hut sells and repairs sunglasses.

**TOBACCO:** Cigarettes are sold at resort gift shops and at select merchandise shops in the theme parks. They are not on display and must be requested. ◆

SHOPPING

SHOPPING & SERVICES

# CROSSROADS SHOPPING CENTER

This shopping center was built and is maintained by Walt Disney World. It is located on State Road 535, across from the entrance to the Disney Village Resorts Area (see "Walt Disney World Overview" map, page 10). Crossroads has over twenty-five different merchants representing both nationally and locally known businesses, including a Disney merchandise store, Character Connection; a U.S. Post Office; and a variety of restaurants. The shopping center is anchored by Gooding's Supermarket, which is open twenty-four hours. This huge supermarket has a pharmacy, full-service florist, and a large deli with prepared foods. Other businesses located here include Sunglass Hut International, Mitzi's Hallmark, Crazy Shirts, Foot Locker, Beyond Electronics, and Pirate's Cove Adventure Miniature Golf Course. The stores listed below offer *Walt Disney World for Adults* readers a twenty-percent discount on selected merchandise (see "Vacation Discount Coupons," page 272).

★ **SUN WORKS:** This store is known for women's leisure fashions designed in comfortable fabrics and eye-catching colors. The styles available here work for both vacation and daily wear. Sun Works also carries a large selection of bathing suits.

★ **WHITE'S BOOKS:** This outstanding independent bookseller carries a wide selection of reading material, ranging from best sellers to local interest books. White's also stocks an array of wonderfully decorative, yet functional items such as picture frames, lamps, planters, bookends, unique timepieces, colorful glassware, pottery, and much more. Shipping service is available.

★ **CHICO'S:** Chico's features women's clothing and accessories that are crafted with natural colors and materials. The clothing here is terrific for casual resort wear.

★ **PACINO'S LIQUORS AND RISTORANTE:** This combination liquor store and restaurant features freshly prepared northern and southern Italian dishes with homemade flavor and presentation. There are separate lunch, dinner, and take-out menus. Don't miss the *Pasta e Fagioli,* a hearty pasta and bean soup. The stuffed veal chop is superb, but you have to ask for it; it's not on the menu. Lunch ranges from $6 to $10; dinner from $12 to $25. No reservations are accepted. The attached annex, Pacino's Liquors, is a fully stocked liquor store that also offers a wide array of miniature liquors and what may be the largest selection of wine in the Walt Disney World area.

★ **KEN DONE FUN AND SUN FASHIONS:** Ken Done's distinctively designed fashions are bright, attractive, and suitable for resort, casual, and everyday wear. The store also features bathing suits and carefully coordinated accessories ranging from tote bags to sunglasses.

★ **FISHTALE FREDDY'S:** Island-style clothing for men, women, and children is the look at FishTale Freddy's. The vivid collection of colors, styles, and attractive accessories, combined with a tropical rain forest decor, make this store a fun place to shop. Freddy's is not for fashion conservatives.

## RESTAURANTS AT CROSSROADS

Walt Disney World visitors have many restaurant choices available to them at Crossroads, including Jungle Jim's (featuring barbecued ribs and more than one hundred hamburger combinations); Chevy's (fresh and tasty Mexican cuisine); Pebbles (fine American cuisine); Perkins Family Restaurant (traditional coffee-shop fare, sandwich platters, and breakfast served all day); Red Lobster (seafood and steak); Johnny Rocket's (hamburgers and diner-style specialties); Pizzeria Uno (pizza and pasta); McDonald's; and Taco Bell. ◆

# WALT DISNEY WORLD TELEPHONE DIRECTORY

*The area code in Orlando and at Walt Disney World is 407. When dialing any of the numbers listed below from outside the Orlando area, you must first dial 407 unless otherwise noted.*
*If you cannot find the number you need listed below, call Walt Disney World Information (407 824-4321).*

## HOTEL RESERVATIONS

**Walt Disney World Reservations** ................................**934-7639**
Switchboard to All WDW Hotels ..................................824-2222
Hyatt Regency, Orlando International Airport .............825-1234
Other Hotels  *(see "Hotels," page 133 ; Off-Site Hotels," page 159)*

## RESTAURANT & DINING EVENTS RESERVATIONS

**Dinner Show Reservations** ........................................**934-3463**
**Disney Dining Reservations** ......................................**939-3463**
MurderWatch Mystery Dinner Theatre ......................828-4444
MurderWatch Mystery Dinner Theatre ................800 624-4109
Other Restaurants *(see "Resort Dining," page 198)*

## ATTRACTIONS INFORMATION

AMC Pleasure Island Theatres, Show Times .................827-1300
Blizzard Beach ............................................................560-3400
Discovery Island .........................................................824-2875
Disney-MGM Studios Production Information ............560-7299
Pleasure Island ...........................................................934-7781
River Country .............................................................824-2760
Typhoon Lagoon .........................................................560-4141
**Walt Disney World Information** ..................................824-4321

## GENERAL INFORMATION

Hearing-impaired Guest Information (TDD) ...............827-5141
Lost and Found at Walt Disney World .........................824-4245
Orlando Airport, Paging .............................................825-2000
Sports Events Information ...........................................939-7810
**Walt Disney World Information** ..................................824-4321
**Weather, Disney** .......................................................**824-4104**

## SPORTS RESERVATIONS

Boating Excursions:
   *The Breathless,* Yacht Club Marina ...........................934-3256
   Fireworks Cruise, Contemporary Marina .................824-1000
   Fireworks Cruise, Polynesian Marina .......................824-2000
   Starlight Cruise, Grand Floridian Marina ................824-2439
Fishing Excursions:
   Buena Vista Lagoon ...............................................828-2461
   Crescent Lake ........................................................934-3256
   Fort Wilderness .....................................................824-2621
   Sassagoula River ....................................................934-5409

Golf Course Pro Shops:
   Bonnet Creek Golf Club Pro Shop ...........................824-2675
   Lake Buena Vista Pro Shop .....................................828-3741
   Magnolia and Palm Pro Shop .................................824-2288
Golf Lessons ...............................................................824-2270
**Golf Reservations, Master Starter** ..............................**824-2270**
Health Clubs and Spas:
   The Spa at Buena Vista Palace ...............................827-2727
   Body By Jake Health Club, Dolphin ........................934-4264
   Hilton Health Club ...............................................827-4000
   Olympiad Health Club, Contemporary ....................824-3410
   Ship Shape Health Club, Yacht & Beach Club ..........934-3256
   Sports and Fitness Center, Disney Institute .............827-1100
   St. John's Health Club, Grand Floridian ..................824-2433
   Swan Health Club, Swan .......................................934-1360
Parasailing, Contemporary ..........................................824-1000
Tennis Reservations:
   Disney Institute ....................................................827-1100
   Grand Floridian ....................................................824-2433
   Contemporary .......................................................824-3578
   Swan and Dolphin .................................................934-4396
Waterskiing Excursions ...............................................824-2621

## GUIDED TOURS

Backstage Magic Tour ..................................................939-8687
Discovery Island Adult Tours .......................................824-3784
**Theme Park Tours** ...................................................**939-8687**
VIP Tours ...................................................................560-6233

## SERVICES

Buena Vista Walk-in Medical Center ............................828-3434
Florist, Gooding's Supermarket ...................................827-1206
Florist, Walt Disney World  ........................................827-3505
House+Med and Medi+Clinic .....................................396-1195
Pharmacy, Buena Vista Medical Center .......................828-8125
Pharmacy, Gooding's Supermarket ..............................827-1207
Sand Lake Hospital .....................................................351-8500

## TRANSPORTATION

AAA Emergency Road Service ................................800 222-4357
Florida Town Car ..................................................800 525-7246
Mears Limousines & Shuttle Service ............................423-5566
Taxi Service at Walt Disney World ...............................824-3360
Town Car Limousine ...................................................299-8696

# READER SURVEY

*Become part of the Walt Disney World for Adults Opinion Bank! Fill out this form and give
us your opinion of the attractions, hotels, restaurants, dinner shows, tours, and more.*

- Was this your first trip to Walt Disney World?   YES   NO   If not, how often have you visited? _____
  What time of year was your most recent visit? _____   How long did you stay? _____
  How many were in your party? _____   Any children?   YES   NO
- Did you make advance dining reservations?   YES   NO
- Did you find the theme parks crowded?   YES   NO
- Where did you stay? _____
  Did you agree with the hotel rating?   YES   NO   If not, why? _____
  _____

- Did we overrate or underrate any of the restaurants where you dined?   YES   NO
  If so, which ones, and how would *you* rate them? _____
  _____
  _____

- Did we overrate or underrate any of the theme park attractions you visited?   YES   NO
  If so, which ones, and how would *you* rate them? _____
  _____
  _____

- If you visited Pleasure Island, did you agree with the nightclub ratings?   YES   NO
  If not, which ones, and why? _____
  _____

- If you attended any dinner shows, did you agree with the ratings?   YES   NO
  If not, which ones, and why? _____
  _____

- Did you follow any of the attraction half-day tours?   YES   NO
  Which ones? _____
  Did they work for you?   YES   NO   If not, how would *you* change them? _____
  _____

- Did you follow one of the 4-Day Vacations?   YES   NO   Which one? _____
  Did it work for you?   YES   NO   If not, how would *you* change it? _____
  _____

- Did you engage in any sporting activities?   YES   NO   Which ones? _____
  Did you enjoy them?   YES   NO   If not, why not? _____
  _____

- Did you take a Disney theme park tour?   YES   NO   Which one? _____
  How would you rate it?   EXCELLENT   GOOD   FAIR   POOR
- Did you attend the Disney Institute?   YES   NO
  If so, how did you like it? _____
  _____

- Did you attend a Disney holiday event? YES NO Which one? _____
  How would you rate it? EXCELLENT GOOD FAIR POOR
- Did you use a discount travel card? YES NO Which one? _____
- Did you use any of the coupons in this book? YES NO Which ones? _____
  How did they work for you? _____
- Was your trip long enough for you to do everything you wanted? YES NO
  If not, what did you miss? _____
  _____
- What was the most disappointing part of your trip? _____
  _____
- What was the best part? _____
  _____
- Besides this book, how did you get information about your trip? _____
  Did you call Disney Information? YES NO If so, how many times? _____
  Did you get the information you wanted? YES NO
  If not, why not? _____
- Was there a strategy or tip in the book that was especially helpful to you? _____
  _____
- Did you discover any insider strategies that you would like to pass on to fellow readers? _____
  _____
  _____
- Will you return to Walt Disney World? YES NO
  If so, when? WITHIN 6 MONTHS WITHIN 1 YEAR WITHIN 2 YEARS DON'T KNOW
- Other comments? _____
  _____
  _____

OPTIONAL

Name: _____
Address: _____
_____

Send a copy of this survey to:
**Walt Disney World for Adults, P.O. Box 1582, Sausalito, California 94966**
Or fax your reply to 415 331-9359

---

VISIT *Walt Disney World for Adults* ON THE INTERNET!

★ FIND OUT WHAT SPECIAL EVENTS ARE HAPPENING DURING YOUR VISIT ★
★ GET THE LATEST OPENING AND CLOSING TIMES AT THE THEME PARKS ★
★ CHECK OUT CURRENT TRAVEL DISCOUNTS AND PROMOTIONAL VACATION PACKAGES ★
★ DISCOVER INSIDER STRATEGIES YOU CAN FIND NOWHERE ELSE ★

http://www.wdw4adults.com/wdw
email for information: info@wdw4adults.com

# READERS' TOURING TIPS

There was a huge response to the Reader Survey that appeared in the last edition of this book. Of those who responded, 22 percent were first-time visitors to WDW and 78 percent were repeat visitors, with an average of five trips each — two couples had returned eighteen times! Respondents' vacations ranged from five to seven days; and 87 percent vacationed without children, while 13 percent brought their kids along and told us that *Walt Disney World for Adults* was very helpful to them in planning their family vacations.

All of our readers' opinions were factored into the ratings that appear in this edition. Among the ratings that many readers felt should be boosted were Jim Henson's Muppet\*Vision 3D, Voyage of The Little Mermaid, The Hall of Presidents, Hoop-Dee-Doo Musical Revue, Disney's Caribbean Beach Resort, Disney Vacation Club, Chef Mickey's Village Restaurant, San Angel Inn Restaurante, Sci-Fi Dine-in Theater, and The Fireworks Factory. Conversely, many readers thought the ratings in the last edition were too high for the Backstage Studio Tour, Jungle Cruise, Universe of Energy, Polynesian Luau, Adventurers Club, and 50's Prime Time Cafe. Almost everyone who responded also sent tips to pass along to you, and many suggestions from our readers enhanced the quality and accuracy of this edition. Here are some of our favorites:

*"We recommend staying at a Disney hotel. Neither of us had before, and there's a huge difference. Staying at Port Orleans, we felt part of the action. You could describe it as a 'total' experience, as though Disney World made a 24-hour effort toward us having a great time."*
— Vicki Sweeney & Terrence Raftery, Arlington, VA

*"We buy an Annual Pass each year and get two trips on one pass. We go in late June one year and in early June the next year. A much better deal than five-day passes."*
— Laura DeMartino, Pittsburgh, PA

*"We needed electric wheelchairs because walking everywhere was too much for us. Guest Relations was not able to help us, but we found that we could rent electric wheelchairs from an outside source and keep them at the hotel. Disney had special vans that took us anywhere we wanted to go, and brought us back. There was even a way not to change monorail trains that a Cast Member showed us."*
— Miriam Comenetz, Floral Park, NY

*"At the water parks, advise people with sensitive feet to wear rubber swim shoes. The walkways in the sun are well over 100 degrees! Also, you can pick up a waterproof container that can be worn around your neck to carry money for food. These are sold at Singapore Sal's (in Typhoon Lagoon)."*
— Peter & Diane Mitros, Iselin, NJ

*"If you are planning to go to Disney World and you are either a Magic Kingdom Club Member or an American Express Card Member, explore the packages that are offered by either group. We used a Magic Kingdom Club package, and it was a great value based on the price of hotels."*
— Catherine Anderson, Long Beach, CA

*"Your hotel reviews often say that WDW transportation can be overcrowded. This really depends on when you visit. We found no problems with transportation during slow periods."*
— Joe & Teresa Droogsma, Circle Pines, MN

*"I recommend the Food 'N Fun Card. We prepaid one price and had a ball. We ate at places and enjoyed water sports activities that we normally wouldn't have. It was a great deal."*
— Bonita Ebenal, Bellingham, WA

*"If time allows, take a day off to relax and unwind from the crowds."* — Martha Harrington, Winston-Salem, NC

*"I'm thirteen and recently assisted in planning my family's first WDW vacation. Since it was my first time, I wanted both my parents and me to enjoy it. Your book could definitely benefit from a companion book for kids. It would help families involve children in vacation planning."*
— Ashley Brown, Circleville, OH

READERS' TIPS

271

# VACATION DISCOUNT COUPONS!

Let us help you stretch your vacation budget with an array of exclusive discounts valued at up to $600 per couple — and even more for families! These offers were carefully selected from among our favorite places at Walt Disney World, and many of these discounts have never been available before. They are designed exclusively for *Walt Disney World for Adults* readers, and are our gift to you with our thanks for helping us continue to make this guide the best it can possibly be.

## Save on Your Airline Ticket — Up to $100 Off!

Start saving money on your Walt Disney World vacation before you arrive! This valuable offer applies to *any* airline and any type of fare.

## 10 to 15 Percent Discount at Dollar Rent A Car
## Plus a Free Car Upgrade and 15 Minutes of Free Long Distance Calling

You won't find a better auto rental offer anywhere! You can use it for any number of days that you rent. Dollar Rent A Car is conveniently located inside Orlando International Airport, and also has a rental counter right on Walt Disney World property. (See page 249.)

## Free Night at DoubleTree Guest Suites Resort at Walt Disney World

Treat yourself to a free night in a spacious one- or two-bedroom suite with kitchenette at DoubleTree Guest Suites Resort, the only all-suites hotel in Walt Disney World. This offer can save you anywhere from $125 to $325! (See page 149.)

## $50 Dining Discount at the Walt Disney World Dolphin

You have a $50 dining credit at any of the terrific restaurants at the Walt Disney World Dolphin, including:
*Sum Chows* — Elegant prix-fixe dinners featuring Asian cuisine. (See page 203.)
*Juan & Only's* — Mexican food served in a fanciful, festive dining room. (See page 202.)
*Harry's Safari Bar & Grille* — Tropical murals, tiger-stripe carpets, and other clever decorations impart an international jungle-explorer flavor to the steaks and seafood served here. (See page 201.)

## Dine Two-for-One at The Outback Restaurant

Enjoy a free entree at the critically-acclaimed Outback Restaurant, located at Buena Vista Palace Resort and Spa. As you dine in this dramatic steak and seafood restaurant, you'll be surrounded by the rustic ambience of Australia's outback. (See page 198.)

## Discounts at MurderWatch Mystery Dinner Theatre

You will receive a $5 per person discount for our favorite dinner show at Walt Disney World, which takes place at the Grosvenor Resort. You'll enjoy an all-you-can-eat prime rib buffet while you help solve an intriguing murder that takes place during dinner. (See page 209.)

## Skip the Line at Planet Hollywood!

Housed inside a dramatic blue celestial sphere, Planet Hollywood is a should-not-be-missed dining experience. Movie props and memorabilia from famous films adorn the walls and ceilings, the food is great, and the razzle-dazzle ambience makes for a truly memorable dining event. (See page 186.)

## 20 Percent Discount at Crossroads Shopping Center

Don't miss this shopping center, located at Walt Disney World. It is filled with many restaurants and fascinating shops, many of which offer you an exclusive discount on selected merchandise. (See page 261.)

## UP TO $100.00 OFF

**Travel Discounters**

18201 Flower Hill Way, Suite D
Gaithersburg, MD 20879
**1-800-355-1065**

**Start your savings even before you get to Orlando with this great air fare offer. Receive up to $100.00 off when you buy an airline ticket from Travel Discounters.**

Call 1-800-355-1065 and mention code **WDW** in order to receive the discount. See reverse for discount prices.

OFFER EXPIRES 12/31/96

---

## 📞 CARD/UPGRADE 🚗

This offer has a nice ring to it.
Receive a free phone card.
**1-800-800-4000**

**Dollar invites you to enjoy 15 minutes of free U.S. long distance calling time and a one class upgrade\*. Rate quoted will reflect a 10%-15% association discount.**
For reservations, call Dollar at **1-800-800-4000**.

Reference your identification number, **PC3007**. \*See back for details.

OFFER EXPIRES 12/31/96

---

## UP TO $50.00 OFF

WALT DISNEY WORLD
DOLPHIN
Logo © The Walt Disney Company

1500 Epcot Resorts Boulevard
Lake Buena Vista, FL 32830
**407-934-4000**

**Walt Disney World Dolphin invites you to dine as their guest.**

Offer is valid in any Walt Disney World Dolphin restaurant during your stay. Limit one coupon per dinner reservation. Coupon must be presented to server at the time of order. Coupon, or any unused portion thereof, is not redeemable for cash or credit, and may not be applied to tax and gratuities. See reverse (up to $50.00 value) for restaurants.

OFFER EXPIRES 12/31/96

---

## GO TO THE HEAD OF THE LINE!

1506 E. Buena Vista Boulevard
Lake Buena Vista, FL 32830
**407-827-7837**

**Please enjoy these privileges when you present this coupon to door host. Immediate access to the bar for cocktails. First available seating in dining room. Good for you and three guest (4 people) Monday-Friday 11:00am-5:00pm.**

Specified hours only.

OFFER EXPIRES 12/31/96

---

## ONE FREE DINNER

The Outback
RESTAURANT

1900 Buena Vista Drive
Lake Buena Vista, FL 32830
**407-827-3430**

**You and your guest are invited to enjoy one complimentary dinner entree when a second dinner entree of equal or greater value is purchased at The Outback Restaurant.**
*(up to $21.00 value)*

BUENA VISTA
PALACE
at Walt Disney World Village

OFFER EXPIRES 12/31/96
Settle to BC8021

---

## $5.00 OFF PER PERSON

MURDERWATCH™
MYSTERY THEATRE

1850 Hotel Plaza Boulevard
Lake Buena Vista, FL 32830
**407-828-4444 Ext. 24**

**$5.00 off each person in your party.**

It could happen to you! Prepare yourself for an evening of Mystery and Intrigue — Anything can happen, and when it does everyone is a suspect!

GROSVENOR
RESORT

OFFER EXPIRES 12/31/96

---

## 5TH NIGHT FREE

DOUBLETREE
GUEST SUITES RESORT™
AT WALT DISNEY WORLD VILLAGE

2305 Hotel Plaza Boulevard
Lake Buena Vista, FL 32830
**407-934-1000**

**DoubleTree Guest Suite Resort invites you to enjoy your 5th night as their guest.**

As the only all suite, full-service resort hotel in the Walt Disney® World Village, DoubleTree Guest Suites offers an ideal location and all the comforts of home. You'll stay in one of our deluxe one or two-bedroom suites with spacious dining area, separate living room, sofa bed, and two color televisions. For your comfort and convenience, each suite also features a hair dryer, refrigerator, coffee maker and microwave oven.

OFFER EXPIRES 12/31/96

---

## 20% OFF

State Road 535 at I-4 (Exit 27)
Lake Buena Vista, FL 32830

**20% off on selected items at**

- ❑ FishTale Freddy's
- ❑ Pacino's Italian Ristorante
- ❑ White's Books & Gifts
- ❑ Ken Done
- ❑ Chico's
- ❑ Sunworks

Check with each merchant for the discounted product covered by this promotion.

OFFER EXPIRES 12/31/96

---

Read each coupon carefully before using. Discounts only apply to the items and terms specified in the offer at participating locations. Remove the coupon you wish to use. Coupons may not be used in conjunction with any other promotion or discount offers.
Example: Special promotional pricing. If in doubt, please check with the establishment.

Make a reservation for a compact or intermediate car, then present this coupon to a Dollar or EuroDollar rental agent upon arrival. You'll receive an upgrade to the next car class at no additional charge. Upgrade subject to vehicle availability and cannot be used in Europe to upgrade to a car with automatic transmission. This coupon may not be used in conjunction with any other coupon or promotion, has no cash value, and expires December 31, 1996. Telephone card and upgrade offers are based on availability while supplies last at participating Dollar locations. Renter must meet Dollar age, driver and credit requirements. Dollar features the quality products of the Chrysler Corporation.

TASTE PUBLICATIONS INTERNATIONAL

Savings are subject to certain
restrictions and availability.
Valid for flights on most airlines.

*Minimum Ticket Price* . . . . . . . . . . . . . . .*Save*
$200.00 . . . . . . . . . . . . . . . . . . . . . . .$25.00
$250.00 . . . . . . . . . . . . . . . . . . . . . . .$50.00
$350.00 . . . . . . . . . . . . . . . . . . . . . . .$75.00
$450.00 . . . . . . . . . . . . . . . . . . . . . . .$100.00

TASTE PUBLICATIONS INTERNATIONAL

There may be times when this
offer cannot be honored.
Subject to change without notice.

TASTE PUBLICATIONS INTERNATIONAL

Restaurants at the Walt Disney World Dolphin
**Juan & Onlys, Sum Chow's
Harry's Safari Bar & Grille,
Coral Cafe, Cabana Bar & Grill
Dolphin Fountain and Tubbi's Buffeteria**

*Guest Name:* _____

*Guest Signature:* _____

TASTE PUBLICATIONS INTERNATIONAL

**"MurderWatch Contempo©"
"Resorting to Murder©"
"The Sock Hop Shock!©"
"Mystery at the USO©"
"The HoeDown WhoDunnit©"
"Mystery, Mayhem, and the Mob©"**

One coupon per visit. May not be
used in conjunction with any
other discount or promotion.

TASTE PUBLICATIONS INTERNATIONAL

Renowned for its succulent seasoned steaks, mouth-watering lobster, savory seafood, and tender baby back ribs smothered with tangy sweet barbecue sauce, The Outback Restaurant at the Buena Vista Palace at Walt Disney World Village boast an elaborate Australian "bush" motif, a beautiful sparkling pond brimming with koi fish, and a shimmering multi-level indoor waterfall.

After dinner you and your guest will receive a complimentary drink in the popular Laughing Kookaburra Good Time Bar.

TASTE PUBLICATIONS INTERNATIONAL

One coupon per visit.
May not be used in conjunction
with any other discount or promotion.

TASTE PUBLICATIONS INTERNATIONAL

Surrounded by magic and merriment, the DoubleTree Guest Suites Resort in Walt Disney World Village is your passport to all the fun and excitement of the Walt Disney World Resort. Of course, every stay begins with DoubleTree's signature greeting — our freshly baked chocolate chip cookies accompanied by a warm welcome. It's all part of the personal attention that sets DoubleTree Guest Suites apart from the rest. Complementary transportation to Magic Kingdom Park®, Epcot® '95, and Disney-MGM Studios. Nightly scheduled service to Pleasure Island and Planet Hollywood. Kids Check-in Desk, Kids Theater and separate KiddiePool. Not valid with any other discount. One coupon per family, per visit.

**Black Out Dates:**
November 21-26, 1995; December 21-31, 1995;
April 1-20, 1996; November 25-30, 1996;
December 20-31, 1996.

TASTE PUBLICATIONS INTERNATIONAL